THINK TWICE!

THINK TWICE!

Sociology Looks at Current Social Issues

LORNE TEPPERMAN
University of Toronto

JENNY BLAIN
Mount Saint Vincent University

With the assistance of Sandra Badin

PRENTICE HALL, UPPER SADDLE RIVER, NEW JERSEY 07458

Library of Congress Cataloging-in-Publication Data

Tepperman, Lorne.
    Think twice! : sociology looks at current social issues / Lorne
Tepperman, Jenny Blain ; with the assistance of Sandra Badin.
      p. cm.
    Includes bibliographical references.
    ISBN 0-13-242322-7
    1. Sociology. 2. Social problems. 3. United States—Social
conditions—1980– I. Blain, Jenny. II. Badin, Sandra.
    III. Title.
    HM51.T4 1999   98-10074
    301—dc21   CIP

Editorial Director: Charlyce Jones Owen
Editor in Chief: Nancy Roberts
Acquisitions Editor: John Chillingworth
Editorial Assistant: Pat Naturale
Marketing Manager: Christopher DeJohn
Project Manager: Serena Hoffman
Buyer: Mary Ann Gloriande
Cover Design: Bruce Kenselaar

This book was set in 10/12 Palatino by DM Cradle Associates
and was printed and bound by Hamilton Printing Company.
The cover was printed by Phoenix Color Corp.

ISBN 0-13-242322-7

Prentice-Hall International (UK) Limited, *London*
Prentice-Hall of Australia Pty. Limited, *Sydney*
Prentice-Hall Canada Inc., *Toronto*
Prentice-Hall Hispanoamericana, S.A., *Mexico*
Prentice-Hall of India Private Limited, *New Delhi*
Prentice-Hall of Japan, Inc., *Tokyo*
Pearson Education Asia Pte. Ltd., *Singapore*
Editora Prentice-Hall do Brasil, Ltda., *Rio de Janeiro*

Contents

Preface

Too many people, even young people, have already made up their minds about many of the pressing public issues of our day. That's because the mass media and other sources present us with information that is one-sided, oversimplified, erroneous, and sometimes even intentionally misleading. Sociology's job is to encourage skepticism about such received opinions—to get students to "think twice" (or more) about what they take for granted, and to think in sociological ways, using the sociological imagination. It is with the aim of encouraging second thoughts, sociological debate, and informed reasoning that we have written this book.

Think Twice! wants to help teach critical thinking skills to introductory sociology students. (In fact, the material in this book has been classroom-tested on thousands of introductory students, and it works!) As a teaching tool, the book can be used as a supplement to a mainstream textbook. *Think Twice!* is also useful as a supplementary text in social problems, social issues, and applied sociology courses. As you will see, *Think Twice!* is made up of 15 chapters, corresponding to the most common topics in an introductory sociology course. Each chapter contains three sections, or "debates." In turn, each debate contains a 2500-word essay and assorted learning aids: discussion questions, writing exercises, and research activities.

In each debate, the discussion is as fair and even-handed as we can manage. After a brief introduction, we look at the best arguments supporting each side. Finally, we draw our own conclusions from the evidence. This approach helps to launch student papers and to promote classroom and tutorial discussion.

In preparing this book, we have read scores of books, papers, and reports on each topic, but we have kept in-text citations to a bare minimum. In doing so, we are not suggesting that students write their own essays without appropriate in-text citation. We have done it to ensure the flow of the argument. In-text citations distract undergraduate readers, and we want, above all, to have the logic of each debate well understood. Sources that have informed our arguments are found at the end of each chapter; students are advised to seek out and read any references that seem intriguing. These selected references can provide a starting point for student essays and literature reviews.

It is not the goal of this book to replace the basic textbook, with its definition of concepts, discussion of founding figures, and comparison of sociological paradigms. Nor does it try to provide a comprehensive review of the literature. Any attempt to do this in so short a space would inevitably prove incomplete, quickly out of date, and therefore misleading.

Nor, again, is it the goal of this book to present the way sociologists actually go about their research, either as individuals or, collectively, as a discipline. Thus there is no attempt to represent the sequencing or give-and-take of arguments as they normally evolve in the research literature. Again, space does not permit such an approach, and this book has another, equally important goal.

Indeed, this book has one job to do, and one job only: to present the reader with compelling debates showing two or more sides of public issues, in this way forcing the student to think twice! Specifically, we show the underlying logic of debates about public issues, the main points that are being made by opposing sides, and (by implication) the kinds of sociological evidence that are relevant to a complete discussion of any issue. What the student can learn from this approach is how sociologists try to move from commonsense or moralistic stances to an approach that emphasizes the usefulness of research and empirical evidence.

In this book, each debate ends by taking a stand. This is to show that sociological reasoning and evidence can take us beyond a mere clash of views on controversial issues. *Think Twice!* is saying, "There really are social problems to be solved. In solving them, social science evidence and reasoning are superior to common sense. That is why students should study sociology." This approach to social issues is not merely a skeptical-person-on-the-street approach. It is also what the founding figures of sociology stood for. Moreover, this approach connects introductory sociology to applied sociology. It hints at the ways sociology can be used in the real world and encourages students to look for other applications.

We hope that instructors find this book helpful and students find it thought-provoking—the beginning of a series of fruitful debates, though certainly not the end. We look forward to comments and suggestions for improvement.

Acknowledgments

This book has benefited from the help and criticism of many students and colleagues. The process began with Sandra Badin, originally an undergraduate in Toronto and now a graduate student at Columbia University, who drafted preliminary arguments for about half the pieces. After a thorough literature search, the arguments were revised and tested on Lorne Tepperman's Introduction to Sociology course during the 1995, 1996, and 1997 academic years, and on Jenny Blain's Introductory Sociology course during 1996 and 1997. They were further revised and written in essay form, then shown to a variety of readers at the University of Toronto, including graduate students Slobodan Drakulic, Sandra Jeffery, and Sandra Colavecchia, and colleagues Jack Veuegelers and Ed Thompson.

After further revision, pieces were read and critiqued by Murray Pomerance, professor of sociology at Ryerson Polytechnic University in Toronto. More revisions were made in the light of criticism received from Professor Pomerance and the following reviewers solicited by Prentice Hall:

Lynn England, Brigham Young University
Allan O. KirkPatrick, Emeritus, Riverside Community College
Larry D. Crawford, Morehouse College
Ralph O. David, Pittsburgh State University

Serena Hoffman, production editor, and Mary Louise Byrd, copy editor, at Prentice Hall both suggested valuable changes, for which we are grateful. Then, last of all, sophomore student Sarah Wittman and graduate student Kathy Osterlund had a look-through the entire manuscript.

Thus the final product you are about to read is the result of many thoughts and second thoughts, and we are grateful to all our students, friends, and colleagues who were so generous with their time.

Lorne Tepperman
Jenny Blain

THINK TWICE!

1. Culture

Culture is our uniquely human environment. In its broadest sense, culture includes all of the objects, artifacts, institutions, organizations, ideas, and beliefs that make up the social environment of human life. This social environment is symbolic as well as material, in the sense that every human group produces meanings that remain in a society's memory.

Culture is a shared symbolic environment, and the people who share a culture are bound to experience the world similarly. Culture structures a person's perception of the world and shapes his or her behavior. A common culture helps to hold a society together. Culture is also something we all reproduce and change every day.

In this chapter we discuss three issues connected with culture. First, we consider whether multiculturalism is a good thing for society, or whether it divides people. Then we examine the debate over the so-called "culture of poverty" and whether some people are poor because of their cultural values. Finally, we discuss a particular subculture—the culture of cities—and decide whether that subculture is worth defending.

1.1

Shouldn't everybody in this country think just like me?

The issue: Should our social institutions recognize more than one acceptable way of thinking and behaving? This question was recently brought to salience over the issue of Ebonics and whether it deserves consideration as a second language in American public schools.

Introduction In the United States, a strong sense of "Americanism" usually unites people of widely varying backgrounds by blurring their cultural differences. But in other societies, cultural variety often poses a problem that cannot be swept under the carpet. Sometimes the difference divides people and sets them against one another. Without a strong, unifying sense of nationhood, cultural differences can lead to conflict.

In such societies people are forced to debate the issue of multiculturalism. For example, communities must decide which language(s) is (are) appropriate for schools, government offices, and other public institutions. Then people are likely to ask themselves: Does multiculturalism bring us together or pull us apart? Do multicultural policies weaken our sense of identity and unity? If so, the cost of multiculturalism may be too high.

And in some countries, people don't know how to deal with large numbers of culturally different immigrants. Sometimes violence erupts. Some politicians call for an end to immigration (of which we say more in a later chapter). But immigration is not the only thing that increases cultural variety. A high rate of childbearing by some groups (for example, Hispanic Americans) shifts the ethnic and cultural balance too. This change has been apparent in large cities like New York and in states like California and Texas.

Some communities welcome and make room for the new cultural mix. Multicultural strategies for doing so vary widely. Community leaders may arrange events to show public interest in and respect for minority cultures. Others help pay for ethnic arts, dance, theater, or mass media productions. Some communities make public services, including education, more accessible by offering them in minority languages. In some countries there have even been efforts to reimburse minority groups for past losses or damages that resulted from prejudice and discrimination. But do these various forms of multiculturalism divide people? Some say they do.

MULTICULTURALISM IS DIVISIVE

Multiculturalism blurs national identity and erodes standards Many societies—like the United States, Germany, and France—have a national identity or national character. Members of these societies believe that, as a group, they share certain characteristics— whether cultural, moral, or temperamental. Often citizens of other countries share this belief. Of course, national identities are stereotypes: Emile Durkheim said that they are "secular totems," meaning that they are ritualistic and idealized; however, like all stereotypes, they have a grain of truth to them. And whether there is such a thing or not, members of the society believe in their national identity. They are proud of it and don't want to lose it.

In some societies multicultural policies cause people to fear for the survival of their nation's unique identity. Such fears are particularly likely among people who suspect that their identity, or the social respect shown that identity, is already threatened. Such fears may arise because of foreign competition, the influence of foreign media on the local culture, or for other reasons.

Critics may also be concerned that cultural standards are falling—for example, that multiculturalism dilutes educational standards and encourages mediocrity. At the extreme, some believe that universities are becoming intellectual and cultural disaster zones, laid waste by racial and cultural differences among the students. Such views pose a problem for liberal universities and for liberal societies generally.

Many feel it is reasonable to expect schools to provide students with "cultural literacy"—that is, a basic familiarity with (Anglo-)American culture. In the eyes of many commentators, this is the key to social and economic success. We do minority-group students no favor by failing to teach them the ideas, terms, facts, and idioms that people commonly use in our society. So it is both practical and sensible to require minority students to learn the majority culture. To do otherwise—to bow to demands that the schools pay more attention to minority cultures—means changing traditional standards of excellence. In the short term this may benefit minority students, but in the long term it fails to prepare them in foundational subjects. It also weakens the integrity of the national culture.

Multiculturalism fosters discrimination A second criticism of multiculturalism is that it fosters discrimination. This view is paradoxical because the intent behind multiculturalism is to strengthen and validate minority cultures, yet the result may nonetheless weaken minority groups. There are several reasons for this. First, both discrimination and multiculturalism encourage people to make ethnic distinctions. Without ethnic distinctions—identifying ancestral differences between people—neither multiculturalism nor discrimination can flourish. So paying attention to group differences may divide us. Making distinctions may invite a hatred, not an appreciation, of cultural differences. It certainly offers a discernible basis for inequality and discrimination. Some believe it was the political radicals of the 1960s and 1970s who, by stressing separateness, started the process of cultural marginalization that is becoming a problem today.

In short, multiculturalism risks churning up unwanted negative sentiments. So if we want to minimize prejudice, discrimination, and ethnic conflict, it may be best to hide ethnic differences, not celebrate them.

A second, related concern is that multiculturalism promotes reverse discrimination. When multiculturalism means making restitution for harm done in the past, it punishes people for something their great-grandparents may (or may not) have done decades earlier. (We have more to say about reverse discrimination in a later chapter.)

Finally, multiculturalism, by attempting to remedy past injustices and inequalities, puts some groups on the offensive and others on the defensive. Instead of pointing to people's common interests, it points to their differences. Instead of promoting activities that people of different backgrounds can share, it calls for a redistribution of wealth, power, and prestige on ethnic grounds. In a variety of ways, multiculturalism promotes expressions of envy and hostility. It encourages a "victim mentality"—too much concern with wrongs done in the past and too little planning for the future.

Multiculturalism slows full social equality   Many people support multiculturalism in the belief that it brings more equality for minority people. However, multiculturalism may have the opposite effect, for two reasons.

First, multiculturalism discourages assimilation into the mainstream of society. In effect, it encourages people to remain part of that little island of activity that they, or their parents or grandparents, created after immigrating. By strengthening traditional ties, loyalties, and values, multiculturalism makes people less suited to get along with others of different ethnic, linguistic, or religious backgrounds. Insulated and isolated, people may get less education than they need (and can handle), thinking that they can earn a living from the crafts and trades available within their own community. Because of too little education, they may not be upwardly mobile, with the result that traditional elites from an Anglo-American background will continue to dominate the society.

Second, by exaggerating the importance of ethnic or cultural ancestry, multiculturalism draws people away from activities that could help to establish equality. People who focus their interest and effort on their own ethnic group are less likely to join with others of the same social class (but of a different ethnic group) to protest unfair working conditions or bad governmental policies. Then the powerlessness due to class is hidden by ethnic differences. Mobilizing people around class issues might do more than multicultural policies to equalize society and benefit minority groups.

MULTICULTURALISM IS NOT DIVISIVE

Diversity already exists   The United States is ethnically and culturally diverse and is becoming more so. Thus, we really have only two choices. We cannot eliminate the diversity; we can either grudgingly tolerate it or embrace and promote it.

Many believe that, in truth, the United States is only a collection of regional and local cultures. By this reasoning, the "American national identity" is artificial—a piece of national propaganda and part of the country's civil religion. It is an article of faith, not a fact, that all Americans share a common set of values, norms, and interests. In truth, America never was a melting pot. The civic culture of the United States has traditionally allowed ethnic minorities to maintain their uniqueness and diversity.

If so, multiculturalism is valuable because it recognizes the country's historic variety and continues to encourage a healthy variety in people's thinking. Cultural variety is not only normal and inevitable; it is fundamental to an open, democratic society and firmly rooted in American history. So the idea that there is *one* national identity (or national culture) that must be protected against any encroachment needs rethinking.

For similar reasons the concern over cultural and educational standards also needs rethinking. We should not view minority demands for varied educational materials as an attempt to evade Anglo-American content. We cannot suppose that students are trying to "get off easy" just because they want to speak in their own language or read stories set in a country where their ancestors were born. On the contrary, minority standards are just fine. At school, other things (such as social class) being equal, immigrants generally outperform native-borns, and non-Anglos outperform Anglos. This difference in achievement is more marked for certain ethnic minorities—for example, Chinese Americans—than it is for others. Yet, in general, to insist that immigrants and non-Anglos meet the prevailing (native-born Anglo) academic standards means asking them to perform worse, not better.

Would the education of students in their own language and cultural context make already high-performing minorities perform better? Or would it have no effect on educational performance levels? We don't know, though it is likely that teaching minorities in their own language would improve their educational attainment and raise their self-esteem as well. All we can say with certainty is that multicultural policies are not intrinsically a strategy to evade tough academic requirements.

Multiculturalism integrates Much has been written suggesting that the United States is an atomized, overly individualistic society. Many Americans, especially those who live in large cities, feel isolated and lacking in community. As we shall see in the section on city life, they also feel little obligation to their neighbors and fear victimization by strangers. What holds people together in this society and gives their lives meaning?

Ethnic culture is one of several important sources of community linkage, which also include associational ties, labor unions, and families. Ethnic ancestry gives minority people a deep sense of community. For this reason a Celtic revival, emphasizing Irish and Scottish culture, has recently enjoyed success among Anglo-Saxons in North America. Thus, ethnic identities are actually unifying, not divisive. A plurality of groups and group memberships can reverse the destructive dissociation of individuals from society.

Like it or not, ethnic sentiments and loyalties often exist far below the threshold of reason. They have a deep meaning for people and won't go away. This is not what rational philosophers like Voltaire and Marx had expected, yet it is so nonetheless. Ethnic identity's survival—generation after generation, century after century—tells us something important. The most recent revivals of ethnic and linguistic identity are responses to a need for collective identity in societies that are unable to provide other forms of membership and identification. They help people to satisfy their need for self-realization, communicative interaction, and recognition. Ethnic cultures thrive because American culture does not suffice.

Organic solidarity Multiculturalism does something else that Durkheim said was necessary in modern societies. It provides *organic solidarity*—social cohesion or connectedness that is based paradoxically on differences between people. Common sense might tell you that it is similarity that ties people together, and this is often true. In many situations it is not true, however. In those cases we gain an advantage by making use of our differences. It is mutual dependency that underlies organic solidarity.

In small, technologically simple societies, people have similar skills and similar ideas. Their similarity ties them together, and they can tolerate little variation in beliefs and actions. By contrast, modern societies are large, fluid, and technologically complex. We cannot expect sameness and cannot bring about total uniformity, even by using force. In the end, crushingly authoritarian societies have failed to do so. Therefore, Durkheim wrote, modern people must learn to tolerate, encourage, and benefit from differences.

There is value in our differences, since differences encourage us to enter into exchange with one another, and exchange helps us all. The Korean-American retailer, the Portuguese-American construction worker, and the Polish-American school psychologist all need each other. Exchanges tie people together in a modern, differentiated society. By showing respect and encouragement for diversity, multiculturalism honors the principle of strength through difference.

Multiculturalism meets society's needs Earlier, we considered the argument that multiculturalism discourages assimilation. However, recent research on ethnic minorities shows that what may be good common sense may not always be true. Today, most minorities participate fully in the country's social and economic life.

What influences participation most is not a person's ancestry but how much education that person received. Typically, highly educated people are better informed and more involved in public affairs. Membership in unions, churches, and other voluntary associations is also important. Holding constant these factors, minority people are as well informed and politically active as any other Americans. The likely effect of a multicultural education on knowledgeability is still being hotly debated.

People can belong to an ethnic group and to the larger society at the same time. Involvement in the ethnic community does not hinder involvement in the larger society. In short, ethnic survival and multicultural policies do no harm to the larger society.

SUMMING UP

Shouldn't everyone be just like me (or you)? Not necessarily. In fact, for most purposes, it's best if there are lots of differences. Of course, multiculturalism may be integrative up to a point and then it becomes divisive. This is suggested by historical instances of cultural distinctiveness leading to secession—Belgium separating from the Netherlands, Norway from Sweden, and Slovakia from the Czech Republic, for example. Today, many in Catalonia want to secede from Spain, many in Quebec to secede from Canada, and so on. Real problems can arise when ethnic differences reflect differences in power, so that ethnic conflict is really a conflict over power. Some of these problems and this conflict will be examined in Section 5.3.

Yet, in the long run, even these conflicts are steps toward a larger integration. Successful multiculturalism will involve sharing power as much as creative cultural diversity. From a global perspective, multiculturalism is a realistic and gracious way to take part in the modern world order. It is, as Durkheim said, a recognition that we are all connected by our differences as well as our similarities.

We are just learning to live with one another as neighbors in the same town and residents of the same globe. Public education should include the teaching of multicultural knowledge about the rights and duties of national and global citizenship. Universities and colleges should help to heal a world torn apart by racial and ethnic conflicts by ensuring that the educational curriculum reflects a diversity of cultural traditions.

Is multiculturalism a divisive policy? The research available provides little evidence that it is. Eventually, multiculturalism may become a heated issue in the United States too, as it has in many other countries. Then it may be useful to study the experience of other multiethnic societies and draw the appropriate conclusions.

REVIEW EXERCISES

For Discussion and Debate

1. Should all primary and secondary school students be forced to learn at least two languages and demonstrate familiarity with the history and customs of at least two ethnic cultures?

2. Should all new immigrants be forced to take a six-week full-time course in the English language and American customs and history before they can get permission to work?

3. Is it a good thing for a country to have a strong national identity? Does it matter what that national identity is?

4. Would the United States have fairer or more progressive social policies if there were fewer cultural differences among its citizens?

Writing Exercises

1. The American national identity: its most attractive and most unattractive features.

2. How American customs (or values) vary from one part of the country to another—for example, between the Northeast and the South or Southwest, or between the East Coast and the West Coast, or between large cities and small towns.

3. "How important my ethnic ancestry is to my personal identity and sense of self."

4. "Cultural differences strengthen (or weaken) my relationship with my best friend."

Research Activities

1. Examine published survey data to find out how much the views on an important social issue—you choose the issue—vary from one minority group to another among people with the same level of education.

2. Make a small questionnaire or interview schedule and use it to find out the attitudes of at least a dozen people toward issues of multiculturalism discussed in this section.

3. Carefully observe and record the interaction between two culturally different people, without being seen, if possible.

What problems, if any, are caused by these cultural differences?

4. Observe and record interactions within a group in which there is clear evidence of the benefits connected with organic solidarity, that is, cohesion based on differences. What do you learn from doing this?

SELECTED REFERENCES

CALABRESE, ANDREW, and BARBARA RUTH BURKE, American identities: Nationalism, the media, and the public sphere, *Journal of Communication Enquiry* (Summer 1992), 16, 2, 52–73.

CONNOR, WALKER, Beyond reason: The nature of the ethnonational bond, *Ethnic and Racial Studies* (July 1993), 16, 3, 373–389.

DUSTER, TROY, They're taking over! And other myths about race on campus, *Philosophy and Social Action* (January–June 1993), 19, 1–2, 30–37.

FUCHS, LAWRENCE H., *The American kaleidoscope: Race, ethnicity, and the civic culture* (Hanover, NH: University Press of New England, 1990).

GITLIN, TODD, The rise of "identity politics": An examination and a critique, *Dissent* (Spring 1993), 40, 2(171), 172–177.

GRAHAM, SANDRA, Motivation in African Americans, *Review of Educational Research* (Spring 1994), 64, 1, 55–117.

HORWATH, PETER, The "dead white male's canon" under attack at American universities: Traditionalist perceptions, *History of European Ideas* (July 1994), 19, 1–3, 553–560.

HUSBANDS, CHRISTOPHER T., Crises of national identity as the "new moral panics": Political agenda setting about definitions of nationhood, *New Community* (January 1994), 20, 2, 191–206.

MELUCCI, ALBERTO, The voice of the roots: Ethnonational mobilizations in a global world, *Innovation* (1990), 3, 3, 351–363.

PATTERSON, ORLANDO, Ecumenical America: Global culture and the American cosmos, *World Policy Journal* (Summer 1994), 11, 2, 103–117.

PORTES, ALEJANDO, and MIN ZHOU, Should immigrants assimilate? *The Public Interest* (Summer 1994), 18–33.

SCHLESINGER, ARTHUR M., JR., *The disuniting of America: Reflections on a multicultural society*, (Knoxville, TN: Whittle Direct Books, 1991).

SCHNAPPER, DOMINIQUE, The debate on immigration and the crisis of national identity, *West European Politics* (April 1994), 17, 2, 127–139.

SMELSER, NEIL J., The politics of ambivalence: Diversity in research universities, *Daedalus* (Fall 1993), 122, 4, 37–53.

SOLARZANO, DANIEL G., Mobility aspirations among racial minorities, controlling for SES, *Sociology and Social Research* (July 1991), 75, 4, 182–188.

STAHL, ABRAHAM, Cultural literacy: A positive view, *Interchange* (1993), 24, 3, 287–297.

TRUEBA, HENRY T., Race and ethnicity: The role of universities in healing multicultural America, *Educational Theory* (Winter 1993), 43, 1, 41–54.

WALZER, MICHAEL, Multiculturalism and individualism, *Dissent* (Spring 1994), 41, 2(175), 185–191.

WAX, MURRAY L., How culture misdirects multiculturalism, *Anthropology and Education Quarterly* (June 1993), 24, 2, 99–115.

WILTERDINK, NICO, Images of national character, *Society* (November–December 1994), 32, 1(211), 43–51.

1.2

Do poor people have bad values?

The issue: Who's responsible for the nation's poor and the resulting costs to the non-poor? Could, and should, the poor learn different values and, in that way, become self-reliant? Or are values beside the point?

Introduction In sociology and anthropology there has been a long-running argument, carried over into the political field, over the origins of poverty. On the one side stand those who follow social thinkers of the last century, social Darwinists such as Herbert Spencer who consider poverty a marker of human genetic "fitness" (or rather, "unfitness"). By this thesis, poor people are poor because they do not have the ability to be anything else. Some people still hold this view, and it appears in stereotypical characterizations of individuals or groups as "naturally lazy" or incapable. However, it has long since fallen out of favor as a sociological or anthropological explanation. There is simply too much that the "fitness" thesis does not explain, such as how the same individual, given a change of circumstances, encouragement, and training, may behave in entirely different ways.

The current debate is about possible links between culture and poverty, and the direction of these links. In this section we first consider the argument known as the *culture of poverty thesis*: that certain types of culture restrict people, prevent them from achieving their potential, and hence act to keep their members—groups or even whole societies—in poverty. The counterargument reverses the direction of causation; it says that people who are poor learn to act in ways that are adaptations to their poverty. Whether either argument fully describes or explains the situation of people in poverty today is assessed at the end of this chapter.

Poverty and how it is measured What is poverty? An inability to pay one's bills? Difficulty in making ends meet? Entrapment by the welfare state? A lack of food and shelter? Being unable to raise a crop that will feed one's family? Being unable to earn enough money to live on?

Definitions of poverty vary from one location to another, depending on what people do in their daily lives. In some areas a few individuals are poor; in others, many people, whole groups, live in poverty. In the United States, in 1991 about 38 million people lived in poverty. An analysis of 1990 census figures shows a variation by congressional district; Kentucky has the dubious distinction of containing the district with highest proportion (18.3%) living below the poverty line. In Canada, 4.23 million live in poverty, representing 15.9% of the population. Other countries also give figures for poverty rates, with a poverty line calculated so that it represents a minimal standard of living, generally higher in cities and lower in rural areas, reflecting the cost of living in these areas. In India, for example, 19% of the population lives below the poverty line; in some other countries the figure would be far higher.

In the United States there has been a small decrease in the poverty rate since 1990. Census figures from 1995 show 36.4 million people, or 13.8% of the U.S. population, living below the poverty line. Some people are more likely than others to be poor; thus, 26.4% of African-American families live in poverty, compared with only 6.4% of European-American families. In Canada 1 in 5 women are poor (up from 1 in 6 in 1988). In 1991, households headed by single parent mothers made up 6% of all families but 30% of poor families.

CULTURE IS A CAUSE OF POVERTY

An examination of who is poor, whether in North America or abroad, is illuminating. Poor families are disproportionately found among black North Americans and among Native North Americans and those headed by female single parents. There are, of course, many poor families and individuals that fall into different categories. How can these variations be explained? And why are some poor people labeled as "underclass," denoting not merely an absence of money but also social disorganization and a lack of sound values?

Some anthropologists doing research in other parts of the world have come up with the answer that culture and poverty are linked. Their work partly echoes that of Max Weber, who in his book *The Protestant Ethic and the Rise of Capitalism* showed connections between the development of capitalist economies in northwestern Europe and religious attitudes influencing people's thoughts and behavior. Weber distinguished between the Calvinist Protestantism of the rising capitalist classes in Britain, Germany, and the Netherlands and the Catholicism of the working class.

According to Weber, Calvinism and Catholicism emphasized different values: work for Calvinists, giving alms or charity for Catholics. Catholics of the day believed that earning interest on loans was inappropriate. According to Calvinism, earning interest, and achieving prosperity by other means as well, were marks of those who were "chosen." Calvinists believed in predestination. They could not earn a place in heaven by good deeds or giving charity, but only by the grace of being chosen before birth; prosperity and success in worldly endeavors were taken as an assurance of grace. Consumption for its own sake was seen as frivolous. Work was a duty. Not working—or having no work—was viewed as immoral. For Weber, the attitudes expressed as part of Calvinist Protestantism facilitated the development of capitalism and can explain why capitalism arose when it did and where it did.

Weber's Protestant ethic implies a reliance on hard work, rationalism, and individualism—especially distinguishing oneself from the masses of other people. For the most part, these are the concepts most highly valued in North America. Cultural goals here include success, and cultural means include individual hard work. However, these goals and means may clash with other values.

If we look at who is poor in America, first we see individuals who have become poor through accidents or bad luck. However, not all of them stay poor; many do recover. Then there are those people who have always been poor. They come from poor families or poor neighborhoods. They have grown up in poverty. Often, as in the case of black or Native Americans, the initial poverty arose out of unequal treatment due to racist attitudes. However, people grow used to living in poverty, and it is now very hard for them to extricate themselves from it.

The concept of a "culture of poverty" arose in the work of the anthropologist Oscar Lewis. Lewis described how people can become trapped by their culture. Capitalism could not have arisen without hard work and the concept of investment, but, said Lewis, different cultures convey different values. For instance, where people do not learn to think of themselves as individuals, they do not act for themselves and may not try to rise above other family members. This is part of the concept of *familism;* another part is the belief in the necessity to have many children.

Lewis considered that the people he studied—Mexican peasants, among others—held values that were not consistent with the need to change their farming practices to more profitable ones. They were not innovative. They valued the family over the individual, were unwilling to place trust in people outside the family, and viewed anybody who did get ahead as unfairly taking other people's shares of the village economic pie. And they were fatalistic, unwilling to believe that they (or, indeed, anyone) could cause change or influence events. At the same time, they were both dependent on and hostile to government policies. All of these traits Lewis saw as handicapping the ability of the villagers to adopt modern farming methods and increase their standard of living.

To repeat, Lewis saw these traits as cultural. People learned them as children when they were socialized into the culture. By the age of 6 or 7, children would have internalized this complex of backwardness, hostility, dependency, fatalism, and familism. The only hope for change and for prosperity came from programs initiated outside the villages. Government workers since Lewis's time have commented on the reluctance of peasant farmers to innovate. The major problems of underdevelopment, Lewis concluded, were cultural ones.

Turning again to North America, we can see how the concept of a culture of poverty can explain many of the problems facing individuals, families, and groups today. Where people are willing to innovate and to work hard, they can often extricate themselves from poverty. Where they are not willing to do this—because they feel that they cannot effect change by their own actions—there is little chance of their escaping poverty. Modern society requires both work *and* initiative, the same values that were instrumental in the development of capitalism.

Unfortunately, whole sectors of society have become caught in a series of poverty traps (including the welfare trap, examined in Section 4.3). Where children grow up seeing their parents dependent and ineffectual, they absorb the culture of fatalism. Educational theorists speak of *cultural deficit*. That is, when children come to school without an orientation to books, or reading, or work, they may fall farther and farther behind. Political theorist Edward Banfield considers that:

Traits that constitute what is called lower-class culture of life style are consequences of the extreme present-orientation of that class. The lower-class person lives from moment to moment, he is either unable or unwilling to take account of the future or to control his impulses. Improvidence and irresponsibility are direct consequences of this failure to take the future into account. (1974, p. 54)

Daniel Patrick Moynihan, noted urbanologist and U.S. senator, and others have long pointed to the high poverty rates within the African-American community and associated it with features of the culture of poverty, such as absent fathers, unwillingness to defer gratification, and spending for its own sake. Some initiatives have attempted to remedy the situation. Educational programs, such as Project Head Start, have helped many American children to break out of the culture of poverty. If we are truly seeing a decline in the poverty statistics today, it may be due to programs such as Head Start that aim to show children that hard work can pay off.

CULTURE IS NOT THE CAUSE OF POVERTY

The culture of poverty argument is a classic example of *functionalist sociology*. In this paradigm, culture is seen as something above and beyond the individual, or even the groups or societies formed by individuals. People are socialized at an early age into the norms, values, and beliefs of their culture, and that socialization affects them for life—at least, according to functionalists.

It is true that in many cases "old habits die hard." We behave in ways that we are accustomed to behave, and we engage in activities from which we have derived pleasure or profit in the past. However, the functionalist argument leaves out much of why we engage in these activities. Socialization is not the entire answer. As people engage in activities, they make plans, form intentions, and foresee circumstances.

On the other hand, although people act with intent, they are not necessarily successful in achieving their intentions. Actions have unintended consequences. As people engage in their actions and practices, they interact with others who may assist their plans, subvert them, or take up some aspects and ignore others. People have their own agendas. If we regard culture not as a system of norms, values, and beliefs that is fixed and that people internalize but as something more fluid, we may see how people in their everyday activities create culture and pass it on to their children. In turn, the children do not accept it uncritically, but modify that culture, so far as they can, according to their own needs.

If socialization were the entire answer, nothing new would ever have been invented, no new forms of government or belief would have been developed. Socialization theory depends on the idea that people internalize their parents' values and beliefs as children and then proceed to act on the basis of them. However, it is not hard to find people who question the values that have been handed down to them. Do you behave like your mother or your father? Or do you, more likely, share some behaviors and some values with your parents and some with other people you have met?

What about social structure? Another strand to this argument is that, while people act with intent, they are constrained in what they can do by social structures and processes. These structures and processes become evident through what other people do and the assumptions they make.

Let us relate this back to the question of a culture of poverty and the assertions that were made about it. We are here engaging in a process of comparison. Poor people and their cultures are being compared to others

and being judged by these others; their culture is found to be lacking, and the epithets of lazy, not innovative, uncaring, improvident applied. This judging occurs without regard to either the processes that made the people poor or what they themselves think about the situation.

What if we view poverty, instead, as a result of the uneven distribution of resources within society? Through taxation and social programs, some societies attempt to distribute resources in a relatively even manner; others distribute them very unevenly. In both types of society, inequalities from the past maintain themselves or even increase. And the sheer physical fact of poverty has implications for the people that deal with it on a daily basis. When money is scarce and not guaranteed in the future, it makes little sense to speak of "improvidence." Survival on a day-to-day basis is more important. Rather than saying that children from poor families have internalized norms of laziness, we can point out that they have to deal with conditions that their wealthier peers do not face: underequipped classrooms, crowded home conditions, the lack of a place to study, or even hunger during the day, which prevents children from giving full attention to their classwork. Saying that a culture of poverty and the people who share it are responsible for this uneven distribution of physical resources, says sociologist William Ryan, is blaming the victim.

The history of victim-blaming in Western society goes back a long way. Some of the ideologies surrounding the current concept of welfare arose around the time of the Poor Law in Elizabethan England, nearly 500 years ago. Over the centuries, seemingly healthy adults who were not employed were variously criminalized, conscripted for work, or relegated to the workhouses of the nineteenth century, which were designed to be as unpleasant as possible.

Victim-blaming, however, fits with the ideas expressed by Weber's Protestant ethic. The idea that unemployment is sinful or immoral is the counterpart to the concept of work as a duty. The idea that people who are not working are sinful or immoral is a counterpart to the concept of worldly success marking those who are "God's elect." The notion that a culture of poverty is responsible for keeping people poor fits with our society's dominant ideology—that poor people deserve to be poor because they have bad values. But though it may fit society's preconceptions, this way of thinking does not explain the phenomenon of poverty very well.

Who are the poor? The culture of poverty theory implies that people in poverty remain there and that the children of poor families themselves stay poor. Sometimes this is the case. However, many people's poverty cannot be accounted for by the theory. It is revealing to look at people who are poor today in North America. Some are unemployed and some are not seeking employment—the stereotypical people on welfare. Many others, however, are in the work force, and U.S. figures for 1996 show a rise in the numbers of the so-called "working poor."

For those not seeking work, it may be instructive to ask why. Some live in areas where there is little work to seek. Moving, which may appear to make sense, may not be an option, particularly where people can contribute to their family economies in ways other than by directly earning a wage (such as by taking care of other family members, children, or elderly relatives). Moving may mean that the expenses for another household have to be found, somehow, with no guarantee of a job. If the only jobs to be found pay a minimum wage, earnings may actually fall below the poverty line for a household with one or more children to support, especially in an expensive city.

Some may have sought work so many times already that they are burned out, dispirited, incapacitated by the experience.

Rather than seeing this as a cultural phenomenon, we may better regard this as a reaction to the material situation of their lives and to the ways that others treat them. Many still have commitments to family. It seems odd that culture of poverty theorists stress familism as a problem when, throughout North American society, women are constantly being told that their first commitment should be to their children and other family members. However, many women on welfare say that they would welcome a chance to work—provided that they can find reliable, affordable child care. Stories in the media tell of women who give up "good" jobs because they calculate that the financial costs associated with these jobs, particularly the cost of child care, are so great as to make the job not worthwhile. (Arguments to do with the "dangers" of welfare are further discussed in Section 4.3. There we find that, on balance, welfare is not a trap but a safety net made necessary by the extreme imbalance of wealth within society.)

What of the other components of the culture of poverty, the idea that the poor are frivolous spenders, concerned only with instant gratification? Middle-class, relatively well-off people often consider that poverty means simply being a bit short of cash and having to do some budgeting. However, for many people in the impoverished areas of Los Angeles or Toronto or Chicago, being poor means not having enough money to pay the rent or power bills on a regular basis. "Budgeting" for them means going to each company to which the household is in debt and explaining, yet again, how much can be paid this month, so that power is not cut off or the family evicted. Going into debt in order to feed and house oneself or one's family means that any money earned is already spoken for, and debt and the interest on it accumulate fast.

Poverty-line calculations include only money for basic housing, food, and minimal clothing. Amusement, sports, medicine, gifts, music, any kinds of comforts are seen as "extras" that can be done without. Yet how many nonpoor people would be willing to live with no comforts or extras, and with no end in sight to this situation?

SUMMING UP

Do poor people have bad values? Like rich people, some poor people have bad values and some don't. But what we have argued here—however much we might wish otherwise—is that there is only a weak fit between values (or worthiness) and rewards. So holding the poor morally accountable for their poverty may make us feel better, but it doesn't square with the sociological evidence.

Poverty is created by society, and individuals and groups deal with it in a variety of ways. Some are more likely to try to find a way out, whereas for others no way out is visible. Rather than look to the individuals for a reason for this incapacitation, we can look to the interaction between individuals and their society: How are they treated by officials and authorities? What rules are made concerning their employment? And how much can they earn before deduction of benefits? What labels are applied to them by officialdom?

Both individuals and groups do become labeled and incapacitated. Rather than blaming the victim, it makes sense to ask how labeling comes about and how society is involved in it, how society constructs dependency in people so labeled, and how some groups have managed to break free of it. Only by looking at the processes by which people struggle to make sense of and overcome their everyday obstacles can we hope to understand the experience of poverty. And only by changing the conditions of that struggle can we hope to reduce the poverty rates. Blaming bad values won't do the job.

REVIEW EXERCISES

For Discussion and Debate

1. "Given the opportunities available to every person in North America today, there is no need for anyone to be poor."

2. Does a strong attachment to family help or hinder individual success? Does it depend on what that "family" is?

3. Members of a religious order used to say: "Give me a child for the first seven years, and he (sic) will be mine for life." True or not?

4. Are early intervention programs worth the effort and expense?

Writing Exercises

1. Describe how people learn to be poor.

2. You are the unemployed single parent of a 2-year-old child. Describe your chief strategies for avoiding poverty.

3. How and why are culture and poverty associated in the popular press?

4. Discuss poverty and the political debate on its causes.

Research Activities

1. Collect media items (such as press clippings) about relationships between

culture and poverty. What views are expressed in the items? Do you agree with these views?

2. Survey your friends and neighbors. How many different views of relationships between culture and poverty can you find?

3. Study speeches of political figures on poverty and culture. Do you find any relationships between the views expressed and the cultural, religious, or ethnic-group membership of the politician?

4. Collect recent poverty statistics. What trends do you observe? Is poverty increasing or decreasing? What groups are becoming more, or less, poor? (*Hint*: The Internet is a good source of current official statistics. Some starting URLs are http://www.marketingtools.com/Publications/NN/96_NN/9606_NN/9606NN03.html and http://www.heritage. org/heritage/cd_ranking/44pover.html.)

SELECTED REFERENCES

BANFIELD, EDWARD C., *The unheavenly city revisited* (Boston: Little, Brown, 1974).

BANTON, MICHAEL, The culture of poverty, *Social Studies Review* (January 1990), 5, 3, 112–114.

BOXILL, BERNARD, The culture of poverty, *Social Philosophy and Policy* (Winter 1994), 11, 1, 249–280.

GANS, HERBERT J., The war against the poor: Instead of programs to end poverty, *Dissent* (Fall 1992), 39, 4(169), 461–465.

———, "Underclass" to "undercaste": Some observations about the future of the postindustrial economy and its major victims, *International Journal of Urban and Regional Research* (September 1993), 17, 3, 327–335.

GIDDENS, ANTHONY, *The constitution of society: Outline of the theory of structuration* (Berkeley: University of California Press, 1984).

JENCKS, CHRISTOPHER, *Rethinking social policy: Race, poverty, and the underclass* (Cambridge, MA: Harvard University Press, 1992).

JONES, DELMOS J., The culture of achievement among the poor: The case of mothers and children in a Head Start program, *Critique of Anthropology* (September 1993), 13, 3, 247–266.

JONES, JACQUELINE, *The dispossessed: America's underclasses from the Civil War to the present* (New York: Basic Books, 1992).

KATZ, MICHAEL B., ed., *The "underclass" debate: Views from history* (Princeton, NJ: Princeton University Press, 1993).

LAWSON, BILL E., ed., *The underclass question* (Philadelphia: Temple University Press, 1992).

LEWIS, OSCAR, *Four families: Mexican case studies in the culture of poverty* (New York: Basic Books, 1959).

MARKLUND, STAFFAN, Structures of modern poverty, *Acta Sociologica* (1990), 33, 2, 125–140.

MASSEY, DOUGLAS S., and NANCY A. DENTON, *American apartheid: Segregation and the making of an underclass* (Cambridge, MA: Harvard University Press, 1993).

MATZA, DAVID, The disreputable poor. In Reinhard Bendix and Seymour Martin Lipset, eds., *Class, status and power: Social stratification in comparative perspective*, 2nd ed. (New York: Free Press, 1966).

MORRIS, MICHAEL, From the culture of poverty to the underclass: An analysis of a shift in public language, *American Sociologist* (Summer 1989), 20, 2, 123–133.

MOYNIHAN, DANIEL P., *The Negro family case for national action* (Washington, DC: U.S. Department of Labor, Office of Policy Planning and Research, 1965).

RYAN, WILLIAM, *Blaming the victim* (New York: Vintage Books, 1976).

WEBER, MAX, *The Protestant ethic and the spirit of capitalism* (London: Unwin University Books, [1904] 1930).

WILSON, WILLIAM JULIUS, *The truly disadvantaged* (Chicago: University of Chicago Press, 1987).

1.3

Do we need to protect the culture of cities?

<u>*The issue:*</u> *The rundown condition of many of the nation's cities. Are the cities worth saving? What do they have to offer that can't be found in smaller towns or newer, cleaner suburbs? And is it worth the cost to recover the culture of these cities?*

Introduction For more than a century, Americans have carried on a love-hate relationship with city life and city culture—in short, a love-hate relationship with "downtown." And for the last 50 years white, middle-class Americans have been leaving the downtown areas of large, old cities for suburbs and for newer, smaller cities. Some have even created enclosed and secure communities of their own, like Levittown and Shaker Heights, Grosse Point and Bel Air. Does this mean they have rejected what we call city culture? Is this city culture good or bad, liberating or enslaving? And do we need to actively protect the culture of cities, which, as we shall see, took a long time to develop?

The debate about the social and cultural value of city life starts in Europe in the Middle Ages. There, cities served as safe havens for serfs, who were virtually enslaved workers. In many parts of Europe, a serf who escaped and managed to live in the city for a year and a day was considered free of his feudal obligations—thus the old saying, "City air makes you free." In those days city life was decidedly liberating. Yet this liberation came at a cost.

Ferdinand Tonnies, an early sociologist, toted up the cost by highlighting the cultural differences between city life (*gesellschaft*) and rural life (*gemeinschaft*). On farms and in small towns, community life was stable, predictable, and enduring, Tonnies observed. Everyone was connected to everyone else through kinship, friendship, neighboring,

and work. Social relations were intimate and deeply meaningful. By contrast, *gesellschaft*, or city life, was fluid, unpredictable, and temporary. City people knew few others and had few connections to them. Many merely exchanged goods and services for money. Their social connections were few and limited. Most relationships were narrow and superficial, shallow and meaningless outside the realm of commerce. The German sociologist Georg Simmel also pointed out that cities are places where we are put in close visual range of people we've never met, and so the stranger is a central figure there.

For Tonnies, the movement from rural to city life signified a loss of community, intimacy, and emotional meaning. But are such losses really inevitable? And are the shortcomings so great that city people are bound to live in fear and emotional isolation—in effect, enslaved by city life? Opinions vary on this topic.

CITIES ARE NOT THE BEST PLACE TO BE

Early American sociology certainly considered the cities enslaving. It linked fast-changing urban industrial life with social pathologies and with social disorganization. The most important theorist in this tradition was the Chicago sociologist Louis Wirth. In his article "Urbanism as a Way of Life," Wirth explained why cities have less social integration or cohesion than smaller communities and why, as a result, cities develop their own culture and way of life like the one Tonnies described.

Three key factors   Three factors combine to produce the characteristic urban culture: a large population, high population density, and population heterogeneity.

A large population ensures that most people won't know one another. Because they are strangers, they do not feel tied to one another in ways that control deviance and support cooperation in a smaller community. As a result, city people are less willing to help one another, especially when helping carries a personal cost. For example, in 1963, Kitty Genovese was brutally slain in Kew Gardens, New York, while many of the strangers who were her neighbors listened to her screams from their apartment windows.

A dense population means that city people will have many interactions and communications. It is virtually impossible to escape other people's notice or influence. The potential for too many interactions, in turn, leads people to develop strategies for avoiding strangers or keeping them emotionally at a distance. It also encourages them to develop institutions, like police forces and subway advertising, that control or pacify strangers in public places.

Population heterogeneity—the presence of people with widely varying values, norms, and interests—is a third problem of city living. Confusion, if not outright conflict, is bound to arise between strangers who see the world differently and compete with one another for jobs, housing, and political influence. Under these conditions, cross-cultural contacts with strangers produce urban misanthropy—a general negative feeling

toward others. This heterogeneity and some of its effects were gently parodied in Bruce Jay Friedman's 1958 play *Steambath*, where God came onstage as a Puerto Rican steambath attendant.

High crime rates   Tonnies and Wirth would have correctly predicted higher crime rates in cities than in small towns or rural areas. And many reasons for high urban crime rates come to mind. First and most obviously, there is more to steal in cities than in small towns or on farms. There are also more places to hide in cities and therefore less risk of getting caught.

Cities also concentrate poverty and unemployment in a small area. In particular, the population density of young men in cities is high, and young men are statistically the most likely to perpetrate common crimes. Cities bring young men together in a critical mass, making it possible for gangs to organize for criminal purposes. In short, crime results because cities marginalize—that is, concentrate, ghettoize, and segregate—both unwanted land uses and unwanted people.

Finally, cities are centers of innovation in everything, even crime. New crimes are always being invented (e.g., computer fraud). And in big cities older crimes, like drug trafficking, prostitution, and illegal gambling, are perfected by organized criminal mobs. As the profitability of crime grows, the scale of criminal activity rises too and criminal organization innovates. Then new crimes and criminal strategies—just like other social and cultural activities—spread from the large cities to smaller cities and rural areas. At least since the last century, the streets of a large city have been an ideal medium in which organized professional thieving can grow.

Above all, Tonnies and Wirth would have emphasized that cities have a weaker normative structure than rural communities. The disruption of social ties and the weakened moral authority of church and community elders lead to weaker social integration and to what Durkheim called *anomie*—a condition of normlessness. Surrounded by so many strangers in an environment that is new and unpredictable, people become self-absorbed and self-protective. They lack empathy and a sense of responsibility for others' well-being.

Finally, social order unravels. Victimless crime, mentally ill people released from institutional treatment, decriminalized public drinking, and the de facto decriminalization of drugs all contribute to a social breakdown of urban public space. The end result is a deteriorated urban standard of behavior and lost public civility. The city, particularly its downtown core, seems like a relatively horrible place to live.

Unhealthy urban culture Tonnies and Wirth would have also predicted higher rates of mental illness in cities. The turmoil, adversity, corruption, and instability that characterize large urban areas all increase the risk of mental illness. In fact, one of the early classic works of sociology, Emile Durkheim's *Suicide*, shows how the seemingly personal act of suicide is social in origin, caused by a lack of moral regulation and social bonding. Others have located the causes of higher urban rates of mental illness and suicide in the stressfulness of modern city life.

Part of the stress is due to fear of victimization. The fearfulness of city life is captured in so-called urban legends, which most of us have heard at one time or another. They are often described as events that happened to a "friend of a friend of a friend." One classic is the alligator-in-the-toilet-bowl story. A pet baby alligator, allegedly flushed down its owner's toilet, survives in the sewage system and shows

up unexpectedly—and fully grown—in someone else's toilet. Such stories are common. More likely than not, their appeal depends on a widespread anxiety (e.g., nature strikes back) and fear of social breakdown and victimization.

It was Georg Simmel—from whom Louis Wirth took many of his ideas—who first intuited how a large city affects people psychologically and emotionally. Life in a city is overstimulating, Simmel wrote. People, especially strangers, surround us on all sides. More than that, we experience countless strange noises, smells, sights, dangers, and opportunities. Walking a city street, we must pay attention constantly. In the long run, sensory overload takes its toll on our nervous systems.

Research has supported at least some of these suppositions. The tempo of life is faster in a large city—more costly, arousing, and engaging than in a small town. People walk faster, talk faster, and even eat faster, mostly because more of them must eat in the same place every hour. They also make more noise; the larger the city, the more car horns there are for irritated people to honk and the more people honk their horns. So in these various ways—isolation, higher risks of crime, and stresses on mental health—people who may have expected to gain freedom through city life are actually enslaved by it. At least, this is one side of the argument. There is another side, however.

CITIES ARE THE BEST PLACE TO BE

People who believe that urban life is liberating may be more conscious of the historic comparison between cities and the rural communities they replaced. For one, Karl Marx was a fan of cities; he referred in passing to the "idiocy of rural life." Marx himself spent much of his adult life in London, perched day after day on the same chair in the great round Reading Room of the British Museum, sifting through books for evidence of patterns in world history. His was a uniquely urban activity, especially in the quasi-aristocratic setting of Great Russell Street in London's Bloomsbury district.

Until recently such scholarly activity was impossible on the farm or even in the suburbs. The advent of the Internet and electronic access to worldwide libraries has begun to change this. In the past, scholarship meant gathering vast knowledge and culture in one place; since at least Alexandria of ancient times, the city has been that place. The vast storehouse of knowledge concentrated in cities liberates people by giving them intellectual freedom.

More freedom in cities   Cities are not only vast accumulations of knowledge; they are also enormous accumulations of people, capital, and corporate institutions. Just about every activity is possible in a city, so just about every activity occurs there. This is because cities also feature weaker social controls than rural areas. People are freer to indulge their whims in large cities. Indeed, city life permits both individualism and nontraditional thinking.

The variety, density, fluidity, and near invisibility of city people mean a greater diversity of activities and ideas. There is also more tolerance for diversity. Ever since feudal times, cities have been less traditional and more open to new ideas than small communities based on *gemeinschaft*, which favors similarity. Urbanism increases tolerance for a variety of groups whose members hold unpopular, if not deviant, ideas and interests, and it increases racial tolerance as well.

More personal fulfilment   Many different types of people and ideas are available in cities.

Whether historical scholars, stamp collectors, religious fanatics, or medical specialists, people find others like themselves somewhere in the metropolis. This means they can interact with others like themselves and build lives that best suit their own interests.

Sometimes this means creating actual geographic communities of people who share unusual or even deviant lifestyles. More commonly it means creating neighborhoods that shelter ethnic, class, or other lifestyle preferences. In short, a greater range of cultural and social facilities means that specialized communities can form in cities. People find support, companionship, meaningful social contact, and a sense of identity in these communities. Though not based on blood ties and ancestral connectedness like the *gemeinschaft* communities Tonnies described, these city communities are no less real or meaningful for all that.

In cities, friends become more important than kin. This means that as a source of social bonding, blood is less important than the language and interests people share. People rely on their friends and acquaintances for help, and usually they get the help they need. The presumption that city dwellers are isolated and miserable as compared with small towners is not supported by empirical evidence. Worldwide survey data even show that city dwellers are happier than rural people. Some of this happiness is due to the greater availability of jobs and wealth. But even controlling for material factors, city dwellers are still happier.

Healthy urban life   The anticity tradition in American culture and American sociology has emphasized city problems, and there are plenty of problems to worry about. Rates of crime, stress, and physical sickness are indeed high. However, as sociologists have gathered more data on rural communities, they have modified earlier views. For example, evidence shows that rates of stress-related neurosis (for example, depression) are higher in urban areas. However, rates of psychosis (typically, extreme breaks from reality) are higher in rural areas. Drug use is all too common among urban youth, but rural children are increasingly using drugs and developing drug-related problems as well.

Density and crowding are pressing urban problems. Yet population size and density do not always cause psychological strain or malaise. Comparative international research shows that some cultures (e.g., the Japanese) have developed strategies for dealing with urban density. Thus there is nothing inevitable about the problems Simmel and Wirth have associated with city life; they can be solved or avoided.

Crime is a major social problem. Yet we must distinguish criminal victimization from the fear of criminal victimization. For many, fear of victimization is caused by too much exposure to mass media sensationalism or to fear of the poor and racial minorities. To the extent that city life frightens people, it is not the city per se that is to blame. Moreover, even when urbanism produces fear and distrust of "foreign" groups in the wider community, it does not affect people's private social worlds—for example, their relations with neighbors.

Research in other parts of the world has shown that city problems like concentrated poverty, crime, and fearfulness can be remedied. Most problems historically associated with city life are political and economic. They can be solved by mobilizing public concern, finding political leadership, and spending public money. Urban fears diminish when public services like transportation, policing, and utilities improve, and poor people have more economic security.

SUMMING UP

Are cities liberating or enslaving? Is downtown the place to be, after all? Do cities offer something—both socially and culturally—that deserves protection? Too many people have made up their minds about how to answer these questions without thinking about them as sociology does.

At first, most people thought that cities were liberating, a far better alternative than feudal life in the countryside. Then, many people came to think that cities were enslaving. Cities seemed far less attractive than a little plot of land in the clean, safe countryside.

As rural life has become an ever smaller part of American life and cities an ever larger part, it is natural that nostalgia for the "good old days" should develop. And surely the media have fostered this nostalgia vigorously. Out of this has come the tendency to blame society's ills on the city and the poorest people who live in cities. Only rarely has there been a willingness to recognize that city problems are largely problems of social inequality and ethnic or racial conflict. Neither problem is due to the mere size or structure of the city. In the end neither problem is solved by ignoring inequality issues or criticizing the culture of cities.

Moreover, the very thing people find enslaving about city life—the threat of strangers—is the flip side of what some other people find liberating—personal freedom. The freedom of city life has always attracted people. It is the reason why few have fled the city for rural life, while many have fled farms and small towns for cities. We have seen that size and density do not inevitably make city life dangerous and limiting. The question is how we can make large, fluid, varied cities safe and healthy enough to provide the full measure of freedom that people have always desired.

REVIEW EXERCISES

For Discussion and Debate

1. Must rural (or suburban or small town) life continue to be as culturally limited as it has been in the past?

2. Would studying city life in other societies teach us how to solve North America's urban problems, or are every society and its problems unique?

3. "The spread of modern information and communication technology has made large cities culturally and economically unnecessary." Do you agree or disagree?

4. "People achieve more of their human potential in small communities than in large cities because scarcity forces them to develop more fully their personalities and their few relationships." Discuss.

Writing Exercises

1. The social experience of moving from a large city to a small town or a small town to a large city.

2. The social experience of moving from a large school to a small school or a small school to a large school.

3. Reasons why deviant (or criminal) behaviors in large cities and small towns are becoming more similar.

4. Why mental illness is both a profoundly personal and social phenomenon.

Research Activities

1. Choose any city with a population of more than 100,000 people. Collect historical data describing how that city's social and cultural life changed as it grew tenfold (e.g., from 10,000 to 100,000 people or from 100,000 to 1 million people). What changes do you find as a result of this growth?

2. Choose any two cities with the same population size, one in North America and one in Africa, the Middle East, or Asia. Collect data that allow you to compare the social and cultural lives of these two same-sized cities. What differences do you find?

3. Choose any two American or European cities: one as it exists today and another when it was the same size at some time before 1700 (e.g., Boston today and Paris, France, in 1635). Collect data that allow you to compare the social and cultural lives of these two same-sized cities. What differences do you find?

4. Get a sample of at least five people to help you research common perceptions of your (nearest) city's social and cultural organization. Ask each person to mark on a map the location of various areas in the city—for example, the richest and poorest areas, the business district, the area of most delinquency, the areas where drugs can be purchased most easily, the gay and lesbian area, the area of most recent immigration, and so on. How much agreement do you find among the maps these people generate?

SELECTED REFERENCES

AMATO, PAUL R., Urban-rural differences in helping friends and family members, *Social Psychology Quarterly* (December 1993), 56, 4, 249–262.

BACHARACH, LEONA L., The urban environment and mental health, *International Journal of Social Psychiatry* (Spring 1992), 38, 1, 5–15.

BEST, JOEL, and GERALD T. HORIUCHI, The razor blade in the apple: The social construction of urban legends, *Social Problems* (June 1985), 32, 5, 488–499.

DURKHEIM, ÉMILE, *Suicide* (New York: Free Press, 1951).

FISCHER, CLAUDE S., *To dwell among friends*, (Chicago: University of Chicago Press, 1982).

———, The public and private worlds of city life, *American Sociological Review* (June 1981), 46, 3, 306–316.

GREENBERG, MICHAEL, and DONA SCHNEIDER, Violence in American cities: Young black males is the answer, but what was the question? *Social Science and Medicine* (July 1994), 39, 2, 179–187.

HEDGE, ALAN, and YOUSIF H. YOUSIF, Effects of urban size, urgency, and cost on helpfulness: A cross-cultural comparison, *Journal of Cross Cultural Psychology* (March 1992), 23, 1, 107–115.

JANG, SUNG JOON, RICHARD D. ALBA, and THOMAS C. WILSON, Urbanism and nontraditional opinion: A test of Fischer's subcultural theory, *Social Science Quarterly* (September 1992), 73, 3, 596–609.

KOWALSKI, GREGORY S., CHARLES E. FAUPEL, and PAUL D. STARR, Urbanism and suicide: A study of American counties, *Social Forces* (September 1987), 66, 1, 85–101.

LEES, ANDREW, *Cities perceived: Urban society in European and American thought, 1820–1940*, (New York: Columbia University Press, 1985).

SADALLA, EDWARD K., VIRGIL SHEETS, and HEATHER MCCREATH, The cognition of urban tempo, *Environment and Behavior* (March 1990), 22, 2, 230–254.

SIEGEL, FRED, The loss of public space, *Responsive Community* (Summer 1994), 4, 3, 43–54.

SIMMEL, GEORG, The metropolis and mental life, reprinted in P. Kaswitz, *Metropolis: Center and symbol of our times* (New York: New York University Press, 1995).

SMITH, EARL, Louis Wirth and the Chicago School of Urban Sociology: An assessment and critique, *Humanity and Society* (February 1985), 9, 1, 1–12.

SQUIRES, GREGORY D., The political economy of housing: All the discomforts of home, *Research in Urban Sociology* (1993), 3, 129–157.

TITTLE, CHARLES R., and MARK C. STAFFORD, Urban theory, urbanism, and suburban residence, *Social Forces* (March 1992), 70, 3, 725–744.

TUCH, STEVEN A., Urbanism, region and tolerance revisited: The case of racial prejudice, *American Sociological Review* (August 1987), 52, 4, 504–510.

WILSON, THOMAS C., Urbanism, misanthropy and subcultural processes, *Social Science Journal* (July 1985), 22, 3, 89–101.

———, Urbanism and tolerance: A test of some hypotheses drawn from Wirth and Stouffer, *American Sociological Review* (February 1985), 50, 1, 117–123.

WIRTH, LOUIS, Urbanism as a way of life, *American Journal of Sociology* (1938), 44, 3–24.

2. Socialization

Socialization is often defined as the social learning process a person goes through to become a capable member of society. The process is "social" because it is through interaction with others and in response to social pressures that people acquire the **culture**—the language, perspective, and skills, the likes and dislikes, the cluster of norms, values, and beliefs—that characterizes the group to which they belong. As a result, socialization is one of the most important processes by which social structure constrains and transforms us.

Primary socialization is learning that takes place in the early years of a person's life. It is extremely important in forming an individual's personality and charting the course of future development. Very often, primary socialization takes place within the context of a family. Here, a young child learns many of the social skills needed to participate in a wide variety of social institutions.

In this chapter we discuss three issues associated with socialization. The first is about primary socialization, specifically, how parents can provide what their children really need. Then we consider whether corporal punishment—in its most common form, spanking—is a good way to exercise discipline over children. Finally, we examine the alleged harmful effects of the media—specifically, whether the mass media, especially television, are to blame for youthful violence.

2.1

Is "Father Knows Best" best for chidren?

The issue: What kind of family—especially what kind of parenting—will help children grow up happy, secure, and competent? Is the so-called "traditional family" really better than any other kind? Or does family structure make no difference whatsoever?

Introduction As we see later in this book, some people believe that families are in decline, as compared with families based on an idealization of the 1950s or the last century. However, even people who believe the modern family is not in decline argue that one kind of family—again, the idealized family of the 1950s or the last century—is best. Specifically, they argue that there is only _one_ kind of family that is best for raising children, but too many families fail to provide the proper kind of parenting. Compared with the past, children today are more often delinquent, do poorly at school, or have low self-esteem. Today's children are said to be unhappy. Critics scan the rates of adolescent drug use and suicide for further signs that modern families are failing their children.

But does one type of family raise children better than another? If so, what is the "best" family type? Critics claim that the best family type for raising children contains two parents and the parents must be heterosexual, for otherwise children develop uncertain sexual identities. And a stay-at-home mother is best, since she provides the nurturing that all children need, especially when they are very young. What is the sociological evidence to support these claims? As usual, there are (at least) two sides to the story.

ONE TYPE OF FAMILY IS BEST

The family has become a convenient political symbol. For example, the phrase "family values" has entered our political vocabulary. In the 1992 presidential campaign, everyone who sought election was in favor of good family life, and each portrayed the opposing candidate as falling on the wrong side of the issue. In truth, there are many ideas about what a "good" family life might be.

Some speakers at the Republican party's 1992 convention took an extreme position on these issues. They held that a mother who works outside the home harms her children, that single-parent households are caused by people not bothering to get married (or, if they had married, not taking their marriage seriously), and that abortion is wrong in almost all circumstances. In short, the extreme family values position suggested that society can solve its problems only if people live in one particular kind of family, with father as the main or only wage earner and mother devoting herself to raising the children and doing housework. This is the "Father Knows Best" image of the American family with which many adults grew up. ("Father Knows Best" was a popular TV show of the 1950s that portrayed idealized family life—wage-earner father and stay-at-home mother.)

This platform persuaded many voters—but not a majority. Perhaps it failed to correspond to their everyday experience of family life. Nonetheless, this family values outlook struck a responsive chord. There is a con-

tinuum of family values positions, and many people resonate to less extreme versions. And that resonance—nostalgia for another kind of family life—leads us to wonder whether there is some truth in this way of thinking.

Sociological support for the view that one type of family is best comes mainly from sociologists who hold a traditional functional view of the family. They note that, other things being equal, children who grow up in single-parent families are more likely to engage in deviant and delinquent behavior. They are also likely to do worse in school and in employment. Children of divorced parents start to date earlier and engage in more premarital sex than other children. They are also less committed to marriage and more readily accept divorce as a solution to marital problems. As a result, they are more likely to divorce and more likely to become single parents.

What critics of divorce rarely admit is that many marriages oppress women and children. Some husbands and fathers put a high premium on obedience at the expense of mutual respect and self-expression. Many marriages are unequal partnerships that the husbands dominate, and evidence shows that unequal marriages are less happy marriages.

Yet, to give critics their due, marital certainty is satisfying, and more caretaking—housework and parenting—does get done in traditional families. Does this mean that stay-at-home wives are better wives and homemaker mothers better mothers? After all, caretaking can be done in lots of ways.

The value of certainty The idealized traditional family is nothing if not certain. In all things, family life included, certainty often reduces friction and gives people comfort and security. First, there are clear roles and expectations. Husbands and wives know what the culture expects of them, as do parents and children. So long as people live up to these expectations, there is certainty within the family and between the family and its social environment.

Second, this certainty is continuous with the past. People who value tradition and justify their behavior on traditional grounds find this family life satisfying and comfortable. Especially at a time when the society, economy, and culture are all changing quickly—even unpredictably—this continuity with families of the past gives people a sense they are anchored in something solid.

Third, a commitment to certainty increases people's stability. Spouses who are dissatisfied with their marriage do not divorce, because they fear or dislike the uncertainty that would follow. Children who are dissatisfied with their parents do not leave or disobey. To do so would leave them feeling guilty and uncertain, feelings they would prefer to avoid.

THERE IS NO "BEST" TYPE OF FAMILY STRUCTURE

Along with certainty comes a trade-off that critics of the modern family rarely discuss. Often, the cost of certainty is boredom, anger, and frustration. For many people, this cost may be too high.

The value of caretaking   Stay-at-home mothers, of whom there are fewer and fewer, spend more hours per week on unpaid housework and parenting than mothers who work for pay. Fathers who work for pay spend the same time on these activities, whether their wives stay at home or work for pay. And other things being equal, family members prefer having more of these services available. Most people like a tidy home, clean clothes to wear, well-cooked meals on the

table, and so on. Similarly, most children value the attention a parent gives them. No one can deny that housework and parenting efforts are worthwhile.

However, the value of a full-time stay-at-home mom is questionable on at least several points. One is whether the time a woman spends on housework and parenting yields a diminishing rate of return. Twice as much time spent on these activities rarely brings twice as many benefits. A too-intrusive parent—mom or dad—may even be irritating. A related point is that someone else can do many of these activities: meals can be cooked outside the home, the home cleaned by a cleaning person, child-care provided by a child-care professional, and so on.

Second is the cost to the family as a whole of providing these services. If there were no psychic or financial costs, we might all want all of these services all of the time. But nothing is cost-free. Many people—male and female—do not want to provide these services all the time. Attitudes regarding work and earning are very similar for younger men and women; both prefer working outside the home, whether part time or full time. Other families simply cannot afford a stay-at-home parent; they need that second earner.

Some parents feel guilty about depriving their family of full-time housework and parenting services. Should they feel guilty? Are their families harmed if they work outside the home? Researchers who believe there is not one "best" kind of family would tell these parents not to worry. They would say it is more important to focus on key family processes.

Many researchers have studied what makes some families more successful than others. What we (and they) mean by "success" includes an absence of marital conflict, a high degree of marital satisfaction or happiness, and avoidance of divorce. Research consistently shows that successful marriages are distinguished from unsuccessful ones by a few important processes. When these processes are working, the marriage succeeds. When they are not working, the marriage fails. In successful marriages, we commonly find:

Expressions of love Spouses show their mates affection, support, and empathy.

Cooperation Spouses cooperate with one another and act in a considerate manner.

Communication Spouses communicate openly and solve their problems together.

Commitment Spouses express a commitment to their spouse and act faithfully toward them.

Agreement Spouses seek agreement on important issues, such as how to spend money and how to raise the children.

Successful marriages, not surprisingly, are more egalitarian than unsuccessful marriages. Neither spouse tries to dominate the other. And also not surprisingly, given what we have said so far, mates in successful marriages indicate a high degree of sexual satisfaction.

These success-producing processes are possible in every kind of marriage: in new and old marriages, legal and common-law marriages, same-sex (homosexual) and opposite-sex (heterosexual) marriages, first marriages and remarriages, marriages with and without children, and so on. Nothing prevents people from having successful marriages if they act in certain ways.

Similarly, success in raising children—success in the sense of raising children who are healthy, happy, and stable—depends on the right parenting processes. Nothing structural prevents people from raising their children successfully. In that sense, there is no one best type of family structure. True, as we noted earlier, the children of single-parent families run a higher risk of problems in school, work, and marriage. But these prob-lems are largely economic (due to poverty) or due to a lack of social supports. With adequate income and social supports, these families work as well as any others—if the family processes are sound.

The sociological evidence is clear: Family processes matter more than family structures. If the family processes are sound, it doesn't matter whether there is one parent or two, and whether the parents are married or cohabiting, same sex or opposite sex, single earner or dual earner, never divorced or remarried. With good family processes, the child turns out fine. With bad family processes, the child is harmed, whatever the family structure.

Which family processes matter, according to the research literature? The answer is so obvious you may feel embarrassed that we had to tell you. The answer is also similar to what makes for success in relations between spouses. Children turn out fine if their parent(s):

Love them Too little love hurts a child's self-esteem, makes the child less assertive, leads to behavior problems, and increases the risk of delinquency. There can't be too much love.

Supervise them moderately Too little discipline harms a child's psychosocial development, lowers school achievement, and leads to behavior problems. Too severe discipline also leads to behavior problems, hostility, and antisocial attitudes. Moderate discipline with both parents agreeing is best.

Cooperate with each other Conflict between the parents harms the children. If there is a lot of conflict, children develop psychosomatic illnesses, psychiatric problems, low self-esteem, and delinquent behavior.

Provide stability Parents should play a regular, predictable role in the child's life. If both parents work for pay, they should keep a stable day-care arrangement. If the parents are divorced, the noncustodial parent should visit the child regularly. Joint custody is best for the child's self-esteem. (Remember, successful couples solve problems together!)

Keep stress under control. When parents are under severe stress, they may become depressed. This increases the risk of domestic conflict, impatience with the children, child abuse, or neglect. The children feel anxious, unhappy, and insecure. Often they become depressed and develop behavior problems.

Seek social support. The children of parents who receive social support from relatives, friends, or neighbors are less likely to suffer these problems. Even under difficult conditions, social support helps parents to cope with stress. This benefit is passed along to children as better parenting.

SUMMING UP

Is "Father Knows Best" best? What type of family is best, and can sociology help answer that seemingly personal question? Yes, it can. Research shows that the "best" family is characterized by certain *processes* (e.g., love and supervision) and not by certain *structures.* If children are to have the best possible upbringing, we should do better than insist on intact marriages and stay-at-home moms. Instead, society must help to ensure that parents know how to control domestic conflict and how to cope with stress, get enough social support, and are able to supervise their children properly.

And society must help more socially and economically vulnerable families—those with insufficient incomes or a single parent—to be able to provide the high-quality parenting that is needed. To raise children well, we must provide support to parents who need it. Some family structures (e.g., single-parent families) need more support than others. Insufficient income is a common source of stress and conflict, and single mothers are most likely to lack a sufficient income. For different reasons, poor or conflictual two-parent families need social support too.

To repeat, the answer is *not* to favor one type of family structure over all others. Here, even the research on same-sex versus opposite-sex parents is consistent. Other things being equal, gay and lesbian parents raise their children as well as heterosexual parents do. There is no evidence that children need heterosexual parents to serve as role models. Nor is there evidence that a child's sexual orientation is shaped by his or her custodial parent(s).

All intimate or close relations, family relations among them, follow a logic that determines the important outcomes. As we have seen, the important social processes include interaction, communication, cooperation, and empathy. They operate similarly in families of different kinds: for example, in a traditional heterosexual marriage, a same-sex marriage, a family without children, or a family with children and one parent. With similar processes, families give their members similar kinds of experience, whatever the family form or composition.

An issue in family life is the interplay among family, school, and work roles. One important concern is the spillover of energy and emotion from family life to work life, and vice versa. Problems in one domain often cause problems in another. Families today are scrambling to invent ways of dealing with role overload, the double burden of work and child care, elder care, and often conflicting demands, as work, school, and family demands all change at once. The best families are the ones that work hardest to find solutions to these problems.

REVIEW EXERCISES

For Discussion and Debate

1. "There are as many types of families as there are actual families."
2. "Certainty in family relationships is far more valuable than any chance of freedom."
3. "It doesn't matter how you raise your children, so long as you are sincere in your beliefs."
4. "The community has no business telling parents how to raise their children."

Writing Exercises

1. "Politicians have no business using family issues to get votes."
2. "Children are captives, no matter how loving the prison."
3. "Parents ought to feel guilty about neglecting their children for paid work."
4. "Poverty is no excuse for raising your children badly."

Research Activities

1. Watch three episodes of at least one "family show" on television. How is the depiction of family life different from the family shows of the 1950s and 1960s mentioned in this chapter?
2. Devise a way to measure family processes in your own family. For example, how much love, supervision, communication, or stress is there? Then try out the measure on your own family and one other family.
3. Examine the data in three published studies that relate family processes to successful marriage or successful parenting. Do the results agree with each other?
4. Examine the findings of three studies on same-sex marriages. Do you find any differences from opposite-sex marriages in what makes the family "work"?

SELECTED REFERENCES

AMATO, PAUL R., and SANDRA J. REZAC, Contact with nonresident parents, interparental conflict, and children's behavior, *Journal of Family Issues* (June 1994), 15, 2, 191–207.

BARBER, BRIAN K., JOSEPH E. OLSEN, and SHOBHA C. SHAGLE, Associations between parental psychological and behavioral control and youth internalized and externalized behaviors, *Child Development* (August 1994), 65, 4, 1120–1136.

CHAO, RUTH K., Beyond parental control and authoritarian parenting style: Understanding Chinese parenting through the cultural notion of training, *Child Development* (1994), 65, 4, 1111–1119.

CONGER, RAND D., XIAOJIA GE, GLEN H. ELDER, JR., FREDERICK O. LORENZ, and RONALD L. SIMONS, Economic stress, coercive family process, and developmental problems of adolescents, *Child Development* (April 1994), 65, 2, 541–561.

DOZIER, BRENDA S., DONNA L. SOLLIE, STEVEN J. STACK, and THOMAS A. SMITH, The effects of postdivorce attachment on coparenting relationships, *Journal of Divorce and Remarriage* (1993), 19, 3–4, 109–123.

ELLIS, GODFREY J., and LARRY R. PETERSEN, Socialization values and parental control techniques: A cross-cultural analysis of child rearing, *Journal of Comparative Family Studies* (Spring 1992), 23, 1, 39–54.

FOXCROFT, DAVID R., and GEOFF LOWE, Adolescent drinking behavior and family socialization factors: A meta-analysis, *Journal of Adolescence* (September 1991), 14, 3, 255–273.

GIEVE, KATHERINE, ed., *Balancing acts: On being a mother* (London: Virago, 1989).

GOETTING, ANN, The parenting-crime connection, *Journal of Primary Prevention* (Spring 1994), 14, 3, 169–186.

GRINGLAS, MARCY, and MARSHA WEINRAUB, The more things change ... Single parenting revisited, *Journal of Family Issues* (January 1995), 16, 1, 29–52.

KURDEK, LAWRENCE, and MARK A. FINE, The relation between family structure and young adolescents' appraisals of family climate and parenting behavior, *Journal of Family Issues* (June 1993), 14, 2, 279–290.

LAMB, MICHAEL E., ed., *The father's role: Cross-cultural perspectives.* (Hillsdale, NJ: Lawrence Erlbaum Associates, 1987).

MCLEOD, JANE D., and MICHAEL J. SHANAHAN, Poverty, parenting, and children's mental health, *American Sociological Review* (June 1993), 58, 3, 351–366.

MCLOYD, VONNIE C., and LEON WILSON, Telling them like it is: The role of economic and environmental factors in single mothers' discussions with their children, *American Journal of Community Psychiatry* (August 1992), 20, 4, 419–444.

METZLER, CAROL W., JOHN NOELL, ANTHONY BIGLAN, DENNIS ARY, and KEITH SMOLKOWSKI, The social context for risky sexual behavior among adolescents, *Journal of Behavioral Medicine* (August 1994), 17, 4, 419–438.

MITCHELL, BARBARA A., Family structure and leaving the nest: A social resource perspective, *Sociological Perspectives* (Winter 1994), 37, 4, 651–671.

OLSON, MYRNA, and JUDITH A. HAYNES, Successful single parents, *Families in Society* (May 1993), 74, 5, 259–267.

PARCEL, TOBY L., and ELIZABETH G. MENAGHAN, Early parental work, family social capital, and early childhood outcomes, *American Journal of Sociology* (January 1994), 99, 4, 972–1009.

SELTZER, JUDITH, Consequences of marital dissolution for children, *Annual Review of Sociology*, (1994), 20, 235–266.

2.2

Should Johnny be spanked?

The issue: **Should parents hit their children as a means of disciplining them?** *And if hitting and other corporal punishment is harmful or ineffective, does the state have a right to interfere in parents' rights to discipline their children this way?*

Introduction Parents do all sorts of things to try to control and discipline their children. One of the things they may try is spanking their children. In this section we treat spanking as one form of corporal punishment and combine the research findings on spanking with the research findings on corporal punishment more generally. We are persuaded that spanking, the mildest form of corporal punishment, predicts more severe forms of corporal punishment. The transition from spanking to worse violence against children is not inevitable—in fact, it may be rare, but there is no physical violence against children that does not begin with spanking.

There may be a continuum of child abuse that ranges from spanking to physical violence and even homicide. In some sense, spanking may be a warm-up for more dangerous and even life-threatening practices. However, experts disagree on this point. Most believe that physical abuses of children, with different degrees of severity, call for different types of management and treatment. They may or may not have different causes.

Spanking remains a common practice in North America, and most North Americans seem to approve of physical punishment. However, many critics view spanking as a kind of child abuse. They claim that spanking can shade into dangerous and life-threatening behavior. Certainly, distinctions between normal and deviant punishments are often hard to make. No wonder strangers feel uncomfortable about intervening when they see a child being punished in public.

Does the practice of spanking predict other, more serious mistreatments? Findings suggest that violence that goes well beyond spanking is widespread and built into many parent-child relationships. Much violence against children is never reported, though many parents who admit to their violent acts may do so in the belief that such behavior is acceptable.

For this and other reasons, we don't know the full extent of spanking in North America, nor of people's acceptance of spanking. Researchers get different results when they study spanking using different methods—for example, by asking about recent behaviors, attitudes toward spanking, or responses to vignettes in which spanking is one possible way of dealing with a fictional child's misbehavior. Nonetheless, the research on spanking and attitudes toward spanking provide some fairly consistent patterns.

PARENTS SHOULD SPANK THEIR CHILDREN

Views about spanking vary with the age of the child involved. Most people would feel it is more acceptable to spank a 2-year-old than an 8-year-old, since the younger child has less developed thinking skills and poorer judgment. It is harder for the parent to reason with a 2-year-old about running into the road, for example. Accordingly, parents of toddlers are more likely to support spanking than parents of older children. Nonetheless, about half of American parents surveyed by M. A. Strauss and D. A. Donnelly reported using corporal punishment on their adolescent child in the past year; they did so an average of six to eight times. For their part, undergraduates surveyed by J. M. Ruane were ambivalent about the use of force to control the behavior of children.

Support for spanking appears to come from three quarters. First, some cultures view spanking and other forms of corporal punishment as appropriate social control. This view is captured by the old adage, "Spare the rod and spoil the child." Second, some religions and cultures also view spanking as moral. This provides the practice with a moral and even supernatural legitimacy. Third, people who were themselves spanked as children tend to support spanking.

Some cultures condone spanking Some research finds little evidence of cultural variations in the use of corporal punishment. However, most research shows that cultures do vary in their acceptance of spanking. Indeed, many cultures currently support spanking—more generally, corporal punishment—for child misbehavior. Remember the American teenager who was flogged naked in Singapore for doing some minor property damage? The public reaction reminds us that, though a majority of Americans consider it okay to hit their own children, they don't approve of other people doing it for them.

Recent studies find spanking is accepted in Indonesia, South Korea, Barbados, and Nigeria, as well as among immigrants to the United States from China, Guyana, and the West Indies. Many industrializing societies appear on this list; yet there is no simple pattern of tolerance for spanking. For example, parents in India generally oppose corporal punishment, whereas parents in the more economically developed United States generally tolerate it. Thus we cannot say that economic development (or literacy or higher education) inevitably makes spanking unacceptable. However, as we will later see, some social factors are indeed correlated with spanking.

Popular acceptance of spanking as a form of child control appears to vary from one culture to another. And, like everything that is culturally variable, spanking raises the ethnocentrism issue: Should members of one culture judge another culture's practices, declaring them to be barbaric, inhumane, or foolish? We will consider this further in a little while.

Some religions support spanking Like cultures, religions vary in their support for spanking. As we noted earlier, religious support for spanking—and, more generally, for corporal punishment—provides moral legitimacy that encourages spanking. More parents spank their children if they know that religious leaders condone the practice than if religious leaders ignore or oppose it.

Survey evidence shows that in the United States, Protestant fundamentalists are the strongest religious supporters of corporal punishment. Most fundamentalists support spanking and other forms of corporal punishment both at home and school. Less fundamentalist religious people, whether Protestant, Catholic, or Jewish, are less supportive. One explanation is that fundamentalist Protestantism (or fundamentalism) is based on a literal reading of the Bible. Fundamentalists interpret the Bible to say that human nature is inherently sinful, that sin demands punishment, and that parents have an obligation to break a child's (sinful) will, to bring it under God's control. From this perspective, corporal punishment is not only a tool by which loving and devoted parents try to lead a sinful child to goodness. It also shows a dedication to God's work of fighting sin, whether or not the punishment succeeds in changing a child's behavior.

Related to this fundamentalist interpretation of the Bible is a belief in absolute right and wrong. Fundamentalism is not a morality in which the same behaviors are sometimes right and sometimes wrong, depending on the situation. According to fundamentalists of any religious denomination, bad behavior is always bad and must always be punished. Good behavior should be approved and emulated. It makes no difference if a child—even your own child—is involved. Nor can we excuse wrongdoing under extenuating circumstances—for example, temptation, poor judgment, or peer influence.

Thus spanking often follows from a particular view of good and evil and a particular notion of parents' responsibility to control their children's evil. Empirical research indicates that physical punishment succeeds only in leading a child to view God as attentive, loving, and all-powerful. However, it does not improve the child's behavior. In fact, spanked children are likely to continue disobeying their parents, since this gains parental attention, and punishment reaffirms the parents' (and God's) love.

People who were spanked support spanking One survey of American college students by A. M. Graziano and K. A. Namaste found that 93% had been spanked as children. The vast majority of "spankees" accepted corporal punishment as a legitimate way to control misbehavior and planned to spank their own children. So, contrary to what we might expect, people who were spanked as children do not generally oppose spanking.

Another survey by S. D. Herberger and H. Tennen helps us understand why. It found that adults who had been spanked as children judge corporal punishment less harshly and critically than adults who did not experience it. Critics may be exaggerating the practice's harmfulness out of ignorance and a lack of firsthand experience. However, there are several other possible ways to explain the support for spanking among Americans who have themselves been spanked.

First, spanking teaches a view of personal responsibility similar to what we noted among fundamentalists. Thus it is part of learning a black-and-white moral worldview. Second, misbehaving boys receive more corporal punishment than misbehaving girls. Thus spanking becomes part of the macho male culture which demands physical pain as the price for independence and masculinity. From this standpoint, corporal punishment is normal and even normative, an early test of manliness. Some fathers may think that spanking their sons initiates them into manhood. However, not all Americans support the practice of spanking. And throughout the world, many people of other countries oppose it as well.

PARENTS SHOULD NOT SPANK THEIR CHILDREN

Some cultures oppose spanking, viewing corporal punishment as an inappropriate form of child discipline. There are reasons why societies oppose or condone spanking, as we shall see. In our own society, we find evidence that corporal punishment— including spanking—indicates family disorganization. Fewer well-functioning families use corporal punishment to control behavior. And, as we shall see, there is evidence that corporal punishment has harmful consequences or side effects.

More developed societies reject corporal punishment We noted earlier that many societies condone corporal punishment. Most societies that accept corporal punishment are less industrialized, but the United States is an exception to the rule. Societies that place a strong emphasis on self-reliance (versus conformity) typically oppose corporal punishment. Indeed, most industrial societies oppose corporal punishment. This shows up clearly when we compare the United States with Sweden, a country well known for its concern for society's vulnerable members and a trendsetter in European social practices.

In 1979, Sweden outlawed corporal punishment at home and in the schools. Since then, survey results show that only 26% of Swedish parents use corporal punishment, compared with 81% of American parents. Swedes believe that the state should intervene in families that abuse their members, physically or otherwise. It puts this belief into practice through laws prohibiting child abuse, and these laws are enforced. Beyond that, Sweden provides families at risk— those in which one or more members are likely to suffer harm—with shelters, counseling, and economic support, for example. The evidence suggests that legislation does succeed in reducing spanking and corporal punishment more generally.

Like other progressive beliefs about sex, marriage, parenting, social welfare, and taxation that started in Sweden, these views about spanking have spread throughout northern Europe. Eventually they may prevail in the industrial world, including the United States.

Corporal punishment indicates family disorganization As we noted, people who were spanked usually condone spanking. People spanked as children, who grew up with friends who were spanked, and who live as adults among people who spank their own children are unlikely to find anything wrong with corporal punishment. As a result, parents use the disciplinary techniques they experienced firsthand when they were growing up. Unless they are taught to do otherwise, people accept their own childhood experiences as normal. They don't evaluate their own behavior unless they can imagine an alternative.

But what conditions lead people who hadn't been spanked to begin spanking their own children? Surely this is key to understanding the origins of spanking when they are other than blind habit. One researcher studied these conditions and found that people used to nonviolent parenting adopt spanking and other corporal punishment techniques when stress becomes extreme—for example, when the husband/father is unemployed, family income is low, or surrounding social norms support violence.

According to this research, the best predictors of corporal punishment, after controlling for whether the parents have been spanked or not, are too many children born too soon, delayed child development, stressful living conditions, and inadequate social support for stressed or inexperienced parents. Mothers are most often the spankers, and sons more often spanked than daughters. Most important perhaps is the finding that parents usually spank their children in desperation, not as a conscious plan.

Spanking is part of a repertoire of disciplinary techniques that are punitive and unreasoning. This means that parents who generally control their children by reasoning or withholding rewards rarely, if ever, spank their children. Conversely, parents who neither reason nor withhold rewards from misbehaving children are likely to resort to spanking and other corporal punishment.

Corporal punishment has negative consequences

We might condone spanking, even spanking carried out for the wrong reasons, if we could show that it improved children's behavior. But there is no evidence that spanking or other corporal punishment does so. On the contrary, boys who receive corporal punishment often become aggressive, girls withdrawn. The practice backfires in other respects too. For example, parents are more likely to punish older siblings than younger siblings for fighting, especially boys when they fight with their sisters. This punishment of the more powerful sibling results in more frequent aggression.

Negative side effects of corporal punishment include depression, anxiety and lower grades in school, aggression and delinquency, and slower physical development. And, not surprisingly, many children who receive corporal punishment come to feel they have little control over their own lives. They are less likely to be ambitious, confident, optimistic, and happy.

The harm caused by corporal punishment merely begins in childhood; it does not end there. Research shows that among adults who were spanked as children we find more crime and racism, a sense of personal injustice, general tolerance for violence and aggression, and belief in the value of extreme solutions to social problems (for example, belief in the death penalty). Corporal punishment in childhood is an even better predictor of violence in adulthood than either social class or viewing violent TV shows.

The negative effects of spanking on later child and adult behavior result from an interaction with other conditions or predisposing factors. After all, the vast majority of Americans are spanked, but only a minority become violently abusive, delinquent, or criminal. Corporal punishment does not always produce negative side effects. For example, corporal punishment mainly causes delinquency when parental discipline is inconsistent, parents' demands are changeable, or discipline is intermittent.

Likewise, corporal punishment mainly causes delinquency when a parent relies nearly exclusively on spanking and rarely tries to reason with the child.

SUMMING UP

Should Johnny be spanked? We don't think so. Spanking usually does not control or reduce misbehavior. At best, spanking drives deviant impulses underground. Often they reappear as violent or delinquent acts or as mental distress. In short, spanking produces undesirable side effects and even stimulates misbehavior. Generally, because it is not correlated with reasoning, spanking gives children little experience in learning to deal reasonably with their impulses.

Are groups or societies that reject spanking right to criticize groups or societies that do accept it? Our answer is mixed. No sociological evidence can prove that one behavior is more ethical or moral than another; sociology does not work that way. Sociology can show that as an informal social control corporal punishment is ineffective. It causes more problems than it solves. This largely explains why most developed societies have rejected corporal punishments like flogging, torture, and execution as formal methods of social control. Even as general deterrents (i.e., to discourage others from wrongdoing) these methods do not work.

Most economically developed, literate, and prosperous societies have rejected spanking and other corporal punishment as acceptable methods of child discipline. As Emile Durkheim showed, societies with a complex division of labor view conflicts in more subtle ways. They tolerate more deviant behavior and punish rule-breakers less harshly. They are more likely to correct the harm done—to make restitution to a crime's victim—than to exact revenge. Whether this indicates a moral development away from repressive justice or merely slack moral standards (as the fundamentalists might charge) is something we cannot answer, for that is a value judgment.

In the end, all we can say is that parents should not spank their children if they want to reduce misbehavior; it doesn't work. Alternate methods, like reasoning with the child and withholding rewards, are more successful if the parents are consistent.

REVIEW EXERCISES

For Discussion and Debate

1. "Capital punishment is a good way to punish serious wrongdoing."
2. "Corporal punishment is more appropriate to use on adult offenders than on children."
3. "Children respond to reasoning better than they respond to threats."
4. "Religion is the source of much of the violence in our society."

Writing Exercises

1. "Spare the rod and spoil the child."
2. The circumstances leading up to the last occasion on which your parents spanked you.
3. Three situations in which torture would be an appropriate form of social control.
4. "What children need most from their parents."

Research Activities

1. Interview at least six people who have witnessed a young child being spanked in public. How did they react?

2. Compare a society in which spanking is widely tolerated with a society in which it is prohibited. How do these societies differ socially or culturally? Collect some published data to illustrate these differences.

3. Make yourself comfortable in a busy public place—a shopping mall, for example—and spend some time observing how parents control and discipline their children. Record your observations. What patterns do you note?

4. Interview a sample of 10 people, using two or more different methods to determine their acceptance of spanking as a method of child discipline. How well do the results of these methods agree?

SELECTED REFERENCES

AGNEW, ROBERT, Physical punishment and delinquency: A research note, *Youth and Society* (1983), 15, 2, 225–236.

CAPPS, DONALD, Religion and child abuse: Perfect together, *Journal for the Scientific Study of Religion* (March 1992), 31, 1, 1–14.

DELEY, WARREN W., Physical punishment of children: Sweden and the U.S.A., *Journal of Comparative Family Studies* (Autumn 1988), 19, 3, 419–431.

DEYOUNG, YOLANDA, and EDWARD F. ZIGLER, Machismo in two cultures: Relation to punitive child-rearing practices, *American Journal of Orthopsychiatry* (July 1994), 64, 3, 386–395.

DUVALL, DONNA, and ALAN BOOTH, Social class, stress and physical punishment, *International Review of Modern Sociology* (January–June 1979), 9, 1, 103–117.

ELLIS, GODFREY J., and LARRY R. PETERSEN, Socialization values and parental control techniques: A cross-cultural analysis of child rearing, *Journal of Comparative Family Studies* (Spring 1992), 23, 1, 39–54.

ELLISON, CHRISTOPHER G., and DARREN E. SHERKAT, Conservative Protestantism and support for corporal punishment, *American Sociological Review* (February 1993), 58, 1, 131–144.

FELSON, RICHARD B., and NATALIE RUSSO, Parental punishment and sibling aggression, *Social Psychology Quarterly* (March 1988), 51, 1, 11–18.

GELLES, RICHARD J., Physical violence, child abuse, and child homicide: A continuum of violence, or distinct behaviors? *Human Nature* (1991), 2, 1, 59–72.

GRASMICK, HAROLD G., ROBERT J. BURSIK, JR., and M'LOU KIMPEL, Protestant fundamentalism and attitudes toward corporal punishment of children, *Violence and Victims* (Winter 1991), 6, 4, 283–298.

GRAZIANO, ANTHONY M., and KAREN A. NAMASTE, Parental use of physical force in child discipline: A survey of 679 college students, *Journal of Interpersonal Violence* (December 1990), 5, 4, 449–463.

HERBERGER, S. D., and H. TENNEN, The effect of self-relevance on judgments of moderate and severe disciplinary encounters, *Journal of Marriage and the Family* (May 1985), 47, 2, 311–319.

LARZELERE, ROBERT E., Moderate spanking: Model or deterrent of children's aggression in the family? *Journal of Family Violence* (March 1986), 1, 1, 27–36.

LENTON, RHONDA L., Techniques of child discipline and abuse by parents, *Canadian Review of Sociology and Anthropology* (May 1990), 27, 2, 157–185.

LIENESCH, MICHAEL, "Train up a child": Conceptions of child-rearing in Christian conservative social thought, *Comparative Social Research* (1991), 13, 203–224.

NEWSON, JOHN, ELIZABETH NEWSON, and MARY ADAMS, The social origins of delinquency, *Criminal Behavior and Mental Health* (1993), 3, 1, 19–29.

RUANE, JANET M., Tolerating force: A contextual analysis of the meaning of tolerance, *Sociological Inquiry* (Summer 1993), 63, 3, 293–304.

STRAUSS, MURRAY A., and DENISE A. DONNELLY, Corporal punishment of adolescents by American parents, *Youth and Society* (June 1993), 24, 4, 419–442.

WELLER, SUSAN C., A. KIMBALL ROMNEY, and DONALD P. ORR, The myth of a sub-culture of corporal punishment, *Human Organization* (Spring 1987), 46, 1, 39–47.

WOLFNER, GLENN D., and RICHARD J. GELLES, A profile of violence toward children: A national study, *Child Abuse and Neglect* (March–April 1993), 17, 2, 197–212.

2.3
Does television cause youthful violence?

The issue: **What do children get from all the television they watch?** Does it do them any harm? And should the state interfere if it does them harm—specifically, if it **leads them to act in aggressive and violent ways?**

Introduction   Almost since the invention and spread of the medium after World War II, television has been accused of producing violent behavior in its viewers, especially younger viewers. And almost since these accusations started, researchers have attempted to find out whether such fears were justified. After all, a lot was at stake. More and more people were spending more and more hours per week in front of the television screen. Moreover, the rise in television viewing appeared to correlate with an increase in teenage rebellion, violence, and crime. In each decade that followed the 1940s, grown-ups voiced more concern about the younger generation—criticizing juvenile delinquents and beatniks in the 1950s, hippies and political protesters in the 1960s, drug users in the 1970s, street gang members in the 1980s, and youthful murderers in the 1990s.

Of course, these grown-ups are (and were) not without their own motives in criticizing young people in the first place; moreover, older generations invariably criticize the younger generation. But to the extent that an increase in both delinquency and TV watching really happened, was this correlation a causal relationship or merely the result of another factor? And if the latter, what might that other factor be? As with the other debates in this book, opinions on this topic varied widely. As we shall see, some of the research supporting one side or another was ideological, and some was also self-serving.

TELEVISION IS NOT TO BLAME

Those with the most to lose in this debate—the television networks themselves—soon became involved in researching the question. They proposed to provide their own thorough and unbiased scientific account of the existing evidence. Not surprisingly, their account showed that television was not to blame. They rested their conclusion on a number of arguments, some of which were hotly disputed by the "independent" research community.

Laboratory studies are not realistic   First, the networks attacked laboratory studies, typically carried out by psychologists, which showed that people (including children) tend to imitate behavior they see rewarded. Thus children watching a television program showing violence are likely to behave aggressively toward one another, or toward their toys, or to express aggression in verbal or projective forms.

However, researchers supporting the networks (call them network people) launched the most common attack on psychological research, which is that behavior in laboratories may or may not be like behavior outside laboratories. After all, laboratories provide a very special—indeed, unusual—environment where one is freed from the constraints of everyday life and surrounded by strangers. This in itself might be enough to incite deviance of one kind or another. How people behaved in a laboratory, however suggestive, was far from the demonstration of a causal relationship, the network people claimed.

Correlation does not prove causation   Laboratory research is often considered better than naturalistic or field research for proving a causal connection between two variables—say, viewed violence and violent behavior. If one accepts the network people's claim that laboratory research is inappropriate, one is then forced to rely on naturalistic or field research, and here the network people used the accusation always leveled at this kind of research, namely that nonexperimental research is incapable of showing a causal connection. At best, it can show that two things co-occur or are correlated.

Imagine, for example, a study comparing two communities. In one, children viewed an average of 6 hours of television a day, and the rate of violent delinquency was 100 offenders per 1000 children. In the other, children viewed an average of 2 hours of television a day, and the rate of violent delinquency was only 25 offenders per 1000 children. This set of figures first poses the problem of the *ecological fallacy*. Are the children in either community who are committing the delinquent acts the ones who are actually watching the most television? If not, television is not to blame. If we get past this hurdle and the children committing

delinquent acts are watching the most television, there is the problem of *logical sequence*: Maybe they started watching violent television *after* they began a life of delinquency. Or there is the problem of *spuriousness*: Perhaps another factor, whether bad genes or faulty socialization, makes them both watch a lot of television and commit delinquent acts. If so, television is not to blame.

With these kinds of correlational data, we can't affix a causal blame. (If you think about it, you will see this is the same kind of methodological problem that arose in the argument over whether cigarette smoking causes lung cancer.)

The research community is undecided   Because of methodological problems, independent researchers for a long time were cautious in interpreting their results and drawing practical conclusions. From this fact, the network people concluded that the research community was undecided about whether television was to blame. Given the enormous stakes—specifically, the cost of regulating the networks and changing their programming—it would be foolish and unfair to make policies about television violence until the research community had reached a clearer, less ambiguous conclusion, said the network people.

TV effects on children's aggression are small   Suppose we ignore all of the points made so far and admit that, yes, there is evidence that viewing violent television programs increases the likelihood of violent behavior, especially by young people. Then, the network people said, the effects of viewing found in research so far were very small. Imagine that studies were turning up the following kind of finding: that doubled television viewing—a change from, say, 2 hours to 4 hours a day—only resulted in a 5%

increase in the probability, seriousness, or duration of violent behavior. In fact, that was the magnitude of effect researchers were finding. Surely it would be inappropriate to spend millions of dollars correcting the "television content problem" if doing so would have so little effect on people's behavior. It would be like killing an ant with a sledgehammer. What's more, such small effects suggest that other factors unconnected with television viewing would be responsible for much more of the problem. "Why not attack those other causes first?" asked the network people.

There is no television effect on viewers' perceptions
If television was indeed warping people's thinking and, in this way, causing violent behavior, it should be possible to show that heavy viewers of television perceived the world in different ways from infrequent viewers. However, network-commissioned research of viewers' perceptions was unable to find any evidence of such a difference.

Television effects are conditional
Even if we gave up on every argument the network people put forward so far, there was still an important one in the wings. It was simply that television viewing, at worst, interacts with other characteristics of the viewer to produce the undesired behavior. Better-adjusted viewers would have less trouble with the existing television content. Let's consider the arguments supporting this notion.

Each year children watch hundreds of millions of person-hours of television, yet relatively few of them become violent delinquents. In fact, the problem seems most marked in the United States; research finds television produces less violence among children from other countries. So we must ask what it is about the United States that causes this pathological reaction to television programs. Likewise, the reaction to televised violence is stronger among boys than among girls and stronger among children from poor and/or violent neighborhoods than among children from nonpoor, nonviolent neighborhoods. Indeed, the reaction to televised violence is strongest among children for whom violence is a normal, everyday experience in the neighborhood or home, or where neighborhood and home values are sympathetic to the use of violence.

Taking this even farther, the context in which a program is viewed also affects children's reactions. If they watch a program alone in a quiet room, they are unlikely to behave aggressively afterward; the same program viewed in a noisy group will more likely produce aggressive and violent behavior.

What this tells us is that television programs interact with, or are conditional on, everyday experience. In a society, neighborhood, or family in which tension is high and violence is common, children will react violently to television violence. But surely, blaming television for this violence is like blaming the mine-shaft canary for dying on us. Children's reactions are simply delivering a message we don't want to hear, that American society needs fixing.

Television only reinforces existing views
Remember, too, that people in real life have the choice of watching or not watching violent programs. There is plenty of evidence that different kinds of people consume different amounts and different kinds of television programming. Important differences include age, gender, and educational level, as well as a number of other factors. If people don't want their children to be violent, they shouldn't let their children watch violent programs. This is the idea behind the newly devised v-chip available on many television sets. Of course, it ignores the fact that other factors besides violent television cause deliquency.

Television violence has already decreased And if all this wasn't enough, the network people went on to claim, finally, that in response to public concern they had been busy decreasing the amount of television violence.

TELEVISION IS TO BLAME

In the face of these persuasive arguments, independent researchers went to work with great energy and resourcefulness. They took exception to virtually every point the network researchers made.

Studies are now more naturalistic, longitudinal These researchers (call them independents) pointed out, first, that reliance on one-shot laboratory experiments was much less common than it had been before. Increasingly, research was *naturalistic*—conducted outside a laboratory setting—and *longitudinal*—following changes over time.

In a longitudinal study, we follow the same people as they change over time, taking repeated measurements of their behavior. We might come back to them once a year to find out how much television they are watching per night and whether they have been in trouble with the law (or some other measure of delinquent thought or action). If we find that an increase in television watching one year is followed by an increase in delinquency the next year, we have grounds for thinking that television had some causal influence on the behavior. So, for example, researchers conducted a 10-year study that found we can predict teenage aggression from the amount and type of television viewing a child did while in the third grade.

Changes in viewing predict changes in behavior Another naturalistic study found that, soon after the arrival of cable television, a community that had previously had no television reception due to surrounding mountains and only low levels of teenage aggression developed high levels of teenage aggression in the schools. Likewise, the homicide rate in South Africa, long without television, increased rapidly after the arrival of television.

The research community is not undecided Findings like these agreed entirely with the earlier findings of laboratory studies. In fact, very few published studies found anything different. All the research pointed to the conclusion that television viewing increases children's aggressiveness and violence. By the 1980s, it would have been impossible to find any independent researchers—indeed, any fair-minded readers of the research literature—coming to any other conclusion.

Small doses add up Even though most research showed only small effects of television violence on children's behavior, these small effects added up—like progressive poisoning by continuously ingesting trace amounts of arsenic. One researcher fitted the available data to a mathematical model and concluded that a mere 8% increase in the average child's level of aggressiveness would double the adult homicide rate 15 to 20 years later.

Television produces generalized fear Research on the views and attitudes of heavy television viewers came to a different conclusion from that of the network people. They found clear evidence that people who watch a lot of television, especially a lot of televised violence (including TV news), are more fearful and mistrustful than people who watch little television. This is particularly marked among groups like the infirm or aged, who are already physically vulnerable and often shut-in at home for long stretches of time. The paradox is that those least likely to suffer from criminal violence, since they are at home in front of the TV a lot of the time, are the most afraid of becoming victims.

Conditional effects revisited   It's true, the independent researchers said, that televised violence has more effect on some people—on young American men living in poor, violent neighborhoods, for example—than it does on others. In a better world, where no one is poor or violent, television might not pose such a problem. However, in the real world, it does. And it is far easier to change television content than it is to change American culture, the class system, the amount of domestic and community violence, or young men's hormones.

The results of content analyses   Researchers also addressed the claim by network researchers that television violence had already begun to decrease significantly. Using the technique of *content analysis*—a systematic method of examining the program content of any communication—they found little evidence that this was so.

SUMMING UP

Unlike many debates in sociology, this one is pretty much over. The evidence is in, and televised violence *does* produce violence in children. The implications for socialization are clear: If you don't want a violent child, restrict his or her viewing of television violence. This is not the only thing you have to do, but it is something that is likely to have an effect, however small.

Further research has also identified the kinds of televised violence that have the largest impact on a child. First, televised programs that show a perpetrator of violence being rewarded or escaping punishment are more likely to produce violent behavior in children (and later, adults). So associating violence with sex, as in pornographic programs, or with glamor and wealth, as in shows about organized crime, will increase the likelihood of violent behavior. Violence that looks sexy, exciting, or like fun is violence that is likely to be imitated.

Second, televised programs that show violence in a setting in which there is no evident pain, sorrow, or remorse, or where violence is shown as justified by some feature of the plot, are more likely to produce violent behavior. We may laugh at action stories in which hundreds of people are mowed down by guns that never run out of bullets, blood gushes like water from a broken fire hydrant, and a never-ending stream of good guys fights a never-ending stream of bad guys. But this fantasy of no-consequence violence increases the likelihood of real-life violence. Violence motivated by revenge or another "basic instinct" of social behavior also increases the likelihood of violent behavior by the viewer. This is one instance of the larger principle that violence that seems justified is more likely to condone and produce real-life violence.

Third, physical violence that occurs alongside verbal abuse increases the likelihood of violent behavior by the viewer. It implies that physical violence is, somehow, a natural or inevitable consequence of verbal abuse.

Fourth, violence that goes uncriticized in the televised story—and by implication seems justified or meritorious—increases the likelihood of violent behavior by the viewer.

Finally, and perhaps most important of all, violence portrayed in a realistic setting with realistic characters—for example, in neighborhoods like the viewer's own neighborhood and heroes that look familiar to the viewer—increase the likelihood of violent behavior. That's why the portrayal of violence in the news is dangerous; it has a disarming tendency to look real.

Of course, one of the reasons television is such a powerful medium is that it remains a magical force. By that we mean it is an institution that has been subjected to remarkably little formal criticism on an ongoing basis. Such criticism—part of our basic experience of painting, music, dance, film, poetry, and literature—could ultimately reveal what we see on television to be not reality but a construction of reality. The criticism of other communication and art forms is far more than philosophical speculation. It is day to day and streetwise; it is regular; it is off the cuff. But when people talk about the television programs they saw last night, they do so without a knowledge of the techniques of the medium: visual techniques, programming techniques, writing techniques, directorial techniques. The effect is to increase the likelihood that they will take what they see on television as realistic and, therefore, as a seamlessly attached part of the world in which they live.

Thus the depictions of life that television programming presents to us in an uninterrupted flow seem less like constructed pictures, less like manipulations, and less affected by canny editorializing than like natural bits of the actual world, which also contains the television set on which we watch them. Beyond that, because television is so graphic and so attractive, we also accord it some authority that is as real as the authority we grant other experts in reality (like doctors and professors of sociology). And if television depictions show us violence in a normal setting, we may be prone to use those depictions as texts for learning basic, and violent, social techniques.

If we could reduce the effects of television by watching less of it, we could perhaps do even better by watching with a critical eye that would help us reveal the presence of the producer, the creator, the instigator behind the image that seems so effortless. The TV depiction would then be someone's view, not a simple statement of "the way things are."

The news is the news, and we can't hope to socialize our children for real life by blotting out reality. However, news coverage also selects and magnifies violent incidents at the expense of nonviolent ones. It would be healthier if the media presented us with a reality that was a more representative crosssection of everyday life, good parts and bad parts together.

The trouble is, people have become accustomed to sex, violence, danger, and excitement as their standard television fantasy fare. It has become addictive, an alternative to everyday lives that may be boring, frustrating, unfair, and unrewarding—as Marx said of religion, an "opiate of the masses." Do we have the right to deny people the kinds of programs they seem to need, even if the research shows long-term harm to their children? Again, the analogy to cigarette smoking comes to mind: Some people want to smoke, and most people believe they should have the right to smoke. But others should have the right to escape the harmful effects of secondhand smoke they haven't chosen to inhale. The cigarette industry has fought back at attempts to limit its profit making through product regulation, and so has the television industry. But it's our lives, our health, our children. Whose interest should prevail? What do you think?

REVIEW EXERCISES

For Discussion and Debate

1. Look at the Selected References for this chapter and you will see that research on television and youthful violence began around 1970 and finished around 1985. By then, the scientific verdict was in: Television causes a violence problem. Why, then, do people still discuss the connection between television and violence as though the question is still unanswered?

2. Which of the "television is not to blame" arguments do you find most persuasive, and why?

3. Do you think this problem needs further study by researchers? If so, why?

4. What other conditional influences, besides those discussed in this chapter, may increase the likelihood that television violence will produce violent behavior?

Writing Exercises

1. "It's impossible to say whether television influences people's behavior. After all, everyone's different."

2. "If people were simply better parents, television wouldn't pose a problem for children."

3. "Trying to regulate television violence means the end of freedom of expression in this country."

4. "Social research, no matter how good, is powerless to bring about social change because. . . ."

Research Activities

Watch (or even better, use your VCR to record) 10 hours of network daytime television and 10 hours of network evening television. Take careful notes of what you see, especially the number and types of violent acts portrayed.

1. How many violent acts and of what type did you count in total? In what kinds of shows were they most frequent? In what kinds of shows were they most violent?

2. Focusing on the violent acts themselves, how often and in what ways were they connected to sexual arousal? How often to revenge or justice? What else were they connected to?

3. What proportion of violent acts portrayed were unnecessary, in the sense that they did not advance the story line or reveal anything new about the characters?

4. Make a count of the demographics of the violent incidents. For example, how many were males against other males? How many were males against females? How many were young people against older people? How many were blacks or poor people committing the violence? Do you see any stereotyping here? Indeed, would you consider racial or gender stereotyping itself to be a form of television violence?

SELECTED REFERENCES

CANTOR, MURIEL G., and JACK ORWANT, Differential effects of television violence on girls and boys, *Studies in Communication* (1980), 1, 63–83.

CENTERWALL, BRANDON S., Television and violent crime, *The Public Interest* (1992), 107, 56–71.

CHAFFEE, STEVEN H., et al., Defending the indefensible, *Society* (September–October 1984), 21, 6(152), 30–35.

COMSTOCK, GEORGE, and VICTOR C. STRASBURGER, Deceptive appearances. Television violence and aggressive behavior, *Journal of Adolescent Health Care* (1990), 11, 31–44.

DONNERSTEIN, NEIL M., ed., *Pornography and Sexual Aggression* (Orlando, FL: Academic Press, 1984).

FIELD, MARTIN, Media and violence—Closing one door: Opening another, *Communications* (1987), 13, 3, 55–63.

FLING, S., L. SMITH, T. RODRIGUEZ, D. THORNTON, E. ATKINS, and K. NIXON, Videogames, aggression, and self-esteem: A survey, *Social Behavior and Personality* (1992), 20, 1, 39–45.

FROST, RICHARD, and JOHN STAUFFER, The effects of social class, gender, and personality on physiological responses to filmed violence, *Journal of Communication* (Spring 1987), 37, 2, 29–45.

GEEN, RUSSELL G., and SUSAN L. THOMAS, The immediate effects of media violence on behavior, *Journal of Social Issues* (1986), 42, 3, 7–27.

GERBNER, GEORGE, LARRY GROSS, MICHAEL MORGAN, and NANCY SIGNORELLI, The "mainstreaming" of America: Violence profile no. 11, *Journal of Communication* (Summer 1980), 30, 3, 10–29.

GITLIN, TODD, Imagebusters: The hollow crusade against TV violence, *American Prospect* (Winter 1994), 16, 42–49.

GREESON, LARRY E., and ROSE ANN WILLIAMS, Social implications of music videos for youth: An analysis of the content and effects of MTV, *Youth and Society* (December 1986), 18, 2, 177–189.

HEATH, LINDA, CANDACE KRUTTSCHNITT, and DAVID WARD, Television and violent criminal behavior: Beyond the Bobo doll, *Violence and Victims* (Fall 1986), 1, 3, 177–190.

IWAO, SUMIKO, ITHIEL DE SOLA POOL, and SHIGERU HAGIWARA, Japanese and U.S. media: Some cross-cultural insights into TV violence, *Journal of Communication* (Spring 1981), 31, 2, 28–36.

MESSNER, STEVEN F., Television violence and violent crime: An aggregate analysis, *Social Problems* (February 1986), 33, 3, 218–235.

PHILLIPS, DAVID P., Airplane accidents, murder, and the mass media: Towards a theory of imitation and suggestion, *Social Forces* (1980), 58, 4, 1001–1024.

RIDLEY, JOHNSON, JUNE E. CHANCE, and HARRIS COOPER, Correlates of children's television viewing: Expectancies, age, and sex, *Journal of Applied Developmental Psychology* (July–September 1984), 5, 3, 225–235.

ROBERTS, CHURCHILL, Children's and parents' television viewing and perceptions of violence, *Journalism Quarterly* (Winter 1981), 58, 4, 4, 556–581.

ROSENTHAL, ROBERT, Media violence, antisocial behavior, and the social consequences of small effects, *Journal of Social Issues* (1986), 42, 3, 141–154.

SAWIN, DOUGLAS B., Aggressive behavior among children in small playgroup settings with violent television, *Advances in Learning and Behavioral Disabilities* (1990), 6, 157–177.

WALKER, KIM B., and DONALD D. MORLEY, Attitudes and parental factors as intervening variables in the television violence-aggression relation, *Communication Research Reports* (June–December 1991), 8, 1–2, 41–47.

WHITE, GARLAND F., JANET KATZ, and KATHRYN E. SCARBOROUGH, The impact of professional football games upon violent assaults on women, *Violence and Victims* (Summer 1992), 7, 2, 157–171.

WURTZEL, ALAN, and GUY LOMETTI, Researching television violence, *Society* (September–October 1984), 21, 6(152), 22–30.

3. Deviance and Control

To sociologists, **deviance** refers to any behavior that leads to a negative reaction by some part of the community. When no one feels threatened by an uncommon behavior—for example, by the wearing of a polka-dot bow tie—people are likely to see it as simply an expression of individuality. But when people do feel threatened, they react in various ways.

Reactions depend largely on how the behavior is perceived. But perception by itself is not enough; for an act to be deviant, perception must be turned into action. How much weight that action carries will depend on how much power people have to enforce their own views of acceptable behavior. **Social control** refers to the institutions and procedures that make sure members of society conform to rules of expected and approved behavior. The operation of social control is most obvious when it is *formal*, especially when laws are enforced through the police and the courts. Formal social control gives specific people (such as police officers) the responsibility of enforcing specific rules or laws while following specific control methods. And formal control varies widely across countries.

In this chapter we look at deviance and control of various types. First we consider whether more poverty in a society translates into higher rates of crime. Then we look at evidence on whether formal efforts to control deviance by imprisoning criminals are effective or desirable. Finally, we consider the pros and cons of legalizing recreational drugs like marijuana, focusing on the likely consequences for both deviance and control.

3.1

Does more poverty equal more crime?

The issue: Is the crime problem a result of poverty, so that increasing poverty increases the danger in our everyday lives? And if so, should we take steps to deal with poverty in order to deal with crime?

Introduction Fear of crime is widespread in North America, and in some communities the fear is increasing. Research has shown that some groups—for example, older people and heavy television viewers—are even more fearful of criminal victimization than others, but that there is little correlation between actual victimization and the fear of it. Nonetheless, the fear remains; and as the research of the early sociologist W. I. Thomas indicates, a thing that is believed to be real is real in its consequences. Thus consequences of this increased fearfulness include public support for more police, stiffer penalties for convicted criminals, and more imprisonment of convicts. Politicians play on this fearfulness to increase their own popularity, even though their actions further increase fearfulness and an openness to extreme solutions.

Less imaginary is the increase among urban poor people of unemployment and desperate economic conditions. Common sense suggests a connection between unemployment (poverty) and crime. If such a connection exists, will a worsening economic situation and the growth of an urban underclass lead to more crime and a more justified fearfulness about crime? Sociologists have researched and debated this question almost as long as the discipline has existed. Yet, strangely, given all the research, there are conflicting points of view on this question. Let's look at them and form our own judgment.

MORE POVERTY DOES NOT MEAN MORE CRIME

Several different kinds of arguments are put forward to explain why we cannot be certain that more poverty means more crime. First, even if more poverty increases the motivation to commit crimes, other factors may have an opposite influence, among them legal deterrence and a lack of opportunity to commit certain kinds of crimes. Second, even if poverty appears to cause crime—therefore, more poverty should cause more crime—there may be other factors that explain this relationship. Third, research that shows poverty and crime are correlated doesn't prove that poverty causes crime or that more poverty will cause more crime.

Motivation isn't everything The reason why poverty may cause crime is best presented by Robert Merton in his famous anomie theory. Merton argues that people who experience a gap between what the culture has taught them to value (society's cultural goals) and the approved method (or "institutionalized means") of pursuing these goals will suffer from *anomie*. One way out of anomie—a way with a long tradition in America—is what Merton calls "innova-

tion." One form of innovation is crime. What crime does, in Merton's eyes, is allow disadvantaged people to pursue the culture's goals by unconventional, often disapproved means. Seen from this perspective, crime is as American as apple pie—a way that disadvantaged groups can pursue the American Dream and thus keep faith with the mythologized American Dream.

However, Merton also points out that people in a state of anomie have other options. For example, they can set lower goals or give up the culture's goals entirely. Or they can continue conforming to society's rules, in hopes that eventually this conformity will pay off. Or they can solve the anomie problem by retreating from both the conventional goals and means—through drugs and alcohol, for example.

Research tells us that people actually do handle their anomie in each of these ways, so crime is not an inevitable consequence of poverty. Therefore, we should not be surprised that some research finds only a weak relationship between poverty and crime. Moreover, other factors enter in. The likelihood of committing criminal or delinquent acts also depends on one's opportunities. Many types of crime (for example, embezzlement and other white-collar crimes) are not possible for poor people. Close policing also makes it difficult to commit some crimes undetected, and the high risk of arrest and punishment makes crime less likely in some communities than in other, poorly policed communities. Also, as sociologist Howard Becker points out in *Outsiders*, rule-breaking behavior must be noticed and labelled to become crime, and poverty might produce rule-breaking action that is not perceived as such.

Appearance may not be reality The relationship between poverty and crime may be only apparent. It depends on how well we have managed to measure the true extent of crime in a given community or group, for example. On the one hand, there is ample evidence of official bias against poor or working-class people—a bias observed in policing, arrest, bail-setting, conviction, and punishment patterns. Some researchers have viewed it, instead, as a bias in favor of middle-class and wealthy people; but either way we view it, the result is a higher rate of recorded criminality by lower-class people. More poverty appears to cause more crime because the formal system of justice criminalizes more poor people, and it is this bias, captured in the official statistics, that leads sociological researchers to conclude that poverty causes crime.

As a result of such biases, many researchers have turned to the use of self-reports of crime or delinquency. These self-reports typically show less difference in class-based rates of crime or other deviance than do the official statistics. However, some researchers claim that this difference shrinks because people misreport their own crime, and the data they provide cannot be believed. And if the data cannot be believed, we cannot assume that they are any better than the official statistics, or reasonably conclude that poverty has little effect on crime.

In the end, we are stuck with two kinds of defective data. It would be foolhardy to draw any conclusion whatever about the link between poverty and crime.

What causes what?   Assume for a moment that the data, whether official or self-reported, are not as flawed as we have been saying. Then suppose that these data show a correlation, or association, between poverty-type variables and crime-type variables. There are now additional problems to handle.

First, in studying the poverty-crime link, researchers have used a variety of different measures. On one side of the equation, some

have focused on poverty (whether absolute or relative), others on class or status level, others on unemployment, and still others on social inequality. These variables are related to one another by anomie theory. Feelings of anomie may be equally intense among poor people, lower class people, unemployed people, and people in the bottom half of a highly unequal society. However, these measures are not all the same, and research using different measures is not strictly comparable. The same holds true on the other side of the equation. Some researchers have studied crime, others delinquency. Of those studying crime, some have focused on crimes of violence, others on property crime, and so on.

Given these variations, how would we reconcile the following three hypothetical findings: (1) poor people are more likely to commit burglary than rich people; (2) there is somewhat more delinquency in highly unequal societies than in less unequal societies; and (3) unemployed people are no more likely to commit murder than employed people. Do these findings show that the poverty-crime linkage is strong or weak, or that we are comparing apples and oranges?

That problem aside, what does a consistent correlation between the poverty measures and the crime measures really mean? It may mean that poverty causes crime; or that criminal activity causes poverty; or that poverty and crime reciprocally cause each other. It may even mean that something else is causing both poverty and crime, so that the relationship between poverty and crime is spurious. For example, past imprisonment, a poor school record, or a concentration of urban young people would each increase the probability that an individual would be poor or be convicted of further crimes.

So, given all these problems, it is risky to conclude that poverty definitely causes crime, and that an increase in poverty will surely increase crime. Before such a conclusion is possible, it is necessary to solve the logical and methodological problems we have just reviewed. However, not every researcher would take this position.

MORE POVERTY MEANS SOMEWHAT MORE CRIME

Another, larger group of researchers would argue that there is little doubt that poverty is strongly and consistently linked with crime. A majority of studies come to this very conclusion, and that can't be accidental. However, the same researchers would disagree among themselves about the importance to attach to this finding, for two reasons. One has to do with the relative importance of poverty, as compared with other causes of crime. And the other has to do with competing theories about the reason poverty is linked to crime.

Competing variables   A common problem in sociology is what is called *overdetermination*. That is, there are too many good, plausible causes for every effect, and usually these causes are related to one another in complicated ways.

There are many good theories about the causes of crime or delinquency. Some stress the importance of early experiences: abusive or neglectful parenting, family conflict, family criminality, or early institutionalization. Other theories focus on the effects of antisocial peers or gang pressures to participate in crime. Still others refer to social or community disorganization or to deviant subcultures. Other theories focus more on the ways labeling (stigmatization) creates a criminal or deviant career. Some theories claim that racial discrimination has a stronger effect on crime than poverty does, whereas others deny it. Some theories focus

less on criminal motivations and more on differential opportunities to commit crimes, or on the deterrent effects of policing and stiff sentences for convicts.

All of these are good variables that have been shown many times to influence the likelihood of criminal behavior. But theorists would disagree on the relative importance of poverty compared to any or all of these other influences. Few would argue that poverty, though important, is surely the most important of the lot.

Competing theories   Not only are there too many variables, there are also too many different theories linking these variables, individually or collectively, to crime. In fact, some of these theories are incompatible with one another. For example, a theory stressing the role of criminal subcultures is not always compatible with a theory stressing social or community disorganization. Likewise, a theory that emphasizes faulty socialization is not always compatible with a theory that emphasizes stigmatization or police bias.

These different theories, with their different important variables, often grow out of different sociological paradigms: structural functionalism, conflict theory, symbolic interactionism, and so on. Some day they may all fit together in a unified theory of crime causation, but so far no one has managed to do that. And part of the reason for this failure is that different paradigms ask different questions and collect different kinds of data. So, for example, some theories seem to call for areal (community level) measures of crime and poverty, and others call for individual level measures. For the most part, there has been little success in linking together the findings obtained from these different kinds of studies.

Given our profusion of variables and theories, once again it seems foolhardy to draw any final conclusion about the link between poverty and crime. All we can say with some certainty is that there is a nontrivial relationship.

MORE POVERTY SOMETIMES MEANS MUCH MORE CRIME

If you are thinking that this section's title is the same as the previous section's title, read them both again. They're not the same. The previous section noted that some sociologists would willingly accept the premise that poverty always has an effect on crime, but it may be a *small* effect. Indeed, they might say that any attempt to predict crime would have to take dozens of variables into account, only one of which would be poverty. The sociologists we want to talk about now take a different position—namely, that under some circumstances poverty has little or no influence, but under other circumstances, poverty has a powerful, overwhelming effect.

This difference in outlooks is not unique to the study of crime. Throughout sociology, some theories assume that a lot of small influences add up to a big influence—call these *additive theories*. Others, however—call them *interactive theories*—assume that any given variable or group of variables will have a big effect only when it interacts with, or varies under, specified conditions. A match and a firecracker in close proximity will not produce anything special unless the match is lit; that's an interactive relationship.

But what *are* the conditions under which poverty (or unemployment, or inequality, or lower social class) likely has its greatest impact? Poverty in a poor, stable country produces less crime than poverty in a poor, rapidly developing country or in a rich country. And poverty seems to have a different effect on boys and girls. Why? Sociologist John Hagan has tried to explain

why there is more difference in the criminality of boys and girls at the bottom of the class structure than there is at the top. He argues that to answer this question we need to know about more than class or poverty. We also need to understand the interaction between class experiences and gender experiences. The result is what Hagan calls a *power-control theory* of crime.

Here's a simplification of his argument: As you go down the class structure from richest to poorest, two-parent families tend to be more *patriarchal*, in the sense that wives have little power relative to husbands, daughters have little freedom relative to sons, and daughters are less delinquent than sons. Gender differences of every kind are diminished in *egalitarian* families, which are more common further up the class structure, where the spouses are also, typically, more highly educated. Power-control theory explains this variation in terms of gender divisions in domestic social control.

Typically, in the more patriarchal families, interpersonal relations featuring shared intimacy, mutual understanding, and caring (among others) are more characteristic of women than men. Mothers in these patriarchal families control their daughters more closely than their sons. This leads daughters to prefer risk taking less than sons; as a result, they are less likely to engage in delinquency. Daughters are also under more pressure to take their schooling and job responsibilities more seriously; in turn, early employment contacts increase their prospects of getting a job and advancing occupationally. By contrast, early involvement in crime isolates boys from schooling and employment that would improve their chances of legitimate adult employment.

This interpretation argues that delinquency results, at least in part, from a lack of familial control and embeddedness in structures leading to economic success. It predicts that any conditions that reduce school or familial control—whether child neglect or poor supervision—or increase the control of nonconforming influences (e.g., delinquent peers) will increase crime and delinquency. Thus homeless people and street kids get involved in more crime than other people, both because they need money and because they are relatively uncontrolled. Paradoxically, children of unemployed parents, though often suffering more poverty than their peers, are more likely to be closely controlled, hence, less delinquent. (Note, however, that the cost of reducing delinquency, according to this scenario, is a domestication of mothers who forgo careers and work in order to tame their children and cater to their husband.)

So in the end, there are factors associated with poverty that motivate delinquency and crime. But to produce criminal behavior, these factors must interact with social conditions such as lax supervision (or for adults, lack of family responsibilities), criminal peers, and/or a lack of legitimate employment opportunities. The effect of poverty on crime is conditional. Therefore, more poverty means more crime only when the social constraints of civil society—family, community, job—break down or disappear.

SUMMING UP

More poverty does produce more crime, under some conditions. For example, more poverty produces more crime under conditions of anomie—a gap between goals and means—as well as under conditions of great inequality or rapid change. All of these conditions excite feelings of uncertainty, frustration, and envy. As a result, they excite the desire to take shortcuts to culturally valued goals or to relieve frustration through aggressive acts.

As well, poverty produces more crime when people's behavior is less effectively regulated, whether because of lax law enforcement or lax parenting. Even under conditions of frustration, people are likely to restrain their desires if doing otherwise will carry great costs. In this respect, bringing shame to one's family may seem as costly to some people as years spent behind bars.

Poverty, while increasing frustration and a desire for shortcuts, may also cut social bonds, thus releasing people from effective control. Take homeless people or street kids. They are certainly poor, and often their poverty leads them to petty crime out of the need to survive. But equally poor people living at home would be less likely to resort to crime, because their family would limit their behavior. So poverty under conditions of relative social isolation will have different effects on crime than poverty under conditions of social integration.

Poverty leads to crime in another sense, one that classic conflict theory would illuminate. It is privilege and advantage that construct the legal system and pay for its enforcement. The very issue of what is "crime" is thus decided by those at a distance from poverty. Some would put it more bluntly, saying that when wealth takes, we call it an "investment strategy"; when poverty takes, we call it "theft."

If worsening economic conditions produce both poverty and family (or community) breakdown, then more poverty will mean more crime. This suggests that government policies aimed at preventing crime need to fight both poverty and family (or community) breakdown. Equally important, it argues the importance of taking steps to promote civil society as an informal buffer against the effects of poverty. (We further discuss the importance of civil society in a later chapter.)

REVIEW EXERCISES

For Discussion and Debate

1. If more poverty equals more crime, why is there much less crime in China or Costa Rica than in the much wealthier United States?

2. How would you account for large differences in the crime rates of the United States, Canada, Japan, and Sweden—all of which have roughly similar levels of per capita income?

3. If you had to choose between official statistics and self-reports on criminal behavior, which kind would you choose? Do you think the data provided by this source would be more reliable for one kind of crime than for another? Explain.

4. Think of another sociological problem besides poverty and crime that requires an interactive or conditional explanation. (For example, how about the effects of divorce on children's well-being?)

Writing Exercises

1. "Eliminating crime means first eliminating poverty."

2. "Stricter parenting is the answer to the delinquency problem in North America."

3. "Differences in the crime rate from one group to another reflect differences in what should be considered a crime."

4. "More gender equality equals more crime."

Research Activities

1. Interview at least two police officers to find out how they decide whether to arrest or merely caution a juvenile who has gotten into trouble.

2. Examine published crime statistics for your community and see how, and by how much, they have changed in the last 10 years. What categories of criminal behavior have changed most?

3. Construct a brief questionnaire to measure opinions about the crime problem in your community, especially how serious it is perceived to be and what should be done about it: Then administer the questionnaire to at least six students in your school and interpret the results.

4. View 10 hours of prime-time television or five recent movies that are about crime or delinquency. What are the implied causes of crime? What kinds of people are the criminals, and what kinds of crime (e.g., street crime vs. white-collar crime) are depicted?

SELECTED REFERENCES

ALLAN, EMILIE ANDERSEN, and DARRELL J. STEFFENSMEIER, Youth, underemployment, and property crime: Differential effects of job availability and job quality on juvenile and young adult arrest rates, *American Sociological Review* (February 1989), 54, 1, 107–123.

CHIRICOS, THEODORE G., Rates of crime and unemployment: An analysis of aggregate research evidence, *Social Problems* (April 1987), 34, 2, 187–212.

DUSTER, TROY, Crime, youth unemployment, and the black urban underclass, *Crime and Delinquency* (April 1987), 33, 2, 300–316.

FARNSWORTH, MARGARET, TERENCE P. THORNBERRY, MARVIN D. CROHN, and ALAN J. LIZOTTE, Measurement in the study of class and delinquency: Integrating theory and research, *Journal of Research in Crime and Delinquency* (February 1994), 31, 1, 32–61.

FIELD, SIMON, *Trends in crime and their interpretation: A study of recorded crime in post-war England and Wales* (London: HMSO, 1990).

HAGAN, JOHN, The social embeddedness of crime and unemployment, *Criminology* (November 1993), 31, 4, 465–491.

———, A. R. GILLIS, and JOHN SIMPSON, The class structure of gender and delinquency: Toward a power-control theory of common delinquent behavior, *American Journal of Sociology* (May 1985), 90, 6, 1151–1178.

———, JOHN SIMPSON, and A. R. GILLIS, Feminist scholarship, relational and instrumental control, and power-control theory of gender and delinquency, *British Journal of Sociology* (September 1988), 3, 301–336.

HARER, MILES D., and DARREL STEFFENSMEIER, The differing effects of economic inequality on black and white rates of violence, *Social Forces* (June 1992), 70, 4, 1035–1054.

HSIEH, CHING CHI, and M. D. PUGH, Poverty, income inequality, and violent crime: A meta-analysis of recent aggregate data studies, *Criminal Justice Review* (Autumn 1993), 18, 2, 182–202.

KLECK, GARY, TRAVIS HIRSCHI, MICHAEL J. HINDELANG, and JOSEPH WEIS, On the use of self-report data to determine the class distribution of criminal and delinquent behavior, *American Sociological Review* (June 1982), 47, 3, 427–433.

MCCARTHY, BILL, and JOHN HAGAN, Gender, delinquency, and the Great Depression: A test of power-control theory, *Canadian Review of Sociology and Anthropology* (May 1987), 24, 2, 153–177.

REINARMAN, CRAIG, and JEFFREY FAGAN, Social organization and differential association: A research note from a longitudinal study of violent juvenile offenders, *Crime and Delinquency* (July 1988), 34, 3, 307–327.

SAMPSON, ROBERT J., and JOHN H. LAUB, Urban poverty and the family context of delinquency: A new look at structure and process in a classic study, *Child Development* (April 1994), 65, 2, 523–540.

SHORT, JAMES F., Poverty, ethnicity, and crime: Change and continuity in U.S. cities, *Journal of Research in Crime and Delinquency* (November 1991), 28, 4, 501–518.

SMITH, M. DWAYNE, JOEL A. DEVINE, and JOSEPH F. SHELEY, Crime and unemployment: Effects across age and race categories, *Sociological Perspectives* (Winter 1992), 35, 4, 551–572.

THORNBERRY, TERENCE P., and R. L. CHRISTENSON, Unemployment and criminal involvement: An investigation of reciprocal causal structures, *American Sociological Review* (June 1982), 49, 3, 398–411.

TITTLE, CHARLES, Social class and criminal behavior: A critique of the theoretical foundation, *Social Forces* (December 1983), 62, 2, 334–358.

3.2

Do we have enough jails?

The issue: How to deal with the crime problem. Will building more jails reduce the crime problem, leave it untouched, or even make it worse?

Introduction Every time we read a newspaper or watch a TV news program, stories and statistics about crime jump out at us. There seems to be a "crime problem" in America. But will prisons solve this crime problem? The research on this question dates back over a century, yet only in the twentieth century did researchers begin to study prisons and prisoners systematically. One researcher, Donald Clemmer, developed his *prisonization theory* out of such careful work. Clemmer states that, by their nature, prisons degrade people, coerce them, and take away their rights.

This treatment is inevitable. Without it, prison officials cannot keep order in such a large community of (usually) young men. Yet this treatment, which keeps peace in the prison, also has unintended and undesirable effects. It alienates prisoners and unites them against the prison administration. A prison subculture, growing out of everyday prison life, reflects and hardens this alienation.

Prisoners learn the prison subculture and antiadministration normative code. Through contact with more experienced inmates, they acquire new criminal skills, often learning to behave in undesirable and violent ways. They end up with an identity that is more deviant than what they had brought into the prison. Thus "prisonization," as Clemmer calls it, produces well-socialized prisoners: people who fit perfectly into the inmate society. However, what works well in a prison subculture works poorly on the outside. The prisoners have been taught how not to adapt to life in the "real world." As their release from prison approaches, they feel great stress. After release, they commit even more crimes—indeed, even more violent crimes—and many end up back in prison. This process is called *recidivism,* or "the revolving door."

A sociological classic by Erving Goffman, *Asylums*, took this argument further. Goffman wrote that all residential facilities that try to shape inmate behavior—including prisons, mental hospitals, concentration camps, military barracks, monasteries, convents, and even boarding schools—are "total institutions." As such, they share many characteristics that Clemmer attributed just to prisons. For example, they all degrade people, strip away old identities, impose uniformity of dress and behavior, limit personal freedom, and in these ways create new identities. The process stamps an inmate with the institution's character and makes him or her less prepared for the outside world.

If this description of total institutions and inmate socialization is correct, we have to ask whether prisons are really a solution to the crime problem or, instead, largely the cause of this problem.

PRISONS CAN SOLVE THE CRIME PROBLEM

Criminals are special Some have claimed that people who wind up in prison are not ordinary, average people. After all, a small minority of people produce the vast majority of offenses. They fit easily into the prison subculture and, upon release, commit more crimes because they were crime-prone before they ever went to prison. Said another way, there are stable, unmeasured differences in the potential for crime within a population. The propensity to commit crime is established early and persists throughout life. Prisons may fail to reform crime-prone people, but neither are they to blame for the commitment to a life of crime. This belief that criminals are a different breed of people leads in several directions. First, it justifies using special, coercive treatment. Anything less fails to keep order among poorly socialized people. Second, it argues that more coercion, not less, is needed.

Some prisoners are what we might call "rational calculators": they commit gainful crimes because the chance of big rewards outweighs the chance of even bigger punishments. Only by increasing the certainty and severity of punishment can we hope to deter these criminals from pursuing a profitable life in crime. Both the risk of being caught and the prospect of increased gain have a significant impact on burglars' decision making. The threat of legal sanctions (fear of arrest) and conscience both inhibit the commission of illegal acts, especially where past accomplishments or future goals may be jeopardized by such an arrest. Where people have a stake in conformity—something to lose by deviance and something to gain by conformity—they are most likely to obey the law.

Many prison administrators still claim that imprisonment's goal is rehabilitation: resocialization into a new, orderly, law-abiding lifestyle. And prisons do provide order, rules, and rule enforcement. In this way they model a new, orderly, law-abiding lifestyle that prisoners can carry to the outside world after release. Unlike other agents of socialization (e.g., schools or the mass media), prisons can forcibly rehabilitate people, or at least appear to do so. They hold up the prospect of early release through parole as a "carrot"—an inducement to cooperate. And as a "stick" there is the threat of punishment for noncompliance. Obviously, forced rehabilitation does not work for everyone. Yet many administrators believe that the right treatment works for the right people.

What the community wants Fear of victimization, crime, and criminals is widespread in America. Though the precise numbers vary over time and from one community to another, a majority of citizens want criminals—especially dangerous or repeat criminals—behind bars. They feel safer knowing that prisons are handling "the problem."

To some degree, the crime problem is a perception problem. People feel there is a crime problem and need to feel that it is being handled. Thus getting criminals into prison helps to solve the problem in their minds. Few harbor the illusion that prisons either deter crime or rehabilitate criminals. However, prisons at least get criminals off the streets for awhile. If prisons don't solve the problem in the long run, they buy time and a sense of greater safety for law-abiding citizens.

Alternatives don't work reliably Many believe that privatizing prisons—putting their administration into private contractors'

hands—increases efficiency and lowers the cost. This makes prisons affordable, despite a rising imprisonment rate. Indeed, many governments, both in the United States and abroad, are considering and/or trying private prisons. Issues that need further study include the use of deadly force by contractors, the effect of additional prisons on sentencing practices, and the problem of prison industries—for example, how to motivate unskilled, uneducated employees and how to avoid competing with outside businesses. These issues aside, privatizing prisons does not improve prisoner rehabilitation. Research shows that in private facilities the treatment—food, living conditions, and skills training, for example—is actually worse, since the chief goal is to make a profit.

Even if they grant that prisons are unable to deter crime, rehabilitate convicts, or keep criminals off the street for long, advocates may still believe that prisons—public or private—are needed because there is no reliable alternative. They point out that other efforts to prevent criminal behavior have failed. Many methods have already been tried. And in some quarters there is skepticism about the effectiveness of alternatives such as intensive probation. Community alternatives to custody (which we discuss shortly) do not necessarily guarantee better results. Some studies even find higher rates of recidivism with noninstitutionalized offenders.

And even if it were possible to prevent crime through efforts of these kinds, many citizens would oppose them. They view crime as immoral behavior. Accordingly, they believe that the criminal (and the criminal's family), not society, should take responsibility and pay the cost. By this reasoning, crimes should be prevented by moral training at home, not by spending public money on costly remedies after the fact.

Others are willing to pay to prevent crime and rehabilitate criminals, but they are concerned about the cost. In particular, they recognize that building more prisons and filling them with more prisoners drains the public purse. (It costs about as much to keep a person in prison as it does to send that same person to a good college.) In the end, many feel that there is no acceptable alternative to prisons. The success of prison alternatives is unknown. Until we can be certain that alternative methods deter and rehabilitate criminals, we may have to continue relying on prisons. At least that is what some people think.

PRISONS CANNOT SOLVE THE CRIME PROBLEM

Other researchers and administrators oppose using prisons to punish routine or nonviolent offenses. People holding this view believe that few criminals are dangerous or unchangeable. On the contrary, a great many people pass through periods of life or circumstances when criminal behavior is quite likely.

Criminals are like everyone else Most criminals are young, especially young men. As they age, they become less likely to commit crimes. Likewise, as the general population ages, a falling proportion of young men will lead to a decrease in the general crime rate. Crime and imprisonment rates will decline naturally.

Demographic factors aside, the view that criminals are just like everyone else is supported by *labeling theories* of deviance. Such theories argue that, at one time or another, most people commit deviant or criminal acts. Few are caught and punished. Most give up their rule-breaking behavior voluntarily, for a variety of reasons: maturation, a change of views or opportunities, or a

stronger stake in conformity due to marriage and employment, for example. But because of the way laws are enforced, some people are more likely to get caught and punished for their rule-breaking. Other factors (such as seriousness of the offense) being equal, race has a strong effect on the chance of incarceration, with blacks and Latinos running the highest risk. Gender also affects correctional practice, with women experiencing stricter rule enforcement and more severe punishment in some prisons. Gender stereotypes also shape the nature of work and vocational training.

Conviction and imprisonment stigmatize people, giving them a deviant identity, reducing their legitimate opportunities, and increasing their tendency to break rules. Sociologists have called this behavior *secondary deviation.* Prison also costs society much more than probation, due to the combined costs of attempted rehabilitation and increased recidivism. Given the risk of secondary deviation, some researchers believe it may be best to put almost no one into prison, and let almost no one out of prison, once in.

What the community doesn't know Average North Americans want as many criminals as possible kept in prison for as long as possible. However, much of the support for imprisonment is based on ignorance of prison conditions and on short-term thinking—a desire for revenge rather than for long-term safety. The social benefits of imprisonment are only temporary. Eventually, most prisoners are back on the streets. We have to ask ourselves, what then?

Movies and television programs show prisons to be unpleasant, but they do not dwell on the variety and seriousness of harms that prisons do. Consider this: Prisons break up families. Imprisonment, therefore, has important unintended consequences for the next generation. Family separation may produce a new generation of criminals. Imprisonment also contributes to child poverty, already a widely recognized social problem.

Prisons increase health risks too. Most American prisons are overcrowded, even by their own reckoning. As a result, prisoners are at greater risk of contracting communicable, often lethal diseases, than are nonincarcerated people. Violence, both mental and physical, is an ever-present feature of prison life (as in other total institutions). This may result from drug use and drug trafficking, ineffective mechanisms of social control and dispute resolution, or new gang subcultures. Rates of HIV and AIDS are high because of drug injection and because many inmates are raped or otherwise forced into sex.

The high risks of abuse and violence translate into stress reactions like sleeplessness, high blood pressure, respiratory problems, and high suicide rates. In many prisons, conditions are unconstitutionally awful. They represent cruel and unusual punishment, whatever the crime a prisoner originally is labeled as having committed.

Alternatives to prison do work For certain types of criminals, community-based alternatives work better than prison; they are cheaper, more humane, and more effective. These alternatives are also less intrusive and disruptive and do not create a dangerous inmate culture. Some, like probation and parole, carry a low risk to public safety. Other alternatives include paying fines, making restitution, and performing community services.

Another alternative to prison is electronically monitored home detention. A recent study, carried out in Cleveland as part of an effort to keep people out of jail, illustrates the potential of this alternative. There,

people awaiting trial for misdemeanors (minor offenses) or non-violent felonies (serious offenses) were allowed to remain in detention at home for 90 days. Each participant wore a coded wristlet that matched a base unit attached to his or her home telephone. Participants were expected to stay at home. To verify their presence, a computer telephoned them at random during the day. They had several seconds to make a contact between their coded wristlet and the telephone receiver. Doing so informed the computer that they were indeed at home. Repeated failure to wear the wristlet or make contact with the ringing telephone violated detention conditions and resulted in jail detention until their trial.

Evaluating the experimental results, researchers found that three-quarters of the participants finished the detention period without any trouble and showed up for their trial as expected. Another 13% were jailed for violating the rules of home detention (e.g., failing to answer the phone regularly). Finally, 14% ran away; a few were still at large when the program ended. What do these results tell us?

- First, money can be saved. For three out of every four accused people, jail or prison is unnecessary. A cheaper, healthier alternative, home detention, works just as well. In fact, it may work better. In one study, house arrestees had lower rates of recidivism and higher rates of social and economic integration than community treatment center residents.

- Second, we know who to choose for this treatment. In the Cleveland study, most people who had previously committed only minor offenses finished the 90-day detention without difficulty. And most people who lived with their families also finished well. Said another way, socially integrated people with little or no previous record of criminal activity are good candidates for home detention. Conversely, people who are socially isolated or who have offended many times in the past are relatively poor risks.

SUMMING UP

Do we have enough jails? We sure do, and then some. Can prisons be relied on to solve the crime problem? The argument on this issue goes back and forth; right now, there is a readiness to believe that something can be done about crime and delinquency. However, the evidence we have examined leads us to doubt that prisons will play an important part. At best, researchers are pessimistic about the effects of prison experience, which often induce what the sociologist David Matza called "drift"—a denial of responsibility. But this is only the beginning of the problem.

First, we have trouble believing that people who end up in prisons are impossible to help and impossible to change. Just as important, prisons cannot be shown to make people better. They probably make them worse, for all the reasons we have noted. Second, the community's desire to imprison convicted criminals—to use capital punishment, too—is real enough. However, it grows out of ignorance, a desire for revenge, and often an excessive fear of victimization. Prison building is an intervention of last resort when people lose faith in the social welfare enterprise. Third, there are alternatives to prison. We have to study them carefully, one at a time, before making final decisions.

However, the early findings are clear enough: For socially integrated people who have been accused and/or convicted of minor crimes, alternative methods work satisfactorily. In any event, people receiving these treatments are not made worse by prison, and they and their families may even bear the costs of detention.

REVIEW EXERCISES

For Discussion and Debate

1. "Most offenders should never go to prison; the rest should never get out." Discuss.

2. The similarities between prisons and other total institutions are more apparent than real.

3. "People don't want prisons to solve the crime problem; they want prisons to punish wrongdoers—something they do very well."

4. "There are good reasons why some social, racial, and ethnic groups are overrepresented in prisons and others

are underrepresented. We have no need for concern on that account." Do you agree or disagree?

Writing Exercises

1. "The three most frightening things about being locked up in a prison are. . . ."

2. "Probably, most convicts would prefer corrective brain surgery—if possible—instead of a year in prison."

3. How I would organize an electronic home detention program for serious criminal offenders (or, for socially isolated offenders).

4. "Prisons of the future": Design your own prison to avoid the problems discussed in this section.

Research Activities

1. Collect some historical information to find out how one particular society (your choice) dealt with lawbreakers before the development of the modern prison system.

2. Using biographies and other published accounts of prison life, find out some of the main elements—the values, norms, rules, and roles—of the prison subculture (e.g., the role of tattoos).

3. Collect statistical data on at least a dozen countries, indicating the fraction of the population that is imprisoned at any given time. Then collect other statistical data about the same countries that would help to explain why some countries have high rates of imprisonment and others have low rates.

4. Collect statistical data to find out whether countries with high rates of imprisonment have low rates of crime. If so, does this prove that prisons solve the crime problem?

SELECTED REFERENCES

DECKER, SCOTT, RICHARD WRIGHT, and ROBERT LOGIE, Perceptual deterrence among active residential burglars: A research note, *Criminology* (February 1993), 31, 1, 135–147.

DRESSEL, P. L., . . . And we keep on building prisons: Racism, poverty, and challenges to the welfare state, *Journal of Sociology and Social Welfare* (September 1994), 21, 3, 7–30.

FARRINGTON, KEITH, The modern prison as total institution? Public perception versus objective reality, *Crime and Delinquency* (January 1992), 38, 1, 6–26.

GEERKEN, MICHAEL R., and HENNESSEY D. HAYES, Probation and parole: Public risk and the future of incarceration alternatives, *Criminology* (November 1993), 31, 4, 549–564.

GOFFMAN, ERVING, *Asylums: Essays on the social situation of mental patients and other inmates* (Garden City, New York: Anchor, 1961).

GOTTFREDSON, DENISE C., and WILLIAM H. BARTON, Deinstitutionalization of juvenile offenders, *Criminology* (November 1993), 31, 4, 591–611.

GRASMICK, HAROLD G., and ROBERT J. BURSIK, JR., Conscience, significant others, and rational choice: Extending the deterrence model, *Law and Society Review* (1990), 24, 3, 837–861.

HUNT, GEOFFREY, STEPHANIE RIEGEL, TOMAS MORALES, and DAN WALDORF, Changes in prison culture: Prison gangs and the case of the "Pepsi Generation," *Social Problems* (August 1993), 40, 3, 398–409.

MATHIESEN, THOMAS, *Prison on Trial* (Beverly Hills, CA: Sage, 1990).

MATZA, DAVID, *Delinquency and drift* (New York: Wiley, 1964).

McCORKLE, RICHARD C., Living on the edge: Fear in a maximum security prison, *Journal of Offender Rehabilitation* (1993), 20, 1–2, 73–91.

McDONALD, DOUGLAS C., Public imprisonment by private means: The re-emergence of private prisons and jails in the United States, the United Kingdom, and Australia, *British Journal of Criminology* (1994), 34, 1 (special issue), 29–48.

MORRIS, NORVAL, and MICHAEL TONRY, *Between prison and probation: Intermediate punishments in a rational sentencing system* (New York: Oxford University Press, 1993).

NAGIN, DANIEL S., and DAVID P. FARRINGTON, The stability of criminal potential from childhood to adulthood, *Criminology* (May 1992), 30, 2, 235–260.

SANDHU, HARJIT S., RICHARD A. DODDER, and MINU MATHUR, House arrest: Success and failure rates in residential and nonresidential community-based programs, *Journal of Offender Rehabilitation* (1993), 19, 1–2, 131–144.

SHERMAN, LAWRENCE W., DOUGLAS A. SMITH, JANELL D. SCHMIDT, and DENNIS P. ROGAN, Crime, punishment, and stake in conformity: Legal and informal control of domestic violence, *American Sociological Review* (October 1992), 57, 5, 680–690.

SHICHOR, DAVID, The corporate context of private prisons, *Crime, Law and Social Change* (September 1993), 20, 2, 113–138.

SMITH, LINDA G., and RONALD L. AKERS, A comparison of recidivism of Florida's community control and prison: A five-year survival analysis, *Journal of Research in Crime and Delinquency* (August 1993), 30, 3, 267–292.

STEVENS, DENNIS J., The depth of imprisonment and prisonization: Levels of security and prisoners' anticipation of future violence, *Howard Journal of Criminal Justice* (May 1994), 33, 2, 137–157.

WALKER, NIGEL, Side-effects of incarceration, *British Journal of Criminology* (January 1983), 23, 1, 61–71.

3.3
Should getting high be legal?

<u>*The issue*</u>: *The nation's drug problem. Are drugs really a problem, and if so what kind of problem: a crime problem or a health problem? What, if anything, should be done about people's perception that there is a drug problem?*

Introduction When people ask questions that begin with the word "should," they are either asking a moral question or an efficiency question. In sociology, *efficiency questions* ask whether or how we can solve a social problem by changing our present laws or practices. In the present case sociologists want to know things like: Should recreational drugs (marijuana, hashish, and maybe even cocaine) be legalized to reduce the costs of arresting and imprisoning drug offenders? Or to reduce health risks? Or to control the quality of drugs sold on the street?

Other times, when people use the word "should," they are asking a *moral question*; in this case: Is it right or proper for society to legalize recreational drugs? What sociologists do to research moral issues is take a social constructionist approach to the question itself. *Social constructionists* study the ways people negotiate meanings for everyday life, given competing interpretations of reality.

Here, constructionists ask: Why do some people want to legalize recreational drugs and others do not? Why does the problem in question seem particularly pressing right now? Is a "moral panic" taking place, and if so why? What kinds of people think that there is a pressing drug problem to be solved? What current ideologies—religious, political, economic, or otherwise—fit well with this idea? And whose political interests are served by promoting the idea that a drug problem needs solving?

With these thoughts in mind, consider the debate about legalizing the sale and use of recreational drugs. Chemicals like THC, found abundantly in marijuana and hashish, are used mainly for pleasure. Unlike alcohol, nicotine, and caffeine—addictive substances that many people with high status frequently use—these recreational drugs are currently outlawed.

WE SHOULD LEGALIZE RECREATIONAL DRUGS

Most arguments in favor of legalizing recreational drugs are efficiency arguments. They support legalizing recreational drugs by emphasizing the practical benefits of legalization or the harm done by failing to legalize these drugs.

Current laws don't work We should legalize drug use because laws aimed at preventing it have no effect. Drug use is widespread. There is no sign that use is declining or that stiff penalties control people's behavior. No consensus exists among drug enforcement critics except that criminal sanctions have little effect on drug use and attempts to control illegal drug use by law enforcement strategies must fail. Thus a great deal of money spent on drug law enforcement is wasted. When, in the 1920s, laws prohibiting alcohol use and sales failed to have an effect they were repealed. Many argue the same should be done today with drug laws.

Prevention works better than arrests Sociologists know that it is usually easier to prevent people from starting a deviant career than to cure or rehabilitate them afterward. So instead of spending money to arrest and convict drug users, we should work at learning how to reduce people's need or desire to use drugs. We should also educate people about the social, economic, and health costs of using recreational drugs.

In short, we should approach this problem as we do cigarette smoking and excessive drinking: as a health problem with economic and social consequences. From a medical perspective, U.S. drug policy should try to reduce harm, increase safety, provide care for those who need it, and foster norms of self-regulation of risky behavior.

Crime is the problem to solve At present neither the medical nor criminal justice approach adequately deals with the problem of dangerous drug use. The public concern about drugs is really a concern about crimes—the production, sale, purchase, and possession of illegal drugs; the commission of crimes to purchase illegal drugs; the commission of crimes while under the influence of drugs; and the violent and corrupt behavior of drug traffickers. And, of course, at least some of that crime is produced by the definition of some drugs as illegal.

A related problem is **drug addiction.** Some recreational drugs, like marijuana and hashish, are not physically addictive. Unlike heroin and cocaine, they do not drive people to commit crimes. There is little evidence that decriminalizing the use of "soft drugs" (e.g., those containing THC) will result in dramatic increases in substance abuse. Nor is there compelling evidence that they lead people to use addictive drugs like heroin or cocaine. States that decriminalized marijuana during the 1960s and 1970s did not suffer epidemics of drug use, compared with other states.

A second problem to be solved is the costliness of addictive drugs. If addictive drugs are cheap or free, addicts do not have to commit crimes to get them. Just like alcohol prohibition in the 1920s, drug prohibition has produced a large criminalized and lucrative industry. A regulated repeal of prohibition would limit overall consumption and put a dent in the revenues of organized crime. Though a radical change in drug policy may not be politically feasible right now, many drug-related crimes would decrease if public health agencies provided free drugs or drug substitutes like Methadone. This has been tried in various countries (e.g., the Netherlands, the United Kingdom), with the predicted reduction in crime.

Research shows that decriminalization of the possession of marijuana since the early 1970s has resulted in decreased costs of enforcement and prosecution of marijuana-related offenses.

Illegal drug use is a health hazard So long as drug use is illegal, we can do little to monitor the quality of drugs available to users or the conditions under which people use these drugs. Where alcohol and caffeine are concerned, food and drug regulations ensure that people don't consume dangerous or poor quality substances. (The same cannot be said of cigarettes, which contain known carcinogens as well as nicotine.) Similarly, health-protective rules should apply to recreational drugs.

One reason for repealing Prohibition was the recognition that, when quality-controlled alcoholic beverages are unavailable, people drink just about anything. In the 1920s and 1930s, people died or went blind from drinking beverages that contained dangerous impurities or the wrong kind of alcohol (methanol instead of ethanol). More recently, some users have died from drug overdoses because they had no way of knowing the strength of the drug. Legalization could prevent this by regulating strength and quality.

When drugs are illegal, users also take fewer health precautions. Needles shared among heroin users spread HIV and AIDS, for example. By driving the drug-user culture underground, the law works against safety, good hygiene, and disease prevention. Programs in other countries have reduced the amount of sharing of contaminated equipment without increasing drug use.

Penalties make things worse What happens to drug users and sellers when they are arrested and convicted? Some are sent to overflowing, underfunded prisons where, to alleviate their horror, they take drugs. For women drug users, the punitive American policy has resulted in gender-biased or inaccessible treatment programs, the prosecution of pregnant drug users, and a rising population of female prisoners.

A second problem is the stigma that comes with an arrest and conviction for a drug offense. Having a record for a drug offense may ruin a person's chances to get a good job or enter a profession. Depressed and desperate, such people turn to drugs. The emphasis on punishment is too expensive in terms of the human costs of incarcerating many people for relatively minor offenses. If our goal is to draw people into law-abiding activity, we want to avoid handing out records. Criminal records exclude people from normal life and in this way increase their chances of committing crimes.

The "war on drugs" hurts foreign relations The "war on drugs" has focused on two main enemies. At home, it has targeted local users and sellers, in hopes that stiffer penalties and more policing would reduce the demand for drugs. It has not. At the same time, U.S. administrations have tried to reduce the drug supply reaching the United States. They have used various means, for example, cooperating with international police efforts to capture large drug producers and traffickers. They have also tried to get the governments of other countries (e.g., Colombia, Panama, Mexico) to control the growth and transport of drugs that otherwise end up in the United States.

Such efforts have undesirable side effects, however. One undesirable side effect is to jeopardize the peace and economic well-being of countries that, like Peru and Colombia, depend economically on producing drugs for the U.S. market. Another side effect is the establishment of friendly relations with corrupt or dangerous rulers (like Noriega of Panama) just because they cooperate, or appear to cooperate, in the "war on drugs." In this way the United States risks being viewed as a country that is "soft" on dictators and tyrants.

Militarization of the drug war in Latin America means increasing economic hardship, repression, and radicalization of the peasantry, as well as further corruption of the military, historically part of the drug problem rather than its solution. Finally, the attempt to repress drug trafficking by war tactics is contrary to democratic ideals.

There is much public support for legalization Survey evidence shows that many still oppose drug use and sales, and some oppose legalization. However, most Americans are indifferent to legalizing non-addictive recreational drugs; they just don't care. They oppose efforts to construct a "war on drugs" which they consider unwarranted. Some strongly favor legalization, for the reasons given earlier. Others actively support the use of marijuana for the treatment of people suffering from terminal illness (i.e., cancer and AIDS). Many researchers claim the drug has medicinal properties in certain situations.

WE SHOULD NOT LEGALIZE DRUG USE AND SALE

People usually oppose legalizing drug use and sales on moral grounds or because they disagree with the efficiency evidence provided by the other side.

Drug use is immoral Some communities consider drug use immoral, and therefore consider drug sales immoral too. The law sometimes uses community standards—for example, what the community considers pornographic—to decide what deviant or marginal behavior to allow. In this case, courts might be reluctant to legalize drug use if they felt this violated the community's moral standard.

People who oppose drug use on moral grounds believe there *is* a drug problem. They support moral and political solutions that include stiffer penalties for wrongdoing and attaching personal blame to wrong-

doers. Conversely, they oppose medicalizing the drug problem by viewing it as a health problem requiring medical treatment. They also oppose legalizing immoral behavior merely because it is hard to control.

Others oppose legalization for a different moral reason: They believe that, by legalizing drug use, we ignore the plight of drug users. We also ignore the social problems that lead people to use drugs in the first place. In other words, legalization lets us forget about the poor and the ill-treated in our society.

Efficiency arguments Some arguments in support of legalization are disputed by people who oppose it. For example, many people opposing legalization claim that drug use, especially the use of hard drugs like heroin, cocaine, and speed, is physically and mentally harmful. Drugs cause health problems for users. They also cause social, psychological, and financial problems for the users' family and friends.

Though soft drugs like marijuana and hashish are less directly harmful, they are said to lead to the use of hard drugs. Evidence indicates that soft drugs are neither necessary nor sufficient for the use of hard drugs, although most hard-drug users have used soft drugs at one time or another. Some opponents are concerned that legalizing soft drugs eases the way for the legalization of hard drugs.

Current efforts are working Some believe that the current policy of zero tolerance is working in the military. For this reason, efforts to eliminate drug and alcohol abuse should be intensified by continuing programs in assessment, deterrence and detection, treatment and rehabilitation, and education and training. The downward trend in marijuana use in high schools also suggests progress in prevention among adolescents. It is argued that a "get tough" policy—including efforts to control cigarette and alcohol consumption at school—offers more promise than legalization.

Legalization might not work here Experiments with legalization have been successful in various places. In Amsterdam, the Netherlands, for example, soft drugs—though not cocaine or heroin—are readily available and consumed in public. The Dutch Opium Act of 1976 allowed for the de facto decriminalization of cannabis in small amounts. It may have resulted from the absence of any clear policy or belated adaptation to already existing circumstances. At best, drug policy was part of a broader health policy based on normalization, treatment, and prevention.

Dutch citizens are for the most part sober, law-abiding, and peaceful. No crime evidently results from drug use or sale. However, opponents say that the Dutch experience with legalized drugs may not apply to North America. There are important social, cultural, and economic differences between the two societies. If the Dutch use drugs moderately despite their availability, the Dutch must have little need for drugs (e.g., they are already happy) or have strong internal constraints on drug use (e.g., a high preference for sobriety). The same needs and constraints may not operate in America.

Market problems remain Some people claim that legalizing drugs will not solve the problems associated with illegal marketing. Judging from past experience with narcotics, alcohol, and tobacco, some illegal markets in drugs will persist. For example, people will continue to buy drugs from unlicensed or unregulated sources if the prices are lower (as they are if there are no sales taxes to pay). They will also continue to buy from illegal sources that offer more varied brands through the illegal production of "designer drugs."

Controlling a legal market may even be harder than controlling an illegal one. Look how difficult it has been to control cigarette manufacturers. Testimony shows they have increased the addictiveness of cigarettes through nicotine additives and worked at addicting children to cigarettes at ever younger ages. Legal drug sellers like these not only have power, wealth, and social respectability, they also have lawyers and legal rights. Thus legalization might make controlling recreational drugs even more difficult than it already is.

SUMMING UP

Should getting high be legal? Yes, but we have to take some steps to make sure that this recreation of choice does not become a full-time lifestyle. A compromise solution is needed, since the two sides are talking past each other. Start by admitting that the "war on drugs" has failed, for the same reasons that Prohibition failed: Too many people want to do what the law forbids, and most bystanders don't mind. At the same time, many people—especially poor young people in the inner cities—are being destroyed by hard (though not by soft) drugs. We need to find out why and do something about it. Prevention and harm reduction, with minimal application of criminal law, may be the most effective public health policy toward drugs.

A compromise includes decriminalizing soft-drug use and finding alternatives to criminalization. Inevitably, psychoactive drugs will be available. So license the production and sales of soft drugs to regulate their quality. Explore the possibilities of a free market versus a government monopoly versus medical control over access to drugs. Tax the profits on legalized drug sales and use the taxes for drug education. At the same time, reduce the penalties for using hard drugs. Treat unlicensed drug selling as a regulatory or tax offense, punishable by huge fines.

Develop a comprehensive public health approach to addressing illegal drug problems. Educate the public against excessive drug use and the use of harmful, illegal drugs. In short, shift the emphasis of drug education to consideration of irresponsible versus responsible drug use. And learn more about the relationship between drug use and socially adaptive or harmful behavior.

Most important, carry out research on ways to reduce the desire to use soft drugs excessively or hard drugs at all. This research may show that people with optimism, a belief in the future, and a stake in conformity usually stay sober. What is needed is grudging toleration, which has fewer disadvantages than either absolute prohibition or uncontrolled legalization. Prohibition cannot substitute for an integrated and well-coordinated approach that includes prevention, treatment, and enforcement and is supported by an educated public.

REVIEW EXERCISES

For Discussion and Debate

1. Should alcohol be made illegal or its use limited to people who need it for medical purposes?

2. "Addiction is a moral problem, not a social or medical problem." Discuss.

3. Should all gambling be made illegal, in view of its addictive tendencies?

4. "It makes no sense to continue a social policy like the 'war on drugs,' which has had no success whatever." (Or "It makes perfect sense to continue the 'war on drugs,' even though it has had no success whatever.")

Writing Exercises

1. "The state has no business regulating how people seek their pleasure, so long as no one else is hurt."

2. "The kind of society in which recreational problems would pose no problem."

3. Why organized crime loves to see the state prohibiting pleasure.

4. How we might more effectively discourage young people from getting addicted to drugs.

Research Activities

1. Collect information on a program designed to discourage young people from using drugs. How successful has the program been? (*Note*: Specify how you are measuring "success.")

2. Review published evidence on the likelihood that a user of recreational drugs will graduate to regular use of heroin, cocaine, or other hard drugs.

3. Interview a dozen students to find out their knowledge of, attitude toward, and use of recreational drugs. What is the connection between their (past or present) use of recreational drugs and their support for legalization of these drugs?

4. Collect published information about the effect of drug production on the economy and politics of any major drug-producing country (e.g., Colombia, Afghanistan).

SELECTED REFERENCES

BROWNSTEIN, HENRY H., The media and the construction of random drug violence, *Social Justice* (Winter 1991), 18, 4, 85–103.

CURRIE, ELLIOTT, Toward a policy on drugs. Decriminalization? Legalization? *Dissent* (Winter 1993), 40, 1(170), 65–71.

DE LEON, GEORGE, Some problems with the anti-prohibitionist position on the legalization of drugs, *Journal of Addictive Diseases* (1994), 13, 2, 35–57.

DICHIARA, ALBERT, and JOHN F. GALLIHER, Dissonance and the contradictions in the origins of marijuana decriminalization, *Law and Society Review* (February 1994), 28, 1, 41–77.

DUNCAN, DAVID F., Drug abuse prevention in post-legalization America: What could it be like? *Journal of Primary Prevention* (Summer 1992), 12, 4, 317–322.

ERICKSON, PATRICIA, The law, social control, and drug policy: Models, factors, and processes, *International Journal of the Addictions* (October 1993), 28, 12, 1155–1176.

FARR, KATHRYN ANN, Revitalizing the drug decriminalization debate, *Crime and Delinquency* (April 1990), 36, 2, 223–237.

GOODE, ERICH, The American drug panic of the 1980s: Social construction or objective threat? *International Journal of the Addictions* (September 1990), 25, 9, 1083–1098.

HEATH, DWIGHT B., U.S. drug control policy: A cultural perspective, *Daedalus* (Summer 1992), 121, 3, 269–291.

INCIARDI, JAMES, ed., *Handbook of Drug Control in the United States* (New York: Greenwood Press, 1990).

JACOBS, JAMES B., Imagining drug legalization, *Public Interest* (Fall 1990), 101, 28–42.

JENSEN, ERIC L., and JURG GERBER, State efforts to construct a social problem: The 1986 War on Drugs in Canada, *Canadian Journal of Sociology* (Fall 1993), 18, 4, 453–462.

KLEIMAN, MARK A. R., Neither Prohibition nor legalization: Grudging toleration in drug control policy, *Daedalus* (Summer 1992), 121, 3, 53–83.

LEVINE, HARRY G., and CRAIG REINARMAN, From Prohibition to regulation: Lessons from alcohol policy for drug policy, *Milbank Quarterly* (1991), 69, 3, 461–494.

NADELMANN, ETHAN A., Drug prohibition in the United States: Costs, consequences, and alternatives, *Science* (September 1989), 245, 4921, 939–947.

NEWCOMB, MICHAEL D., Substance abuse and control in the United States: Ethical and legal issues, *Social Science and Medicine* (August 1992), 35, 4, 471–479.

REUTER, PETER, Quantity illusions and paradoxes of drug interdiction: Federal intervention into vice policy, *Law and Contemporary Problems* (Winter 1988), 51, 1, 233–252.

SINGLE, ERIC W., The impact of marijuana decriminalization: An update, *Journal of Public Health Policy* (Winter 1989), 10, 4, 456–466.

SKOLNICK, JEROME H., Rethinking the drug problem, *Daedalus* (Summer 1992), 121, 3, 133–159.

TONRY, MICHAEL, and JAMES Q. WILSON, eds., *Drugs and crime (Crime and justice: A review of research,* vol. 13), Chicago: University of Chicago Press, 1990.

WINICK, CHARLES, Social behavior, public policy, and nonharmful drug use, *Milbank Quarterly* (1991), 69, 3, 437–459.

4. *Class and Stratification*

By **class**, sociologists mean a group of people who share similar *life chances*—opportunities to attain what they need and want in life. According to theorists who follow the Marxist paradigm, these life chances are structured mainly by people's control over the means of production by which we earn a living. According to theorists who follow the Weberian paradigm, life chances are also structured by people's position in the hierarchies of status and power which are not directly connected with economic domination.

Stratification refers to the layering of society that results when people have different life chances. Within each layer, people often come to share a common awareness of their condition and a willingness to act in terms of their common problems and common interests. This may reveal itself in voting patterns, lifestyle choices, and acts of resistance or protest.

In this chapter we examine three issues associated with class and stratification. First, we consider the functional theory of stratification, which argues that inequality and stratification are not only inevitable, they are socially beneficial. Then we consider whether the middle class—traditionally, the bulwark of American society—is disappearing, as Marx would have predicted, and if so, whether this is a problem. Finally, we return to an earlier theme, the poverty problem, and whether social welfare makes the problem worse.

4.1

Shouldn't poor people be happy that others are rich?

The issue: *The wide inequality between the poor and the rich: Is it natural and inevitable, or can it be decreased? And if it can be decreased, would it improve society to decrease inequality, or would doing so stifle people's ambition?*

Introduction Many people are accustomed to economic inequality and accept it as normal and natural. For example, we are all aware of differences due to accidents of birth or inborn abilities (e.g., being born into a rich family or with an aptitude for drawing). However, our views about economic equality vary, in part because economic equality itself varies. Simple societies are much more egalitarian than complex societies. Some industrial societies are more equal than agricultural societies, while others are less so. And some industrial societies, like Sweden, are more egalitarian than other industrial societies, like the United States. So inequality varies, and because it varies, people (especially sociologists) look for explanations. They also ask whether more equality is better or worse.

Likewise, economic opportunity varies over time. For several decades after World War II, economic growth meant that almost everyone was doing better financially. Under these conditions, people paid less attention to inequality. But in the last decade, economic growth has declined, wages have stagnated or fallen, and unemployment has grown. Many middle-class people have lost ground financially. The rich have gotten richer while the poor have gotten poorer, so inequality has increased. Under these conditions of changing inequality, people once again look for explanations. With these variations in mind, people hold strong views about the need for, and acceptability of, wide economic inequalities.

ECONOMIC INEQUALITY BENEFITS SOCIETY

A theory proposed by sociologists Kingsley Davis and Wilbert Moore about 50 years ago provides one explanation of why people are unequal economically. It also implies that inequality is necessary and suggests reasons why inequality varies from one society to another. Society's members agree on which social roles contribute the most to society's survival and are, therefore, the most valuable roles. In any society valuable talents and abilities are always in short supply. We must motivate people to train for and commit themselves to the most valuable roles. Large amounts of money and prestige provide the necessary motivation, and wide inequalities of income and prestige result. Society prospers largely because economic inequality has supplied the talent society needs. Looked at another way, because the poor don't have money, there are doctors, lawyers, architects, and movie stars.

Inequality varies over time or from one society to another, because of: (1) variations in the degree to which some roles are viewed as more valuable than other roles, and (2) variations in the scarcity of talent needed to perform the most valuable roles. By this reasoning, military leadership should be valued more highly in wartime than in peacetime. And societies that have a warlike culture or prosper mainly by warring on other societies should reward military leaders more highly than peace-loving societies. Likewise, societies that place a high value on artistic performance should reward concert pianists more highly than less artistically inclined societies do. But when highly talented concert pianists become numerous, the rewards paid to individual pianists should start to decline (unless they have a "union," as doctors, lawyers, and many other professionals do), and the expected proficiency of high-income pianists will increase.

This functional theory is like the economist's theory that prices reflect the supply and demand for particular goods and services. It differs in proposing that there is a social consensus about which goods and services are most highly valued. You may be able to think of reasons why the functional theory often makes wrong predictions and feel that these wrong predictions tell us that functional theory, if not completely wrong, at least needs modification. But let's begin by considering why its predictions are sometimes right and why one could, therefore, believe that economic inequality benefits society.

Let's narrow our terms of reference and ask why an increase in economic inequality might bring a society increased benefits. In 1992, the wealthiest 20% of Americans received 11 times more after-tax income than the bottom 20%. By contrast, the wealthiest 20% of Japanese received just under five times more after-tax income than the bottom 20%. On this basis, the United States has more economic inequality than Japan—indeed, twice as much.

Is the United States too unequal? Is Japan unequal enough? The following arguments provide reasons for thinking that more inequality is better than less and that inequality is good for society:

Inequality motivates effort Poverty and inequality are necessary functional aspects of capitalism. They serve to induce workers to perform alienating work for pay, warn workers of the consequences of labor militancy, and maintain a reserve army of unemployed workers who depress the wages of employed workers, keep down the prices of goods and services supplied by underpaid workers, and keep marginal enterprises afloat. The trick is to find the right balance between work incentives and low-wage labor markets and between the preservation of order and the amelioration of discontent. For example, too little inequality or poverty is unprofitable for capitalists; too much undermines work incentives or provokes the poor to militant action.

Inequality reveals talent The drive for upward mobility on a tall ladder produces a competition in which everyone tries hard to win. Only the most talented are successful. Thus the most valuable positions in society are filled with the most talented, hard-working people. Merit is rewarded, and the most meritorious hold positions of the greatest importance to society.

Inequality promotes investment If America's wealth were shared equally, everyone would be comfortable but no one would have enough money to invest heavily. Large enterprises, however, need large amounts of capital. A high degree of income inequality produces personal fortunes that can be invested in new technologies or to build new factories. This investment creates thousands of new jobs for people lower down the ladder. Even conspicuous consumption by the rich creates work for many thousands of people.

Inequality promotes philanthropy Since the Middle Ages, the wealthiest citizens have patronized the arts, the church, colleges and universities, hospitals and orphanages, and other deserving public institutions. Without this patronage, society would be worse off. More inequality creates more millionaires and, in this way, creates more philanthropy.

Inequality maintains labor supply A rapidly changing economy requires some poverty and unemployment. Poor and/or unemployed people are available to fill new jobs as they are created. That is why Marx called them a "reserve army of labor." Thus a high degree of inequality produces highly motivated poor people who are willing and able to enter new jobs. In this way inequality contributes to rapid, even explosive, economic growth.

Inequality produces economic development In the long run, everyone benefits from economic inequality and from capitalism, which increases economic inequality. The poor struggle to escape poverty. The middle class struggle to move up the economic ladder, year by year and generation by generation. The wealthy demonstrate the rewards of hard work and invest in the economy. The net result is economic development. These are the reasons people put up with economic inequality. There is no reason to limit inequality. More is better. It is because of twice as great inequality that, in some years at least, the U.S. economy was growing twice as fast as the Japanese economy—not, however, in the last three decades.

Under capitalism, business is motivated by greed and self-interest. However, it is premised on confidence in society, and it invests in anticipation, though not knowledge, of return. Capitalism's confidence, optimism, and faith are positive qualities that produce altruism and economic growth, as well as inequality and poverty. However, many challenge these arguments. They hold the view that economic inequality may not be natural or inevitable. But even if it is, less inequality is better.

ECONOMIC INEQUALITY DOES NOT BENEFIT SOCIETY

Research on this topic raises many questions about the validity of arguments made earlier. Let's consider the counterarguments in roughly the same sequence as before.

Inequality motivates effort Up to a point it may be true that the greater the degree of inequality, the more people are motivated to escape the bottom rungs and reach the top rungs. However, there are limits to this principle.

It is widely argued that high pay is needed to attract competent managers, but it had not been needed in utilities, nationalized industries in the United Kingdom, or government positions. Further, these highly paid executives all come from the same class which traditionally has managed big businesses in the United States. Little incentive is needed to recruit them.

Top performers in a variety of fields—entertainment and sports, but also law, journalism, fashion, and academia—reap a disproportionate share of financial rewards for their work. The disparity in salaries is due to market imperfections that depress competition at the top and a culture of greed that became fashionable in the Reagan era.

People too far down the economic ladder become demoralized. They are preoccupied with the day-to-day problems of mere survival. Also, they lack opportunities for education and entry into good jobs, without which they have little chance to move upward as far as their talent and energy warrant. What Karl Marx called "false consciousness"—a delusional picture of reality disseminated by an apparatus of ideology—surely holds many to the belief that one can move easily from rags to riches if only one is lucky enough. Their thwarted ambitions soon die, turning them to bitterness or laziness.

Inequality reveals talent Are only the most talented successful in such a system? In a system of equal opportunity, the most talented would indeed profit most. However, plenty of evidence shows barriers to the education, hiring, and promotion of intelligent and ambitious people—among them, women, racial minorities, people with handicaps, and people from impoverished backgrounds. As a result, we find a weak fit between success and the usual signs of talent or merit—namely, intelligence, drive for success, aptitude, or commitment to the job.

If talent is not the best way to explain success, what is? Probably a combination of influences that includes high social class origin (i.e., one's parents' position), good social contacts, a good education, location in a thriving country, industry, and organization or line of work.

Inequality promotes investment In principle, a high degree of income inequality produces personal fortunes and jobs for people lower down the ladder. Indeed, this idea underlies "supply-side economics," which was popular in the 1980s under the Republican (Reagan and Bush) administrations. Supply-side economics justifies cutting government in order to cut taxes. What monies the rich had previously paid in taxes, they could now invest, thus creating jobs for the poor. However, evidence from that period does not support the theory's predictions. Wealthy people do indeed invest their earnings. But they may not do so in ways that produce jobs.

First, much personal wealth is invested in financial activities—acquisitions and mergers, buyouts and sell-offs, and stock market, currency, and land speculations—all of which earn profits for the investor but create no new jobs. They often actually destroy businesses and jobs and wipe out other people's savings. Thus these activities merely redistribute wealth upwards from the poor and middle classes to the (already) rich.

Second, most investment in new jobs is offshore, in low-wage, developing countries. It produces jobs, but not here. As well, many wealthy people use tax loopholes and tax havens (offshore residence) to avoid paying taxes on their earnings. So investments profit wealthy shareholders but bring fewer benefits—either as jobs or taxes—to ordinary Americans.

Inequality promotes philanthropy Does more inequality mean more philanthropy? The evidence questions this assertion as well. Some wealthy people contribute lavishly to cultural, educational, and other institutions. They receive tax breaks for doing so; their philanthropy costs them little or nothing and it advertises their business. But what percentage of their personal wealth do they give away in socially beneficial ways? The amount is small, and the percentage they donate varies little with the extent of economic inequality. Further, the poor give proportionately more through their taxes.

Corporate philanthropy, like many other corporate activities, is best explained as a form of imitation or contagion, not as a selfless or moralistic activity. Corporate giving serves to create and maintain businesspeople's positions within the business elite or improve their public image. Further, philanthropic foundations work to maintain the social order rather than change it. This has been visible in the effects of philanthropic foundations on the development of the social sciences. Since the degree of inequality has little impact on the amount of philanthropy, there is no justification for a high degree of inequality on philanthropic grounds.

Inequality maintains labor supply How about the claim that inequality produces highly motivated poor people willing to enter new jobs, thus contributing to economic growth? A "reserve army of labor" may have been useful a century or even a half-century ago. However, today there is little industrial advantage to having many poor and/or unemployed people. More probably, new industrial investment can go into Third World factories, where labor is cheaper than it may ever be again in America. The rest can go into development in automation, which substitutes machines for people, with the result that overall production costs can plummet.

Thus maintaining extreme economic inequality in America means not challenging a reserve labor market but reproducing a large impoverished underclass. The poor lack spending power; hence, they contribute little to the economy, and they need public support merely to survive. The middle class pays to support this underclass while the rich invest overseas.

Inequality produces economic development Is the net result of inequality more economic development? As we have seen, more inequality does not automatically produce more economic development, at least not in America. The wealthy profit from their investments, and on the surface these profits look a lot like economic growth, but the average American's income is dropping. It would drop faster if not for the payment of public moneys—Social Security, welfare, and AFDC, among others—to the neediest. In the middle-class household, incomes would drop too if not for the ever-increasing contribution by second-income earners (typically, wives) and longer working hours for people who do have jobs.

In recent years, there has been rapid economic development in Europe and Japan, countries with less economic inequality than the United States. Even the Pacific Rim countries, such as Korea, Taiwan, and Hong Kong, which began with higher levels of economic inequality, have reduced inequality in order to promote development. Low inequality stimulates growth in four ways: by inducing large increases in the savings and investments of the poor, by contributing to political and macroeconomic stability, by increasing the morale and efficiency of low income workers, and, with higher rural incomes, by increasing market demand for domestic products.

SUMMING UP

Shouldn't poor people be happy that others are rich? Well, if you believe that extreme inequality is an incentive to try harder, we guess they should be happy. But in the end, the functional theory of stratification leaves many unanswered questions. Also problematic, it provides justification for a status quo in which large numbers of people are left to go destitute while a relatively small number bathe in luxury.

As we said in an earlier section, inequality is not primarily a result of differential merit. Mainly, it is caused by the capitalist economy that determines the precise amount of poverty and degree of inequality. Conflict theorists note that the institution of private property gives rise to class relationships. In a class system, poverty stems from reliance on labor income, and wealth flows from ownership of property. The stratification of the labor market relegates the propertyless to different positions of relative poverty, depending on their credentials. And credentials are a form of capital themselves, unequally distributed. The state reinforces unequal power relations emerging from the interaction of class and labor market operations. Public programs to aid the poor (which we discuss in a later section) are compatible with the capitalist system's defining institutions, perpetuating poverty and the system that creates it.

Are high incomes and prestige the best motivations for hard work? It is doubtful they are. What about altruism? Duty to one's family or community? A drive to create something meaningful in one's life? All of these motivations affect people at every level of the social order. Sometimes they bring wealth and prestige. Often they do not. But are they less important or less real for being less lucrative?

And how much economic inequality is too much? There is no evidence that an income ratio of 100 to 1, where the top boss earns 100 times what the average worker does, produces more economic growth or social well-being than a ratio of 20 to 1, which is more typical of other industrial societies. If the same social benefits can be achieved with less social inequality, then more inequality is too much.

REVIEW EXERCISES

For Discussion and Debate

1. Do inequalities of power benefit society? How are they related to economic inequalities?

2. "Fear of loss is a stronger motivator than the promise of gain." Discuss.

3. Does the functional theory of stratification account for economic inequalities among nations of the world? Why or why not?

4. What kind of evidence would prove that equality—economic or otherwise—is better for societies than inequality?

Writing Exercises

1. What is a "fair" system of economic inequality?

2. The reasons why hunter-gatherer societies are economically equal.

3. Why greed is more socially useful than unselfishness.

4. Is economic inequality becoming more or less important?

Research Activities

1. Collect data to determine whether the most functionally important players on a professional sports team (you choose the sport) earn the highest wages.

2. Collect data from at least six industrial societies to determine whether economic inequality (use the Gini Index, if possible) is correlated with high or low rates of annual growth in productivity (use the GNP per capita to measure this).

3. Collect data on wages within an industry (you choose the industry) to find out whether labor conflict (e.g., strikes) increases with an increase in economic inequality.

4. What role, if any, did economic inequality play in the downfall of a major society or civilization? Use historical sources to find the data you need.

SELECTED REFERENCES

ABRAHAMSON, MARK, A functional theory of organizational stratification, *Social Forces* (September 1979), 58, 1, 128–145.

———, Functionalism and the functional theory of stratification: An empirical assessment, *American Journal of Sociology* (March 1973), 78, 5, 1236–1246.

ALLEN, MICHAEL PATRICK, Power and privilege in the large corporation: Corporate control and managerial compensation, *American Journal of Sociology* (March 1981), 86, 5, 1112–1123.

BETZ, MICHAEL, KEMP DAVIS, and PATRICK MILLER, Scarcity, income advantage, and mobility: More evidence on the functional theory of stratification, *Sociological Quarterly* (Summer 1978), 19, 3, 399–413.

BLUMBERG, PAUL, Another day, another $3,000: Executive salaries in America, *Dissent* (Spring 1978), 25, 2(111), 157–168.

BOK, DEREK, *The cost of talent: How executives and professionals are paid and how it affects America,* (New York: Free Press, 1993).

BROOM, LEONARD, and ROBERT G. CUSHING, A modest test of an immodest theory: The functional theory of stratification, *American Sociological Review* (February 1977), 42, 1, 157–169.

CULLEN, JOHN B., and SHELLEY M. NOVICK, The Davis-Moore theory of stratification: A further examination and extension, *American Journal of Sociology* (May 1979), 84, 6, 1424–1437.

EHRENREICH, JOHN, and BARBARA EHRENREICH, Hospital workers: A case study in the "new working class," *Monthly Review* (January 1973), 24, 8, 12–27.

FISHER, DONALD, The role of philanthropic foundations in the reproduction and production of hegemony: Rockefeller Foundations and the social sciences, *Sociology* (May 1983), 17, 2, 206–233.

———, American philanthropy and the social sciences in Britain, 1919–1939: The reproduction of a conservative ideology, *Sociological Review* (May 1980), 28, 2, 277–315.

GALASKIEWICZ, JOSEPH, *Social organization of an urban grants economy: A study of business philanthropy and nonprofit organizations* (Orlando, FL: Academic Press, 1985).

———, and RONALD S. BURT, Interorganization contagion in corporate philanthropy, *Adminis-*

trative Science Quarterly (March 1991), 36, 1, 88–105.

GILDER, GEORGE, Moral sources of capitalism, *Society* (October–September 1981), 18, 6(134), 24–27.

GORDON, DAVID M., American poverty: Functions, mechanisms and contradictions, *Monthly Review* (June 1972), 24, 2, 72–79.

HARRIS, WILLIAM T., Rule changes and the earnings of National Football League field goal kickers, *Sociology of Sport Journal* (December 1992), 9, 4, 397–402.

SIMPSON, MILES, Political rights and income inequality: A cross-national test, *American Sociological Review* (October 1990), 55, 5, 682, 693.

WACHTEL, HOWARD, Capitalism and poverty in America: Paradox or contradiction? *Monthly Review* (June 1972), 24, 2, 51–64.

4.2

Is the middle class disappearing, and if it is, who cares?

The issue: *Signs of shrinkage of the middle class, leaving society polarized between a large poor group and a much smaller rich group. Is class polarization a bad thing? Would the loss of a middle class, if it occurs, change society significantly?*

Introduction Debate over whether the middle class is disappearing is timely and important. The difficulty in answering this question stems in large part from a lack of agreement about what counts as "the middle class." There are at least four competing definitions of "middle class." We shall call them the statistical, relational, cultural, and institutional definitions.

♦ People who use a *statistical definition* answer the question about the disappearance of the middle class by examining the shape of the income distribution. By middle class these statistically minded analysts mean people whose incomes are near the average—for example, people who earn between 50% and 150% of the average annual income. The ques-

tion is, what percentage of people are in this middle range, and is it declining?

♦ Other analysts use a more distinctly *relational definition*. They follow Karl Marx's notion of social classes, focusing on power and control. They answer the question about the disappearance of the middle class by examining the working and life conditions of these white-collar people. In particular, they look for evidence of "proletarianization" of the middle class, about which we say more shortly.

♦ A third group of analysts use a *cultural definition*. They build on Max Weber's research on the Protestant ethic and its contribution to capitalism's growth, focusing on distinctive class values. They answer the question about the disappearance of the middle class by looking for signs that the traditional Protestant ethic virtues are losing their hold.

♦ Still others use an *institutional definition*. They are concerned with whether people identify themselves as middle class and with the ways institutions create and maintain class identities. People who take an institutional approach look for signs that middle-class people are more or less separated from capitalists or working-class people than they once were.

As we shall see, the different definitions of middle class lead us to answer our question in slightly different ways.

THE MIDDLE CLASS IS DISAPPEARING

Statistical: The gap between the rich and poor
Some who say that the middle class is disappearing note a widening gap between the rich and poor in America and, to a lesser extent, in Europe. The percentage of the population that earns between 50% and 150% of median income is decreasing. That is, a smaller percentage of people are middle-income earners.

With downward pressure on their jobs and incomes, increasing numbers of middle-class Americans are calling for assistance from public welfare agencies that were originally established to serve poor people. This decline in real wages and salaries, which brought about the shrinkage in number of middle-class families, has only been partly offset by the contribution of working wives to family incomes.

Personal incomes have become more unequal in the United States since the 1970s. Working-class incomes have stagnated while managerial sector income, especially compensation for corporate executives, has risen. Data from the Panel Study of Income Dynamics confirm that, between 1977 and 1987, the middle class shrank in size, the income distribution became more skewed toward lower incomes, and mobility out of the middle class was more likely to be downward than upward, so that the class system became more divergent, or unequal and polarized.

One common measure of income equality is the *Gini Index*, which ranges between 0 (indicating that everyone has an equal share) and 1.0 (indicating that one person controls all the wealth). The United States has the highest Gini Index of all industrial countries, followed by Australia, New Zealand, and Switzerland. Japan, Sweden, Belgium, and Holland, by contrast, have the least income inequality. Evidence shows that the Gini Index for earned incomes in the United States has risen continuously since 1980, from about .38 to .42, which indicates that the middle class is, indeed, shrinking.

Relational: Proletarianization of white-collar jobs
Since the 1950s, there has been a shift in the kinds of occupations that are considered to be middle class and working class, respectively. While the boundary was once easily drawn between manual and nonmanual labor—the former being working class and the latter middle class—the distinction between the two classes has come to be based on additional features of work. These include income (both the amount and whether it is paid in wages or as salary), job security, opportunity for upward mobility, and degree of autonomy given to do the job.

Jobs that are secure and well paid, that provide an opportunity for upward mobility and allow people to exercise autonomy are considered middle-class occupations. Jobs that score low on these criteria, even if they do not involve manual labor, have fallen into the working-class category. Examples include clerks, secretaries, and day-care workers.

Since the start of the 1980s, downward mobility has become a common experience for middle-class Americans. Many have lost their jobs and have great difficulty finding new ones. Along with this, many have lost their faith in the ideology of hard work being rewarded. Some even claim that many professionals—lawyers, pharmacists, architects, engineers, and even doctors—have been proletarianized in this way; in general, they have been made less autonomous, secure, or well paid. Aspects of proletarianization for clerical labor include the actual removal of supervisory functions from a position, the loss of reasonably assured career prospects, loss of the opportunity to play a part in decision making, and the loss of autonomy.

Thus, to whatever extent people identify with their jobs, some who were once considered to be middle class now no longer are so considered. Given that there has been no trend in the opposite direction—that is, there are no occupations that used to be considered working-class that have now been granted middle-class status—it is safe to conclude that there are fewer middle-class people around.

Cultural: The decline of middle-class culture One defining feature of the old middle class was that it differed culturally—that is, in beliefs, values, attitudes, and lifestyle—both from the rich and the poor. Not only were these middle-class values distinctive, they were also the dominant values in the political arena and mass media.

Middle-class culture was characterized by the belief that family life should be held in high priority, by the so-called Protestant work ethic, by respect for the law and for government, and by a strong belief in individualism as a philosophy of life. (There was also at least lip service paid to tolerance and respect for differences among people.)

The past two decades have witnessed a decline in general support for some, if not all, of these values. Widespread economic insecurity has made people less tolerant of others, particularly if these "others" are believed to pose a threat to their economic well-being. Family life is now an ideological battleground in which some forms—for example, poor, single-parent families—are singled out for criticism and close observation. (More will be said about family forms in a later chapter of this book.) Government no longer commands people's unthinking respect in this post-Watergate era. And the philosophical value of work has been degraded in a culture of job insecurity and widespread occupational hazards.

Institutional: The blurring of class lines The visible decline in income equality we spoke about earlier is a result of corporate downsizing, more unemployment and underemployment, and downward social mobility for many upper-middle-class people. At the same time, there has been a progressive reduction in union membership among blue-collar workers. This is due mainly to the relocation of industrial jobs to low-wage, traditionally nonunionized areas of the United States and threats to relocate jobs offshore in case of difficulties with the local work force. White-collar jobs have also become more numerous. Traditionally, these jobs have rarely been unionized. Unionizing them has become more difficult than ever in the face of an economic recession.

Stagnant or falling wages and weaker middle-class prospects for upward mobility and working-class protections against unemployment have blurred traditional lines that separated the two classes. It is also harder for middle-class people to maintain other distinctions, like different neighborhoods, clubs, or schools for their children. Increasingly, the line between working-class and middle-class people has disappeared or is at least smudged.

THE MIDDLE CLASS IS NOT DISAPPEARING

Statistical: The gap between the rich and poor Statistically speaking, the middle class is far from having disappeared. Though the fraction has fallen, most American households still earn between 50% and 150% of the average income. Though there has been a small decline in wages since the early 1970s, the average worker is not worse off in terms of total pay per hours of work, nor has there been any significant change in the shape of the distribution of earnings for the labor force as a whole. This should not be a cause for middle-class complacency. The changes we described in the previous section are indeed occurring. However, they may be halted or slowed by an upsurge in economic growth.

Relational: White-collar jobs are still more autonomous People who say that the middle class is not disappearing point out that in recent years, industrialized countries all over the world have entered the Information Age. This change has meant a significant job loss in the manufacturing sector. At the same time, there has been a noticeable increase in the number of jobs that require technical knowledge. However, research also suggests more "bad" jobs are being created (in the service sector) than "good" (i.e., technical) jobs. There has also been a shift in the occupational structure, so that more people provide services, particularly professional and helping services. An increasing proportion of the population is employed in white- as opposed to blue- or pink-collar work. This means that the middle class is swelling, not shrinking.

Indeed, Daniel Bell claims in his classic book *The Coming of Post-Industrial Society* that we have only begun to transform the economy from one that is based on capital and labor to one based on expert knowledge and information technology. Class categories developed to describe the old industrial order may no longer capture the new economic reality. In any event, by this account the fortunes of highly educated middle-class people will improve, not worsen, with the shift Bell describes.

The withering away of the middle class is, therefore, not on the horizon. The distribution of income has not changed significantly; rather, the composition of the middle has changed, with a decreasing number of opportunities for low-educated, low-skilled workers and increasing educational stratification of the work force. The condition of the core middle class continues to differ very clearly from that of the working class; the situation of the marginal middle class combines both working-class and middle-class features.

Cultural: Only a changing middle-class culture By some accounts, middle-class culture is not in decline; it is merely changing, due to sociostructural and economic changes. Though tempered by a greater realization of society's role in shaping opportunities and influencing destinies, individualism is still alive and well. Nor has the work ethic been lost. Most middle-class people still believe that one must work for a living and work hard to get ahead. Indeed, many sociologists voice a concern that individualism is excessive in the United States (we say more about this in a later section). So long as individualism remains central to the American Dream, it is hard to show that middle class culture is truly dead.

Millions of middle-class Americans are still hardworking, ambitious, thrifty, and tolerant. We also find much evidence of middle-class culture as a lifestyle distinct from working-class culture. So, for example, travel is increasingly significant to the new middle classes. Green (environmental) politics is also of particular interest. So are natural fabrics. Advertising campaigns to shift consumers away from polyester were a process of gentrification marked by gentle class warfare and snobbery.

Historically, middle-class life has been characterized by distinctive approaches to work, consumption, residential location, voluntary associations, and family organization. These have largely been aimed at distinguishing middle-class life and thought from that of the peasantry and working class. Central to middle-class culture are compartmentalization of the world and an obsession with achieving control in their own lives. Even today well-educated middle-class or professional parents are more likely than working-class parents to expose their preschoolers to lessons and conversations and to encourage early goals related to independence, self-control, and environmental control. By contrast, nonprofessional parents place a higher value on good manners, obedience, and getting along with other people.

These values are sufficiently strong that they cut across ethnic identities, allowing Americans to see a vast structural similarity among members of the middle class. Middle-class values also compete with ethnic and racial identities, and some believe that the quest for middle-class positions by African Americans is devastating the African-American community. African-American men and women who work in company management positions, like their white counterparts, live in integrated communities and have small families, an egalitarian ethic in marital arrangements, and neolocal family residence—hence, minimal kinship linkages, especially of the extended type. In short, taking on middle-class values drives a wedge between African-American poor and African-American nonpoor.

Institutional: Enduring class institutions As the "new economy" takes its toll on personal lives and class institutions, one thing continues to amaze us: the tenacity of optimism and faith in the future. Historically, the expansion of the middle class was closely linked to a growing economy and increasing equality of opportunity. The reversal of these conditions, evident from the 1970s, may undermine the well-being of the middle class and its correlative social values, notably tolerance and civility. For middle-class people, a sense of powerlessness produces opposition to economic redistribution, whereas for the working class it produces support. As a result, powerlessness produces political polarization between social classes and support for different political parties.

Middle-class people have tried, despite adversity, to maintain a distance from the poor and from the working class. Note that it is precisely with the downward pressure on middle-class incomes and the blurring of actual differences between classes that we have seen a middle-class backlash against welfare recipients and other vulnerable people.

Abram Swaan, writing about middle-class opposition to labor legislation in nineteenth century Europe, called this phenomenon "downward jealousy." Those whose status is in the greatest danger—people who are downwardly mobile or already in the lower middle class—are most willing to use any means to draw distinguishing class lines. Though not benefiting financially by treating people below them more harshly, these marginal superiors gain status by pushing others downward, symbolically or concretely.

The welfare backlash shows that middle class people are still acting as though they are different from working-class people and from the poor. New institutional boundaries between classes are being established in the political arena, just as they still are in schools, clubs, and neighborhoods.

SUMMING UP

Is the middle class disappearing? However we define middle class, the answer is the same: no, it's not. People who say that the middle class is disappearing point out that a smaller percentage of the population are middle income earners, that fewer people fit the middle-class label, and that middle-class culture is not as prominent as it once was. Those who say that the middle class is not disappearing note that while working-class jobs are being lost due to the automation and computerization of production and service delivery, the same forces are creating new middle-class jobs. They add that middle-class culture is not in decline; it has merely changed key.

Karl Marx, in his classic work *Capital* and elsewhere, predicted that in the long run the middle class must disappear. This prediction is part of the "logic" of capitalism, as later Marxist theorists agreed. According to this theory, capitalists seek ever-higher profits by lowering the costs of production in a variety of ways: by substituting machines for human workers and lower-paid foreign or nonunionized workers for local, unionized workers; by tightening managerial control and speeding up the work process; and by proletarianizing costly professional and managerial work. The result of these processes is to increase the wealth of the capitalist class and decrease the wealth of the rest, thus separating society into two camps ("haves" and "have-nots") and eliminating the middle class.

Around this generally downward trend in incomes (at least, as experienced by the majority), short booms and busts—recurring periods of brief, widespread prosperity followed by returns to economic decline and impoverishment—are to be expected. And as we have seen, the 1980s brought hardship for many and unparalleled wealth for a few; the late 1990s show a general improvement in people's financial fortunes. The theory predicts an eventual return to the downward spiral.

Our analysis has suggested that so far the middle class is far from disappearing statistically, culturally, relationally, or institutionally. This tells us a lot about the inertia and resilience of social forms. In societies, institutions and major groupings change very slowly indeed. Moreover, the U.S. economy is in the middle of a boom right now; there is no way of knowing how long it will last. Should we care if the middle class is in danger of disappearing? Probably yes, since most of us are either in the middle class or aspire to be so. But so far the signs don't warrant a lot of concern, except among Marxists and others who take the "long view."

REVIEW EXERCISES

For Discussion and Debate

1. Is the working class disappearing?
2. "The middle class is mainly a state of mind, not a material reality." Do you agree or disagree?
3. "It is precisely the threatened disappearance of the middle class that accounts for the upswing in racial and gender conflict." Discuss.
4. "With the disappearance of the middle class will come the beginning of extreme class warfare that Karl Marx predicted." Agree or disagree?

Writing Exercises

1. The class of neighborhood I live in is . . . because . . . .
2. I believe my lifestyle is working/ middle/upper class because . . . .
3. Why it is important to me to be in the working/middle/upper class.
4. Why "working/middle/upper class" doesn't mean what it did in my parents' time.

Research Activities

1. Devise a questionnaire that asks about the furnishings of people's living rooms. Administer this questionnaire to at least a dozen people of different social classes. What differences do you find in the furnishing styles of people who belong to different classes?
2. Collect some published data showing that people's social class affects their noneconomic behavior or attitudes.
3. Examine research to find out whether people who are upwardly mobile into the middle class (i.e., were born into a lower class) are different from people who were born into the middle class.
4. Examine the research on at least three different countries to find out whether countries with a large middle class are different socially, politically, or economically from countries with a small middle class.

SELECTED REFERENCES

ARCHER, MELANIE, and JUDITH R. BLAU, Class formation in nineteenth century America: The case of the middle class, *Annual Review of Sociology* (1993), 19, 17–41.

BELL, DANIEL, *The coming of post-industrial society* (New York: Basic Books, 1973).

ECKERSLEY, ROBYN, Green politics and the new class: Selfishness or virtue? *Political Studies* (June 1989), 37, 2, 205–223.

EVANS, GEOFFREY, Class, powerlessness and political polarization, *European Journal of Social Psychology* (September–October 1993), 23, 5, 495–511.

FRYKMAN, JONAS, and ORVAR LOFGREN, *Culture builders: A historical anthropology of middle-class life,* trans. John Gills (New Brunswick, NJ: Rutgers University Press, 1987 [1979]).

GILLMAN, KATHERINE, and JOY DUNKERLY, Is the middle class shrinking? *Futures* (April 1988), 20, 2, 137–146.

KELLOGG, SUSAN, Exploring diversity in middle-class families: The symbolism of American ethnic identity, *Social Science History* (Spring 1990), 14, 1, 27–41.

KELLY, MICHAEL P., and ROBIN ROSLENDER, Proletarianisation, the division of labour and the labour process, *International Journal of Sociology and Social Policy* (1988), 8, 6, 48–64.

KIVINEN, MARKKU, The new middle classes and the labour process, *Acta Sociologica* (1989), 32, 1, 53–73.

KLOBY, JERRY, The top-heavy economy: Managerial greed and unproductive labor, *Critical Sociology* (Fall 1988), 15, 3, 53–69.

KOSTERS, MARVIN H., and MURRAY N. ROSS, A shrinking middle class? *Public Interest* (Winter 1988), 90, 3–27.

LERMAN, ROBERT I., and HAROLD SALZMAN, Deskilling and declassing: Wither the middle stratum? *Society* (September–October 1988), 25, 6(176), 60–66.

LEWIN, ARTHUR, A tale of two classes: The black poor and the black middle class, *Black Scholar* (Summer 1990–1991), 21, 3, 7–13.

MUNT, IAN, The "other" postmodern tourism: Culture, travel and the new middle classes, *Theory, Culture and Society* (August 1994), 11, 3, 101–123.

MYLES, JOHN, and ADNAN TUREGUN, Comparative studies in class structure, *Annual Review of Sociology* (1994), 20, 103–124.

NEWMAN, KATHERINE S., *Falling from grace: The experience of downward mobility in the American middle class* (New York: Free Press, 1988).

NIGGLE, CHRISTOPHER J., Monetary policy and changes in income distribution, *Journal of Economic Issues* (September 1989), 23, 3, 809–822.

SCHNEIDER, JANE, In and out of polyester: Desire, disdain and global fibre competitions, *Anthropology Today* (August 1994), 10, 4, 2–10.

SHEAK, ROBERT J., and DAVID D. DABELKO, The declining middle class: More evidence, *Free Inquiry in Creative Sociology* (May 1993), 21, 1, 29–35.

SWAAN, ABRAM, Jealousy as a class phenomenon: The petite bougeoisie and social security, *International Sociology* (September 1989), 4, 3, 259–271.

WILKINSON, DORIS Y., Afro-Americans in the corporation: An assessment of the impact on the family, *Marriage and Family Review* (1990), 15, 3–4, 115–129.

WILLIAMS, MELVIN D., The black church in a midwestern university twin city: An Afro-American dilemma, *Research in Race and Ethnic Relations* (1991), 6, 27–47.

WRIGHT, ERIK OLIN, and BILL MARTIN, The transformation of the American class structure, 1960–1980, *American Journal of Sociology* (July 1987), 93, 1, 1–29.

4.3

Isn't welfare dangerous?

The issue: Have attempts to help the poor through the payment of welfare benefits created new problems that are worse than the poverty itself? Has the institution of welfare become an economic, social, and political nightmare?

Introduction Since 1970, the conditions of the poor—even the conditions of poor children—have gotten worse, despite the ameliorative efforts of public assistance, or welfare. Is welfare likely to solve the problem of poverty, or is it part of the problem? Answering this question takes us into the domain of such concepts as the feminization of poverty, the marginalization of the poor, the poor underclass, and the culture of poverty.

The emergence of the term *underclass* represents a continuing readiness to charac-

terize what the sociologist David Matza called "the disreputable poor." In explaining poverty, many continue to search for "cultural deficiency," whether in the form of flawed values, family relations, or welfare rules. The poor wouldn't be poor, in other words, unless something were wrong with them.

The argument against welfare and other forms of assistance arises from the fact that, for various reasons, many people who are not poor believe the poor are very different from themselves. In a society based on the idea (if not the fact) that merit is rewarded, they think of the poor as people who may not have tried hard enough to succeed, people who are in some sense disreputable or undeserving, or at least, lazy.

Just below this public perception is the notion of an *underclass*. The poor do not just lack money, according to this concept; they lack the social and moral virtues that lead those who have them to get money. Besides poverty, the underclass is characterized by long-term unemployment, a high proportion of households with one parent (typically, a mother), and intergenerational dependence on welfare. Concentrated in rundown sections of towns and cities, the underclass produces crime and delinquency, drug dealing and drug use, low educational achievement, and teenage pregnancy. And all of this, principally because the underclass does not desire to achieve better. This underclass is located below the working poor and middle class, both financially and morally. It is also seen as an underachieving and underconforming social group. The concept of the black underclass, like that of the culture of poverty, places much of the responsibility for black poverty on blacks themselves, asserting that reform has failed.

Does welfare create or perpetuate the underclass? If so, it does harm—perhaps more harm than good. Let's look at the evidence on both sides.

WELFARE DOES MORE HARM THAN GOOD

Those who believe that welfare perpetuates an underclass make various arguments to support their view. Their arguments fall into three main categories: concern with the harm done by dependence on welfare, concern with the economic costs of paying welfare to the underclass, and concern with the ineffectiveness of welfare as a way of dealing with poverty.

Dependence on welfare Those who believe welfare does more harm than good claim, first, that welfare payments create a disincentive to work. They also argue that the welfare state, in expanding its responsibility for public needs, results in the atrophy of individual moral responsibility.

It is argued that the welfare system has created behavioral disincentives that trap many recipients in poverty across generations by fostering dependence and a culture of poverty. The process also reduces work effort and diminishes the sense of work ethic. Increased dependence also has strong negative effects on children's intellectual abilities and life prospects. Children raised by families on welfare are more likely to fail in school, be engaged in criminal activities, and end up on welfare themselves than those raised with more privileges. By this reasoning, the only long-term solution is to get rid of the welfare program.

Since many people on welfare have little education and few skills, their chances of getting a well-paid job are slight. The jobs they can hope to get pay minimum wage or even less. Though welfare pays less than the minimum wage, a rational person would still choose welfare over a week's hard work for just a few dollars more.

It is in this context that we can understand the current wave of so-called workfare programs. With some local variations, they all require welfare recipients to spend part of their week at unfamiliar jobs from which they gain no marketable job skills. Supporters argue that workfare programs ensure that valuable public work gets done and that welfare recipients maintain a routine of doing productive work.

Available evidence suggests that various workfare approaches rapidly increase earnings, lower unemployment rates, and reduce welfare benefits. However, using welfare recipients in this way promotes the laying off of workers who were formerly paid to do this work. As well, such jobs encourage relatively little development of skills. The effectiveness of such programs is questionable, and programs emphasizing job search appear to fare better.

A second aspect of this concern about welfare dependence is the perception of recipients as poorly socialized. The underclass is seen as lacking in personal responsibility. High rates of divorce and unwed pregnancy are ascribed to irresponsible attitudes. In short, paying welfare encourages laziness, sexual promiscuity, and reckless procreation. No wonder, critics say, that cities and states with higher welfare payments draw large numbers of poor migrants from other cities and states.

The cost of welfare   Other critics focus less on the worthiness of recipients and more on the cost of welfare programs. First, they argue that welfare and associated programs for the poor are too expensive. They may have been tolerable in earlier days, when the economy was growing and there was less global competition and public indebtedness. Today, the middle class cannot afford to pay high taxes to service debts for earlier welfare programs while also paying welfare to growing numbers of current recipients. Welfare and other public programs must be put on the back burner until the debts are paid.

Second, critics argue that welfare and related programs require a huge, costly bureaucracy to administer. Almost by definition, bureaucracy produces red tape, delay, and waste. Until we can figure out how to deliver programs more efficiently, we may have to cut out or cut back the programs themselves.

Third, welfare and other social programs are so costly in many cities and states that they impose heavy tax burdens on business to pay for these programs. High taxes reduce the profits these businesses can make, so many of them are forced to move to less taxed municipalities—often out of the country—in order to survive. By increasing taxes, welfare drives out business and reduces job creation. People on welfare thus become even less likely to get a job because of welfare.

Effectiveness   Finally, critics point out that despite its cost and longevity, welfare has not succeeded in reducing the number of poor or improved their chances of escaping poverty. For 50 years, public welfare has overpromised, failed to evaluate and separate effective from ineffective programs, and hidden its setbacks. For many, welfare—a plan designed to deal with an emergency—has become a way of life. Public welfare professionals need to educate political leaders and the public that welfare is not a subsidy of people but of systems, and that the key to changing welfare lies not in reducing welfare entitlements but in increasing the reward for work.

It should be possible, critics say, to devise a program for the poor that does more than provide temporary support on a long-term basis. To become viable again, social welfare policy should emphasize specific themes: productivity (getting people back to work), reciprocity (something given for something taken), community (a sense of responsibility for others), and privatization (less spending on welfare by government). These are indeed the themes emphasized in the welfare reform bill signed into law by President Clinton in his first term in office.

WELFARE DOES MORE GOOD THAN HARM

People who take the opposing view draw different conclusions about each issue we have addressed so far.

Dependence on welfare   First, they emphasize that few people are on welfare by choice. They are not to blame for being poor, nor is there much they can do to escape poverty. In a society with high unemployment rates, due mainly to globalization and automation, many people are bound to be out of work at any given time. And with low minimum wages, prevalent part-time work, and little job security, many people are unable to save money for the times when they are out of work. Welfare recipients, therefore, cannot be characterized as lacking in moral responsibility or a desire to work.

The cost of welfare   We cannot deny that welfare and related programs carry huge costs. Nor can we deny the need to deal with the public debt—in small part a result of past spending on social services and in large part due to the poor economy. However, it is unfair to focus on welfare as the chief source of present financial problems, and it is unreasonable to imagine these problems are remedied by reducing or eliminating public welfare. In fact, most public spending benefits the middle class and wealthy, not the poor. Consider higher education. The working poor pay taxes to support college education, yet their children are unlikely to get much of it. The main beneficiaries are middle-class children. Likewise, investors, businesspeople, and self-employed professionals have many legal opportunities to reduce their taxes, depriving the state of needed revenues, but the working poor have virtually no tax loopholes to exploit.

To solve society's financial problems, we must not focus only on benefits paid to the poor. We must also take into account benefits paid to the nonpoor and see to it that everyone contributes a fair share to taxes. More than 90% of the trillion U.S. dollars spent on welfare every year are spent benefiting middle- and upper-income individuals and corporations in the form of Social Security, Medicare, and wealth redistribution to business. Other examples include farm subsidies, below-market government loans, tax breaks for the wealthy, and subsidized government insurance. Cutting poverty programs while maintaining this "upside-down welfare" program seems hypocritical at best.

Effectiveness   Just as its critics say, current welfare programs are ineffective. They neither prevent nor eliminate the conditions that drive people on to welfare. Nor do they help people get off welfare. They simply keep people alive from one month to another. However, research shows that spells on welfare are shorter, inheritance of dependency is less common, and welfare fraud is rarer than most people believe. The welfare abuses that become public are not typical and, like most news in the media, are interesting precisely because they aren't typical.

The best that can be said for welfare is that it does what people thought it would when they invented it. Welfare provides a moderating influence on the economy and on social life during an economic depression. Remember that modern welfare took its present form during the Great Depression of the 1930s, when unemployment was even higher than it is today. The main purpose of welfare was to keep unemployed people alive and, secondarily, to pump money into the economy. As a matter of historical fact, welfare was a plan to jump-start an economy that had nearly been killed by reckless speculators. Government hoped that welfare would bring security and order to a chaotic, frightening, and dangerous situation. Many feared surges of crime and violence and political upheaval. Welfare helped to control all these threats to the social order, though it did not, and could not, eliminate them.

The expansion of the welfare state from 1935 to the mid-1970s meshed well with the needs of profitable production, political legitimacy, and patriarchal control. With the economic crisis of the 1970s, the welfare state became too competitive with capital accumulation and too supportive of empowered popular movements. Women, persons of color, and the poor ranked high among the victims of the new austerity plan.

Today welfare is controlling the threats to order, but it is not—and cannot be—a solution in itself. Since the 1960s, the welfare state has been failing due to a combination of slowed economic growth, greed for high profits, and unreasonably high wages that reduce distributable surpluses. In the past decade we have seen that neither a planned nor a competitive economy works particularly well without substantial modification. In this context, welfare pluralism acts as a form of damage limitation in which the deficiencies of one approach are more or less balanced by the strengths of others.

Response to recent changes Those who view welfare in a more positive light may not agree on the ways to reform current programs in order to solve long-standing problems of poverty and unemployment. However, they do agree that under current economic conditions, reducing welfare is extremely harmful, especially to women and children, who are among the main recipients. Single mothers with preschool children in particular have the least opportunity to find and keep jobs if welfare is cut. The history of the national welfare rights movement has been, and is increasingly, an ongoing revolution for and by women.

Welfare supporters also agree that nothing is to be gained by privatizing welfare provision by the voluntary, informal, and commercial sectors. One facet of a change to privatization has been the emergence of fees and sales as the principal source of nonprofit growth, not only among hospitals and universities but also among social service and civil organizations. Although these trends may have positive results, they raise serious questions about the future of the nonprofit sector and about access to care on the part of the disadvantaged.

Contrary to the welfare critics, these analysts believe that reducing welfare would not lower the teenage pregnancy rate. Nor would it reduce the divorce rate or bring back traditional, stable family life. None of these problems is caused by welfare, so none is solved by reducing welfare. Instead, they are part of a large transformation of family life in all social classes and all industrialized Western countries.

Finally, reducing welfare payments would not reduce poverty. To reduce poverty, we need to make more jobs available. And despite the arguments of supply-side economics (discussed in an earlier section), there is no evidence that more jobs are automatically created when public spending is reduced. If unemployment becomes long term and increases sufficiently, many economic victims may be forced into a permanently stigmatized underclass.

SUMMING UP

Isn't welfare dangerous? No; the absence of welfare would be far more dangerous. In the end, the decisive argument against viewing welfare as harmful is a historical argument: Welfare is a stage in the evolution of the idea of "social citizenship." T. H. Marshall, an

English sociologist, pointed out that the concept of citizenship has been evolving for at least five centuries. The status of "citizen" began to develop in medieval cities. The idea was that citizenship makes a person free and, in important respects, equal to everyone else.

With the rise of nation-states, the citizenship idea expanded in three ways. First, in the seventeenth and eighteenth centuries came *civil citizenship*. It guaranteed liberty of the person; freedom of speech, thought, and faith; the right to own property and to conclude valid contracts; and the right to full justice in the courts. *Political citizenship* developed next, in the nineteenth and twentieth centuries, with the spread of universal suffrage—the right of all adults to vote in elections and run for office.

The concept of *social citizenship* began to develop only in the present century. It reflected an understanding that economic disadvantages limit people's ability to enjoy full civil and political citizenship. If people are to be full citizens, they need economic security: a minimum wage, the right to unionize, the right to a job, and fair treatment on the job. In all industrial societies, social citizenship has become a goal of social development and the mark of a civilized society.

In many respects, the United States is distinctive. For example, in contrast with most other liberal democracies, the U.S. Constitution did not establish affirmative welfare rights or obligations. And the structure of the U.S. welfare system—pensions, health insurance, and the like—is to a large degree privately organized. Though supportive of values central to the political culture behind welfare, Americans are ambivalent in their interpretations of individualism, humanitarianism, and the role of big government. Economic development produces not only efficiency and growth but also market failures, socioeconomic and political conflict, and general economic insecurity. Social programs are needed to help individuals cope with the problems accruing with economic success. Seen from this perspective, modern welfare is not a gift to the lazy or unlucky; it is one of the defining characteristics of a modern society.

REVIEW EXERCISES

For Discussion and Debate

1. What would be some likely social consequences of a 50% reduction in the welfare payments in your community?

2. What is workfare, and how does it fit into the Protestant work ethic?

3. Why would someone prefer to depend on welfare rather than have a job? What evidence supports your argument?

4. How does the payment of welfare and other social programs to equalize people's life chances actually help to maintain the existing system of inequality?

Writing Exercises

1. Welfare handouts kill people's desire to work hard and get ahead.

2. People have a natural desire to work as a means of expressing themselves and making contact with other people.

3. The tax system provides far more handouts to rich people than it does to poor people.

4. The development of social responsibility for the poor is a major step in human history.

Research Activities

1. Collect data on how three poor families and three middle-income families budget their income each month. What proportion, in each case, goes to food, shelter, and other necessities?

2. Analyze three political speeches about poverty or the poor from the 1930s, showing what has or hasn't changed in the way politicians approach the topic.

3. Collect and compare information about the welfare benefits provided to poor families with two children in two American states and two foreign countries (e.g., Sweden, Japan, Nigeria). Explain the differences.

4. How do chronically unemployed people spend their time? Devise a research strategy for collecting data to answer that question. Time permitting, collect some data and analyze them.

SELECTED REFERENCES

AXINN, J. M., and A. E. HIRSCH, Welfare and the "reform" of women, *Families in Society: The Journal of Contemporary Human Services* (November 1993), 74, 9, 563–572.

BEITO, DAVID T., Mutual aid, state welfare, and organized charity: Fraternal societies and the "deserving" and "undeserving" poor, 1900–1930, *Journal of Policy History* (1993), 5, 4, 419–434.

BESHAROV, DOUGLAS J., Beware of unintended consequences: Too many questions remain unanswered, *Public Welfare* (Spring 1992), 50, 2, 18–19.

BEVERLY, CREIGS C., and HOWARD J. STANBACK, The black underclass: Theory and reality, *Black Scholar* (September–October 1986), 17, 5, 24–32.

BIRDSALL, NANCY, DAVID ROSS, and RICHARD SABOT, Inequality and growth reconsidered: Lessons from East Asia, *World Bank Economic Review* (1995), 9, 3, 477–508.

CUSHING, BRIAN J., The effect of the social welfare system on metropolitan migration in the U.S., by income group, gender, and family structure, *Urban Studies* (March 1993), 30, 2, 325–338.

DATTALO, P., The gentrification of public welfare, *Social Work* (September 1992), 37, 5, 446–453.

GLAZER, NATHAN, Is welfare a legitimate government goal? *Critical Review* (Fall 1990), 4, 4, 479–491.

GOODIN, ROBERT E., Moral atrophy in the welfare state, *Policy Sciences* (May 1993), 26, 2, 63–78.

GRIFFEN, SARAH, Poor relations: The backlash against welfare recipients, *Dollars and Sense* (May 1992), 176, 6–8.

GUERON, JUDITH M., Work for people on welfare, *Public Welfare* (Winter 1993), 51, 1, 39–41.

JENSEN, LEIF, DAVID J. EGGEBEEN, and DANIEL T. LICHTER, Child poverty and the ameliorative effects of public assistance, *Social Science Quarterly* (September 1993), 74, 3, 542–559.

KARGER, HOWARD JACOB, The global economy and the American welfare state, *Journal of Sociology and Social Welfare* (September 1991), 18, 3, 3–20.

KERLIN, A. E., From welfare to work: Does it make sense? *Journal of Sociology and Social Welfare* (March 1993), 20, 1, 71–85.

KUTNER, NANCY G., and MICHAEL H. KUTNER, Ethnic and residence differences among poor families, *Journal of Comparative Family Studies* (Autumn 1987), 18, 3, 463–470.

LIEBMANN, GEORGE W., The AFDC conundrum: A new look at an old institution, *Social Work* (January 1993), 38, 1, 36–43.

MARSHALL, T. H., *Class, citizenship, and social development* (Garden City, N.Y.: Anchor Books, 1965).

MATZA, DAVID, The disreputable poor. In Reinhard Bendix and Seymour Martin Lipset, eds., *Class, States and Power: Social stratification in comparative perspective*, 2nd ed. (New York: Free Press, 1966).

MAY, EDGAR, Social policy and the poor: Fifty years of looking ahead, *Public Welfare* (Winter 1993), 51, 1, 32–34.

MOYNIHAN, DANIEL PATRICK, Toward a post-industrial social policy, *Public Interest* (Summer 1989), 96, 16–27.

MURRAY, C., Discussing welfare dependency is irrelevant, *Public Welfare* (1992), 50, 2, 24–25.

NORTHROP, EMILY M., The feminization of poverty: The demographic factor and the composition of economic growth, *Journal of Economic Issues* (March 1990), 24, 1, 145–160.

STOESZ, DAVID, A new paradigm for social welfare, *Journal of Sociology and Social Welfare* (June 1989), 16, 2, 127–150.

VEDDER, RICHARD, and LOWELL GALLOWAY, Declining black employment, *Society* (July–August 1993), 30, 5 (205), 57–63.

ZINN, MAXINE BACA, Family, race, and poverty in the eighties, *Signs* (Summer 1989), 14, 4, 856–874.

5. Race and Ethnic Relations

From a sociological point of view, both **ethnicity** and **race** are socially constructed. They are ideas we have about ourselves and others that affect how we perceive and interact with one another. They are similar in that both terms imply some kind of common biological origin that ties people together. People who share a common ethnicity or race are usually considered to be related by "blood" or to have had some common ancestor. They differ in that ethnic identity is likely to form among people with a common culture, language, religion, or national origin. Members feel they are culturally and socially united, and that is how others see them. In contrast to ethnicity, members of a race are identified on the basis of presumed physical traits, especially appearance. A race could include members from many ethnic and social backgrounds and is defined in terms of shared appearance rather than shared history or culture.

Neither race nor ethnicity is an objective concept. Interethnic and interracial contacts have been taking place for thousands of years. As a result, no supposed racial group is genetically pure, and racial divisions do not reflect genetic realities. Rather, they reflect the assumptions, biases, or stereotypes with which people categorize one another.

The first section in this chapter considers whether problems often associated with race and ethnicity—namely, prejudice and discrimination—are diminishing. The second section examines affirmative action—a set of legislative actions taken to reduce discrimination—and asks whether it is merely another form of discrimination against the majority group. Finally, the third section considers whether ethnic nationalism, which is flourishing around the world, is a positive or negative social force.

5.1

Is love all you need?

The issue: **Is discrimination decreasing, or are ethnic and racial minorities as disadvantaged as they were a generation ago,** *when today's baby boomers were listening to the Beatles sing "All You Need Is Love"?*

Introduction The study of ethnic and race relations has its own set of terms and phrases, used at different times by minority and majority groups, governments, and social agencies. In the first section of this chapter, the focus is on discrimination, prejudice, and stereotyping. In the next, it shifts to systemic discrimination, racism, and the process of being racialized. The third section examines the intersection of ethnicity with nationalism.

Discrimination refers to the process of making a selection based on some criteria.

For instance, we may discriminate between two pieces of music based on the criteria of style and tonality. Fifty years ago, to say someone was "discriminating" would mean that the person made fine distinctions regarding quality. In fact, it was paying a compliment, for it suggested the person chose high-quality products. The word later became used for making distinctions based on criteria that were not strictly relevant. In particular, it came to refer to the making of choices between people based on **stereotypes** or **prejudices**. So, to discriminate, used popularly, has come to mean looking not at the individual but at images and stereotypes. Thus a Scot or a Norwegian or a Nigerian is judged not on her or his own talents and abilities but on characteristics popularly associated with Scots or Norwegians or Nigerians as a group.

For instance, some evaluate individual Scots according to the stereotype that, as a group they are stingy and penny-pinching, nicely represented by Disney's Scrooge McDuck. Jokes, cartoons, and common phrases and sayings illustrate this stereotype. If someone believes it and thinks of Scots in that way, we say that that person is prejudiced. If she acts on the prejudice by not admitting Scottish people to her circle of friendship because she considers they are likely to be stingy, she is engaging in discrimination that is unfounded in two ways. First, she is applying a group stereotype to an individual, without examining whether the individual is typical of the group. Second, she is assuming that the group label, or stereotype, does hold, though she has not tested that either. If she were to visit Scotland, she might meet examples of another tradition, hospitality, which might change her mind. However, it is likely that while she makes assumptions about Scots based on the stereotype, her behavior will not attract many friends, for the Scottish

people she meets will also have assumptions about Americans, based on stereotypes that are familiar to them and their own prejudices. So it is easy for a prejudice to be self-fulfilling.

To examine whether discrimination and prejudice are decreasing, we must examine not only how they operate but how people get their prejudices. Because of limited space, for the most part we will focus on relations between African-American and European-American groups.

DISCRIMINATION AND PREJUDICE ARE DECREASING

If we look at the situation in the United States today, we can see clearly that race relations have changed. Fifty years ago there were few nonwhite professionals. The important people in a community—the mayor, leading politicians, elected officials, industrialists, doctors, and lawyers—were almost certain to be white. Television shows were about white, European-American people, with people of color shown only in minor supporting roles.

In 1954 came the Montgomery, Alabama, bus boycott and the emerging civil rights movement. By 1964, the call to eliminate racial discrimination was heard loudly. The Civil Rights Act of 1964 removed many unfair hiring practices and guaranteed access to public accommodations and federal organizations. The Voting Rights Act of 1965 made it much more possible for the voices of African Americans to be heard in the political sphere, not only as electors but as those elected. Since then, the number of African Americans in the public eye has risen, and almost all major political offices have had African Americans elected to them (the only exceptions being president and vice president). In 1990, there were almost five times as many African-American elected officials as in 1970, a mere 20 years before.

Along with legislation have been public education programs to reduce prejudice by attacking stereotypes. In addition, television now presents images of successful black Americans, not only in programs such as "Oprah" and "The Cosby Show" but through advertising showing African-American men and women in many varied roles, including executive positions. Finally, if we look at today's children of all ethnicities and races, their heroes very often include the sports figures they see on television, many of whom are African Americans. The names of basketball stars are household words. Today, it seems, doors are open to people of all ethnicities to work and study and reach their full potential.

There are many reasons why reductions in prejudice and discrimination have occurred. One is simply that people have realized how unfair such discrimination is. Another is that people have realized that we need the contributions of every member of society, to their fullest potential, in order to remain competitive in a global economy. We can look at the changes to advertisements, which now show people of color making important decisions about their futures and daily lives. This development is no more than a recognition by advertisers that African Americans and other minorities hold responsible jobs and merit the same treatment and recognition as anyone else.

A few prejudiced individuals do remain, and they continue to pose a problem. When members of minorities experience prejudice and discrimination, generally it is because they have encountered one of these prejudiced people. Gradually, with education, we can expect their numbers to become fewer and fewer, until prejudice based on race or ethnicity is finally a thing of the past.

PREJUDICE AND DISCRIMINATION ARE NOT DECREASING NOTICEABLY

Christopher Bates Doob makes the case in his book *Racism: An American Cauldron* that racism is very much present today, and that stereotyping, prejudice, and discrimination are still with us. Let us reexamine some of the statements made earlier, starting with the political scene since the 1960s, in the light of what Doob has to say. In 1964, civil rights was seen by some as the most important problem facing the country. By 1966, its importance had declined in the popular eye, and it has never since been viewed as so important.

Was this because the problem had been solved? Let us look again at the numbers of black elected officials. In 1970, there were 1479; in 1985, 6312; and in 1990, 7335—certainly an advance. But the figure for 1985 represented only 1.2% of all elected officials. There are currently (in 1997) 39 members of the Congressional Black Caucus: 38 members of the House of Representatives and one senator. These numbers have grown from 13 House members who in 1970 founded the Caucus. The increased numbers now permit Caucus members to form "a pivotal voting bloc, whose power allows them to dramatically influence the creation, direction and enforcement of public policy." However, the increased numbers are in large measure the result of boundary changes to create majority African-American electoral districts. In the southern states, except for judicial office, no African-American holds a statewide elected position, and European-Americans still appear reluctant to vote for black candidates.

Let us look at another area, that of the presence of black actors and black issues on television. Has there been an advance? Or are African-American actors only given work when they have to portray black characters? Again, it seems clear that there has been some advance. More black actors are visible, particularly in advertisements. How far-reaching, however, has this advance been?

Research indicates that, for the most part, black characters are still portrayed in stereotypical situations. We might think there are key exceptions, like the successful middle-class characters typified by the Huxtables on "The Cosby Show." But the two parents were rarely, if ever, portrayed at their employment as doctor and lawyer. Nor were issues of race or ethnicity addressed. The effect, says Doob, is to create the impression that blacks, like whites, can be successful if they choose, and they have only themselves to blame if they are not. If commercials showing people of color in many kinds of occupations are an advance—and certainly there are many reasons why they have become prevalent—they would likely not exist without extensive lobbying by African-American organizations and threats to boycott products if African Americans continued to be shown only in a negative light. In this area, as in others, equality has not come without a struggle.

The Public Broadcasting System airs many discussions about issues concerning African Americans, and its documentaries such as "Eyes on the Prize" have received high praise. Yet they are watched by a relatively small proportion of the population, as compared with the numbers who watch situation comedies on major networks.

While there have been notable advances in some areas, for many African Americans today these advances have little effect on their daily lives. True, they have some rights that before were denied: rights to equal treatment under the law, rights to receive an education, rights to vote. But sometimes exercising these rights becomes difficult. Doob gives examples dealing with education and interactions with police and the legal system. Let us first look at education.

Black youths in a white education system

Sociologist George Dei comments that black youths are encouraged to see themselves as failures. They are surrounded by media portrayals in which they are in trouble with the law, unemployed, or failing at school. At school, teachers often see their students in terms of the media portrayals. This is prejudice. However, we must ask where this prejudice comes from and how it is constructed, and also how it affects those young African-American women and men themselves.

Many schooling practices have been constructed on the assumption that black youths do not need advanced education. It is still common to find black students disproportionately in vocational classes. Studies of the distribution of students (tracking) point to decisions taken by administrators hurriedly, without a knowledge of the individual students, and based on these kinds of assumptions. An academic class has three students too many in it. Who can be dropped? Who will not need it? This is where prejudice enters the decision making, often unthinkingly. Perhaps the administrators do not mean to be racist, but the effect of their actions is to create yet another generation of black youths who do not have the qualifications to move on to more advanced education or to get good jobs when they leave school.

The effects of such discrimination are compounded. Students see that few African Americans are in the educational fast tracks. They may believe this is because of race. There is still research being conducted that purports to show difference in intelligence among races, and reports of this difference are still periodically displayed in the popular media as part of the discourse on race. Some black students will believe they are simply less intelligent, that they cannot be expected to do academic work, and drop out of school or take vocational courses. Other black students will see through the workings of the school system and be well aware of the discrimination they face. They may feel it is not worth fighting the system, that regardless of their own abilities or how well they do in school, the cards are stacked against them. Similarly, they will be likely to drop out or to take less rigorous courses. Still others who attempt to continue with high-level courses report dealing with incredulous administrators and constantly having to prove themselves and their abilities.

Some students have pointed to the culture of the school as a source of discrimination. When they are in the classroom, dealing with the textbook material, they are assumed to be individuals, processing material according to their own intelligence. But the material very often is alien, based on European-American/Canadian views of the world. When the student who is not European American enters the classroom, she or he must set aside culture, tradition, personal history, racism faced in the world outside the school, and even the racism expressed in the graffiti in the school's own washrooms, to deal with this European-American material. Protests from activist groups have led to some changes in class-room material, but often schools are short of money and therefore cannot acquire many of the excellent new materials available.

Teachers, of course, have a part to play here. Some are quite frankly prejudiced. Many others, themselves from a wide variety of ethnicities and cultures, are open to suggestions about how to make students who are not European American feel at home in their classrooms. Often, however, their solutions rely on the students them-selves providing material, giving talks to the class, and so on. While class participation is important and interesting, is it fair to use renowned books and films to present a European-American perspective, and then expect a grade 10 student to present a dif-ferent perspective, and call this "giving equal time"? Some school students are highly literate and very knowledgeable, but few could expect to win a debate with the "great thinkers" whose books are routinely used in school systems.

Some schools, however, do attempt to give their students an education that is based on their own cultural backgrounds and that enables them to appreciate cultural and ethnic diversity as a strength of their community and society. The Rafael Hernandez School is a "school of choice" in the Boston area to which parents from the African-American, Puerto Rican, and European-American communities can send their children. This school has a waiting list from all three groups. Another is Clara Barton High School in Brooklyn, where all students are treated with respect.

Interactions with officialdom Our second set of examples of present-day discrimination and prejudice comes from interactions of members of visible minorities with officials of the state, notably police officers, judges, and others involved in legal and law enforcement systems. First, however, a short example from Canada.

Internationally known journalist Jan Wong, returning from the Atlanta Olympic Games, found herself separated from other Canadians passing through passport control and detained for several hours for reasons that were never made entirely clear to her. Her long wait ended with an apology from a senior official. She concluded that the only reason she was detained was that she looked different from a junior official's conception of "Canadian." When she published an account of her experience in *The Globe and Mail* newspaper, a stream of letters to the editor gave other examples. A few, written by European Canadians, stated that racism could not be the reason for her detention, because such things simply did not happen. Clearly, perceptions of whether racism exists and what constitutes racism differ.

Interactions between members of visible minorities and officialdom (largely European American) may erupt into violence. Very often, officials believe that minority-group members are more likely to be violent or more likely to have engaged in criminal behavior; to be black becomes to be suspect. Instances in both the United States and Canada indicate that many police officers, seeing a black, Hispanic, or Native American, will fit that person's appearance to that of a suspect or make assumptions based only on the person's minority status. In extreme cases this has resulted in the shooting of innocent, law-abiding citizens. More often it results in a beating or an arrest. The "suspect" may be engaging in the ordinary activities of walking down the street, talking to friends, or being part of a crowd, as in this case, cited by Doob from an article in *The New York Times* in 1990:

> In September 1990 John Andrews, a black man, was standing in an otherwise all-white crowd whose members were asking two white police officers to stop a tow truck from hauling off a woman's car, which had been parked illegally. According to witnesses, even though Andrews was acting just like everyone else in the crowd, the officers pulled him out, slammed him against the car, and arrested him. One of the witnesses explained that "the younger cop . . . totally lost control. He punched the kid in the stomach and at one point unsnapped his holster. And the kid never laid a hand on the officer."

SUMMING UP

When, in the late sixties, the Beatles sang "All You Need Is Love," most members of the baby boom generation wanted to believe that war, poverty, and strife, as well as prejudice and discrimination, really could be made to disappear easily. Now, 30 years later, with the baby boomers in charge, it hasn't turned out to be quite so easy after all.

In some areas of life, it appears that prejudice and discrimination against members of minorities are declining. In others, there is little evidence for a decline, and much to indicate that prejudices and their acting out in discrimination are still very much with us. Talking about prejudice, however, does not give the whole picture. We need to ask why particular, widely shared prejudices have come about. We need to ask why, in an advanced, multiethnic society such as the United States, the same old prejudices are so widely shared. In the next section we investigate the social, as opposed to individual, nature of discrimination or oppression, and whether the concept of affirmative action can help in countering some of the social problems associated with systemic discrimination.

REVIEW EXERCISES

For Discussion and Debate

1. "Racial violence is everywhere you look in our cities."

2. "Minority groups should learn that their best hope is in the ballot box."

3. "Minority-group members are more likely to engage in crime."

4. "Prejudiced people are just ignorant."

Writing Exercises

1. "How I would go about overcoming prejudice."

2. "The role of legislation in preventing discrimination."

3. "White folks don't see the racism in society."

4. "What today's children learn about the civil rights movement."

Research Activities

1. In your favorite television sit-coms or soaps, how are members of the majority and minorities shown? Document the number of times minority actors appear, indicating whether or not their character must be played by a minority actor in order to fit the story line. How does this compare with the situation of majority actors?

2. Canvass your friends. How many of them can give examples of discrimina-

tion they have experienced or witnessed against members of minorities?

3. List the high school and college or university classes you have participated in, with the approximate proportions of minority and majority students in each. Now find out the statistics on minority and majority proportions in your geographic area. Is there a difference? If so, why?

4. Examine one stereotype about an ethnic, racial, cultural, or religious group of which you are a member. How is this stereotype shown in popular culture? How do you feel when you think of this stereotype being applied to yourself?

SELECTED REFERENCES

BANTON, MICHAEL, The nature and causes of racism and racial discrimination, *International Sociology* (March 1992), 7, 1, 69–84.

DEI, GEORGE J. SEFA, *Anti-racism education: Theory and practice* (Halifax, NS: Fernwood, 1996).

DOOB, CHRISTOPHER BATES, *Racism: An American cauldron* (New York: HarperCollins, 1993).

EGGERS, MITCHELL L., and DOUGLAS S. MASSEY, A longitudinal analysis of urban poverty: Blacks in U.S. metropolitan areas between 1970 and 1980, *Social Science Research* (June 1992), 21, 2, 175–203.

GONZALES, JUAN L., JR., Race relations in the United States, *Humboldt Journal of Social Relations* (1993), 19, 2, 39–78.

GOZA, FRANKLIN, Differential income attainment among Asians in the United States, 1960 to 1980, *International Review of Modern Sociology* (Spring 1990), 20, 1, 1–31.

HILL, HERBERT, and JAMES E. JONES, *Race in America: The struggle for equality* (Madison: University of Wisconsin Press, 1993).

JONES, EVONNE PARKER, The impact of economic, political and social factors on recent overt black/white racial conflict in higher education in the United States, *Journal of Negro Education* (Fall 1991), 60, 4, 524–537.

KELLOUGH, J. EDWARD, and EUEL ELLIOTT, Demographic and organizational influences

on racial/ethnic and gender integration in federal agencies, *Social Science Quarterly* (March 1992), 73, 1, 1–11.

KILBOURNE, BARBARA, PAULA ENGLAND, and KURT BERON, Effects of individual, occupation and industrial characteristics on earnings: Intersections of race and gender, *Social Forces* (June 1994), 72, 4, 1149–1176.

LI, PETER, Race and gender as bases of class fractions and their effects on earnings, *Canadian Review of Sociology and Anthropology* (November 1992), 29, 4, 488–510.

MURTY, KOMANDURI, JULIAN B. ROEBUCK, and GLORIA R. ARMSTRONG, The black community's reactions to the 1992 Los Angeles riot, *Deviant Behavior* (January–March 1994), 15, 1, 85–104.

RANSFORD, H. EDWARD, and BARTOLOMEO J. PALISI, Has there been a resurgence of racist attitudes in the general population? *Sociological Spectrum* (July–September 1992), 12, 3, 231–255.

SANDEFUR, GARY D., and ANUP PAHARI, Racial and ethnic inequality in earnings and educational attainment, *Social Service Review* (June 1989), 63, 2, 199–221.

SHORT, GEOFFREY, Prejudice reduction in schools: The value of interracial contact, *British Journal of Sociology of Education* (June 1993), 14, 2, 159–168.

TAYLOR, PATRICIA ANN, Education, ethnicity, and cultural assimilation in the United States, *Ethnicity* (1981), 8, 31–49.

THOMAS, MELVIN E., Race, class, and personal income: An empirical test of the declining significance of race thesis, 1968–1988, *Social Problems* (August 1993), 40, 3, 328–342.

———, CEDRIC HERRING, and HAYWARD DERRICK HORTON, Discrimination over the life course: A synthetic cohort analysis of earnings differ-ences between black and white males, 1940–1990, *Social Problems* (November 1994), 41, 4, 608–628.

YETMAN, NORMAN R., and FORREST J. BERGHORN, Racial participation and integration in intercollegiate basketball: A longitudinal perspective, *Sociology of Sport Journal* (September 1993), 10, 3, 301–314.

ZIPP, JOHN F., Government employment and black-white earnings inequality, 1980–1990, *Social Problems* (August 1994), 41, 3, 363–382.

5.2

Are two wrongs trying to make a right?

The issue: Affirmative action, which some call "reverse discrimination." Have efforts to discriminate in favor of racial and ethnic minorities and women taken a wrong step, creating a white backlash (including rejection of the policy by voters in California)?

Introduction Affirmative action has a bad name today in many quarters. The task of this section is to indicate why, and whether this bad reputation is deserved. In the process, we hope to clear up some misconceptions about discrimination, prejudice, and attempts to counter them.

Affirmative action is most often discussed with regard to hiring practices. It can also be found in assigning housing and in admission to courses at the high school and college levels. Other forms of affirmative action, not necessarily named as such, may be seen in selection of television programs to be screened, or programs for a community radio station, or texts in a school course.

Often affirmative action is seen as an attempt to right an old wrong. Because it is popularly associated with hiring, we will offer an example here. In the past, let us say, members of a particular minority group have been excluded from jobs in a department store (or at least from jobs where they would be visible to customers). Now the owners of the store wish to remedy this situation, perceiving it as unfair. How should they go about it? Several options are open, including among others:

- Attempt to ensure that substantial numbers of minority-group members apply for jobs in the store, then give the jobs to the most qualified applicants, irrespective of ethnicity, race, or gender.

- Attempt to ensure that substantial numbers of minority-group members apply for jobs in the store, then apportion the jobs so that highly qualified members of the minority group at least get some of them.

- Select a group of best qualified applicants and award jobs first to the minority-group members among them, then to other members of the best qualified group.

- Hire only qualified members of the minority for a period of time, until the minority group becomes represented in reasonable numbers in the store's work force.

The concept of affirmative action is broad and general, stretching over a long period of time. It goes further than one instance and implies that the store has made a commitment to a long-term plan based on one or more of the options we've listed here.

Is this practice unfair, a case of "reverse discrimination"? Or should it be seen as necessary? Is there something going on here that goes beyond the concept of discrimination against the individual? If someone achieves a position through affirmative action, has this compromised the concept of jobs being awarded on merit?

AFFIRMATIVE ACTION IS REVERSE DISCRIMINATION

In the past, many people did not get the jobs they merited because of racism. Today we should be attempting to make sure that the only criterion for hiring is individual merit. Society requires that the best qualified people get the best jobs, regardless of race.

Very often, when you see a member of a visible minority in a professional or managerial job, you wonder how the person got there. Often people say it happened as a result of affirmative action. Sometimes you have to wonder just how good people are at their jobs, if they gained them through affirmative action. It doesn't help people to be treated as if they are special and have jobs or university places made just for them. People need to be able to stand on their own feet. It does them much more good to be able to compete on equal terms, and if they achieve the positions in an open competition, it is much better for their self-esteem. Also, other employees will respect them more.

So-called affirmative action means that well-qualified people may be overlooked in favor of those who are less well qualified. Surely it would be better to help members of minorities to gain qualifications and become competitive, not give them special treatment. After all, the people who are overlooked have to live too and have to make ends meet for their families.

There are some jobs now for which white people know they needn't bother applying. This situation is not going to promote harmony among different ethnicities or between minority and majority. Affirmative action programs are seen as reverse discrimination and arouse a lot of resentment. Those who promote affirmative action are well-meaning, but are not taking account of the realities of life today. Affirmative action only encourages hatred and divisiveness, because so many people see it as being unfair.

AFFIRMATIVE ACTION IS A NECESSARY ATTEMPT AT FAIRNESS

All of the opinions we've just cited have likely been heard by many of you. These are commonly expressed beliefs about affirmative action. Here we examine some of them to see whether they hold truth.

Hiring should be on individual merit Individual merit is often given as the ideal criterion for hiring. The implication is that in today's world, other considerations should not matter. However, researchers who have examined hiring practices indicate that in reality, people are hired for a variety of reasons, not all concerned with individual merit. In general, people who have responsibility for hiring tend to hire people who are most like themselves or who are recommended by other people like themselves, in terms of culture, behavior, and the ability to make conversation. Those who are seen as "different" have several strikes against them. In an interview situation they may display cultural differences that the hirer finds confusing or worrying, because he or she does not recognize them, or the hirer may simply assume that they will be "difficult to get along with."

These assumptions take many forms, as we saw in the previous section. What makes them especially problematic is that they form part of, and reinforce, structures of racism or oppression that persist throughout much of North American society. Also, they take place within a framework where members of the majority—the ones doing the hiring—are, for historical and structural reasons, more likely to be in positions of power. Without some kind of affirmative action, there is no guarantee that well-qualified members of minorities will be hired, even when their qualifications are superior to those of other candidates, or that they will gain admittance to educational programs. Even when members of minorities are carrying out the hiring, they may be under pressure to not hire other minority members. Doob cites one case where an African-American manager felt unable to hire an African-American secretary because of how his department would be viewed. He feared that people would say, "That's a black operation over there, so it can't be too effective."

Advances in hiring for senior positions since 1979 have been so scant as to be negligible. A 1979 survey of 1708 senior executives of Fortune 1000 corporations indicated that 3 were African American, 2 Asian, 2 Hispanic, and 8 women; a 1985 survey of 1362 senior executives found 4 African Americans, 6 Asians, 3 Hispanics, and 29 women. It seems that only when large corporations are engaged in affirmative action will they hire people who are minority members, women, or especially minority women to high positions. This barrier to advancement, so subtle as to be almost invisible, is known as the "glass ceiling." In Section 6.1 we examine its operation with special reference to gender; it operates similarly where race and ethnicity are concerned.

Hiring should be based on individual merit. Affirmative action helps level the playing field to make this possible. Perhaps one day we can dispense with the mechanics of affirmative action and focus only on merit—but certainly not yet.

People who have benefited from affirmative action cannot be the best   This belief indicates a lack of understanding of most affirmative action programs. In general, these programs work by first selecting people who meet a standard for the job that is considered adequate to high, then choosing from among them— bearing in mind the criteria of the affirmative action program and its long-term goal, which is often to eventually have a work force that reflects the character and diversity of the population of the local area. At times, the standard is reconsidered and adjusted upward or downward; therefore, affirmative action can result in what can be seen as a lowering of standards, but the original standards were set higher than the content of the job required.

An example comes from a gas-pipe construction company. The company would not hire anybody who did not have a grade 12 education, which was beyond the qualifications of most of the Native American people of the area, for historical and structural reasons. Federal affirmative action consultants examined the content of the job and pointed out that it did not require a grade 12 education. The company itself admitted that there was no good reason for the grade 12 requirement, except that it had always been there. Given the pattern of education in the area, the grade 12 requirement was discriminatory, an example of *systemic discrimination*. Educational practices and job hiring practices were intersecting to deny jobs to Native peoples. When it was changed, many more Native Americans were hired on the construction project.

However, the charge that people who benefit from affirmative action cannot be the best is generally leveled at those who occupy senior positions. We have already mentioned the phenomenon of the glass ceiling. It would seem more logical to state that where a company has no members of minorities and few women in senior positions, then the senior executives must have reached their position through preference and favoritism, having been protected from the competition that minority members might give them. There are many African Americans, Asian Americans, Native Americans, and women who graduate from universities with high awards, so that we should reasonably expect them to appear among the holders of top-ranked jobs. Affirmative action programs are an attempt to level the playing field, so that the achievements of candidates of all races and ethnicities can be taken into account.

People need to be able to stand on their own feet
The concept of individualism is very strong in North America (it is discussed further in Chapter 11). Often, people look only at the individual and individualism, neglecting the social world within which each individual exists. This concept fits in with the "American Dream." Anyone can be successful, get ahead, and achieve a lifestyle that will support a family in relative comfort, as long as they work, study, apply themselves, and act respectful, while at the same time standing up for themselves as individuals—at least so goes the Dream.

When we look at society, however, we see that it is not so simple. Success is far more attainable by people in some sectors of society than in others. Furthermore, some people do not stop at modest achievements, but go on to amass fortunes. Again this can be part of the Dream, but in a capitalist society one person's fortune is predicated on the assumption that many others will have relatively little. In other words, as society is currently structured, not everyone can succeed.

Many of the laws, norms, practices, and institutions of society have come from a past in which racism was not only common but legal—in fact, a past in which racism was constructed by leading members of society as a protection of their own privileged position. This "scientific racism" of the eighteenth and nineteenth centuries has been discussed by, among others, Stephen J. Gould in his book *The Mismeasure of Man*. The goal of scientific racism was to demonstrate the superiority of one group of people—European males of the scientists' countries of origin and of the middle and upper classes—over all others, using indexes such as brain size (cranial capacity) and head proportions (cephalic index). To many people today this goal makes no sense whatsoever. In the context of eighteenth- and nineteenth-century colonialism, it did make sense to those people who saw themselves as having a right to control the lives of others. The rulers of the English and French colonial empires saw themselves as superior to the Irish or Scots or East Indians or Ghanaians or Native Americans they were attempting to control. They used terms such as "savage" or "barbarian" to describe these people and to justify their rule. They constructed a scale from highest (themselves) to lowest (Africans and people of African descent).

Of course they were not doing something entirely new. Throughout history, people have attempted to vilify those whose land they wanted to invade or whom they saw as enemies or threats. The persistence of

European anti-Semitism indicates how this has been done, and of course eighteenth- and nineteenth-century rulers drew heavily on anti-Semitism as part of their system. What was new, according to Gould, was the "scientific" nature of the enterprise. As part of this view, many Africans were enslaved and brought to the United States and Canada. Slavery was not a new phenomenon, but its linkage with scientific racism was. In the areas where slavery was most economically profitable, a series of laws was instituted to prohibit the education of slaves. Even after the abolition of slavery, segregation supported by law remained strongly in force in many parts of North America.

Seen against this historical background, many of the acts of discrimination of the present day begin to fall into place as part of a racism that underlies many North American institutions. Members of minorities are still seen as "different," implying a difference from a European-American norm. But that difference often appears less intrinsic in them than in the ways they are treated by society and in the assumptions that are made about them. A word sociologists and social activists use to describe this is *racialized*. African Americans or Native Americans or Asian Americans are treated and thought of as being different, and when most people of any ethnicity are asked to think of an American, they think of a European American. Yet the majority of Americans are not only of European descent.

To say that people must "stand on their own two feet" implies that an individual person, unaided, can combat the system of racialization and win. However, if we look at the very real advances that have been made toward the elimination of racism, we see that they have taken place through collective, rather than individual, action. The Montgomery bus boycott is one example of collective action. Where affirmative action programs have been put into place, they have come about through the action and protests of minorities. Affirmative action is the result of members of minority groups coming together to say, "Enough!"

SUMMING UP

Are two wrongs—prejudice and affirmative action—trying to make a right? The answer is "no," if you accept the notion that affirmative action is a social response to a historically constructed situation of inequality, not discrimination against individuals.

Problems associated with affirmative action typically relate to its portrayal in the media and to the current economic situation. Put simply, in many areas jobs are scarce. Many people are unemployed or underemployed. Members of privileged groups in society have grown up with the assumption that they will be able to find a job. When they cannot, it is easy to find a scapegoat. If there is only one job available, and that job goes to a minority-group member, other candidates rationalize their disappointment, saying that they have lost out because of affirmative action. They receive support from the media, which focus on the ethos of individualism and success.

In actuality, relatively few people are the beneficiaries of affirmative action. In the United States affirmative action showed some success in the 1960s and 1970s. In later years, the shortage of jobs has posed a major problem for members of all ethnic groups. In Canada, employment equity, as affirmative action is known, is mandatory in the federal public service but voluntary in the private sector, and federal jobs are currently being downscaled.

Affirmative action can be a useful tool in the attempt to create a more fair and just society. It cannot work in isolation, but requires a population that understands the process and understands the need for it. We advocate antiracism education, so that people of all ethnicities can understand how historical processes of racialization and gendering affect North American society. Racism remains one of the major problems today. Affirmative action programs can help, but they cannot do the job alone.

REVIEW EXERCISES

For Discussion and Debate

1. "Racial discrimination is all in the eye of the beholder."

2. "American democracy is another word for majority rule."

3. "Governments and elected assemblies should have the same proportions of minority group members as there are in the community electing them."

4. "Nobody could feel proud of getting a job through affirmative action."

Writing Exercises

1. "People should be hired on their own merits."

2. Popular views of affirmative action, and why these arise.

3. "Today, everybody has the same access to the education system, and so anybody can get the qualifications they need to succeed."

4. Getting ahead as a minority group member.

Research Activities

1. Find accounts in the media about a court case involving alleged discrimination in hiring or promotion. Who was involved, and how was the case reported? Try to find accounts of the same case in media targeted for different audiences, and compare the reports.

2. Examine a copy of a newspaper that gives information about business and finance. Look at the pictures of people selected for executive positions. What do these tell you about race and gender patterns of hiring? Explain your findings.

3. Examine representation of minorities at the local government level in your area over the past 10 years. What changes do you find, and why?

4. What laws regarding hiring discrimination apply in your area? What jobs do these apply to—all, or only some? What groups are protected by these laws, and are there some (e.g., religious minorities) that are not protected?

SELECTED REFERENCES

BARKER, KATHLEEN, To be PC or not to be? A social psychological inquiry into political correctness, *Journal of Social Behavior and Personality* (1994), 9, 2, 271–281.

BOBO, LAWRENCE, and JAMES R. KLUEGEL, Opposition to race targeting: Self-interest, strat-ification ideology, or racial attitudes? *American Sociological Review* (August 1993), 58, 4, 443–464.

BURSTEIN, PAUL, Affirmative action, jobs, and American democracy. What has happened to the quest for equal opportunity? *Law and Society Review* (1992), 26, 4, 901–922.

BUTLER, JOHN SIBLEY, Affirmative action in the military, *Annals of the American Academy of Political and Social Science* (September 1992), 523, 196–206.

CALLISTE, AGNES, The struggle for employment equity by blacks on American and Canadian railroads, *Journal of Black Studies* (January 1995), 25, 3, 297–317.

CUNNINGHAM, SUSAN, The development of equal opportunities theory and practice in the European community, *Policy and Politics* (July 1992), 20, 3, 177–189.

DITOMASO, NANCY, and DONNA E. THOMPSON, The advancement of minorities into corporate management: An overview, *Research in the Sociology of Organizations* (1988), 6, 281–312.

DOOB, CHRISTOPHER BATES, *Racism: An American cauldron* (New York: HarperCollins, 1993).

DRAKE, W. AVON, and ROBERT D. HOLSWORTH, Affirmative action and elite racial reconciliation, *Research in Race and Ethnic Relations* (1994), 7, 57–82.

EDWARDS, JOHN, Group rights v. individual rights: The case of race-conscious policies, *Journal of Social Policy* (January 1994), 23, 1, 55–70.

EPSTEIN, RICHARD, *Forbidden grounds* (Cambridge, MA: Harvard University Press, 1992).

GAMSON, WILLIAM A., and ANDRE MODIGLIANI, The changing culture of affirmative action, *Research in Political Sociology* (1987), 3, 137–177.

GLAZER, NATHAN, *Affirmative discrimination* (New York: Basic Books, 1975).

GOULD, STEPHEN J., *The mismeasure of man* (New York: Norton, 1981).

GRAHAM, HUGH DAVIS, Race, history and policy: African Americans and civil rights since 1964, *Journal of Policy History* (1994), 6, 1, 12–39.

HENRY, FRANCES, and CAROL TATOR, Racism in Canada: Social myths and strategies for change. In *Ethnicity and ethnic relations in Canada*, ed. Rita M. Bienvenue and Jay E. Goldstein (Toronto: Butterworths, 1985).

HIRSCHMAN, ALBERT, *The rhetoric of reaction* (Boston: Belknap, 1991).

KILLIAN, LEWIS M., Gandhi, Frederick Douglass and affirmative action, *International Journal of Politics, Culture and Society* (Winter 1991), 5, 2, 167–182.

LIPSET, SEYMOUR MARTIN, Equal chances versus equal results, *Annals of the American Academy of Political and Social Science* (September 1992), 523, 63–74.

————, Two Americas, two value systems: Blacks and whites, *Tocqueville Review* (1992), 13, 137–177.

MENTZER, MARC S., and JOHN L. FIZEL, Affirmative action and ethnic inequality in Canada: The impact of the Employment Equity Act of 1986, *Ethnic Groups* (1992), 9, 4, 203–217.

OLIVAS, MICHAEL A., The attack on affirmative actions: Lives in parallel universes, *Change* (March–April 1993), 25, 16–20.

SKOCPOL, THEDA, JIM SLEEPER, ROBERT S. BROWNE, and JONATHAN RIEDER, Race, liberalism, and affirmative action (II), *American Prospect* (Summer 1992), 10, 86–97.

STARR, PAUL, Civil reconstruction: What to do without affirmative action, *American Prospect* (Winter 1992), 8, 7–14.

5.3

Is too much national spirit a bad thing?

The issue: **Has nationalism—an extreme love of one's nation or ethnic group—done more harm than good in human history,** and will it engulf us in wars and genocidal acts until people learn to reject such extreme sentiments?

Introduction   The phrase *ethnic nationalism* conjures up images of the horrors of war in the former Yugoslavia, of "ethnic cleansing," of the struggle between Hutu and Tutsi peoples in Central Africa. It can also refer to the longstanding attempts of the Basques of the boundary between France and Spain or the Kurdish people of the Middle East to achieve international recognition. Closer to home, we can examine the situation of Native groups in Mexico. What about the United States and Canada? Does ethnic nationalism occur there, and how should we, as sociologists, view it?

But what are both "ethnicity" and "nationalism"? Very often these words are used without definition, in the implicit understanding that everyone knows what they mean. Yet the word *ethnicity* may mean something different for different ethnic groups, and its meaning changes as we move from North America to Europe. The concept of ethnicity includes both subjective and objective components. People feel that they belong to an ethnic group. Others perceive them as part of this group. They may claim a common ancestry, or language, or religion, or race, or some or all of these. They may base their group membership on culture. One useful definition is that ethnicity refers to:

> an involuntary group of people who share the same culture or to descendants of such people who identify themselves and/or are identified by others as belonging to the same involuntary group. (Isajiw, 1985, p. 16)

Nationalism refers to loyalty to one's nation. Michael Ignatief, in his book *Blood and Belonging: Journeys into the New Nationalism*, outlines two kinds of nationalism, civic and ethnic. In his view, *civic nationalism* is constituted by a community of citizens who, as equals, express loyalty and patriotic attachment to a shared set of values, both social and political. *Ethnic nationalism*, however, is loyalty based on inheritance rather than values. In this section we examine Ignatief's distinction and its usefulness.

ETHNIC NATIONALISM IS NOT DESTRUCTIVE

People have a deep-seated need to belong. Humans are social beings who come together to construct communities based on shared cultural values and traditions. In the United States and Canada we can easily see how different cultural groups construct communities that differ from each other. Often, therefore, Italian Americans will identify with other Italian Americans, Vietnamese Canadians with other Vietnamese Canadians.

Here in North America, many of these groups meet, at least theoretically, as equals. For a long time, the prevailing ideology in the United States was that of the "melting pot," where all cultures would "melt" to create a new society and a new culture. Although in practice some cultures have been more represented in the resulting "mix" than others, North Americans in general share many of the same pursuits, tastes, hobbies, and recreations as other North Americans. Baseball, football, skating, volleyball, hockey, jazz, or country music are enjoyed by many people regardless of their background. People whose ancestors come from China, Finland, or Kenya play with the local symphony orchestra. Pop music is listened to by almost all teens.

Ethnicity and identity   Yet, when we walk through the streets of a city such as Los Angeles or Toronto, we are amidst sights and scents and sounds that indicate multiple ethnicities. We hear several languages being spoken. People use clothing, hairstyles, and jewelery to proclaim their ethnicity. If asked, some will identify themselves as American or Canadian, but others construct their identities as African American, Italian American, or German Canadian. For some, this is a simple statement of identity, reflecting family ties, language, religion, tradition, and culture. For others, this claiming of group membership is a declaration of resistance against being treated as an "other," outside the bounds of society, by those who are considered mainstream.

We have so far only considered people who have come as immigrants. What about the people who see themselves not as immigrants or as the great-great-granddaughters and sons of immigrants but as indigenous inhabitants of their country?

Ethnicity and nationhood The term *ethnic group* has less often been used sociologically in Europe than in North America. Groups of people that in North America would be considered ethnic groups are in Europe spoken of as nations. This term is often associated with political boundaries. The words *nation* and *state* do not have the same meaning, but in Europe a nation often controls its own state or is at least a potential candidate for statehood. Alternatively, the nation may be a national minority within a state. In either case, there is a political dimension to the word *nation* that is lacking for *ethnic group*. In many cases, though not all, a nation will have its own land base. There are Scots living all over Europe, but they have their own land base in Scotland. It may surprise some North American readers to learn that although Scots consider themselves a nation, Scotland is not a nation-state.

Ethnic nationalism for such groups is a search for identity, a tracing of roots to a shared cultural past, together with a search for political recognition. To continue with European examples: All over Europe there have been movements seeking national autonomy. Basque, Scottish, and Welsh nationalism are only three examples. When the former Soviet Union split apart, it did so along national lines, and groups with shared cultural links and their own land bases become the new nation-states of Georgia, Belarus, Ukraine, and others.

In many parts of the world, people are calling for the right to govern themselves as they see fit. They claim this right based on their concept of nationhood, rooted in their culture and history. In making their claims,

they speak not only of the traditions and customs they share but also legal, educational, and political systems and institutions that they consider as uniquely their own.

In North America there are groups that claim nationhood rather than ethnic group status—most notably, the people of Québec, many of whom consider that they constitute a distinct society, and the many aboriginal nations who point out that they were governed by their own political and legal systems long before Europeans landed on North American soil. Not all Québecois seek independence from Canada. Just over half of those who voted in the Québec Referendum of 1995 voted to remain part of Canada. Many, however, including many of those who voted against separation, define themselves as Québecois rather than Canadian. As Michael Ignatief points out, the provincial assembly of Québec is called L'Assemblée Nationale. Similarly, while many people of Native ancestry consider themselves Native American or Native Canadian, others see themselves first as Mohawk or Mi'kmaq or Navaho.

Where people with a geographic land base believe they form a nation, feel strongly loyal to that nation, and form or maintain their own political, legal, and educational systems, there seems little reason to insist that they are not a nation. Surely it is more productive to spend time and energy working out how economic and political links can be formed or maintained between the new nation and others around it than endlessly arguing over whether such a nation has a right to exist.

ETHNIC NATIONALISM IS DESTRUCTIVE

So far we have considered the case of people with a geographic land base who consider themselves to form one nation. This, however, may be rarely found, or the geographic land base may be very small. Different ethnic groups share an area, either living amongst each other or in small enclaves. In the former Yugoslavia, one village might be predominantly of one ethnicity, the next of another.

In 1990, across Canada attention was drawn to Kanehsatake, otherwise known as Oka, where many Mohawk people took a stand to protect a wooded area, a burial ground, from being turned into a golf course. In the initial police raid on a small barricade across a little-used road leading to the area, a police officer was shot and died. People of the nearby reserve of Kahnawake joined in the dispute, barricading the Mercier Bridge leading to Montreal. European Canadians from a nearby town came to the barriers to protest, and their activities included burning an effigy of a Mohawk warrior and throwing rocks at carloads of people—pregnant, sick, or elderly— being evacuated from Kahnawake. This resulted in the death of an elderly veteran who was, paradoxically, a European Canadian who had married into a Mohawk family. In Kanehsatake, Mohawks and European Canadians had lived next door to each other. Over the next few weeks, many Europeans left the area. Some of their houses were looted. Some of these residents did not return.

Ethnic nationalism is not the same as simple patriotism, or love for one's country, or culture. Ethnic groups are found in a situation of multiple ethnicity where more than one such group is present. The Kanehsatake Mohawks are ethnic only with respect to their French-Canadian or English-Canadian neighbors who, sociologically speaking, are equally ethnic. The expressed nationalism of one group arouses fear, distrust, and an equal nationalism in others. Many English Canadians today speak in tones of wounded

pride at the idea that Québecois would want to separate, as if it is a personal affront. They perceive it as an attack on the concept of Canada as a tolerant, peaceful, and all-inclusive country, and hence an attack on themselves as good citizens of such a country. They cannot understand why French Canadians (or for that matter Native Canadians) do not share their view of Canada.

We have mentioned Ignatief's distinction between ethnic and civic nationalism. Ignatief defines himself as a cosmopolitan, a member of a global society, part of a global economy. He speaks several languages and feels at home in the diversity of a big city. He points out, however, that the ability to be cosmopolitan is fragile. People can only be cosmopolitan if they have their own cosmopolitan state or if they live in states that can guarantee order and peace to their citizens. As Ignatief says:

> Globalism in a post-imperial age only permits a post-nationalist consciousness for those cosmopolitans who are lucky enough to live in the wealthy West. The Bosnian Muslims are perhaps the most dramatic example of a people who turned in vain to more powerful neighbours to protect them. The people of Sarajevo were true cosmopolitans. (Ignatief, p. 9)

But the Bosnian Muslims did not live in a strong nation-state that could guarantee peace and tolerance within its bounds.

Ignatief also defines himself as one who favors civic nationalism. In his view, a nation should be a community of equals held together by law and by respect, not by the ties, real or supposed, of blood. Within a community of equals, each can be free, can be herself or himself. The goal of multiculturalism is a community in which people can express themselves through culture, religion, and language, respecting and valuing the cultures, religions, and languages of others. Such respect and value, however, are fragile.

It is too easy for a demagogue to gather a following through boosting his or her own culture by denigrating others. Old prejudices compound this, so that it seems not only that another's culture is inferior but that "they," the others, must always create inferior cultures.

Ethnic nationalism is a fantasy constructed out of rhetoric that denies basic humanity to others. The rhetoric is full of contradictions. There are many stories in Bosnia of people who recount the evil of their neighbors, then in the next breath speak longingly of the days when they could live in harmony side by side. This rhetoric feeds the fantasies of power, particularly for those who wield their power through weapons. Ignatief writes "most nationalist violence is perpetrated by a small minority of young males between the ages of 18 and 25. . . . I met lots of young men who loved the ruins, loved the destruction, loved the power that came from the barrels of their guns" (Ignatief, p. 187).

It would be a mistake, however, to trace the destructiveness of ethnic nationalism to the power complexes of these young men. They did not invent the rhetoric or the nationalist fantasy, though they do maintain it. The only real defense against this destructiveness is a political system that prevents the buildup of nationalism by denying the demagogues a platform. If this is so, then ethnic nationalism, however it arises, should be seen as inherently destructive, and resisted.

Another look at ethnic nationalism Ignatief speaks of ethnic nationalism as inherently destructive and wishes to promote civic nationalism. Yet when he looks around the world, he sees increasing numbers of places in which the strife of ethnic nationalism is occurring, and he sees reasons for it to occur. Where people are ruled by others, where they live with fear, where they have little say in their own lives, they are easily swayed by a simplistic nationalism that seeks to put down others.

This section has reviewed arguments for seeing ethnic nationalism as positive pride in heritage or as simplistic and destructive. In our view, these arguments do not give the whole picture. Ethnic nationalism is a complex phenomenon, and it emerges differently under different conditions. Here are some examples:

The war in Chechnya has been brutal. At the time of this writing, it appears to be over, at least for the present. News reports from Chechnya, however, indicate that people are working to maintain a level of hatred of all things Russian—for instance, viewing videos of atrocities committed on both Russians and Chechens. At the same time, the Chechen people are going to the polls to elect or give elected legitimacy to their new government of independence. Chechen nationalism is defined in opposition to Russia. The Chechen people were forcibly relocated by Stalin, and attempts were made to suppress their culture and religion. Suppression contained but did not eradicate resistance, and when the iron hand of the Soviet state was removed, resistance to Russian rule became nationalist uprising.

In Spain, the Basque people had zealously protected the medieval charters that guaranteed them a measure of autonomy and local self-government. During the nineteenth century, these charters were abolished by Spain. Finally, during the Spanish Civil War, General Franco targeted the Basques with the bombing and partial destruction of the town of Guernica, in which 1500 died, and the closing of schools, newspapers, and other cultural institutions and prohibiting public use of the Basque language. Fifty thousand Basques died during the Spanish Civil War. After the war, Basques retaliated with growing underground resistance movements, including the terrorist movement *Euskadi ta Askatasuna* (ETA), which was responsible for a number of attacks. Franco's death brought political change in its wake, and eventually the granting, or regranting, of a measure of autonomy to the Basque community.

Although some Basques remain political prisoners, there are signs that the period of Basque terrorism may be over. A 1996 article in *National Geographic* states, "Nearly every Basque now agrees on one thing: The future should be decided by negotiations, not violence" (Abercrombie, 1996, p. 256). Yet, as this chapter was being written, violence by ETA members once again was making headlines.

SUMMING UP

Is too much national spirit a bad thing? In one sense, the answer is simple: Too much of anything is usually a bad thing. But some would say that, where virtue and justice are concerned, the same rules do not apply. Gerald R. Alfred, a Kahnawake Mohawk, writes in *Heeding the Voices of Our Ancestors* of his own nation and its nationalism. This nationalism has arisen in response to conditions over centuries. It draws upon traditional Mohawk symbols and concepts and Mohawk history to create a distinctive identity. It is a community response, and it changes as ideas arise within the community and people attempt new ways of dealing with the conditions of their lives, including relations between their community and the Canadian government.

Mohawk nationalism cannot be understood unless its historical roots are considered. We can trace three phases in the development of Mohawk nationalism, after a starting point when Mohawks and their institutions were trading partners and allies of Euro-American colonists. During the "latent" phase, colonists, who now had less need of their Native allies, began the process of disregarding and dismantling Mohawk institutions and culture. Native communities, generally isolated, attempted to maintain their institutions on a piecemeal basis. "Revival nationalism," the second phase, did not arise until the colonists' goal of removing Mohawk institutions and identity became clear. This period was marked by various forms of confrontation and focused on the reconstruction, on a traditional basis, of Mohawk identity and institutions. Now, in the third phase of complex nationalism, the community is drawing on both traditional and modern concepts, seeking to develop a Mohawk state based on a modified version of the old institutions of the Iroquoian Confederacy.

> Where most Native communities seek redress in the reform of Canadian constitutional law, the Mohawks of Kahnawake seek to re-structure the relationship in a more essential way through the creation of a truly confederal Canada and the re-implementation of a Native-Canada relationship based on the principles of the Kahswentha—the Two-Row Wampum, embodying the ideal of mutual respect for the cultural and political autonomy of each society. (Alfred, 1995, p. 185)

Mohawk nationalism is a problem for the Canadian state as presently constituted, and this problem is not going to go away. This is not a simplistic nationalism founded on demagoguery. Here, as elsewhere, denial or suppression of the rights of a minority that constitutes itself as a nation is not a solution. The only eventual solution can be some form of restructuring. The question is whether this restructuring can come about peacefully, or whether ethnic nationalism, generating further competing ethnic nationalisms, must result in destruction. Rather than being an argument to be debated in this section, the question of whether ethnic nationalism becomes destructive is one to be determined by the actions of peoples and governments.

REVIEW EXERCISES

For Discussion and Debate

1. "Can't we all just be American?"
2. "Nationalism is a response to oppression."
3. "Native people should join the mainstream."
4. "Every group has the right to self-determination."

Writing Exercises

1. "Cultures meeting"—an imaginary reconstruction of the first encounter between Native people and Europeans in your area.
2. "Ethnicity and identity: Can they be separate?"
3. "Nationalism is about power."
4. "Who am I? Factors important in my own identity."

Research Activities

1. Trace the ethnic history of your geographic area, describing the groups that have settled in the area. Go as far back as you can.
2. Trace your own ethnicity. (Don't just settle for "American!") How does this form part of your identity? If, like most North Americans, you can trace descent from more than one cultural group, which is more important to you, and why?
3. Search the World Wide Web for statements of ethnicity and nationhood from any one group you wish to know more about. (Be specific in your search; name the group you intend to find.) How do you react to the statements? Why?
4. Find media reports of conflict associated with ethnic nationality. What terms are used to describe the participants? Which side do the media favor, and why?

SELECTED REFERENCES

ABERCROMBIE, THOMAS J., The Basques, *National Geographic*, November 1996, 74–97.

ALFRED, GERALD R., *Heeding the voices of our Ancestors* (Toronto: Oxford University Press, 1995).

BAUMANN, ZYGMUNT, *Modernity and the Holocaust* (Ithaca, NY: Cornell University Press, 1989).

DADRIAN, VAHAKN, The anticipation and prevention of genocide in international conflicts: Some lessons from history, *International Journal of Group Tensions* (Fall 1988), 18, 3, 205–214.

———, The role of the Turkish military in the destruction of Ottoman Armenians: A study in historical continuities," *Journal of Political and Military Sociology* (Winter 1992), 20, 2, 257–288.

DANFORTH, LORING M., Claims to Macedonian identity: The Macedonian question and the breakup of Yugoslavia, *Anthropology Today* (August 1993), 9, 4, 3–10.

DEBELJAK, ALES, The disintegration of Yugoslavia: Twilight of the idols, *International Journal of Politics, Culture and Society* (Fall 1994), 8, 1, 147–161.

DENITCH, BOGDAN, Learning from the death of Yugoslavia: Nationalism and democracy, *Social Text* (1993), 34, 3–16.

DERLUGIAN, GEORGI, "Ethnic" violence in the post-communist periphery, *Studies in Political Economy* (Summer 1993), 41, 45–81.

DIETLER, MICHAEL, "Our ancestors the Gauls": Archaeology, ethnic nationalism, and the manipulation of Celtic identity in modern Europe, *American Anthropologist* (September 1994), 96, 3, 584–605.

ERIKSEN, THOMAS HYLLAND, A future-oriented non-ethnic nationalism? Mauritius as an exemplary case, *Ethnos* (1993), 58, 3–4, 197–221.

FEIN, HELEN, Genocide: A sociological perspective, *Current Sociology* (Spring 1990), 38, 1–126.

GHEORGHE, NICOLAE, Roma-Gypsy ethnicity in Eastern Europe, *Social Research* (Winter 1991), 8, 4, 829–844.

IGNATIEF, MICHAEL, *Blood and belonging: Journeys into the new nationalism* (London: Vintage, 1993).

ISAJIW, WSEVOLOD W., Definitions of ethnicity. In *Ethnicity and ethnic relations in Canada*, 2nd ed., ed. Rita M. Bienvenue and Jay E. Goldstein (Toronto: Butterworths, 1985).

JAMES, CARL, *Talking about difference: Encounters in culture, language and identity* (Toronto: Between the Lines, 1994).

———, *Seeing ourselves: Exploring race, ethnicity and culture* (Toronto: Thompson Educational, 1995).

LINGLE, CHRISTOPHER, Collectivism and collective choice: Conflicts between class formation and ethnic nationalism, *Ethnic Groups* (1992), 93, 3, 191–201.

LUKES, STEVEN, Five fables about human rights: What would it be like if, . . . *Dissent* (Fall 1993), 40, 4(173), 427–437.

NAGEL, JOANNE, Ethnic nationalism: Politics, ideology, and the world order, *International Journal of Comparative Sociology* (January–April 1993), 34, 1–2, 103–112.

NAGI, SAAD Z., Ethnic identification and nationalist movements, *Human Organization* (Winter 1992), 51, 4, 307–317.

RYAN, STEPHEN, Ethnic conflict and the United Nations, *Ethnic and Racial Studies* (January 1990), 13, 1, 25–49.

SMYTH, FRANK, Cashing in on Rwanda's genocide, *New Statesman and Society* (July 1994), 7, 313, 16–17.

STAUB, ERVIN, *The roots of evil: The origins of genocide and other group violence* (Cambridge: Cambridge University Press, 1989).

VAN DEN BERGHE, PIERRE L., The modern state: Nation-builder or nation-killer? *International Journal of Group Tensions* (Fall 1992), 22, 3, 191–208.

ZUKIER, HENRI, The twisted road to genocide: On the psychological development of evil during the Holocaust, *Social Research* (Summer 1994), 61, 2, 423–455.

6. Gender Relations

In contrast to biological sex, **gender** refers to culturally learned notions of masculinity and femininity. **Gender roles** are learned patterns of behavior that a society expects of men and women, and they are a widespread aspect of social life. By **masculinity**, then, we mean that package of qualities that people in our society expect to find in a typical man. By **femininity**, we mean that package of qualities people expect to find in a typical woman.

Since gender is learned, gender roles vary from one culture to another. In short, beliefs about masculinity and femininity are not linked to sex in the same way in all societies. Like race, gender is a social construction that varies across societies. And like race, gender is largely an imposed social construction that confers more benefits on some people (in this case, men) than it does on others (namely, women).

In this chapter we examine three issues associated with gender and gender relations. The first is concerned with discrimination against women in the workplace, and whether women experience a "glass ceiling" that sets limits on their career possibilities. The second section considers whether men are able to participate in parenting children as effectively as women. The third section examines how the media influence our notions of masculinity and femininity—and particularly whether the media have negative effects on women.

6.1

Do employers treat women like second-class men?

The issue: **Do women have an equal opportunity in the workplace,** *or do they still hit a "glass ceiling" when they take their ambition and talent to the maximum and strive for advancement?*

Introduction The possibility that there is a glass ceiling on women's jobs is a topic that is argued by employers and employees, sometimes through the court system. On the one hand, many claim that all barriers to women's hiring and promotion have been eradicated. On the other, women in many walks of life point to instances when they were denied promotion. Many claim this is because of their gender and the assumptions that were made about them, that they were asked questions that indicated they were being evaluated differently from men and against different standards.

In the 1960s and 1970s, the women's movement took as its goal that women should have the same opportunities as men. Has this goal been met? Is it true that women's career advancement opportunities are, like those of men, determined only by a woman's own ambition and qualifications? On the other hand, can we consider "ambition" and "qualifications" without also wondering why women may have been encouraged during high school years to set their sights lower, to be less ambitious, and so obtain fewer qualifications? What of sexual harassment, which some women have said plays a part in keeping them out of occupations that have traditionally been considered "male"?

This topic ties in with that of affirmative action—as we have seen, a highly divisive question. If there is no restriction on women's participation in the labor force, surely there is no need for affirmative action, as women will be hired or promoted according to their merits. Some women find offensive the suggestion that they should be hired because of affirmative action. To them this concept reduces the value of their qualifications. Other women and men point out that where affirmative action programs are not in place, women are not hired to the extent that their qualifications deserve. They speak of this as *systemic discrimination,* which is not necessarily based on the personal prejudices of employers but on the accumulated weight of habit, assumptions, and the precedents of past hiring decisions.

Take an example: A number of years ago we became aware that several young female science students had been turned down for summer employment in a field camp. Each was interviewed and rejected individually, on the basis that while her qualifications were good, she would be the only woman in the camp, which was considered a bad idea. The key word here is *individually*. If all three had been hired, they would clearly have had female company! This kind of summer employment was a valuable work experience, but now, at the end of their university program, these women have fewer qualifications for permanent employment than their male classmates who were hired. An affirmative action program stating that, all other

academic qualifications being equal, women should have preference in hiring, would have resulted in the hiring of these women (and some men).

THERE ARE NO LONGER ANY CEILINGS ON WOMEN'S WORK

In the past there were many barriers against the employment or promotion of women. Men were seen as breadwinners who had to support a family, so that many people felt that women should not compete for men's jobs. Perceptions about different skills and abilities of women and men led also to the idea that there were jobs women could not do, as well as those they should not do. Even as recently as 20 years ago, it was common for women to be paid less than men for doing the same work because the men had to support families, and for women seeking promotion to be told they were not eligible for high-position employment.

In reality, many women also had to support families, but social assumptions overlooked this. Women, it was thought, would not be able to give the same attention to difficult or complex tasks because of their responsibilities to their spouses and children. And in any case, if women's abilities were different, women would not be capable of the sustained concentration required for high-performance jobs. For example, in a letter to John Stuart Mill, Sigmund Freud objected to Mill's championing of women's rights by saying that it would not be right for him to assume that "my own dear child" could or should undertake the intellectual pursuits that he himself engaged in. He was referring to his fiancée. His attitudes were typical of the time and persisted well into the twentieth century.

These barriers, however, have now been removed. As the twentieth century progressed, women demonstrated that their capabilities paralleled those of men, and that they too could excel in math, science, politics, and other "male" fields of endeavor. Further, society showed that it needed the skills of talented women, as well as men. In many parts of the Western world it is illegal for employers to discriminate against women in their hiring practices, and jobs are commonly advertised as "open to women and men." In today's schools, girls as well as boys study math, sciences, and arts, and barriers to the entry of women in law schools and medical schools have long been gone.

However, if we look at the distribution of occupations, we find that there are fewer women than men in high-paying positions, and on average women still earn around 75 cents for every dollar earned by men, calculated on the basis of hourly wages. This need not, however, indicate that women experience barriers to promotion. The highest wages are earned by people in senior positions. The average age of chief executive officers of the leading 1000 most valuable, publicly traded U.S. companies, according to a 1992 *Business Week* analysis, is 56. These senior men (and a few women) commenced their careers over 30 years ago, in the 1950s and 1960s, when the women's movement was just getting underway and prejudices against women's careers were still in effect. There was indeed a ceiling on women's careers at that time, which now, thanks to changed attitudes and legislation, has been removed. Thus we should look not at the highest earners but at people who are currently working their way up the corporate and professional ladders. Many women are graduating from universities with degrees in accounting, management and finance, engineering, and economics, and they are the ones we will expect to see at the top of the employment tree in the future.

Many women still seek entry into the traditionally female occupations of stenographers and secretaries, sales clerks, bookkeepers and accounting clerks, cashiers, nurses, elementary school teachers, general office clerks, and janitors and charwomen. "Job ghettos" still exist. However, if women do take these jobs, it is because they choose to do so. Many women still enter into occupations that are relatively low paid or that do not lead to promotions and career paths. They do so for a variety of reasons. Sometimes they are attracted to the content of the job. Sometimes they consider the job will fit in with their family responsibilities. At more senior levels, women may postpone career plans in order to bear and raise children. If they do so, they will take longer to achieve senior executive status. The existence of the so-called "Mommy track," however, indicates not that a supposed glass ceiling prevents women from reaching the upper levels of management, but that the women themselves make choices about their lives, which obviously affect their career plans. For any given woman, raising a family may take priority at one point in her life, and her career may be highlighted later on. Recently, the *Wall Street Journal* reported, "after decades in the trenches, women are finally moving into Madison Avenue's executive suites." It takes time to reach the senior positions, that's all.

A GLASS CEILING EXISTS, AND SOME WOMEN BREAK THROUGH IT

It is true that the imbalance in salaries at present is caused partly by an overabundance of men in senior positions. But this is only part of the picture. At all levels of age and experience, men continue to earn more than women. Either they are in occupational fields that pay better or they hold job titles that are seen as "higher." For instance, salaries in engineering are higher than those in nursing, and managers are paid more than secretaries. Some of these job "choices" lead to promotion, while others do not. Further, U.S. statistics show women earning around 75 cents to the male dollar, for full-time employment, but only 60 cents at the higher levels, indicating that when women do reach the upper echelons, they are paid less for their contributions.

Many women do go into occupational "ghettos," seeking jobs in traditionally female fields. We can raise questions, however, as to whether this is purely by their own choice. What causes women to become secretaries? Also, why should secretaries be seen as less important and less eligible for promotion than other people in their industries? And why, when we open the business section of a newspaper and look at the new executive appointments, are the photographs almost all of men?

Women seeking employment or promotion in a variety of fields have commented that they still have to prove they can do the job to a level superior to that of men. In discrimination cases appearing before the courts, women have brought evidence of being told jobs were not open to women or being asked for higher education qualifications than were male applicants. Further, women say they are judged by different criteria. In some occupations—such as television news anchors—the standards of age and attractiveness applied to women and men differ, with women being removed from public view at a much younger age. In other cases, women have to demonstrate not only that they have the required job skills but also that their family, if they have one, will not interfere with their job commitment. If they have no children, they may be asked if they plan to have children.

In some jurisdictions such questions are illegal, but they are still being asked. A recent article in Toronto's *The Globe and Mail*

newspaper quoted a senior executive officer as saying that he judged women's performance by stricter criteria than men's. Junior men are still groomed for promotion, taken to conventions, and shown the mechanics of decision making, while it is rarer for aspiring women to be prepared in this way.

The U.S. government's Glass Ceiling Commission is currently working to produce strategies for women and minority members to break through the glass ceiling. The commission has produced a series of papers that explain how the glass ceiling operates. Some women do make it to the top, the commission says, but they are rare, very determined, and often without families. Those women who do hold high-level executive positions are often found in staff functions, such as personnel, as are women in mid-management positions. A similar pattern is found for male minority-group members. The question becomes not why only a few women are found in high-level positions, but how and why women and minority members continue to be "ghettoized" into the less prestigious areas of staff functions (or in medicine, pediatrics; or in law, family law).

In a case recently before the U.S. courts, a woman was denied partnership in a large legal firm in the area of litigation, despite the glowing recommendations of several male partners in the litigation group where she had worked and her excellent track record. Less highly recommended male candidates were successful. The firm did, however, offer her a partnership if she would manage the domestic relations department, an area in which she had little interest and less expertise. She did not accept. Another lawyer, commenting on the hiring situation for women generally, has said, "They expect perfection of women, but not of men."

The Glass Ceiling Dataline is another fact-finding organization, created in 1991 as a newsletter to "report on the 'glass ceiling' in

American corporations" (http://cyber-werks.com/dataline). The organization has observed that:

- The rate at which women and minority men are moving up has slowed.
- Ghettoization of women and minority men in areas like human resources and staff jobs has increased.
- Retaliation against anyone who complains of discrimination at management levels is swift and terrible.

This organization has gathered data on academia as well as on corporations, and has followed and documented the progress of lawsuits brought by people who were discriminated against or who were subjected to sexual harassment at work.

The U.S. Department of Labor's report on "The Glass Ceiling Initiative," focusing on employment practices among nine federal contractors, stated:

> The OFCCP (Office of Federal Compliance Programs) initially anticipated concentrating on the executive suite and the highest levels of management. As the pilot project progressed, however, the reviewing team discovered that much of the investigative questioning and many areas of prospective analysis became irrelevant because there were no minorities and women at these levels. To put it plainly, the glass ceiling existed at a much lower level than first thought. . . . All of the companies reviewed had a level beyond which few minorities and women had either advanced or been recruited, and minorities tended to be found at lower levels of management than women." (*Dataline*, August 1992)

SUMMING UP

Do employers treat women like second-class men? Does a glass ceiling exist? If so, is it an artifact of the age structure and demographics of the working population?

Does it exist in some fields but not in others? Has progress been made, or has progress ceased? The evidence bearing on these questions is read differently by observers, depending on where they are positioned in the political and social structure within which employment and promotion occurs.

The U.S. federal government thought sufficiently about the glass ceiling to create a commission to study it. However, critics say that the commission was created to placate feminists and minority leaders rather than to study a real phenomenon. The work done by this commission and by other researchers suggests that a glass ceiling does exist. Though gains have been made by women and minority-group members in the past 30 years, they will not persist automatically; indeed, the numbers of women and minority-group members being promoted may be decreasing rather than increasing.

In some areas, however, there do seem to be gains. In the field of education, there is still an imbalance in the ratio of women to men who are elementary school teachers and the ratio of men to women who are principals of secondary schools. However, the imbalance is lessening, with more women becoming principals. Whether the same pattern is found in other areas of education—secondary schools, colleges, and universities—is another matter. There remain few female university principals.

On balance, therefore, we consider that a glass ceiling does exist. Individual women manage to breach it, and still others may, too, if legislative initiatives are maintained. But we are unlikely to see large numbers of female top-executives while current hiring practices (such as hiring women middle managers predominantly within staff functions) persist. Only when a substantial number of women and minority-group members are present in management and executive positions at all levels will we see the automatic hiring of women and minority-group members to these positions, and until then the work of organizations such as the Glass Ceiling Dataline will be required. We hope for a future in which restrictions on hiring will truly be a thing of the past.

REVIEW EXERCISES

For Discussion and Debate

1. "There are no more restrictions on women's employment."
2. "Pressures in the workplace discourage women from competing."
3. "If women choose to take part-time jobs while they're raising their kids, that's not the fault of employers."
4. "Women don't want the responsibility of holding top jobs."

Writing Exercises

1. Sexual harassment in the workplace, and its effect on the jobs people hold.
2. "Who mentors women in the workplace?"
3. The Mommy track.
4. Pink-collar ghettos.

Research Activities

1. Examine a newspaper that prints announcements of the hiring and promotion of top executives. What proportion of those appointments are of women?
2. Search the World Wide Web for discussions of the glass ceiling for women.
3. Interview 10 graduates of your college, 5 women and 5 men. Who is in full-time employment? Who has achieved promotion, and how long did it take them? Has gender been a factor? What other factors may have been operational here?
4. Watch your favorite TV sit-coms or soaps. Document the number of female and male characters who are in professional or executive careers. Does the show portray these characters at their work?

SELECTED REFERENCES

ALDRIDGE, ALAN, Discourse on women in the clerical profession: The diaconate and language-games in the Church of England, *Sociology* (February 1992), 26, 1, 45–57.

BRINTON, MARY C., HANG YUE NGO, and KUMIKO SHIBUYA, Gendered mobility patterns in industrial economies: The case of Japan, *Social Science Quarterly* (December 1991), 72, 4, 807–816.

BURKE, RONALD J., and CAROL A. McKEEN, Career priority patterns among managerial and professional women, *Applied Psychology: An International Review* (October 1993), 42, 341–352.

BURRIS, BEVERLY H., Technocratic organization and gender, *Women's Studies International Forum* (1989), 12, 4, 447–462.

DRAPER, ELAINE, Fetal exclusion policies and gendered constructions of suitable work, *Social Problems* (February 1993), 40, 1, 90–107.

ETZKOWITZ, HENRY, CAROL KEMELGOR, MICHAEL NEUSCHATZ, and BRIAN UZZI, Athena unbound: Barriers to women in academic science and engineering, *Science and Public Policy* (June 1992), 19, 3, 157–179.

EVETTS, JULIA, "Women and careers in engineering: Continuity and change in the organization, *Work, Employment and Society* (March 1994), 8, 1, 101–112.

GIBELMAN, MARGARET, and PHILIP H. SCHERVISH, The glass ceiling in social work: Is it shatterproof? *Affilia* (Winter 1993), 8, 4, 442–455.

GLASS, JENNIFER, The impact of occupational segregation on working conditions, *Social Forces* (March 1990), 68, 3, 779–796.

HEWARD, CHRISTINE, Academic snakes and merit ladders: Reconceptualizing the "glass ceiling," *Gender and Education* (October 1994), 6, 3, 249–262.

LOPATA, HELENA ZNANIECKA, Career commitments of American women: The issue of side bets, *Sociological Quarterly* (Summer 1993), 34, 2, 257–277.

MONK-TURNER, ELIZABETH, Sexual nuances within internal labor markets: "The politics of being known," *Social Science Journal* (April 1992), 29, 2, 227–232.

SPURR, STEPHEN J., Sex discrimination in the legal profession: A study of promotion, *Industrial and Labor Relations Review* (April 1990), 43, 4, 406–417.

STEWART, JAMES B., and JUANITA M. FIRESTONE, Looking for a few good men: Predicting patterns of retention, promotion, and accession of minority and women officers, *American Journal of Economics and Sociology* (October 1992), 51, 4, 435–458.

THARENOU, PHYLLIS, and DENISE CONROY, Men and women managers' advancement: Personal or situation determinants? *Applied Psychology: An International Review* (January 1994), 43, 1, 5–31.

TIENDA, MARTA, KATHARINE M. DONATO, and HECTOR CORDERO-GUZMAN, Schooling, color, and the labor force activity of women, *Social Forces* (December 1992), 71, 2, 365–395.

TRUSS, CATHERINE J. G., The secretarial ghetto: Myth or reality? A study of secretarial work in England, France and Germany, *Work, Employment and Society* (December 1993), 7, 4, 561–584.

WADDOUPS, JEFFREY, and DJETO ASSANE, Mobility and gender in a segmented labor market: A closer look, *American Journal of Economics and Sociology* (October 1993), 52, 4, 399–412.

WARING, MARILYN, *If women counted* (San Francisco: HarperCollins, 1990).

WENK, DEEANN, and RACHEL A. ROSENFELD, Women's employment exit and reentry: Job-leaving reasons and their consequences, *Research in Social Stratification and Mobility* (1992), 11, 127–150.

YODER, JANICE D., Rethinking tokenism: Looking beyond numbers, *Gender and Society* (June 1991), 5, 2, 178–192.

6.2

Are men fit to be dads?

The issue: Are men able and willing to be good fathers and help their wives raise their children? Or, seen from the wife's standpoint, will the coming of babies mean new burdens and worries for her alone?

Introduction This question and related ones have caught the public's attention through such books as Arlie Hochschild's *The Second Shift*, which indicates that women are still doing much of the work of the household and in particular retain primary responsibility for parenting. There are many ways in which this question may be approached. Do both women and men have the skills and temperament, including the patience, that parenting requires? Do the practicalities of running a household and making ends meet economically permit both women and men to specialize in parenting?

Other factors have a bearing on this topic: custom and culture, availability of child-care facilities, what the neighbors think, and not least, the availability of work outside the household for women or for men. In many households, of course, one parent has to cope with all eventualities of paid work, housework, and child care. According to the U.S. Bureau of the Census, single-parent households formed approximately 15% of all households in the United States in 1989. The majority of single-parent households are headed by women, with a substantial minority (3.1% of all 1989 households, or 21% of single-parent households) by men.

When parents are asked how they divide the responsibility of the household, women are described as doing more tasks related to child care, particularly if having responsibility for events or tasks is inquired about. Thus, though men will take children to doctor's appointments, often the appointments will have been made by women. Statistics from time-budget studies show that the work of the household is not allocated equally. When parents are asked why this discrepancy arises, they give many reasons. In this section we investigate some of the reasons they give, in an attempt to answer the question of whether child-care responsibilities can, or should, be shared.

MEN AND WOMEN CAN, AND OFTEN DO, SHARE PARENTING

Few sociologists today would go along with Talcott Parsons's categorizations of *instrumental male* and *expressive female* roles within a household. From studies of small groups of students engaged in short-term tasks, Parsons and Bales generalized findings to all small groups, particularly to families, saying that in any small group involved in task performance, two "leaders" would emerge. In families, they said, the father would undertake the "instrumental" tasks of decision-making, making a living in the outside world and representing the family to that outside world, while the mother would become the "expressive" leader, carrying responsibility for the mental and physical well-being of family members and nurturing relationships as well as people. Parsons did acknowledge that a number of women worked for pay outside their homes, but saw this as a small-scale phenomenon, a trend that would never catch on. Events since the 1950s have proved him wrong.

In the Western world, large numbers of women and men work outside the home. Many of the women in the paid work force have young children. By the end of the 1980s in the United States, over 60% of married women were officially working for pay. If we include women who engage in "unofficial" paid work (looking after other people's children in their homes, cleaning houses, and so forth, without declaring income from this) the proportion becomes still higher.

Many women are taking on breadwinner activities as part of their daily lives. If they are in the paid work force, who looks after their children while they work? There is no single overall pattern. Some families make use of day care provided by professional caregivers. More, however, rely on less formal methods, such as babysitters who come to the parents' houses, small-scale child-minding facilities, or family members' voluntary care. Although most babysitters are female, some are male; male teens, like female teens, are beginning to regard babysitting money as a sizable proportion of their income. While most non-household family members who help with child care are female, some are male. Often grandfathers, who may feel that they did not see enough of their own children when the children were young, are pleased to care for their children's offspring.

A further solution for many couples is that of structuring their daily lives so that one or another parent is generally available to do child care. These parents take turns in the house, sometimes taking part-time work in order to facilitate this. The growing availability of paternity leave also gives men more opportunity to spend time with their very young children, and men who do so say that they very quickly learn how to perform basic caregiving tasks, such as changing diapers, preparing and giving feedings, and taking infants for medical appointments. Sometimes men consider themselves insulted if their abilities in these areas are questioned.

The sight of a man pushing a stroller, rare 30 years ago, is now commonplace. Fathers are seen with children in many public places, from parks and playgrounds to art galleries. Some may play only a minor part in the raising of their children, but others look after their children for many days at a time, while mothers are away on business trips or military tours of duty. And an increasing number of fathers, in the eventuality of a separation, expect to spend at least part of each year with their children, caring for them. In short, there are no reasons for men not to give care to children. And those that do often find this a rewarding part of their lives.

THERE ARE SOME AREAS WHERE PARENTING IS NOT SHARED

We indicated that men are quite capable of looking after children, their own or those of other people. This section does not dispute these findings but instead points to what is missing from them.

Often the ability to give child care or to perform specific child-care tasks is confused with carrying responsibility for those tasks. Michael Lamb, in studying child care and fatherhood, has looked at three levels of task performance. The first of these concerns

basic supervision of children. An adult may be in the same room with children and "keeping an eye on them," or possibly engaging in an activity with the children. Much of the child care performed by men, says Lamb, falls into this category. Further, when men are "looking after children" in this sense, this is often all they are doing (other than personal activities such as reading the newspaper or watching television), whereas women will be simultaneously involved in cooking or housework or activities relating to paid work.

The second level relates to basic physical care: feeding, bathing, diapering, and so forth. Men perform these activities, says Lamb, but not to the same extent as women, nor to the extent in which they engage in category one activities such as play. But the most telling examples, says Lamb, come when we look at the third category of activity. Feeding children is an important task, but who ensures that there is food of a suitable kind for them to eat? Who ensures that there are diapers on the shelf and clean clothes in the closet? These tasks Lamb categorizes as taking responsibility for children, and in his findings they are performed very infrequently by men.

Why this difference? From the still very small number of men who do take responsibility for planning and organizing child care, it is clear that there are no physical or mental reasons why men cannot do this. However, there may be social reasons. In a recent study, Jenny Blain (1993b) questioned parents about how and why they apportion domestic responsibilities. Several findings emerged. Some parents talked about "the mother's role" and "the father's role," suggesting that there were things that women should do (like laundry and dealing with children's nightmares) and that men should do (like taking out the garbage and shoveling snow). Some parents talked in terms of different abilities for males and females and of household skills in terms of different learning during childhood, saying, for instance, that men had less ability to do laundry, because they didn't know what was required or didn't care as much about the outcome. Some men said they didn't know how to use the washing machine and therefore couldn't do laundry. Of course, a few men did laundry regularly and did it well, and also did household planning, and they had learned all this on the job. Some men said that they would not telephone doctors, or babysitters, or other parents (whom they referred to as "mothers") about their children, because they "wouldn't feel comfortable" doing so. And some parents said that, while men could look after children and often did, women always had an advantage because they were bonded with their children and therefore were more able to understand the children's needs.

Anthropologist Meg Luxton has discussed similar patterns of talking about household duties in terms of how they give men who do not want to do child care a way out. Earlier, Kathryn Backett saw such patterns as coping mechanisms that act to maintain harmony by hiding a discrepancy between what people say they believe in (such as equality within the household) and what they actually do. Describing washing machines as beyond male comprehension means that a man can show he is willing to do housework but shouldn't do this bit because he would get it wrong. Instead, he can offer to "keep an eye on the kids" while his spouse gets on with the washing.

SUMMING UP

Our discussion may make it sound as if Lamb's findings about the lack of male participation in child care are the result of a conspiracy of males who have plotted to do all they can to get out of doing housework. Of course, this is not the case. To understand why men do not take more responsibility and why women often accept their excuses, we have to look at their social milieu.

Despite the increased participation of women in the work force, popular ideas of men and women often still show them as doing different sorts of things. In the popular press, "the family" means one man who is a breadwinner, one woman who is portrayed in the home although she may also have a work-place job, 2.4 children, and a dog. When men are mentioned in news stories, they are described by their occupations. When women are mentioned, they are described by how many children they have.

In light of this, when schools, day-care centers, or other institutions need to contact "a parent," they are likely to telephone the mother. If a father makes the initial contact with an organization, he may be viewed with some suspicion. An example: Many hospitals prepare cards for their young patients, routinely giving the mother's name as the first contact. Derek, a computer programmer, took his daughter to an outpatient clinic one night, when she had developed a persistent cough. He saw the card and questioned the practice of putting his wife's name at the top and his at the bottom, when he had offered both names as contacts and as caregiving parents. The response was, "Oh, you're living apart then." He attempted to explain that they were not living apart, that he regarded himself as a caregiving parent, and that his wife was at home dealing with other children. He was told that the software that generated the card had to put the mother's name at the top if she was living in the same household as the child. His offer to examine the computer interface, as someone with expertise in programming, was treated as a joke.

In a circumstance such as this, the father's request to be the first contact is treated as strange, frivolous, or as implying the mother's unfitness for parenting or the parents' not getting along. Sometimes parents speak (as they did when interviewed by Blain) of how taking time off work to care for sick children is regarded by employers. On the whole, employers are more likely to see this as a female responsibility. Some men do take time off, but call in to say they themselves are sick. Other men have family sick leave built into their contracts of employment, but when they claim it, they experience incredulity from employers and co-workers.

REVIEW EXERCISES

For Discussion and Debate

1. "Mothers and children bond. This explains why women do child care."
2. "Men who care for their families are more than willing to help out with the housework."
3. "Men just don't have the skills to do housework and child care."
4. "In all cultures, it's the men who do the hunting."

Writing Exercises

1. "Gendered patterns in my childhood, and how they've affected my life today."
2. How parents can combine child care with a paid job.
3. "Lots of men would like to do more in the house, if only their wives would let them."
4. "Society makes it difficult for women raising children today."

Research Activities

1. Observe adults with young children in one of the following locations: a doctor's or dentist's waiting room; a playground in a park on a sunny day; a store that sells children's clothes. Observe for one hour, noting what adults accompany children, and the interactions between children and the adults.
2. Make a list of common household and child-care tasks. Interview six people who are parents of young children, and ask them who, in their household, does what. Ascertain how many adults are in the household and their relationships to the children. How do patterns of housework and child care vary from one household to another?
3. Collect a file of newspaper clippings that mention parents. Make a list of common words used to refer to mothers and to fathers, noting whether these words are the same or different. What does this tell you about the ways mothers and fathers are spoken of today?
4. Look at three magazines dealing with parenting. How many of the articles are directed toward mothers? Toward fathers? What, according to the articles, are the responsibilities of being a parent?

SELECTED REFERENCES

ALWIN, DUANE F., Changes in family roles and gender differences in parental socialization values, *Sociological Studies of Child Development* (1991), 4, 201–224.

BACKETT, KATHRYN C., *Mothers and fathers* (New York: St. Martin's Press, 1982).

BLAIN, JENNY, I can't come in today, the baby has chickenpox! Gender and class processes in how parents in the labour force deal with the problem of sick children, *Canadian Journal of Sociology* (1993), 18, 407–431.

———, The daily construction of fatherhood: Men talk about their everyday lives. In *Canadian men and masculinity*, ed. Tony Haddad (Toronto: Canadian Scholar's Press, 1993).

BURNS, AILSA, and ROSS HOMEL, Gender division of tasks by parents and their children, *Psychology of Women Quarterly* (March 1989), 13, 1, 113–125.

CHODOROW, NANCY, *The reproduction of mothering: Psychoanalysis and the sociology of gender* (Berkeley: University of California Press, 1978).

CROUTER, ANN C., et al., Processes underlying father involvement in dual-earner and single-earner families, *Developmental Psychology* (1987), 23, 431–440.

DE LUCCIE, MARY F., and ALBERT J. DAVIS, Do men's adult life concerns affect their fathering orientations?" *Journal of Psychology* (March 1991), 125, 2, 175–188.

DEVAULT, MARJORIE L., Doing housework: Feeding and family life. In *Families and Work*, ed. Naomi Gerstel and Harriet Engel Gross (Philadelphia: Temple University Press, 1987).

DUFFY, ANN, NANCY MANDELL, and NORENE PUPO, *Few choices: Women, work and family* (Toronto: Garamond, 1989).

GERSON, KATHLEEN, A few good men: Overcoming the barriers to involved fatherhood, *American Prospect* (Winter 1994), 16, 78–90.

HAWKINS, ALAN J., SHAWN L. CHRISTIANSEN, KATHRYN POND SARGENT, and E. JEFFREY HILL, Rethinking fathers' involvement in child care: A developmental perspective, *Journal of Family Issues* (December 1993), 14, 4, 531–549.

HOCHSCHILD, ARLIE, with ANNE MACHUNG, *The second shift: Working parents and the revolution at home* (New York: Viking, 1989).

ISHII-KUNTZ, MASAKO, Are Japanese families "fatherless"? *Sociology and Social Research* (April 1992), 76, 3, 105–110.

———, Paternal involvement and perception toward fathers' roles: A comparison between Japan and the United States, *Journal of Family Issues* (March 1994), 15, 1, 30–48.

LAMB, MICHAEL E., Introduction: The emergent American father. In *The father's role: Cross-cultural perspectives*, ed. Michael E. Lamb (Hillsdale, NJ: Lawrence Erlbaum Associates, 1987).

LUXTON, MEG, Two hands for the clock: Changing patterns in the gendered division of labour in the home. In *Through the kitchen window: The politics of home and family*, ed. Meg Luxton and Harriet Rosenberg (Toronto: Garamond, 1986).

MARSIGLIO, WILLIAM, Contemporary scholarship on fatherhood: Culture, identity and conduct, *Journal of Family Issues* (December 1993), 14, 4, 484–509.

MITCHELL, G., STEPHANIE OBRADOVICH, FRED HERING, CHRIS TROMBORG, and ALYSON L. BURNS, Reproducing gender in public places: Adults' attention to toddlers in three public locales, *Sex Roles* (April 1992), 26, 7–8, 323–330.

PARSONS, TALCOTT, and ROBERT F. BALES, *Family, Socialization, and Interaction Process* (Glencoe, Ill.: Free Press, 1955).

POPENOE, DAVID, Parental androgyny, *Society* (September–October 1993), 30, 6(206), 5–11.

SELTZER, JUDITH A., and YVONNE BRANDRETH, What fathers say about involvement with children after separation, *Journal of Family Issues* (March 1994), 15, 1, 49–77.

SILVERSTEIN, LOUISE B., SUSAN SPERLING, JAY BELSKY, VICKY PHARES, and MICHAEL E. LAMB, Primate research, family politics, and social policy: Transforming "cads" into "dads," *Journal of Family Psychology* (December 1993), 7, 3, 267–282.

SORENSON, ANN MARIE, and DAVID BROWNFIELD, The measurement of parental influence: Assessing the relative effects of father and mother, *Sociological Methods and Research* (May 1991), 19, 4, 511–535.

TUTTLE, ROBERT C., Determinants of fathers' participation in child care, *International Journal of Sociology of the Family* (Spring 1994), 24, 1, 113–125.

WILLIAMS, EDITH, NORMA RADIN, and THERESA ALLEGRO, Sex role attitudes of adolescents reared primarily by their fathers: An 11-year follow-up, *Merrill Palmer Quarterly* (October 1992), 38, 457–476.

6.3

Do we imitate the males and females we see on TV?

The issue: **Do portrayals of girls and women in the mass media—especially on television—keep gender stereotypes alive** and **thus keep women from achieving equality with men, at home or at work?**

Introduction All around us in the mass media are images of women and men, boys and girls. By definition, almost every time a person is portrayed or described, that person's gender is evident. Does this matter? Opinions differ. Some research indicates that presentation of gender does matter, that people often imitate what they see on television or read about in the papers. Others suggest that people do not merely slavishly imitate what they see, and that the media can usefully present people with a range of expressions of gender from which they can choose. More opportunities are available to women and men than ever before, and the media alert us to these opportunities.

Still other researchers indicate that the effect of media presentations of gender is highly complex. Media images may influence small details of people's lives by suggesting to them what is culturally approved or possible and what is a goal to aim for. A further complexity is that different agencies of the media aim images toward different sectors of the population. Often, the media target a male reader or viewer, but sometimes images are produced for the "female gaze." Race and sexuality intersect with gender in these arguments.

In this section we indicate some of the complexities of the arguments surrounding the question of whether gendered media images affect people's daily lives. Inevitably, some of the discussion will lean more toward a constructionist perspective than in other parts of the book. Indeed, this topic can provide a useful introduction to some aspects of constructionist approaches to the world, which students may wish to pursue at a later stage in their careers.

MEDIA IMAGES AFFECT OUR DAILY LIVES

When we look around us, we see gendered images: women and men, boys and girls, even animals are presented as gendered. The word *gender* as used by many social scientists implies a social component to a distinction between male and female, so let us be clear on what is meant here. Many items that people use—toys, clothes, books, and magazines—are presented as appropriate for people of one or the other biological sex to use. As social scientists, we perceive this presentation to be based on social assumptions about what generalized male people and female people do, rather than following directly from the people's biology. We therefore discuss it in terms of socially constructed gender, not biological sex.

For example, I go into a store to buy a birthday present for one of my children's friends, aged 8. I wander around the aisles, my eyes glazing over with the variety of items. An assistant approaches me and offers to help. "I'm looking for a present for an 8-year-old, maybe around $8 to $12," say I. The inevitable response is, "Is it for a girl or a boy?" This reaction can be pursued through several levels of experiment. If I have time, and if the store is not too busy, I may say, for example, "It's for a child who really likes bugs." The response is usually either an assumption of gender, whereupon the assistant starts calling the child "he," or asks again, "Yes, but is it for a boy or a girl?"

Why does the assistant ask this? Is it because she or he assumes that gender is the most salient characteristic a child can have—that being male or female takes precedence over whether the child likes bugs? Or is this a marketing technique suggested by representatives or required by store managers? Often it is a required sales technique, but one that fits in with the assistant's own conception of how the world is divided into male and female people, rather than people who do and do not like bugs, even in second grade.

So what is the connection here with the media? Take a look at Saturday morning children's television—cartoon shows interspersed with commercials. The commercials are aimed directly at girls *or* boys, typically matched to the type of show—Barbie dolls, or GI Joe figures. The result can be seen in the gender-specific demands from child viewers for this toy or that toy. Children are not only being entertained but are also learning which toys are appropriate for them, how they as girls or boys are expected to behave, and what they are expected to want in a gendered way.

The messages from TV are clear. Boys will fight and push aside others they don't respect and expect to make decisions about themselves and their actions. Girls will wait, play with dolls, and expect to be chosen. It's the same in storybooks and movies. Ten years later, the stereotypes are acted out, as young women plan to follow the men they feel have chosen them, trying to appear not too aggressive, not too successful, in case they are perceived as a threat and thereby rejected. Meanwhile, in the popular media, women are described in terms of the number of children they have, and men in terms of their occupations or political affiliations. A

woman who emphasizes politics in her life, or a man whose first priority is his children's care, is pointed out as a curiosity, not as a role model.

Some branches of the media see their role differently, as forerunners and agents of change. They will deliberately show a female engineer or a male nurse or elementary school teacher not as curiosities but as experts in their fields, deliberately chosen as role models. These programs and magazines show awareness of diversity in race and ethnicity, as well as gender. But these programs are themselves stereotyped by the rest of the media as "educational" or "feminist," and are watched, read, or listened to by relatively small numbers of people. However, some attempts are being made by socially conscious agencies to use commercial media (television advertisements) to promote change. Therefore, we see male sports stars talking about problems of violence against women, in an attempt to promote models of masculinity that are concerned, caring, and nurturing while at the same time being strong.

These attempts are based on long-standing research that shows the power of imitation in constructing social behavior. Certain kinds of people are more likely to be imitated than others: those who are close to the individual, those who are perceived as warm and caring, those who are perceived as powerful and important. Hence the use of well-known, admired figures in advertisements, who seem to look directly at the viewer and to speak to him or her. These are the people we look up to, and we copy their appearance and behavior.

WE'RE NOT SO SUSCEPTIBLE TO THE MEDIA

Much research indicates the importance of imitation. However, the concept of a *direct* imitative influence of media images on viewers, and hence on society, may be too simplistic. It is true that we can identify stereotypes of masculinity and femininity, and it is true that these stereotypes are all around us, and it is true that we can present children and adults with models of what seems to be socially acceptable and expected. But the counterargument is that people do not merely imitate. Socialization theories such as those of Albert Bandura are too mechanistic; no one is consciously planning and making decisions. Other, more sociological theories, such as social action accounts of socialization, allow for people to engage in interaction with others. People creatively shape their behavior and learn from their previous interactions.

Are we saying then, that media images have no impact? No, indeed. We are saying that it is hard to measure their impact, and that there isn't necessarily a straightforward imitation process at work. What many theorists today look to is how media images are put together, why they appear as they do, and how people associate themselves with the social relations portrayed in the images, rather than just copying the actions.

There is an argument, often heard, that media portrayals do not shape people's actions. The media's job is to reflect the social world in news stories, cartoons, and literature. The media's job is also to "give people what they want." If violent masculinity is reflected in TV shows, this is because it is there in the real world. If women appear indecisive or passive, say proponents, this is because many women want to act that way for at least part of the time. And as evidence that the media reflect the world, they will point to stories in which women are brave and courageous, or in which people of either gender perform community service such as rescues.

It is not hard to demolish this argument. Though many real-life actions are portrayed,

countless others are not. What are omitted are the ordinary, everyday activities, the ways people spend most of their time. This is when the second argument on behalf of current media productions is made, the argument that the media give people what they want. People do not want to see "ordinary" activities, because these are boring.

This is where the question of "gaze" arises. What people are movies made for? Who are assumed to be the chief viewers of television material, the chief listeners to radio, the chief readers of newspapers? It is still common to discover that newspapers are directed at male readers, perhaps male readers of a particular social class, with incidental pages containing what women are assumed to want (fashion, not politics). We still talk of "the man in the street" as meaning the ordinary viewer, the ordinary person, obscuring the fact that over half of ordinary people are female. People conducting media studies find that the majority of Hollywood films present women—and women's bodies—as objects for the male gaze. There may have been some change in the presentation. In the 1950s, women appeared as domesticated, passive objects; in the 1990s, they are sometimes wild, "liberated," or sexy. Nonetheless, they are still objects. Few films are made for a female gaze, even when the filmmakers include women.

If we turn our attention to media other than films, we still find the male gaze or male readership predominating. Authors of children's books are still advised by their publishers that because girls will read books about boys, but boys will not read books with leading female characters, they should make their leading characters male. The majority of newspaper stories remain about males. In Canada in 1991, Media Watch found that fewer than one-fifth of newspaper reports mentioned women. Perhaps this can be seen as a dictatorship of the market, or of what the market is assumed to be: a largely male readership or viewership. And it is true that adult men have more income on average than adult women, to spend not only on books, magazines, and movie-going, but also on the products that are advertised in magazines and on television.

When a news story is told from a male point of view, particularly a European-American male point of view, the standpoint of the reporter or editor is not noted. It is assumed to be a general, unbiased, objective point of view. When a story is told from the point of view of a Native American woman, it is common for both her Native-ness and her femaleness to be pointed out in some way. She is deemed to represent a *special interest*, and her standpoint is seen as "not objective." Her words are modified to present them to a European male gaze.

Even when we look at areas deemed to be of interest specifically to women, we can find an objectification. A case in point is the advertising of menstrual products. We see women in these commercials determined to hide any evidence of menstruation and deny that the physical body changes associated with it need have any effect on their daily lives, particularly in terms of their ability to "have fun." In short, these advertisements make plain that to be seen as interesting or important, women must deny any relationship to their own bodies and the cycles of their lives.

SUMMING UP

Do we all just imitate what we see on television? No, not in any simple, monkey-see, monkey-do fashion. But don't underestimate the importance of the media. Media images of gender have a vast impact on women and men in their daily lives. This impact, however, is not simple. It is not merely a question of a girl seeing female children on TV playing with a dollhouse and copying their actions, or a boy seeing GI Joe and performing an exact imitation—though sometimes these things may happen. Both young and old people process information presented to them in light of what they already know about the world. Some of the girls who watched stereotyped TV shows in the 1950s and 1960s grew up to be the feminist activists of today. Others are now quite antifeminist. Clearly, there is more going on here than merely a copying of activities. People engage with the information given them and construct their own ways of behaving, sometimes imitating, sometimes resisting models offered them.

More important, media images present us with ideas of how the world is organized, the social relations that prevail, and the assumptions about men and women, maleness and femaleness, that people use when they construct their own everyday behavior. In this section we have used gendered social relations as the example. Clearly, these are not the only relations in North American society or its mass media. But whether we focus on gender, or on race, ethnicity, religion, or social class, the media show us the dominant, or *hegemonic*, social patterns of who is important, whose words are worth more air time, whose gaze is considered to be *the* gaze, who has power.

We can challenge this in many ways—by promoting other forms of presentation, by showing we want news stories told from a female perspective, a Native-American perspective, an African-American perspective, by showing that regardless of our own blackness or whiteness, maleness or femaleness, we find such stories interesting and important to know about. But more important still will be the entry of females and minority persons into powerful jobs in the media industry. In a society that claims all people are individuals, no one group has a monopoly on objectivity, and in order to work toward a society that is truly fair and just to all, we all need to understand how other people perceive the social world.

REVIEW EXERCISES

For Discussion and Debate

1. "Today, women are trying to be just like men."
2. "Women always have to have the last word."
3. "Boys will be boys."
4. "TV is simply entertainment. It shouldn't try to change the world."

Writing Exercises

1. "How gendered stereotypes affect and influence me."
2. "Two people who have been my role models."
3. "Women are encouraged to view themselves through men's eyes."
4. "Violence against women on TV should be censored."

Research Activities

1. View two installments of a TV sit-com. Note the behaviors of women and men. What behaviors are stereotypically male or female? Do any women use stereotypically male behaviors or men use stereotypically female behaviors? What makes the humor in this sit-com?

2. View Saturday morning children's TV for two hours. Time the commercials, noting gender of participants, product, whom the product is aimed at, and the title of the show. Present the results as a table. What does this tell you about gender?

3. Draw up a short interview schedule on self-presentation—dress, jewelery, makeup. Include questions on how and where people learn about these things, who they imitate, and the chief influences on their appearance. Choose a convenient site, such as a shopping mall or a park, interview four people, and present your findings in the form of a short report.

4. Invite a group of friends to discuss the latest movie they've seen. Ask them about how women and men are portrayed in the movie. Is there any stereotyping? While they are talking, watch the gendered dynamics of their talk—who speaks the most and who interrupts. What have you learned? Did the subject of the conversation influence who spoke?

SELECTED REFERENCES

BANDURA, ALBERT, *Aggression: A social learning analysis* (Englewood Cliffs, NJ: Prentice Hall, 1973).

BONNER, FRANCES, and PAUL DU GAY, Representing the enterprising self: Thirtysomething and contemporary consumer culture, *Theory, Culture and Society* (May 1992), 9, 2, 67–92.

BRINSON, SUSAN L., TV fights: Women and men in interpersonal arguments on prime-time television dramas, *Argumentation and Advocacy* (Fall 1992), 29, 2, 89–104.

COUTTS, L. BLOCK, and D. H. BERG, The portrayal of the menstruating woman in menstrual product advertisements, *Health Care for Women International* (March–April 1993), 14, 2, 179–191.

FURNHAM, ADRIAN, and NADINE BITAR, The stereotyped portrayal of men and women in British television advertisements, *Sex Roles* (1993), 29, 3–4, 297–310.

FUSS, DIANA, Fashion and the homospectatorial look, *Critical Inquiry* (Summer 1992), 18, 4, 713–737.

GRIFFIN, MICHAEL, K. VISWANATH, and DONA SCHWARTZ, Gender advertising in the U.S. and India: Exporting cultural stereotypes, *Media, Culture and Society* (July 1994), 16, 3, 487–507.

KELLER, KATHRYN, Nurture and work in the middle-class imagery from women's magazines, *International Journal of Politics, Culture and Society* (Summer 1992), 5, 4, 577–600.

KRAY, SUSAN, Orientalization of an "almost white" woman: The interlocking effects of race, class, gender, and ethnicity in American mass media, *Critical Studies in Mass Communication* (December 1993), 10, 4, 349–366.

LIVINGSTONE, SONIA, Watching talk: Gender and engagement in the viewing of audience discussion programmes, *Media, Culture and Society* (July 1994), 16, 3, 429–447.

LOTTER, ILSA, MARTIN WEINBERG, and INGE WELLER, Reactions to pornography on a college campus: For or against? *Sex Roles* (1993), 29, 1–2, 69–89.

McROBBIE, ANGELA, Shut up and dance: Youth culture and changing modes of femininity, *Cultural Studies* (October 1993), 7, 3, 406–426.

Media-Watch, Two years of sexism in Canadian newspapers: A study of 15 newspapers, *Resources for Feminist Research* (Spring 1991), 20, 1/2, 21–22.

MEYERS, MARIAN, News of battering, *Journal of Communication* (Spring 1994), 44, 2, 47–63.

PERIMENIS, LOUISA, The ritual of anorexia nervosa in cultural context, *Journal of American Culture* (Winter 1991), 14, 4, 49–59.

RUDMAN, WILLIAM J., and AKIKO F. HAGIWARA, Sexual exploitation in advertising health and wellness products, *Women and Health* (1992), 18, 4, 77–89.

SHAW, DONALD L., and SHANNON E. MARTIN, The function of mass media agenda setting, *Journalism Quarterly* (Winter 1992), 69, 902–920.

TANNEN, DEBORAH, *You just don't understand: Women and men in conversation* (New York: Morrow, 1990).

TIEFER, LEONORE, The medicalization of impotence: Normalizing phallocentrism, *Gender and Society* (September 1994), 8, 3, 363–377.

TRENEMAN, ANN, Cashing in on the curse. In *The female gaze*, ed. Lorraine Gamman and Margaret Marshment (Seattle: Real Comet Press, 1989).

TURNER, G., *British cultural studies: An introduction* (Boston: Unwin Hyman, 1990).

WALTERS, SUZANNA DANUTA, Material girls: Feminism and cultural studies, *Current Perspectives in Social Theory* (1992), 12, 59–96.

WHITE, JANE H., Women and eating disorders. 1. Significance and sociocultural risk factors, *Health Care for Women International* (October–December 1992), 13, 4, 351–362.

7. Family

A **family** consists of a group of people who are related to one another through marriage, descent, or legal adoption. Family members have institutionalized roles that define what they can expect from one another and what duties they owe each other. The nature of these rights and duties is determined by cultural values. In turn, they are influenced by economic realities and in many cases backed up by the laws of the state.

Adult family members have a legal duty to take care of their dependent children. This means taking care of their basic survival needs, like food and shelter. Ideally, it includes providing love, comfort, and a sense of security. Good families also teach their children the language, customs, beliefs, norms, skills, and values they will need to fit into their society. To a degree, most families do these things. Yet real families fall short of the ideal in many ways, and this can cause problems. Just like the society that it mirrors, a family can display selfishness and cruelty, inequality and violence.

In this chapter we examine three issues that have generated a lot of debate. The first section considers whether, in modern societies, the family is in decline—not providing its members with what they expect and need. The second examines evidence on mating to determine whether one kind of mate works better—provides more satisfaction or a better chance of the marriage's survival—than another. Finally, the third section asks whether family violence—whether directed against spouses or children—is increasing and, if so, whether that is further evidence of the decline of the family.

7.1

Do families have a future?

The issue: Are families in decline, as so many critics have said in the last two decades? If so, what's wrong with them, and can they be fixed? If they're not in decline, what can we do about the critics who say they are?

Introduction In the past decade, there has been a lot of talk about the supposed "decline of the family." This results in part from a concern about the growth of an underclass, which we discussed earlier. It is also related to concerns about what some have called the "sexual revolution" and the "second demographic transition." Both changes, related but distinct, reflect a separation of sexual activity from marriage and procreation and the development of contraceptive technology that makes this separation possible.

A third concern is due to problems of parenting, educational quality, and the future of our children. In the past 30 years, rising divorce rates and rates of women's participation in the paid work force, combined with a traditional absence of fathers from active parenthood, have raised the fear that children are not getting the parenting they need. The weak influence of schools and churches on young people and the strong media influence prompt concern about delinquency and vocational incompetence.

Given the rapid changes in people's intimate lives and work lives, many fear for the future of the family. They declare that the contemporary family is in decline and urge that we return to earlier forms of family life. But is the family in decline? As always, to get a full picture we have to look twice.

THE FAMILY IS IN DECLINE

Anthropologists and historians know that there are scores, if not hundreds of different family types already on record. American families today are not the way they were 40 years ago, but neither were families 40 years ago the way they were 80 years or 200 years before that. What's more, families existing at a given moment always vary from one society to another, one social class to another, one ethnic group to another, and so on. Thus variability, not uniformity, is the norm in family life, and it always has been. So when people speak about "the family," they have in mind an abstraction and an ideal. There is no such thing as "the family," only families. There has always been diversity, but in the past there was a stronger, wider acceptance of the nuclear family as the ideal or optimal type of family.

So when people say that families are in decline, they are taking that particular nuclear family type as the reference point. If we probe deeper, we usually find that this reference point is the idealized family of the baby boom years—the 1950s. The 1950s nuclear family—only possible with labor-saving household appliances and public education, among other things—was a short-lived phenomenon. It, in turn, was an idealized version of the nineteenth-century, rich, urban family in which the husband (and father) was earning an income.

In this idealized family, a father, mother, and children all live together. Mother and father are married "'til death do us part." Divorce is rare or impossible. These are the biological parents of the children they live with. Father is the income earner, and mother stays home to keep house, care for the children, and take part in community activities. The idealized relationship between spouses, between parents and their children, and between siblings is loving and nurturant. There is a clear division of labor and a hierarchy of power. Each family member has a role to play, and each plays it faithfully—at least according to this script. Dick runs. Jane runs. Dick and Jane run.

It is against such a backdrop that critics of modern families declare that "the family is in decline." And they are right. Few families today look like this idealized family—if families ever did. The statistics show us that today fewer people are marrying, staying married, or having many children.

- First, people are delaying marriage or avoiding it entirely, choosing *cohabitation*, or common law marriage, instead. Cohabitation, which has spread rapidly in the last 20 years, is even more firmly established in northern Europe than it is in America. And there is every indication that cohabitation will become more common still in the future.

- Second, fewer people are staying married. Said another way, the divorce rate is high. Estimates vary, but most researchers predict that 40 to 50% of American marriages will end in divorce. Cohabiting couples are not especially likely to stay together. As a consequence, many people have two or more marriage-like relationships in their lifetime, along with many shorter-lived pairings.

- Third, people have fewer children today. The baby boom period—roughly 1945 to 1965—was America's last childbearing frenzy, and it interrupted a century-long slide in birth rates. It is not that today more couples have no children whatever. Couples delay childbearing and produce one or two children rather than three or more, as in the past. Of course, these patterns vary too. Poorer people, less educated people, and rural people have always had higher fertility rates, and they still do. But everyone's average childbearing has fallen.

So today's family is less likely than its predecessor to contain two married spouses and three or four children. In fact, a household fitting that description is likely to be a product of *remarriage*. Then, one or both adults live with their spouse's biological children, not merely their own—again, not the idealized or traditional pattern. And family size is also, even in remarriages, often limited by social factors. In Westwood, a suburb of Los Angeles, for example, many couples who can afford large families in fact have small ones because housekeepers refuse to take jobs where they must care for more than one or two children.

Recent years have seen dramatic increases in the percentage of mothers—even mothers of pre-school children—who work for pay.

Since the 1970s, full-time housewives have been in the minority. For the most part, these are older women, women without work experience, or women who cannot get suitable day care. As a result, most families today have at least two income earners. Given the drop in real incomes since the 1970s, generally one income is not enough to maintain a middle-class lifestyle. In many cases, it is not even enough to maintain a modest working-class lifestyle. The drop in income is one important reason—though not the only reason—why mothers have entered paid work in large numbers.

Women's large-scale entry into paid work has had important consequences. One is that it further reduces the number of families that rely on a single income earner. Another is that fewer wives are economically dependent on their husbands than in the past. This makes it easier for wives to escape from an unsatisfying marriage or an abusive husband. Third, families serve fewer purely economic functions today than they once did. People, especially women, do not need to live in families if they don't want to; they can make it on their own. (Among other causes, this change reflects antidiscriminatory hiring laws, more egalitarian views about males and females, and more education for women.) Thus people who live in families today are there, more often than in the past, because they choose to be. More than ever before, marriage and parenthood are based on choice. This means they are contingent and somewhat unpredictable—not permanent and rooted in tradition, as in past families.

So, on virtually every dimension, the idealized family of the past is in decline. Indeed, though idealizations of this family remain, the actual family type is disappearing and just about gone. But is that bad, as critics of modern families believe? Let's take a closer look at these idealized families, characterized by distinct gender expectations and limited opportunities for women in education and the labor force. For example, let us look at family life in nineteenth-century America, before the major changes we have mentioned all took place. That may help us better understand why traditional families died out as quickly as they did. It may also help us judge whether the change is a decline or an improvement.

THE IDEALIZED FAMILIES WERE IMPERFECT

Imagine a small town in America 100 or so years ago. In those days, what were people's prospects for a happy family life? There was little choice of mate, for people had little contact with the world outside their community. On reaching their late teens and early twenties, they would have known only a few dozen potential mates. Often, they met at church. Some were deemed unacceptable on class or racial grounds. Others were already engaged, in fact or in the eyes of the community. To end up with a mate they found attractive and compatible was, for most young folk, a matter of very good luck.

Once married, a woman was financially dependent on her husband. Women who did not marry were just as dependent on their father or brothers. Culturally, legally, and financially, men dominated their wives and children. This meant women and children had little protection against abuse or neglect. With shorter life expectancies than today, many men died, leaving their wives as widows and single parents. Indeed, single parenthood was as common in those days (due to death) as it is today (due to divorce). Widows and orphans were often left without financial protection and forced to rely on charity or kin for help.

Family life was dominated by the uncertainties of childbearing. Poor birth control technology meant many unexpected or even unwanted children. Pregnancies and deliveries risked a woman's life. Child raising was a strain that lasted through most of a woman's adult years. Naturally, each child had many brothers and sisters. This limited children's privacy, chances for education, access to parental attention, and other benefits that children in smaller families take for granted today. And the life chances were worse for daughters than for sons.

Would you want to be part of this "ideal" family? No wonder people changed their family relations as quickly as opportunities permitted. But change was not entirely in their own hands. Much of the work was done for them, unexpectedly, by demographic change.

Demographic change   A century ago, many constraints on family life were economic and demographic (a result of births, deaths, and location). As the economic and demographic factors changed, so did family patterns. Take one example: the effects of a falling death rate. Over the last 100 years, people's lives have lengthened. We are less likely to die in infancy and more likely than ever to live into our seventies, eighties, and nineties. Today, death is less salient than before. We spend less time observing or anticipating death. So we can focus our thoughts and efforts on the future, and the future has grown longer for everyone. One result is that we spend more time planning for the future.

For example, more people today plan their families: how many children they want to have and when they want to have them. This is possible thanks to improved methods of contraception. And because fewer children die, fewer births are needed to reach the desired family size. A higher proportion of children born are actually wanted, so parents today have a stronger emotional attachment to their fewer, longer-living, wanted children than in the past.

With reduced fertility and generally improved living conditions, wives come to outlive their husbands by wider margins than in the past. This means a longer period of widowhood.

From a child's point of view, parents are less likely to die in early or middle age than a century ago. This means there are more parents (even grandparents) living into old age. Consequences include the establishment of retirement communities for both single and married elderly people, emotional dependence on adult children that lasts many decades, and for people without children, financial dependence on the state.

Parents are less likely to die in early or middle age, and lone female parents aren't discouraged from keeping their children, so there are fewer orphans today. Most children today have living parents, even if those parents do not live with one another or with the child.

Most dramatic of all, since spouses are unlikely to die in early or middle age, unsatisfied husbands and wives face a new dilemma. In the past many unhappy marriages ended when one or the other spouse died. Today, they end this way less often. Married people today face many years spent in an "empty nest," alone with their spouse. It's either that or divorce. High current divorce rates reflect this new demographic reality as much as they reflect women's greater economic independence and fewer young children.

Today, if not ended by divorce, about 4 marriages in 10 reach a fiftieth anniversary (compared with half as many in 1851). Marriages not ended by divorce are likely to last about 20 years longer than they did in 1851. Of these, 14 years are spent in the empty nest, compared with an average of 0 years in 1851. These are average figures, and they ignore the variations. In the past some couples did have an empty-nest period, and for some of them it may have been long and happy. But when the empty-nest period is even longer and more certain, marital happiness cannot be taken as a matter of course. Today, marriage is not centrally concerned with child bearing and child raising any more than it is centrally concerned with economic production, as it was in farm families of 1851. Marriage is about companionship, affection, and emotional support between spouses.

SUMMING UP

For the purpose of this discussion, we will ignore class-based and race-based differences in the modern family; they are interesting and important but not decisive for the argument that follows. In every modern family, life is a series of choices: whether to marry, when to marry, whether to have children, when to have children, whether to divorce, when to divorce, whether to remarry, when to remarry, and so on.

These choices are never easy, but people like having choices. What's more, people choose differently, and the result is a vast variety of intimate relations we call families. To capture this variety, our definition of family must be broader than in the past. Here's one possible definition of family that reflects the new reality: a family is two or more people in an intimate, meaningful relationship marked by mutual, enduring responsibility. Family members may or may not live together, may or may not have sex with one another, may or may not have children or a spouse present, and may or may not be of opposite sexes.

This modern family—immensely variable and based on personal choice—is not in decline. People still form families, though their ideas about family life vary widely. As noted, people form families for less instrumental reasons today than in the past, and they form different kinds of families than in the past. Yet they still use the traditional language of family life—speaking of husbands, wives, parents, children, brothers, and sisters—even when the reality is far more complicated.

Are families going bad? Have they become unimportant and even harmful to people's well-being? As never before, people are rethinking what is meant by "family life" and what one can expect from "family" as a social institution. One wonders whether earlier expectations are still appropriate, and if not, what we can reasonably expect modern families to offer their members. To answer this, we must explore the various ways that people live in families. In talking about families, we must be careful to consider how earlier expec-

tations of family fit together with times past. As well, we must draw contrasts between what we expect from families and what families can actually give us.

Family life is becoming more, not less, important. For this reason, people want families to succeed as much as possible. Success depends on a family's ability to provide its members with security, identity, companionship, and other important resources. A successful family life produces social, economic, and psychological well-being—even increased longevity and good health. Healthy families are productive families and they benefit society at large as well as the individual family members. Much is known about how healthy and successful families are nourished and what works to make them successful. However, old expectations and old solutions to family problems—indeed, old-fashioned family forms—do not always work as desired. In many areas, we need to find new solutions to family problems. The deeper we look into the family-decline question, the more we realize that for people in modern societies, family is both part of the problem and part of the solution.

REVIEW EXERCISES

For Discussion and Debate

1. What's better about families today than families 50 or 100 years ago?

2. What are the likely disadvantages in the reduction of childbearing in North America in the last 30 years?

3. "Demographic change explains all the important changes in family life." Agree or disagree?

4. What kinds of data could show that families are becoming more important than they were in the past?

Writing Exercises

1. "Divorce has proved an unmitigated social disaster and should be prevented at all cost."

2. "Only under special circumstances of financial need should women with young children be encouraged to work for pay."

3. "In the good old days, marriage really meant something."

4. "Today, family life is based almost entirely on choice."

Research Activities

1. Collect the most recent statistics you can on cohabitation: Who does it, for how long, and why? How often do cohabiting couples marry?

2. Read a published memoir, diary, or biography of a nineteenth-century "ordinary" woman. What was her view of family life?

3. Examine old photographs or paintings to see how they express family relationships in the nineteenth or early twentieth century.

4. Develop a short questionnaire measuring what young people expect from their future marriage and parenthood. Try out the questionnaire on at least six people and tabulate the results.

SELECTED REFERENCES

BERNARD, L. DIANE, The dark side of family preservation, *Affilia* (Summer 1992), 7, 2, 156–159.

BURGESS, ROBERT L., The family in a changing world: A prolegomenon to an evolutionary analysis, *Human Nature* (1994), 5, 2, 203–221.

CHERLIN, ANDREW, Changing family and household: Contemporary lessons from historical research, *Annual Review of Sociology* (1983), 9, 51–66.

COLEMAN, JAMES S., The rational reconstruction of society, *American Sociological Review* (February 1993), 58, 1, 1–15.

CURRIE, DAWN H., "Here comes the bride": The making of a "modern traditional" wedding in Western culture, *Journal of Comparative Family Studies* (Autumn 1993), 24, 3, 403–421.

DICKSON, LYNDA, The future of marriage and family in black America, *Journal of Black Studies* (June 1993), 23, 4, 472–491.

GILLIS, JOHN R., Ritualization of middle-class family life in nineteenth century Britain, *International Journal of Politics, Culture and Society* (Winter 1989), 3, 2, 213–235.

GUBRIUM, JABER F., and JAMES A. HOLSTEIN, *What is family?* (Mountain View, CA: Mayfield, 1990).

HALSEY, A. H., Changes in the family, *Children and Society* (1993), 7, 2, 125–136.

JALLINOJA, RIITTA, Alternative family patterns: Their lot in family sociology and in the life-worlds of ordinary people, *Innovation* (1994), 7, 1, 15–27.

LASLETT, PETER, *The world we have lost* (London: Methuen, University Paperbacks, 1971).

OKIN, SUSAN MOLLER, *Justice, gender, and the family* (New York: Basic Books, 1989).

PALERMO, GEORGE B., and DOUGLAS SIMPSON, At the roots of violence: The progressive decline and dissolution of the family, *International Journal of Offender Therapy and Comparative Criminology* (Summer 1994), 38, 2, 105–116.

POPENOE, DAVID, Family decline in the Swedish welfare state, *Public Interest* (Winter 1991), 102, 65–77.

———, Scandinavian welfare, *Society* (September–October 1994), 31, 6(212), 78–81.

RITALA-KOSKINEN, AINO, The family structures are changing—but what about the idea of the family? *Innovation* (1994), 7, 1, 41–49.

ROSEN, DAVID M., What is a family? Nature, culture, and the law, *Marriage and Family Review* (1991), 17, 1–2, 29–43.

ROSSI, ALICE S., The future in the making: Recent trends in the work-family interface, *American Journal of Orthopsychiatry* (April 1993), 63, 2, 166–176.

SCANZONI, JOHN, and WILLIAM MARSIGLIO, Wider families as primary relationships, *Marriage and Family Review* (1991), 17, 1–2, 117–133.

SMITH, DANIEL SCOTT, The curious history of theorizing about the history of the Western nuclear family, *Social Science History* (Fall 1992), 17, 3, 325–353.

———, The meanings of family and household: Change and continuity in the mirror of the American census, *Population and Development Review* (September 1992), 18, 3, 421–456.

TILLEY, LOUISE A., and JOAN W. SCOTT, *Women, work and family* (New York: Holt, Rinehart & Winston, 1978).

VINOVSKIS, MARIS A., Death and family life in the past, *Human Nature* (1990), 1, 2, 109–122.

7.2

Does a happy marriage mean finding Mr. or Ms. Right?

The issue: A high and worrisome rate of divorce and, some believe, a rejection of stable marriage in favor of cohabitation, singlehood, or sequential monogamy—none of which are supposed to be good for children. Can this trend be reversed by better mating practices?

Introduction   Our culture puts a great deal of emphasis on romantic love. We are bombarded by stories and images of love every time we turn on the television, go to the movies, or open a magazine. And our culture also places a lot of importance on the family as a source of personal meaning and happiness. These two themes come together in our culture's mating rituals. According to popular thought, people search for the best—even the perfect—mate. In marrying that mate they are supposed to come as close to married happiness as is humanly possible. This romantic marriage is presumably the best place to develop personally and raise children. Divorce results when this romantic love disappears.

Are these cultural assumptions about mating and marriage sociologically valid? Do people really mate in this way, and are successful marriages really based on finding the single best mate—Mr. or Ms. Right? If so, what makes one potential mate better than all the others? And how do people go about finding that one best mate? As usual, sociologists disagree about the answers to these interesting and important questions.

THERE IS NO MR./MS. RIGHT

From a purely mathematical standpoint, it seems impossible that there is one best mate or, if there were, that we would be able to find that person. And from a sociological standpoint, that is probably why research has found no correlation between the number of partners dated before marriage and marital satisfaction.

If marital satisfaction were really a "shopping problem"—that is, a problem of finding the best bargain among available mates—then people who had shopped more and longer would stand the best chance of finding the bargain. Think about buying a new car. You don't buy the first one you see. You study the cars available, talk to friends, visit different dealers, test-drive a lot of models—all aimed at increasing the likelihood you find the car that will please you the most. And before marrying we all do the same kinds of things: study possible mates, talk to friends, and date different people. But the survey evidence on mating collected by Martin Whyte finds that extensive "shopping" (i.e., dating) does not produce a happier marriage than less extensive shopping. And this finding suggests that the shopping metaphor is inappropriate.

There are other reasons to think so. Consider the arithmetic of the problem with the help of a few scenarios. Suppose you made a list of the five most important qualities you were looking for in a mate, say, attractive appearance, good sense of humor, intelligence, honesty, and kindness. And suppose that you required that your best possible mate score in the top 20% of the population on each of these qualities. If these qualities are uncorrelated, or independent of one another, only $(.2)(.2)(.2)(.2)(.2) = .00032$—or one person in 3125—could fill the bill. If you're even more particular and consider only people in the top 10% of the population on each of these five qualities, only one person in 100,000 could fill the bill.

But what about this "perfect mate"? Would he or she rate you in the top 20% on each of his or her own five desired dimensions? Suppose this person does. Then each of you is searching for the other; but each of you is rare and, therefore, unlikely to be found by chance. In fact, the likelihood of your wanting and finding each other by chance alone is less than $(.00032)(.00032) = 1$ in 10 million (approximately). The chances are even worse if you're both looking for someone with the same shopping list as your own. Those are not very good odds, are they? Few of us have time for 10 million dates (though film and television portray a world where everyone apparently does).

How might you deal with this shopping problem? One way would be to search systematically (not randomly) by going places and joining groups where people with the desired qualities are most likely to be found. That makes sense. You *should* go to certain places, not others, if you want to maximize the chances of meeting someone rich, or well educated, or of Italian descent, for example. However, this process is time-consuming and it is also chancy. Sure, you can increase the likelihood of meeting someone rich, but how about the chances of meeting someone honest, kind, intelligent, or funny? Would you know where to go to find lots of people with those qualities?

Another search strategy is to cast your net as widely as possible. Some people put advertisements or answer advertisements in newspapers or magazines. Some even advertise on the Internet. Advertising increases the total number of people who will come to know that you are a potential mate with particular desirable qualities; and that is an improvement on the random mate search. However, many people feel uncomfortable about adver-

tising in this way; others have difficulty evaluating the responses they receive. Some unpleasant surprises may be in store.

A more realistic strategy may be to lower your sights. Settle for Mr. or Ms. Almost-Right. So, for example, settle for a candidate who is in the top 50% of the population on all of your five desired qualities. Doing this improves your chances considerably. Now the chance of your bumping into each other is $(.5)^5(.5)^5 = 1$ in 1000 (roughly). And maybe you can even improve on this by systematic searches (i.e., joining groups) and advertising. But still, even if you get the chances of meeting Mr. or Ms. Right up to 1 in 500, you are still very unlikely to meet. And what this tells us is that *most people do not meet and marry this way.*

It seems much more conceivable that you will meet and marry someone who just happens to be nearby. You don't shop for a mate at all. Instead, often without expecting it, you fall in love with someone you like, get married, and if you're lucky, live happily ever after. Let's call that the "potluck" scenario. However plausible this scenario may seem, there is still another way to think about mating.

THERE IS A MR./MS. RIGHT

If the potluck scenario were valid, people would meet their mates by chance and settle down with them mainly because they were there and both were ready to settle down. But if that was how people mated, married people would be different from their mates as often as they were similar. In other words, marriages "made in heaven" would look like a blindfold God (or chance) had randomly selected pairs of people from a big sack of candidates.

But that isn't what the literature on mating shows. Rather, the research finds that most interpersonal attraction between people—

whether for purposes of mating or merely friendship—is based on similarity. That is to say, people like other people who are like themselves; when applied to marriage this principle of like attracting like is called *homogamy*. There is one major exception to this rule: Men and women differ from each other in a variety of ways, including what they look for in a mate. More often than not, research finds that men are looking for an attractive appearance, whereas women are looking for the ability and willingness to support a family. That aside, the research finds that marriages are usually homogamous. How is that possible, and why does it happen?

Some research shows that spousal similarity is not due to homogamy, or the initial similarity between mates before marriage. Rather, it is due to a convergence—a growing similarity—of spouses' qualities after marriage. The longer people live together, the more alike they become—in their interests, activities, views, even their appearance. This may sound perfectly dreadful to the person who is seeking independence and selfhood and hopes that marriage can be an opportunity for free growth and personal expression. This, in most instances, is not how marriage works. On the other hand, the research literature shows that homogamous marriages are happier and more satisfying than *heterogamous* marriages (in which the spouses are very dissimilar). In turn, the literature shows that marital satisfaction produces life satisfaction—an overall satisfaction with all aspects of life. A happy marriage spills over into other domains: how people view their work, for example.

But similar spouses do not have to be similar in every respect; some similarities are more important than others. It used to be said that ethnic or racial differences posed a serious problem for couples who decide to marry outside their own group. However current research does not support this view. Unless the friends and relatives of the couple create a problem, such differences don't seem to matter much. That is, they have no effect on marital satisfaction or the likelihood the couple will break up.

Educational similarity is much more important for marital satisfaction—and perhaps increasingly so. The same is true of a similarity in ages. This marks a major change in the conditions necessary for an enduring marriage. In the nineteenth and early twentieth centuries, when divorce was almost impossible, men often married women who were much younger and less educated than they were. We don't know how satisfying these marriages were, but they lasted. Today, when divorce is easy, marriages rely a lot more on spouses wanting to be with one another; and increasingly, people are marrying spouses who are similar in age and education. These factors seem to draw people together and keep them together—at least more than a common ethnicity or race. A common religion makes a difference if one or both spouses are seriously committed to their religion, its practices, and beliefs.

Much less is known about the common social, political, or sexual attitudes that draw people and keep people together, or about the personality differences that are tolerable in a successful marriage. So it is hard to say whether two insecure mates fit together better than a secure mate and an insecure one, or whether there is a problem if a Republican marries a Democrat, or even if a feminist marries a male chauvinist. Here is room for those of you still active in the mating game to do your own research.

Let's allow that some mates are probably better for you than others; in that sense, there is a Mr. or Ms. Right. More properly, there may be many Mr. or Ms. Rights, but a vastly larger number of Mr. or Ms. Wrongs.

Given the impossible shopping problem we discussed earlier, how do (did) you and your suitable mate manage to find each other? Why are homogamous marriages more likely to be satisfying, and how do they happen far beyond the realm of chance?

- *First, a geographic or locational explanation:* Most social interactions between single people—especially young single people—take place in relatively homogamous settings. Take your primary school, high school, or college. Though there are many kinds of people in each of these places, they are far more similar to you in every respect than a random sample drawn from the world at large. Most important, they are roughly the same age and at the same educational level as you are. Less important but also notable, they represent only a few of the world's ethnicities, races, social class levels, language groups, and cultures. You are far more likely to find someone very much like you sitting at the next seat in the cafeteria than, say, working in a match factory in southern India, or growing yams in the Amazon River valley. For their part, young tribal yam growers in Brazil don't stand much chance of finding homogamous—or any other—mates in the cafeterias of North American colleges.
- *Second, a clinical psychological explanation:* Perhaps people in homogamous marriages are more satisfied with each other and with life overall because satisfied people are more likely to fall in love with similarly satisfied people. Imagine two scenarios. In the first, a person who hates himself or herself (i.e., has low self-esteem) tries to escape unhappiness by marrying someone very different, who possesses all the self-esteem that that person lacks. The likely result for both mates is a tense, depressed, and disappointing heterogamous marriage. In the second scenario, two people—each of whom has high self-esteem (i.e., loves him/herself) is attracted to someone with similar, lovable qualities. The likely result: a relaxed, possibly boring, but satisfactory homogamous marriage.
- *Third, a social psychological explanation:* Perhaps more satisfied people consciously and unconsciously manufacture the appearance of homogamy. They don't want to look like or feel like losers. Beyond that, they identify with their spouse, search for and develop similarities, and even exaggerate similarities—all because this strengthens the marital bond and increases marital satisfaction. And if the marriage is indeed satisfying, the longer the spouses live together and the more interactions they have, the more similar they will become.
- *Fourth, another social psychological explanation:* People who are capable of happiness or satisfaction with life do not spend a lot of time comparing what they have with what they don't have. So people who are capable of settling for a nearby mate with whom they likely have much in common will be much happier than people who continue to shop for the perfect mate—as we have seen, an impossible goal. The result: a world split into happy homogamous couples, unhappy "still-looking" singles, and late-marrying, never-satisfied heterogamous couples.
- *Fifth and finally, a more sociological explanation:* Emile Durkheim, in his book *Suicide*, does not make a case for homogamy but he does make a case

against what he calls *anomie,* or norm-lessness, and *egoism,* or lack of integration into social groups. He argues, for example, that single and divorced people, especially men, commit suicide far more often than married people, again especially men, because marriage roots people and sets limits to their desires and aspirations. Unlimited desires are dangerous, socially and psychologically—hence, the urge to suicide. If indeed homogamous marriages are easier to achieve and maintain—that is, lower maintenance relationships—than heterogamous marriages, they will more readily bring people satisfaction.

SUMMING UP

Several important things must be said in concluding this section. One is that all marriages are homogamous to some degree and heterogamous to some degree. So we are talking about differences of degree—that is, about more and less homogamous marriages. Also, we have really looked only at socially homogamous marriages. Less is known about psychologically homogamous marriages. Possibly, the "best" marriages are homogamous in some important social respects (e.g., similarities in age and education) but heterogamous in some important psychological respects (e.g., differences in emotional volatility or expressiveness).

Furthermore, this section is not aimed at sending people out to shop for people who are clones of themselves, any more than it is aimed at sending people out to shop for mates who are vastly different. In general, we oppose the notion of there being a single Mr. or Ms. Right and the idea that "shopping" is a possible, rational, or conscious mating strategy for the majority of people.

Our point is not so much that you *shouldn't* mate by shopping; it is that most people *can't* mate by shopping, and extensive shopping does not produce better outcomes. Neither are better outcomes apparently produced by settling quickly for a nearby mate and then spending your lifetime struggling to live with that choice.

Finally, it is not at all clear that some marriages work better than others because some people have chosen more suitable mates than others. Ultimately, what makes marriage work is what happens after marriage, not before it; that is, some participants *work at* marriage. In particular, working on marital communication is enormously important.

The research shows that marital satisfaction is lower for couples with frequent disagreements and infrequent shows of affection, and this is not surprising. Typically, people who are happily married kiss frequently and fight relatively little. Anyone would rather kiss than fight. Happily married couples look on themselves as best friends and are very accepting of each other; they work hard on their marriage. They also confide in each other very often, a habit whose frequency has a positive effect on marital satisfaction. Satisfied spouses understand each other's desires for change, more often than not agree with one another, and believe that they are better understood by their spouse than by anyone else.

The *quality* of communication matters as much as the quantity. Happy marriages are marked by an ability to deescalate arguments and dispel bad feelings, not simply communicate good feelings. Frequent low-intensity interactions, such as sharing the events of the day, are the key to good marital communication. Happily married couples usually communicate in a friendly, open, relaxed, and attentive way. Unhappily married couples communicate in less varied and satisfying ways. Some research suggests that couples increase their marital satisfaction by spending leisure time together. However, shared leisure activity increases marital satisfaction only if the couple communicates satisfactorily in the course of that activity. High stress couples are rarely capable of this.

Spouses who do not like or love each other do not communicate adequately and will not experience what contemporary Western culture defines as a "happy marriage." No amount of work on their communication will change the fact that they do not like each other. At the same time, spouses who like each other should be able to develop good communication patterns, if they take the trouble to think about it and do it. Good interaction and communication patterns are what make a marriage work, no matter who you've married. So put away your shopping list.

REVIEW EXERCISES

For Discussion and Debate

1. Do you find the very idea of mating as a "shopping problem" offensive? Why or why not?

2. Do people get jobs by shopping? Is "job search" a typical or useful way of thinking about how most people end up in jobs? What are alternative explanations?

3. Do you find the very idea that mating is a "potluck" process offensive? Why or why not?

4. What kinds of differences between mates are likely to make for a happier marriage? Why do you think so?

Writing Exercises

1. "When I meet Mr. or Ms. Right, I'll know it right away."

2. "Marriages between similar people are bound to be boring."

3. "I'll never meet someone who's right for me. It's mathematically impossible."

4. "High divorce rates in our society are a direct result of our mating ideology."

Research Activities

1. Interview six males and six females in your college to find out what qualities they are looking for in a mate. How do males and females differ in this regard? How much similarity in desires do you find *within* each gender group?

2. Make your own list of the qualities you are looking for in a mate. Then collect some data—either published or obtained through interviews—that allow you to calculate how many eligible people with these qualities probably live in your community.

3. Interview six married or cohabiting couples—three who seem to be happy in their relationship and three who seem to be unhappy. By observing them interact during the interview, and by what they say about their relationship, what factors seem to differentiate one group from the other?

4. If you are in a love relationship, do a small experiment. For one week, change your behavior (i.e., improve your communication and interaction style) and see what effect, if any, it has on the quality of your relationship. If you are not in a love relationship, try this experiment with a close friend.

SELECTED REFERENCES

BUSS, DAVID M., Human mate selection, *American Scientist* (January–February 1985), 73, 1, 47–51.

CASPI, AVSHALOM, and ELLEN S. HERBENER, Continuity and change: Assortative marriage and the consistency of personality in adulthood, *Journal of Personality and Social Psychology* (February 1990), 58, 2, 250–258.

CROHAN, SUSAN E., Marital happiness and spousal consensus on beliefs about marital conflict: A longitudinal investigation, *Journal of Social and Personal Relationships* (February 1992), 9, 1, 89–102.

DEAL, JAMES E., KAREN S. WAMPLER, and CHARLES F. HALVERSON, The importance of similarity in the marital relationship, *Family Process* (December 1992), 31, 4, 369–382.

GLENN, NORVAL, Interreligious marriages in the United States: Patterns and recent trends, *Journal of Marriage and the Family* (August 1982), 44, 3, 555–566.

HALLER, MAX, Marriage, women, and social stratification: A theoretical critique, *American Journal of Sociology* (January 1981), 86, 4, 766–795.

HEATON, TIM B., and EDITH L. PRATT, The effects of religious homogamy on marital satisfaction and stability, *Journal of Family Issues* (June 1990), 11, 2, 191–207.

KALMIJN, MATTHIJS, Shifting boundaries: Trends in religious and education homogamy, *American Sociological Review* (December 1991), 56, 6, 786–800.

KRUEGER, ROBERT F., and AVSHALOM CASPI, Personality, arousal, and pleasure: A test of competing models of interpersonal attraction, *Personality and Individual Differences* (January 1993), 14, 1, 105–111.

LIAO, TIM FUTING, and GILLIAN STEVENS, Spouses, homogamy, and social networks, *Social Forces* (December 1994), 73, 2, 693–707.

LYKKEN, DAVID T., and AUKE TELLEGEN, Is human mating adventitious or the result of lawful choice? A twin study of mate selec-tion, *Journal of Personality and Social Psychology* (July 1993), 65, 1, 56–68.

MANCIE-TAYLOR, C. G., and S. G. VANDENBERG, Assortative mating for IQ and personality due to propinquity and personal preference, *Behavioral Genetics* (May 1988), 18, 3, 339–345.

MARE, ROBERT D., Five decades of educational assortative mating, *American Sociological Review* (February 1991), 56, 1, 15–32.

MCPHERSON, J. MILLER, and LYNN SMITH-LOVIN, Homophily in voluntary organizations: Status distance and the composition of face-to-face groups, *American Sociological Review* (June 1987), 52, 3, 370–379.

PAGNINI, DEANNA L., and S. PHILIP MORGAN, Intermarriage and social distance among U.S. immigrants at the turn of the century, *American Journal of Sociology* (September 1990), 96, 2, 405–432.

QIAN, ZHENCHAO, and SAMUEL H. PRESTON, Changes in American marriage, 1972 to 1987: Availability and forces of attraction by age and education, *American Sociological Review* (August 1993), 58, 4, 482–495.

RYTINA, STEPHEN, PETER M. BLAU, TERRY BLUM, and JOSEPH SCHWARTZ, Inequality and inter-marriage: A paradox of motive and con-straint, *Social Forces* (March 1988), 66, 3, 645–675.

VEENHOVEN, RUUT, The growing impact of mar-riage, *Social Indicators Research* (January 1983), 12, 1, 49–63.

WEISFELD, G. E., R. G. H. RUSSELL, C. C. WEISFELD, and P. A. Wells, Correlates of sat-isfaction in British marriages, *Ethology and Sociobiology* (March 1992), 13, 2, 125–145.

WHITE, LYNN K., Determinants of spousal interaction: Marital structure or marital hap-piness, *Journal of Marriage and the Family* (August 1983), 45, 3, 511–519.

WHYTE, MARTIN KING, Choosing mates—the American way, *Society* (March–April 1992), 29, 3(197), 71–77.

7.3
Is the modern family a danger zone?

The issue: Increasing reports of family violence. Is violence really increasing? If so, what can we do about it?

Introduction People's concern about the decline of the family grows partly out of a fear that family violence is increasing. Recent research on family (or domestic) violence has revealed various types of violence that received little attention earlier in this century—verbal abuse, physical abuse, and sexual abuse, for example. Victims of these abuses are chiefly children, wives (or female partners, in the case of cohabitation), and elderly parents.

In this section, we will not discuss *patriarchy*—the domination of women by men— as a cause of family violence, even though patriarchy is central to a feminist theory of the problem. The reason we will not discuss it is because it is not a variable; that is, it does not seem to vary much from one society to another, or over time within our own society. According to feminist theory, our society has always been patriarchal and it still is; so, with no change in that variable, patriarchy can hardly be the explanation of any perceived increases in violence against women, or against any other family members.

But is family violence increasing? Or is it a perennial family problem that is only now gaining the attention it deserves? An increase in violence would indicate that the family is in trouble. On the other hand, if family violence is age-old and just starting to get public attention, it is still a pressing problem. However, our diagnosis of the problem, and of ways to deal with it, will be different.

Normally, at this point we would begin a section titled "Yes, the family is a danger zone," followed by another section titled "No, the family is not a danger zone." But for reasons that will become apparent as you read along, this chapter is organized a little differently. Mainly, this has to do with the availability of credible information.

Sources of information The main reason people debate family violence is because relevant information is lacking. The chief sources of information about family violence fall into three main categories: clinical studies, official statistics, and random sample surveys.

Clinical studies of family violence are based on victims who become known to social work, medical, and psychiatric professionals. Usually, these victims come for help and advice voluntarily. They are probably no more than a fraction of all victims, perhaps an unrepresentative fraction. As in all clinical studies, we gain a detailed picture of their lives and, from this, a detailed picture of the conditions leading up to their abuse. But because these victims may be unrepresentative, we cannot safely infer that the causes of their abuse are general causes of family violence.

Official statistics on family violence are gathered by police, courts, hospitals, and women's shelters, among others. Though less detailed than clinical studies, these statistics provide a fuller count of the abuse victims. Here, too, we run into questions about the quality of the information. First, careful statistics on domestic violence are relatively new, dating back only a decade or two. Before then, most institutions ignored domestic violence as a rare and/or private concern. Second, even now many victims avoid becoming statistics. For example, many abused wives refuse to phone the police, or, if police are involved, refuse to press charges. Others avoid doctors, shelters, and hospitals. Abused children are even less likely to report abuse or seek help.

Victims of abuse often feel degraded and devalued, even deserving of blame for what has happened to them. Some also feel that the domestic problem can be mended if they take no formal action. They may feel that the stigma attached to filing a report or pressing charges will hurt them personally. Others fear that filing a report or pressing charges will destroy their relationship with the abuser. For all these reasons, official statistics underestimate the extent of family violence and may be biased toward recording only certain kinds of victims.

A third source of data is *random sample surveys* of victims. The last decade has seen a growing use of these surveys to measure more fully the extent of victimization. These surveys ask a random sample of adults to indicate how many times in the past year they have experienced or perpetrated any one of many domestic verbal, physical, or sexual abuses. Typically, the survey results show a widespread occurrence of domestic violence. Verbal abuse is more common than physical abuse, and minor physical abuse (e.g., slapping or kicking) more common than major physical abuse (e.g., stabbing or choking). Though some studies find abuses by women to be as common as abuses by men, the abuses by men are typically more physical than verbal, and more major than minor.

Where husbands and wives are concerned, victimization surveys show that official statistics seriously underreport the true extent of domestic violence. These findings

are also less biased than clinical studies and official statistics. As a result, we can use survey studies to paint a picture of typical victims and typical abuse conditions. However, even the results of random sample surveys cannot fully answer our question: Is family violence increasing? First, there is still self-selection in what respondents are willing to write on a questionnaire or report to an interviewer, especially when something as personal as domestic violence is concerned. Second, the survey results only go back about 10 years or so. We have no comparable data for earlier decades, let alone earlier generations or centuries. As a result, we can only use the recent data to speculate on family violence in the past.

Reformulating the question Since we cannot answer it in a direct way, let us consider three indirect ways of answering the question: Is family violence increasing?

- *Changes in reporting:* First, some believe that official reports of domestic abuse have increased in the last 20 to 30 years because people are more willing to report their victimization to authorities. If the reporting of domestic violence has increased, we need other evidence to show there has been a *true* increase in family violence.
- *Cross-national comparison:* Second, we can employ the strategy of cross-national comparison to stand in for a historical analysis. Social scientists often do this when historical evidence is lacking. To do this, one assumes that other contemporary societies are, in important ways, like our own society used to be 50 or 100 years ago. In turn, this assumes a pattern of progress from one type of society to another as a result of modernization or economic development. If today's

survey reveals that earlier or less modern societies have less domestic violence than our own, we can suppose that our society probably had less domestic violence when it was also less modern. On the other hand, if societies with different degrees of modernity vary little in their frequency of domestic violence, we have no reason to believe domestic violence in America was less (or more) common in the past.

- *Changes in causative conditions:* Finally, we can use the recent results of victim surveys to draw a "model"—or create a theory about—the conditions producing domestic violence. Then, we can ask whether these conditions were more or less common in the past. To take an example, many studies of domestic violence find that abusers drink too much, and their violent episodes are preceded by drinking. If we can show that people drink more alcohol today than they did in the past, then it is likely (other things being equal) that domestic violence is more common today than it was in the past. This approach to the question assumes that, regardless of the society or point in history, the same mix of causes produces domestic violence. What varies is the prevalence, or commonness, of these causes. This assumption may be wrong. If it is right, we can make sensible guesses as to whether family violence is increasing.

HERE'S THE (CONJECTURAL) EVIDENCE

As we noted, some people, especially critics of modern families, believe that domestic violence really is increasing. Let us examine the evidence supporting that view.

Supposed changes in reporting   Official statistics show increases in the occurrence of domestic violence. If they are *not* due to increases in the willingness to report and record abuses, then they must be true increases in occurrence. But do we have any reason to think changes in the official statistics are merely a result of increases in reporting and recording? In a word, yes. Many factors contribute to recent increases in the reporting and recording of violent incidents.

- First, we have seen the development of a broader definition of what constitutes domestic violence than in the past. Now included in this definition are verbal as well as physical acts. As well, most people now understand that even husbands can rape their wives. This acknowledges that women are *not* sexual property. One cannot assume a willingness to perform sexual acts merely on the basis of a marital relationship.
- Second, most people now understand that domestic violence is a problem. Police and medical professionals, among others, are looking out for signs of abuse. In many jurisdictions they are obliged to report any occurrences they learn about.
- Third, victims of abuse are less stigmatized than in the past. That means people, especially adult women, are less reluctant to report victimization or to come forward for help. And they are less embarrassed to do so, though they may still be frightened about the consequences.
- Finally, victims receive more help than in the past, so they are more likely to benefit by coming forward.

For all these reasons it seems that today victims are more willing to report, and authorities more willing to record, occurrences of domestic violence than in the past. We cannot assume that domestic violence is increasing on the basis of official statistics alone.

Results of cross-national comparison   However, we come to a somewhat different conclusion using cross-national statistics. Here, the key work is by the sociologist Rosemary Gartner, who analyzed homicide rates in a large number of societies at different levels of development. Gartner used homicides against women—an extreme form of gendered violence—to represent the entire range of gendered violence. Compared to statistics on other types of physical abuse, statistics on homicide are the most complete and trustworthy. Variations in homicide rates are likely to reflect variations in other types of physical abuse which are harder to measure thoroughly and consistently.

In the United States and Canada, the rates of homicides against women compared with homicides against men haven't changed much in the last few decades. But if we look at societies that are less economically developed, societies closer to the way America used to be, we see wide variations in homicide rates by sex. Gartner (1989; 1991) finds that in countries still sharply stratified by gender (e.g., Italy, Iraq, or India), where families are patriarchal, women's risk of death by homicide is much less than men's. On the other hand, women's and men's risks of death by homicide are much more equal in societies like the United States, where many women have left their traditional family and reproductive roles.

Said another way, women are safer from violence when they remain within traditional women's roles, especially within the family roles of wife and mother. When large numbers of women enter the public realm (e.g., by getting more education and working for pay),

they run a greater risk of violence. Yet, paradoxically, other research by Gartner shows that little of the violence against women occurs in the public sphere. For women, the greatest risks of violence—in this case, homicide—are found in the home. By entering the public sphere, women increase their risk of violence in the private sphere.

Still more research by Gartner shows that the circumstances leading up to violence (homicide) are particular for women, whether they are wives, cohabiting female partners, or girlfriends. Most commonly, a man murders a woman—usually a woman with whom he has been intimate—when she leaves or threatens to leave the relationship. Often, then, men also kill their children and themselves. Economically developed, modern societies make leaving a mate possible for larger numbers of women.

Gartner's research leads us to think that domestic violence does indeed increase with economic development. It is therefore conceivable that domestic violence in the United States has increased over the last 50 years as women have gained in independence. Gartner's cross-national evidence also suggests that the added risk of violence diminishes once women achieve a foothold in the public sphere and establish their intimate relationships on a more equal footing.

Supposed changes in causative conditions   What about the conditions that are today associated with wife battering, a common form of domestic violence? Have these conditions become more common, making family violence an increasing social problem?

The research on abusive husbands is voluminous and consistent. A typical abusive husband drinks too much alcohol, dominates the marital relationship, views his wife as sexual property, and acts possessive and jealous toward her. Some abusive husbands are also violent and competitive in relationships outside the home. Many grew up in homes where the father battered the mother and children. Research on marriages characterized by wife battering is voluminous and consistent. Violent marriages are preceded by violent pre-marriages, whether as violent dating or cohabiting relationships. However, some research indicates that violence is more common in cohabiting relationships and remarriages than it is in first marriages.

The typical abusive relationship is deeply troubled. Domestic violence is merely the tip of the iceberg, a symptom of marital difficulties. Multiple problems besides violence are present, and the couple has trouble coping with them all. Sometimes the problems are economic, like unemployment or a shortage of money. Sometimes too many young children, an addiction, a health problem, or the pressures of business are sources of stress. Whatever the source, this couple doesn't know how to cope with its problems. Interactions between the spouses are rare, negative, and conflictual.

Yet despite these problems and the violence they cause, the wife doesn't leave. She is emotionally or financially dependent or, for various reasons, remains committed to making the relationship work. Besides, she may have tried to leave but decided against it out of fear of more violence, even murder. So the violence continues and, in some cases, escalates. Gartner finds that, generally, a wife will only kill her husband after he has abused her repeatedly, threatened her life, and/or kept her from leaving.

Do we have reason to think these causal factors are more common today than they were 50 or 100 years ago? If so, we are justified in thinking that domestic violence is increasing.

Yes, these problems are more common   It is likely that intimate relations are stressed more today than they were in the past. Spouses, especially women, occupy more roles than they once did. Usually, both spouses have work and family responsibilities. The economic strains may also be worse today, after nearly two decades of economic and job uncertainty. Finally, today more couples cohabit and more are remarried; in both types of relationship, violence is statistically more likely than it is in a first marriage.

No, these problems are not more common   On the other hand, many other things have not changed. Feminists argue that our society has always been patriarchal and it is patriarchy—the social domination of men over women—that is at the root of the problem. It is doubtful that, compared with the past, society is more patriarchal than it once was, or even that men today drink more and are more possessive, jealous, domineering, or violent outside the home. It is also doubtful that intimate relations today are more marked by rare, negative, or conflictual interactions. We have no solid data, but it is hard to think of reasons why spousal interaction would have worsened in these ways.

SUMMING UP

Is the modern family becoming a danger zone, a place that is hazardous to your mental and physical health? We don't know. Sociology lacks hard evidence of increases or decreases in family violence. Therefore, we have to develop conjectural strategies to study the problem. These strategies tell us the following: The reporting of violent domestic incidents has increased dramatically. There is also reason to think that domestic violence is more common in a society like our own than in an earlier society like the one that existed in America a century ago. Finally, the evidence on factors contributing to domestic violence is mixed. Some evidence points to a likely increase in domestic violence, whereas other evidence points in the opposite direction.

Given the evidence available, we cannot reach a final, conclusive answer to this question. What is to be learned from this incomplete exercise? The answer is that just as *we* don't know whether domestic violence is increasing, neither does anyone else. Anyone who claims to know the answer is speaking out of turn. Anyone who criticizes modern families on the grounds that they are more violent than earlier families is talking through his hat. And anyone who proposes political actions that depend on knowing the right answer to this question should be told to think again.

There are many things we need to understand better. More research will bring us closer to answering our question: Is family violence increasing? But for the time being, we have to keep studying and admitting our uncertainty.

REVIEW EXERCISES

For Discussion and Debate

1. "Concern about family violence is excessive."

2. "There is far too much concern about domestic violence against women and not enough concern about domestic violence against men."

3. "Family violence that doesn't show up in official statistics is not to be believed."

4. "There is no one type of abusive person: All family violence is a response to stressful situations, and anyone is capable of violence."

Writing Exercises

1. "Women could avoid much domestic violence if they simply stayed in the home."

2. "Gendered violence is primarily a result of changes in marital and sexual expectations."

3. "We know from our parents that domestic violence was really less common in the past."

4. "Domestic violence is all in the eye of the beholder."

Research Activities

1. Read at least one novel from the nineteenth or early twentieth century, looking for evidence of domestic violence.

2. Devise a brief questionnaire tapping people's attitudes to the circumstances under which wife battering might be justified. Try out the questionnaire on six people and report your findings.

3. Interview at least two police officers to find out how they handle reports of domestic violence.

4. Find evidence that violence against elderly parents is, or is not, increasing.

SELECTED REFERENCES

BERK, RICHARD A., ALEC CAMPBELL, RUTH KLAP, and BRUCE WESTERN, The deterrent effect of arrest in incidents of domestic violence: A Bayesian analysis of four field experiments, *American Sociological Review* (October 1992), 57, 5, 698–708.

BROWNE, ANGELA, and KIRK R. WILLIAMS, Gender, intimacy, and lethal violence: Trends from 1976 through 1987, *Gender and Society* (March 1993), 7, 1, 78–98.

CARP, E. WAYNE, Hits and misses: The literature of family violence, *Criminal Justice Review* (Autumn 1993), 18, 2, 236–240.

EASTEAL, PATRICIA, Violence against women in the home: How far have we come? How far to go? *Family Matters* (April 1994), 37, 86–93.

ERCHAK, GERALD M., and RICHARD ROSENFELD, Societal isolation, violent norms, and gender relations: A reexamination and extension of Levinson's model of wife beating, *Cross Cultural Research* (May 1994), 28, 2, 111–133.

GARTNER, ROSEMARY, Patterns of victimization, in L. Tepperman and J. Curtis, eds., *Everyday life: A reader* (Toronto: McGraw Hill Ryerson, 1989), 138–147.

GARTNER, ROSEMARY, Family structure, welfare spending, and child homicide in developed democracies, *Journal of Marriage and the Family* (1991), 53, 231–240.

GELLES, RICHARD J., Family violence, *Annual Review of Sociology* (1985), 11, 347–367.

GORDON, LINDA, *Heroes of their own lives: The politics and history of family violence* (New York: Viking, 1988).

HUDSON, JOE, *Single parent families: Perspectives on research and policy* (Toronto: Thompson Educational Publishers, 1993).

HUTCHINGS, NANCY, Family violence, *Peace Review* (Fall 1992), 4, 3, 24–27.

JOHNSON, NORMAN, ed., *Marital violence* (London: Routledge and Kegan Paul, 1985).

LINDSEY, DUNCAN, and NICO TROCME, Have child protection efforts reduced child homicides? An examination of data from Britain and North America, *British Journal of Social Work* (December 1994), 24, 6, 715–732.

PALERMO, GEORGE B., and DOUGLAS SIMPSON, At the roots of violence: The progressive decline and dissolution of the family, *International Journal of Offender Therapy and Comparative Criminology* (Summer 1994), 38, 2, 105–116.

PLASS, PEGGY S., African American family homicide: Patterns in partner, parent, and child victimization, 1985–1987, *Journal of Black Studies* (June 1993), 23, 4, 515–538.

PLECK, ELIZABETH, *Domestic tyranny: The making of American social policy against family violence from colonial times to the present* (New York: Oxford University Press, 1987).

SAUNDERS, DANIEL G., A typology of men who batter: Three types derived from cluster analysis, *American Journal of Orthopsychiatry* (April 1992), 62, 2, 264–275.

SHEPARD, MELANIE, Predicting batterer recidivism five years after community intervention, *Journal of Family Violence* (September 1992), 7, 3, 167–178.

SHERMAN, LAWRENCE W., DOUGLAS A. SMITH, JANELL D. SCHWARTZ, and DENNIS P. ROGAN, Crime, punishment, and stake in conformity: Legal and informal control of domestic violence, *American Sociological Review* (October 1992), 57, 5, 680–690.

STITH, SANDRA M., and SARAH C. FARLEY, A predictive model of male spousal violence, *Journal of Family Violence* (June 1993), 8, 2, 183–201.

STRAUS, MURRAY A., Sociological research and social policy: The case of family violence, *Sociological Forum* (June 1992), 7, 2, 211–237.

———, Family violence, *Encyclopedia of Sociology*, ed. Edgar F. Borgatta and Marie L. Borgatta, Vol. 2 (New York: Macmillan, 1992).

WOFFORD, SHARON, DELBERT ELLIOTT MIHALIC, and SCOTT MENARD, Continuities in marital violence, *Journal of Family Violence* (September 1994), 9, 3, 195–225.

8. Work and the Economy

We all know something about **work**, whether from firsthand experience or the accounts others provide to us. Young people work at going to school, then most move on to work at a job or career. Some people work in the home, keeping house or caring for children; normally, they get no pay for doing this. Others work at home and earn an income by selling a good or service outside the home. Most of us work in large organizations—in factories or offices—to earn a living. Working together in large numbers, we create goods and services, earn a wage for ourselves, and produce a profit for the company.

The daily work routine is so common that people who break the pattern seem abnormal. No wonder so many unemployed and retired people feel like outsiders to the "real" business of society. For the same reason, many people have trouble relaxing at night, on the weekend, or on holidays. For some, stress and sleep disorders have become a constant problem. For many full-time housewives, the problem is boredom and a sense of worthlessness; they look to alcohol or antidepressants for solace. In short, as work has become more and more central to our society, it has also become a main source of stress in our lives.

In this chapter, we look at three issues related to work and the economy. First, we ask whether, given what we can predict about the future, people are still likely to have jobs as we know them in the next century. The second section examines the role of education in a recession-ridden, postindustrial economy and asks whether higher education is still a good investment. Finally, the third section looks at formal work organizations and considers whether the "tall" impersonal bureaucracies of the twentieth century are likely to survive.

8.1

Will your grandchildren have jobs to go to when they grow up?

The issue: Increasing rates of unemployment and underemployment, especially among young people and middle-aged to old people who are seeking work. Does this signal a growing trend and even more joblessness in the future?

Introduction Few professional sociologists have shown much ability to predict the future. Yet trying to predict or at least to project the future is important. (*Projections* are predictions that take current trends to their logical conclusion, as though nothing else will change.) Without predictions and projections, we cannot see the likely consequences of our present actions, and without them, we cannot make good social and economic policies. Making good predictions means taking a modest time frame—long enough to be interesting but short enough to have some hope of accuracy. A hundred years is probably too long, 5 years too short. In this section we settle for 50-plus years and ask: Will Americans still have jobs in the year 2050?

This question is important, for most people take having a job for granted. Most of our ancestors worked for pay throughout their adult lives. Our status system is based on occupational prestige. Our educational system prepares us to get, hold, and carry out jobs. Our economic system assumes we will have money to spend, which we get mainly by working for pay. Our political system assumes that most of the money we need in life will come from wages and salaries paid to us by a job.

If few people will have paid jobs in the year 2050, we will need new social, economic, political, and cultural institutions. And the year 2050 is not far off. So let's think about your children's future and ask: Will Americans still have jobs in 2050?

FEW WILL HAVE JOBS IN 2050

No crystal ball is needed to foresee the migration of American jobs. This is especially true of manufacturing jobs, although service jobs—record keeping, computer programming, and telephone services, for example—can also migrate. Already, hundreds of thousands of jobs have migrated due to economic globalization and the lowering of trade barriers.

As workers, we all want high-paying jobs, but as consumers, we all want cheap products resulting from low-paying jobs. Asked to choose between a car made by well-paid workers in America and an equally good, cheaper car made by poorly paid workers in, say, Korea, most people choose the latter. As the Korean firm sells Americans more of its cars, it hires more Korean workers, and as the American firm sells fewer cars, it lays off American workers. The result is a booming economy in Korea and a slump in industrial America.

The governments of high-wage countries have tried various strategies to reverse this trend—among them, threatening countries that enjoy a huge export surplus (like Japan), insisting on favored access to foreign markets, or slapping tariffs on the exports of trading partners (like Canada). In the long run, none of these strategies works. America's wealthy investors don't want them to work. They want the freedom to invest their capital wherever it can earn the biggest profit, inside or outside the United States. Trade barriers and trade wars interrupt the flow of capital and profit making by investors.

For these reasons, lower-paid foreign workers will continue to take manufacturing jobs away from Americans. The only way to reverse that trend is for Americans to lower their standard of living and settle for the same wages paid in, for example, Korea, Mexico, or Poland.

Technology takes jobs too Machines have been taking people's jobs since the Industrial Revolution began, over two centuries ago. That's the whole point of machines: to do a job more quickly, cheaply, and uniformly than people can do it. And on balance, the mechanization of work has benefited humanity. Today, we live better materially than even the richest people lived three centuries ago. Generally, our work is also safer, cleaner, quicker, and often more interesting than it was in the past. Machines have done away with a lot of drudgery.

The replacement of people by machines has not pleased everyone, however. In England, the Luddites began attacking machines almost as soon as they made an appearance, for Ned Ludd and his followers foresaw the loss of jobs to machines. They were ridiculed for their shortsightedness. It was clear to consumers, if not to Luddites, that mechanization was a good thing. Many people also felt that machines could go only so far. They would take away the horrible jobs and leave the interesting ones for people to do. Work life would improve as a result.

Many people still think so today. However, increasingly, computers are taking even white-collar (clerical and managerial) jobs. With the refinement of "expert systems," machines will also take professional jobs, like diagnosing illness, giving legal advice, or drafting plans for an office building. Computers in one city will control room lights, air conditioning, and heating in buildings on the other side of the continent. Perhaps your grandchildren will get their education at home, studying from a compact disk library or by interacting with a mechanized "teacher" over the Internet. This sounds exciting if you are a consumer, but menacing if you are a job holder or job seeker. But, of course, most of us are both.

In this way, entire professions are reduced to semiprofessions and paraprofessions or eliminated altogether. Already we see a surplus of engineers, architects, teachers, nurses, pharmacists, lawyers, managers—even doctors. Where these professionals are still employed, many are underemployed—working below their level of skill and training. *Proletarianization* has significantly reduced the status, salary, autonomy, and security of what used to be good jobs.

Displaced workers lack skills   Machines and global competition will not take all the jobs. Some, like haircutting, still need to be done here, where the customer is. Other jobs are too complicated to be mechanized at present. For example, programming a computer to provide toddlers with day care would be incredibly expensive; hiring live caregivers is much cheaper.

Competition will intensify for jobs that remain, for there will be more people seeking fewer jobs. The "information economy" will also provide new kinds of jobs—eventually even the job of programming a machine that cuts hair (to replace barbers) or plays with infants (to replace caregivers). However, most displaced workers will lack the education and skills needed to do these new jobs. An unemployed barber knows a lot about cutting hair, but he doesn't know how to program a machine to do it.

To judge from recent experience, the shortage of skilled people will coincide with a large number of unemployed, underskilled people, a migration of skilled people to skilled jobs overseas, and the creation of machines to do human work. In the end, it may be a machine—not an ex-barber or human programmer—that figures out how to program another machine to cut hair.

Consequences   In a future with few jobs to do, more people will rely on welfare or a guaranteed annual wage. And given the popular view of welfare (discussed in earlier chapters), more of us are likely to be poor. The underclass will grow, further increasing the gap between the unemployed poor and the employed well-to-do. Under these conditions, we can expect the economy to collapse through overproduction. There will be lots of products to buy, but no one to buy them. The economic system crashes. In the event of an economic disaster, we will see the behavior associated with demoralization: more addiction, violence, and crime, among other things. We will also see more behavior associated with rapidly rising unemployment: escapes into fantasy, political extremism, religious fanaticism, hatred of foreigners, and racism. All this happened in the 1920s and 1930s. We know how the story turns out: Right wing political movements like Nazism flourish. A bleak picture, yes. But not everyone imagines the future in this way.

MOST PEOPLE WILL STILL HAVE JOBS IN 2050

There are at least two reasons why people will still have jobs in the future. First, people will want to avert the disaster associated with a large-scale loss of work. Second, work has always changed, so it will continue to change.

Averting disaster Without a reorganization of work, capitalism will collapse. No one, especially capitalists, wants this to happen. Governments will collapse too. No one, especially politicians, wants this to happen. And without reorganization, society will collapse. No one, not even the consumers of cheap goods and services, wants this to happen. No one wants an upsurge of fanaticism and racism, crime and poverty. When it is clear that these are on the way, people will take the appropriate steps.

Work has always changed The reason for thinking so is that education and work organization have always changed to meet new needs and opportunities. Just over a century ago, most Americans farmed. With the rise of manufacturing, farmers' children became blue-collar workers. With the rise of clerical and managerial work, blue-collar children became white-collar workers. And with the rise of employment in the public sector—in government, teaching, social services, policing, and the like—white-collar children entered public service.

Each shift was wrenching, at the time. But seen in retrospect, each seems perfectly natural, almost inevitable. We cannot easily see ahead to the next major shift. But we can assume that, as in the past, the children of today's workers will flow into new kinds of work as new opportunities open up.

Expected Changes in Work

A shorter work life Over the past century people have reduced the fraction of their lives they spend at paid work. Today, people get more education and enter paid work later and retire from work earlier than their great-grandparents did. The average workday is only 7 or 8 hours, the workweek only 5 days. It takes little effort to imagine the coming of a 4-, 5-, or 6-hour workday, a 3- or 4-day workweek, and a work life that is only 30 instead of 40 or 50 years long, as it was in the past. However, it may turn out, as many are discovering today, that we have to work longer and harder when we are working at all.

More job and income sharing One way to solve the shortage of jobs is to share them. Sharing fits well with people's competing obligations: needs for more schooling, job training, and child care, among others. People with the most family obligations have led the way in job sharing and, accordingly, income sharing. Parents of young children have been the most likely to take part-time work for part-pay—sometimes willingly and sometimes not so willingly. (Critics say this is just another way of exploiting a powerless group.) What began as exceptions—part-time work and work sharing—are gradually becoming more common. As they become more common, people find them somewhat easier to take and easier to do. The same can be said of increasing numbers of people who piece together a living from a combination of part-time jobs.

Expanded nonprofit work Public sector work expanded rapidly in this century, in response to the Great Depression and World War II. People needed jobs and the state supplied them—at least to certain groups of people. For example, better public services—roads, sewers, teachers, social workers, police, and so on—were needed, and large numbers of workers were hired to provide them.

The concept of public service will expand in the foreseeable future. In the past, many community services were provided informally or voluntarily. Housewives were particularly active in this way. They provided attention, care, and assistance to the neediest and most vulnerable community members: the old, the young, the infirm, the newcomers. However, as large numbers of women have entered paid work, less community work has been done voluntarily. Critics fear the loss of community spirit and communal association.

To fix that, the state will have to pay people for community work that they once did voluntarily. Unlikely as it may seem, the state will do so because the work is important and it is not being done. So, for example, people will be paid to tutor school dropouts, take meals to shut-ins, help organize community activities, and welcome immigrants who don't speak English. The state will pay an annual income for this "nonprofit" work, expanding the nonprofit sector. Doing so will prepare us to replace welfare (or workfare) with a guaranteed annual income for everyone.

Consequences   *If* work life changes in these ways, *then* there will be important consequences. First, the relationship between work and leisure will change. Fewer hours will be spent in paid work, so people will take their leisure more seriously, spending more time visiting friends and relatives, joining voluntary associations, and just relaxing in public places. Second, communal, cooperative activities will count for more and individual, competitive activities for less. Finally, the relation between industry and schooling will change. For example, educators will make a clearer distinction between schooling for jobs and schooling for education, a topic we discuss in the next section.

The individualization of work lives   In 2050, most adults will still have jobs. However, their work lives will be much more varied than they are today. We have seen this "individualization" process in the lives of women, who entered the work force in rapidly growing numbers in the last two decades. What we notice about the lives of American women is the variety, fluidity, and idiosyncrasy of their job patterns. Compared with their mothers and husbands, women do a wider variety of jobs today. Over their work lives, they often move in and out of jobs. As we have noted, temporary, short-term, and part-time employment is increasing, especially for women. Finally, it is becoming ever harder to predict who does what kind of job. Education, marital status, parental status, and age are no longer the good predictors of a woman's job status they once were.

Following this pattern to its logical conclusion, in 2050 each person will uniquely mix education, domestic work, and paid work over a lifetime. No two patterns will be the same. Few people will have a single lifelong career. People will need to be educated, reeducated, and retrained, as the market changes its demands for job skills. This pattern of individualized work lives, already evident among millions of American women, will come to characterize the work lives of more and more American men.

With so much variety, fluidity, and idiosyncrasy, it will be hard to identify people's social class. As a result, class identification and cohesion will be even weaker than they are today. One consequence is that labor unions, which depend on stable class identification, will also be weaker than they are today.

As men's and women's lives individualize, gender lines will blur further. The life chances of women and men will be more similar than they have been. As a result, male domination will diminish and gender identities will weaken.

Educational institutions, particularly colleges and universities, will contain an even more varied and fluid mix of people. No longer primarily places for young people, they will increasingly bring together people widely experienced in the "real world" and people lacking such experience. Under these conditions, students will challenge their teachers more. Teaching will be much less the transfer of information, much more the negotiation of new ways to learn.

SUMMING UP

Will your grandchildren have jobs to go to when they grow up, say, around the middle of the twenty-first century? Probably they will, but they won't be the jobs we are familiar with. The America in 2050 we have imagined is an exciting place, and we may get there sooner than expected. But we will not get there without conflict and stress. The major changes we have described are on their way, yet no one is really ready. Delayed public responses to what appear to be personal problems—unemployment, poverty, and demoralization, among others—will hurt people. An awareness of these coming changes and the need to prepare makes the process easier. One thing is certain: The change is coming and we have to get ready.

The next section discusses education's role in this changing work world. As we have noted, formal education has an important part to play, but no one is quite certain what that role is and how to play it. Looking back to Chapter 7, we see that family life will have to change too, and it is already changing. With large numbers of women entering paid work, the connection between family life and work life is better studied and better understood than it once was. The individualization of work life reflects and promotes an individualization of family lives too. People's marriages are also more varied, fluid, and idiosyncratic than ever before. One reason people delay and minimize childbearing is to maintain flexibility in their work lives and marriages.

In conclusion, our answer to the question originally asked is that most Americans will still have jobs in 2050, but their jobs and work lives won't be familiar to us. Some readers will feel we are unduly optimistic, others that we are unduly pessimistic. Only time will tell. Already American adults are struggling as never before to create their unique work lives, family lives, and educational lives. In this, the past offers us little guidance or assurance.

REVIEW EXERCISES

For Discussion and Debate

1. "Dire predictions about the future have usually proved wrong."

2. "Eventually, machines will replace people in almost every kind of work."

3. "Work is far more important as a source of personal fulfilment than as a source of income."

4. "Work in the future is going to be mainly make-work, not necessary for society."

Writing Exercises

1. "The individualization of work is a good thing for everyone."

2. "It's getting harder to distinguish between work and leisure."

3. "Women are likely to suffer the worst consequences of change in the workplace."

4. "Where work is concerned, past experience is always a good indication of future trends."

Research Activities

1. Collect data on the individualization of work careers in your own family or among your friends.

2. Study the history of a particular job or occupation to see how that job has changed with automation.

3. Compare the history of that particular job or occupation in the United States with the history of the same job in another country to see whether changes due to automation are inevitable.

4. Read at least one set of published predictions about the future of work from 50 or more years ago. How correct have these predictions turned out to be?

SELECTED REFERENCES

BELL, DANIEL, The third technological revolution and its possible socioeconomic consequences, *Dissent* (Spring 1989), 36, 2(155), 164–176.

BLOCK, FRED, *Postindustrial possibilities: A critique of economic discourse* (Berkeley: University of California Press, 1990).

BOGENHOLD, DIETER, and UDO STABER, The decline and rise of self-employment, *Work, Employment and Society* (June 1991), 5, 2, 223–239.

BRAVERMAN, HARRY, *Labor and monopoly capital: The degradation of work in the twentieth century* (New York: Monthly Review Press, 1975).

CASTELLS, MANUEL, and YUKO AOYAMA, Paths towards the informational society: Employment structure in G-7 countries, *International Labour Review* (1994), 133, 1, 5–33.

COATES, JOSEPH F., JENNIFER JARRATT, and JOHN B. MAHAFFIE, Future work, *Futurist* (May–June 1991), 25, 3, 9–19.

GALLIE, DUNCAN, Patterns of skill change: Upskilling, deskilling or the polarization of skills, *Work, Employment and Society* (September 1991), 5, 3, 319–351.

GANS, HERBERT, From "underclass" to "undercaste": Some observations about the future of the postindustrial economy and its major victims, *International Journal of Urban and Regional Research* (September 1993), 17, 3, 327–335.

GERSHUNY, JONATHAN, Post-industrial convergence in time allocation, *Futures* (June 1993), 25, 5, 578–586.

GUILLEMARD, ANNE-MARIE, and MARTIN REIN, Comparative patterns of retirement: Recent trends in developed societies, *Annual Review of Sociology* (1993), 19, 469–503.

HEYDEBRAND, WOLF V., New organizational forms, *Work and Occupations* (August 1989), 3, 323–357.

IDE, THOMAS, and ARTHUR J. CORDELL, Automating work, *Society* (September–October 1994), 31, 6(212), 65–71.

KASARDA, JOHN D., Urban industrial transition and the underclass, *Annals of the American Academy of Political and Social Science* (January 1989), 501, 26–47.

LALIVE D'EPINAY, CHRISTIAN, Beyond the antimony: Work versus leisure? The process of cultural mutation in industrial societies during the twentieth century, *International Sociology* (December 1992), 7, 4, 397–412.

LERNER, SALLY, The future of work in North America: Good jobs, bad jobs, beyond jobs, *Futures* (March 1994), 26, 2, 185–196.

MANZA, JEFF, Postindustrial capitalism, the state, and the prospects for economic democracy, *Journal of Political and Military Sociology* (Winter 1992), 20, 2, 209–241.

MOYNIHAN, DANIEL PATRICK, Toward a postindustrial social policy, *Public Interest* (Summer 1989), 96, 16–27.

RIFKIN, JEREMY, *The end of work: The decline of the global labor force and the dawn of the post-market era* (New York: Putnam, 1995).

ROBERTS, K., S. C. CLARK, and CLAIRE WALLACE, Flexibility and individualization: A comparison of transitions into employment in England and Germany, *Sociology* (February 1994), 28, 31–54.

SWINNERTON, KENNETH A., and HOWARD WIAL, Is job stability declining in the U.S. economy? *Industrial and Labor Relations Review* (January 1995), 48, 2, 293–304.

Szafran, Robert F., Occupational growth and decline, *Sociological Spectrum* (October–December 1991), 11, 4, 379–393.

Whittaker, D. Hugh, The end of Japanese-style employment? *Work, Employment and Society* (September 1990), 4, 3, 321–347.

8.2

Is college a waste of my time?

<u>The issue</u>: *Given the problems of finding a job, many young people are coming to doubt the value of a higher education. Would they be better off getting into the job market right after high school? Or is higher education still worthwhile?*

Introduction Since you are reading this book, you must be a college student. That means you have already thought about the question, "Is higher education a good investment?" What's more, you have answered the question with a "Yes." So it may seem pointless to raise this question. On the other hand, many people have started to doubt the value of a higher education. Some students wonder whether the sacrifices they make for an education are worth it, especially when they hear about the numbers of unemployed and underemployed graduates. Taxpayers also seem to have doubts about the value of higher education, as it costs more and more. They are much less willing to invest large amounts of public money in schools than they were a generation ago. And employers are often heard to complain about the quality of graduates on the job.

So it's time for another look at this question. Is higher education still a good investment, compared with other ways you could spend your time (e.g., gaining on-the-job experience)? To answer it, we'll do more than rely on personal experience and mass media reports. As in the rest of the book, we'll look at sociological evidence.

And as with every topic we discuss, there are arguments on both sides of the issue. We begin by considering the view that today higher education is a poor investment of time and effort.

HIGHER EDUCATION IS A POOR INVESTMENT

In 1967, people graduated from college to enter a booming job market. They were the first wave of the so-called "baby boom generation" (or even "pre-boomers"), and because there were so few of them, they didn't need outstanding talent or effort to succeed. Employers were waiting to snap them up. Most industries and professions were growing, and they needed highly educated employees. Most graduates quickly got jobs at good starting salaries and in the field they had trained for. Their investment in higher education quickly paid large dividends. People who had borrowed money to finance an education were able to pay off their loans. Soon, many were able to buy a home, raise a family, and enjoy the American middle-class way of life.

Today, the picture is different. Graduates enter a slow-growing job market in which organizations have flattened to eliminate managerial staff (we discuss "flattening" in a later section), and many workers are involuntarily self-employed. Few industries or professions are growing, so few need lots of highly educated employees. People take longer to find jobs in the field they trained for, and starting salaries are often disappointing. People who borrowed money to finance an education will have trouble paying off their loans. It will be longer until they can buy a home, raise a family, and enjoy the American middle-class way of life.

These two snapshots, taken 30 years apart, describe different worlds of experience with education. The experiences of American parents and their children—a mere difference of one generation—are worlds apart: a real generation gap! How difficult it is for young people, under these circumstances, to understand the enthusiasm of their parents for higher education. How difficult it is for parents to understand their children's skepticism and doubt.

There are at least four reasons to think that today, higher education is a poorer investment than it used to be or than people believed. One is the cost of higher education; another, the declining financial return on these costs; a third, the low return in job satisfaction and finally, a low return in the form of upward social mobility.

- *Costs:* Since 1967, the costs of education have risen, with higher tuition fees at most institutions. Yet student loans have not, typically, become more generous or easier to get. And relative to wages, living costs have risen. So many recent graduates have gone into debt, even poverty, to complete their schooling. The cost of education has been high and constantly rising.
- *Financial returns:* In purely financial terms, today's college education returns a lower percentage profit on the money invested than it did a generation ago. With more competition for fewer jobs, today's graduates can

expect more unemployment, more unwanted part-time work, a lower starting salary, and lower lifetime income than graduates in 1967. The graduate in 1997 has no guarantee of work, income, or job security; though never guaranteed, these were all more certain in 1967.

- *Job satisfaction returns:* The 1997 graduate is more likely than a graduate 30 years ago to have to take work for which he or she was not trained, or work that makes little use of the graduate's skills, aptitudes, and knowledge, or even work that could be done by a high school dropout.
- *Mobility returns:* The 1967 graduate was likely to walk out of college into a job that was better than his or her parents had—a job with more security and prestige, better pay and working conditions, for example. Then, the graduate would improve his or her income and status for another 25 or so years, plateauing in the late 40s or early 50s. Today, many graduates start out worse than their parents and don't progress at all. Some people call this *underemployment*, since it underemploys the graduate's talents. Sociologist Ivar Berg, in his well-titled book *Education and Jobs: The Great Training Robbery*, concludes that many jobs that employ college graduates have little need for such highly educated personnel.

Why, then, are graduates hired? Because bosses value the "credential." A college degree tells them something about the stability and middle-class aspirations of a prospective employee and the person's ability to learn. Also, large numbers of college graduates give the organization an air of prosperity and respectability. This has nothing to do with the content of the education or the job, however. Many graduates hired for these reasons feel frustrated. Their morale and productivity suffer as a result. The problem is partly due to inflated expectations and inflamed desires. To see how this works, consider two typical cases—an engineering graduate and a sociology graduate.

The engineering graduate has spent 4 years solving hard mathematical problems. She has honed her computer skills so that she can write complicated programs in several current languages. She has done great work in graphic representation, built complex (imaginary) bridges or electrical circuits, and simulated complex chemical reactions. She loves engineering. Upon graduation, she is hired to analyze the flow of inventory at WalMart; this uses (maybe) 1% of her knowledge.

The sociology graduate has spent 4 years reading imaginative, critical analyses of societies past and present, including, five or six times over, the book you are reading right now. Among other things, he knows how to study a small group or a large organization and how to analyze survey data or evaluate historical evidence. He knows the major schools of social thought, can argue both sides of a debate on any social topic, and writes clearly and forcefully. He loves sociology. But after graduation, he will need "job training" at a graduate school, teacher's college, law school, social work school, or business school. Otherwise, he may be hired to sell educational software for a major manufacturer; this uses (maybe) 1% of his knowledge.

For both the engineering graduate and the sociology graduate, educational returns in the form of job satisfaction are low. Higher education creates expectations and desires that are beyond what most jobs can satisfy. Often, being a student is a lot more fun and a lot more challenging than working at a job.

HIGHER EDUCATION IS A GOOD INVESTMENT

You can think about the payoffs of a higher education in at least two ways: in terms of the benefits to you and the benefits to society.

Benefits to society Where society is concerned, the benefits of a higher education are clear: More education improves society.

- First, the more education people get, the more the civic culture improves. More educated people are better informed and more politically active. Thus the spread of education, especially higher education, strengthens democracy.
- Second, education brings other social changes. For example, highly educated people are more open to changes in family life. They marry later, plan their families more carefully, bear fewer children, and raise them more thoughtfully. Highly educated men also grant more equal status to their wives and children. This makes for more marital satisfaction (as we saw in an earlier chapter) and better adjusted children. Highly educated women demand, and take, higher status.
- Third, some important positions in society—jobs carrying much responsibility and reward—actually are allocated by educational attainment. More access to higher education weakens the stratification system by giving poor young people more opportunity. And this means that, to some degree, talented, hardworking, and well-informed people will gain social positions of the greatest responsibility.

Benefits to you What about your own well-being? Here, too, the evidence is clear: You will benefit from a higher education.

- First, higher education can be very satisfying. School is a challenge—a workout for your brain—and when you're in good mental shape, meeting the challenge feels pretty good. Like physical exercise, mental exercise makes you stronger. When you finish a tough assignment, you know you've accomplished something. As one student said, "School is empowering."
- Second, higher education gives you the credentials, sometimes even the contacts, you need to get a job and get ahead. If you were born rich, you don't need this; stop reading and go on to the next section. But if you weren't born rich, college education is the best investment you can make. Compared to high school graduates, let alone high school dropouts, college graduates have less unemployment, less underemployment, a higher income, more job security, and a better choice of jobs.

In the postindustrial (information) society, more jobs demand a college education. There are fewer jobs to be had in manufacturing and few new jobs for people with less than a college degree. This trend will not change direction. In the future, more and more jobs—in the professions, management, service, and sales—will require a college degree or two. (Re-read the previous section if you don't know why.) Current statistics show that the number of new jobs going to college graduates has been increasing while the number of new jobs going to less educated people has been decreasing.

WHAT KIND OF EDUCATION DO YOU NEED?

Often it seems that the evolving job market wants new employees to have specialized skills. However, sociologist Daniel Bell, in *The Coming of Post-Industrial Society*, argues otherwise. He claims that jobs of the future will require a combination of general and job-specific skills. Job-specific skills will be gained on the job, in training programs provided by the employer or in short college courses. General skills, however, will still be available only through a lengthy course of college studies. Bell believes that in the postindustrial society, knowledge and theory, not capital and labor, are the new sources of value and productivity. Everyone needs to become a good learner to survive in the new world of work, and general skills make learning job-specific skills easier.

What general skills do students gain at college, and how do they facilitate the learning of both theories and job-specific skills? General skills include literacy, cultural literacy, and learning (or cognitive) skills. Two other products of higher education—cultural capital and interpersonal skill—also fit into the category of general skills.

Literacy   Literacy no longer just means the ability to puzzle out a simple page of text. At the least, it means an ability to master large amounts of written material quickly and accurately. It also means reading between the lines—understanding what the writer has left unsaid and the reasons why. This also means understanding the writer's ideological bias, and it always means understanding the flow of an argument.

Cultural literacy   A term invented by historian E. D. Hirsch, *cultural literacy* means familiarity with a large number of common facts and references. Hirsch shows that this fact-vocabulary changes slowly, and people of all classes and ancestral backgrounds use it. To be unfamiliar with these common facts and references—to be culturally illiterate—

means trouble communicating with a large part of the population. Colleges all teach cultural literacy.

Here's a very tiny and quick informal test of your cultural literacy: Who are Lorne Tepperman and Jenny Blain? (a) U.S. figure-skating pairs champions, 1995; (b) O.J. Simpson's accountants; or (c) the authors of this book?

Learning (or cognitive) skills Primary and secondary education are mainly concerned with teaching us facts and how to use those facts. A college education, by contrast, teaches us *analysis* (the ability to break down arguments); *synthesis* (the ability to make arguments); and *evaluation* (the ability to judge the quality of competing arguments). As you can see, we practice all of those skills in this book. Analysis, synthesis, and evaluation are part of every good essay you write—whether in history, English, science, sociology, or otherwise. The grade you get on an essay depends on how well you demonstrate these skills, far more than on the facts you gather or number of books you cite.

Like good reading, good writing is an essential tool in all learning and communication. Learning to write well helps you think well, and vice versa. Valuable as a medium for communicating with others, good writing is even more valuable as a way to communicate with yourself. The process of writing tells you what you think and helps you figure out why.

Cultural capital French sociologist Pierre Bourdieu coined the term *cultural capital*. It refers to knowledge that is rarer than the facts and references possessed by the culturally literate. People who have lots of cultural capital think of themselves as "cultured" (or refined) and they value contacts with other people who are cultured. Bourdieu shows that, in France, elites spend a lot of time together showing off their cultural capital. When finished, they trust each other and can transact their business quickly and smoothly.

Colleges provide cultural capital, though not always intentionally. By watching and talking to others, students learn how to dress, talk, eat, walk, joke, date, and so on in more "worldly" ways. They can banter about Kirkegaard, or at least about Woody Allen bantering about Kirkegaard. And they can drop Kurt Cobain's lyrics into a conversation at McDonald's. But here is an interesting paradox. Knowledge like this with no job value—usually acquired for its own sake—often becomes cultural capital. Eventually, it is useful for getting ahead. But knowledge acquired for its immediate usefulness—for example, a job-related skill—is rarely cultural capital. In the long run, it is less useful for getting ahead.

Interpersonal skill One last benefit of a higher education—interpersonal skill—overlaps with cultural capital. Understanding people and communicating well (i.e., tactfully, empathetically) is important in all professional, managerial, sales, and service jobs. Since many jobs in the information economy fall into these categories, in the future interpersonal skills will be even more important in getting jobs, keeping them, and doing well. College teaches us to communicate in various ways. Generally, college programs let us make painless mistakes while learning interpersonal and communication skills. If we make them on the job, the same mistakes might hinder our future.

SUMMING UP

Is college a waste of your time? No way; but you're not surprised to hear us say that, are you? Since the authors of this book are professional educators, it cannot surprise you that we think higher education is a good investment. We admit that the obvious returns to this investment—cash payoffs immediately after graduation—are lower than they once were. In fact, they are lower than we think they ought to be and lower than Daniel Bell thinks they will be in the future. We will be able to judge better the quality of Bell's theory when the postindustrial future arrives and the evidence is in.

For the time being, arguments in favor of a higher education seem more compelling than the arguments against. If you are one of many people born without a "silver spoon in your mouth" (a term that displays a bit of ancient cultural literacy), higher education is the best investment you can make. But don't think you can simply put your money into this particular account and wait for the interest to accumulate. An investment in higher education has to be active: an ongoing series of choices, efforts, and reformulations. Given who you are and what you hope to accomplish, some educational strategies—some schools, some programs, some courses—are better than others. The best education for you may not be the best education for someone else. And remember that, often, learning for its own sake brings the biggest payoffs. If you've already forgotten why, reread the discussion on cultural capital.

REVIEW EXERCISES

For Discussion and Debate

1. "Some kinds of education are more of a waste of time than others."

2. "Financial returns to education are far less important than people make them out to be."

3. "The more educated a society becomes, the better it becomes."

4. "Cultural capital is not something you can learn at school."

Writing Exercises

1. "The interpersonal skills I have gained from going to school."

2. "What ought to be included in a measure of cultural literacy."

3. "Anyone with the right credentials can get ahead, whether he or she knows anything or not."

4. "People get far more education than they really need these days."

Research Activities

1. Examine data on the average educational achievements of people in a particular occupation. How do you account for the education "required" for this job?

2. Read the want ads in your local newspaper to determine what education is required for the most attractive jobs. Why is educational requirement often unstated?

3. Interview six recent graduates of your college to find out what job(s) they got after graduation, and whether they consider their education was a waste of time.

4. Find evidence from 100 years ago that professional job holders—doctors, lawyers, engineers—were less skillful at their job than people holding the same job today.

SELECTED REFERENCES

AINLEY, PAT, *Class and skill: Changing divisions of knowledge and labour* (London: Cassell, 1993).

BELL, DANIEL, *The coming of post-industrial society* (New York: Basic Books, 1973).

BERG, IVAR E., *Education and jobs: The great training robbery* (Boston: Beacon Press, 1971).

BIDWELL, CHARLES E., The meaning of educational attainment, *Research in Sociology of Education and Socialization* (1989), 8, 117–138.

BLAU, PETER, et al., *The American occupation structure*: Reflections after twenty-five years, *Contemporary Sociology* (September 1992), 21, 5, 596–668.

BOWLES, S., and HERBERT GINTIS, *Schooling in capitalist America* (New York: Basic Books, 1976).

COLLINS, RANDALL, *The credential society: An historical sociology of education and stratification* (New York: Academic Press, 1979).

FINKELSTEIN, MARVIN S., Combining the liberal and useful arts: Sociological skills in the global economy, *American Sociologist* (Fall 1994), 25, 20–36.

GRANFIELD, ROBERT, and THOMAS KOENIG, Learning collective eminence: Harvard law school and the social production of elite lawyers, *Sociological Quarterly* (Winter 1992), 33, 4, 503–520.

HALABY, CHARLES, Overeducation and skill mismatch, *Sociology of Education* (January 1994), 67, 1, 47–59.

HALSEY, A. H., Educational systems and the economy, *Current Sociology* (Autumn–Winter 1990), 38, 2–3, 79–101.

HAMILTON, STEPHEN F., and JANE LEVINE POWERS, Failed expectations: Working-class girls' transition from school to work, *Youth and Society* (December 1990), 22, 2, 241–262.

HUNTER, ALFRED A., and JEAN MCKENZIE LEIPER, On formal education. Skills and earnings: The role of educational certificates in earnings determination, *Canadian Journal of Sociology* (Winter 1993), 18, 1, 21–42.

KERKHOFF, ALAN C., Educational pathways to early career mobility in Great Britain, *Research in Social Stratification and Mobility* (1990), 9, 131–157.

LEWIS, DARRELL R., JAMES C. HEARN, and ERIC E. ZILBERT, Efficiency and equity effects of vocationally focused postsecondary education, *Sociology of Education* (July 1993), 66, 3, 188–205.

MONK-TURNER, ELIZABETH, The occupational achievements of community and four-year college entrants, *American Sociological Review* (October 1990), 55, 5, 719–725.

ROSENBAUM, JAMES E., TAKEHIKO KARIYA, RICK SETTERSTEN, and TONY MAIER, Market and network theories of the transition from high school to work: Their application to industrialized societies, *Annual Review of Sociology* (1990), 16, 263–299.

SAKAMOTO, ARTHUR, and MEICHU D. CHEN, Inequality and attainment in a dual labor market, *American Sociological Review* (June 1991), 56, 3, 295–308.

SMITH, CLIFTON L., and JAY W. ROJEWSKI, School-to-work transition: Alternatives for educational reform, *Youth and Society* (December 1993), 25, 2, 222–250.

SPENNER, KENNETH I., ALAN C. KERKHOFF, and THOMAS A. GLASS, Open and closed education and work systems in Great Britain, *European Sociological Review* (December 1990), 6, 3, 215–235.

STERN, DAVID, MARTIN MCMILLION, CHARLES HOPKINS, and JAMES STONE, Work experience for students in high school and college, *Youth and Society* (March 1990), 21, 3, 355–389.

TREIMAN, DONALD J., and HARRY B. G. GANZEBOOM, Cross-national comparative status-attainment research, *Research in Stratification and Mobility* (1990), 9, 105–127.

8.3

Do large organizations turn people into robots?

The issue: Alienation from work in large organizations and a lack of commitment to work, especially work in large organizations. Has the large organization, especially, the bureaucracy, outlived its usefulness?

Introduction We spend more and more of our lives dealing with large organizations—colleges, governments, hospitals, department stores, and so on. Few of our experiences with these organizations, whether as workers or customers, are pleasurable. In fact, sometimes they make us feel fake and inhuman, as if we have to become robots to fit in with the game plan.

Why is this? Because large organizations are like the cities we discussed in an earlier chapter. They all have their own cultures, and because they bring together large numbers of strangers, they need special ways of maintaining social control. So large organizations develop large bodies of rules and regulations. Often, the normative order of a large organization is so complex that no one knows all the rules. The result—a huge, powerful collection of strangers following rules that almost nobody knows—can be frightening.

It was this image of the "organization" that terrified the novelist Franz Kafka and that he captured in his surrealist novel *The Trial*. Once the terror passes, we see that large organizations are familiar and that they are everywhere. Yet large organizations of the kind we see today are still relatively new to human history and they are a major human accomplishment. At least this was the view of the sociologist Max Weber. Weber points out that bureaucracy—the most developed type of formal organization—has only reached its maturity since the nineteenth century. Its early ancestors were the Prussian army of Frederick the Great (eighteenth century) and the British civil service (nineteenth century). Like bureaucracies today, each reflected a conscious effort to raise efficiency and increase success: to gather better information, make better plans, and win more battles.

Twentieth-century research has revealed a number of weaknesses in bureaucratic organization. Many experts on management and administration have noted that other forms of organization perform better than bureaucracies in such an uncertain, rapidly changing economy as ours. So we have to consider whether large bureaucratic organizations have outlived their usefulness. As usual, there are two sides to the debate.

LARGE ORGANIZATIONS HAVE OUTLIVED THEIR USEFULNESS

People who believe that large organizations have outlived their usefulness base their view on a huge body of literature that criticizes bureaucracies. Critics note that bureaucracies cost too much, are bad places to work, maintain a distance from their clients, and adjust too slowly to changes in the environment. In short, after reaching a certain size, the inefficiencies of the organization simply exceed the benefits.

Cost too much Often, what large organizations (including bureaucracies) produce—whether goods, services, or decisions—cost a lot, since the organization producing them is so large. Some critics believe that results just as good could be achieved at a lower cost by cutting the red tape, the middle managers, and the numbers of clerks and faceless bureaucrats, as well as the fringe benefits that usually come to these folk with long-term (career) employment.

Bad workplaces Large organizations are awful places to work. Governed by a huge number of rules and long chains of command, they are both impersonal and stifling. The size and scale of a large organization are inhuman, offering people little room for variety, spontaneity, or creativity.

Distance from clients In large bureaucracies, people who make the policies are separated by many organizational levels from the front-line staff who apply these policies. This creates two problems. First, policy-makers know little about the customers or clients to whom their policies apply. Second, from the customer's (or client's) point of view, the organization seems unaware of, and unresponsive to, their needs and opinions. This unresponsiveness breeds resentment.

An added problem is the tendency of organizations to displace their goals or to forget their original purpose. So, for example, an administration forgets the policies it was originally elected to implement. Once in office, its main concern is to gain reelection, not to govern. So the Congress (or President or Parliament) turns its efforts to *appearing* to make changes, without taking the risks of actually making them.

Slow to adjust Most large organizations change slowly, despite rapid changes to their operating environment. In part, this is because of the distance between policy-makers and clients mentioned above. It is also due to the difficulty of changing a large, complicated body of rules and practices. And within any organization, some managers have a vested interest in keeping things as they are. They stand to lose if the organization changes, so they obstruct any efforts to make changes.

LARGE ORGANIZATIONS HAVE NOT OUTLIVED THEIR USEFULNESS

Many of the arguments supporting large, bureaucratic organizations are the same today as they were in Weber's time. They include the following: Bureaucracies maintain a well-trained work force, they make effective and predictable decisions, and they provide a clear, continuous flow of information.

Good staffing Bureaucracies excel in selecting and training their employees. They have elaborate rules for avoiding *nepotism* (hiring and promoting friends and relatives), and so they are open as institutional structures. They provide training to develop the staff's skills. And despite some evidence of continued discrimination against women and minorities, such practices are rarer in large, bureaucratic organizations than in any others.

Effective, predictable decisions In effect, bureaucracies are assembly lines for the production of decisions. And because of the detailed division of labor, hiring by merit, careful training, and elaborate rules that govern decision making, good decisions usually result. Bureaucratic decisions are "good" in the sense that they usually solve problems or provide services for which the organization was created. Similarly, they are "good" because they help the organization survive in an often hostile environment. In both cases, they are "good" because they are predictable and consistent with earlier practice.

A clear flow of information Good decision making depends on the flow of reliable information to the right people. To ensure this, a good organization has a clear chain of command. It is clear who gets information from whom and who gives orders to whom. In these respects, bureaucratic organizations achieve great clarity.

Clear patterns of information flow may seem trivial until you consider the possibilities for error. Imagine Joe's Plumbing Company—a small, simple organization with only three levels of authority (the boss, the master plumbers, and the apprentice plumbers) and a span of control of three (i.e., each superior controls three subordinates). Joe controls 12 workers, and the chain of command is clear:

Joe commands the master plumbers, who command the apprentice plumbers.

The path of information flow is also clear. Joe receives reports from only three employees: his master plumbers. This limits confusion and gives Joe time to find new customers and think about company policy. In turn, each master plumber receives reports from only three employees: his or her apprentice plumbers. This limits confusion and gives the masters time to deal with customers and supervise the apprentices' work. The apprentices do most of the work, and don't have time for anything else.

Even in such a small organization with 13 members, there are 78 possible *dyadic* (pairwise) communication paths. But with a clear chain of command and reporting, only a few paths are used formally. And the maximum communication distance from the bottom of the hierarchy (an apprentice plumber) to the top (Joe) is two links—the number of levels in the organization minus one.

But now let's apply the same logic to a larger organization with a similar tree-shaped communication structure. Imagine the Wootten Motor Car Company, with a span of control of six (not three) workers and nine (not three) organizational levels from top to bottom. Do the calculations and you will learn that the CEO of this company, Ted Wootten, has roughly 2 million employees. With only nine levels of organization and only six subordinates reporting to each superior, Wootten commands a work force the size of, say, Philadelphia. Yet he receives reports from only six subordinates, leaving him free to pursue new business and lunch with important people.

The maximum distance from Wootten to his lowest-level worker—the front-line of the operation—is only eight links. This means that if a problem arises on the factory floor, there will be no more than eight telephone calls before Wootten hears about it. Some

might say that's seven phone calls too many. On the other hand, only eight calls is not bad. In the Wootten Motor Car Company, the number of possible dyadic communications is 2×10^{12}, or 2000 billion—a number that is unfamiliarly, unimaginably large.

The point is that a "tall" (many-level) bureaucracy with a clear chain of command and information flow effectively controls vast numbers of workers and conveys vast amounts of information upward and downward. For its size, no other kind of organization could do better.

COULD A FLAT ORGANIZATION DO BETTER?

Some organizations have to be large. For example, automobile companies have to be larger than plumbing companies. But do large organizations also have to be "tall," and if not, what are the advantages and disadvantages of tallness?

Two organizations compared Whatever its size, any organization can be tall and narrow or flat and broad. These variations are achieved by shifting the number of levels and the span of control. So, for example, Johnny's Bread Company (with 126 employees) has a *tall* and narrow structure. There are seven levels and the span of control is two (i.e., each superior has two employees reporting). By contrast, Sarah's Bread Company (with 132 employees) has a *flat* and broad structure. There are three levels (like at Joe's Plumbing Company) but the span of control is eleven (i.e., each superior has eleven reporting employees).

Other things being equal, the better organization should produce better outcomes. So which company makes better bread? Has more satisfied employees? More satisfied customers? Higher profitability? Given two companies of roughly the same size—

Sarah's and Johnny's—which type of organization works better?

Ideally, Sarah's, with its flat and broad structure, should work better. With only three organizational levels, there are few middle managers. This means that a higher percentage of employees meets the public and bakes the bread. In turn, this should mean better service to retailers and more feedback from customers about what's liked and disliked. Finally, this should mean a faster response to criticisms and faster introduction of new products. In short, flat-and-broad Sarah's should be more responsive and adaptable than tall-and-narrow Johnny's.

The maximum communication distance in a flat organization, from the bottom level up to Sarah Brown, CEO and owner, is only two steps. (Compare this with the six steps needed to reach Johnny Smith, CEO of the competing company.) A short communication distance means less chance that incoming information will get distorted or lost as it travels from the bottom level up to the boss. So Sarah Brown gets better (i.e., more accurate and faster) information from her front-line workers than Johnny Smith does from his.

Finally and conversely, at Sarah's the maximum distance downward is also just two steps. This means less distortion of commands coming from the top. Front-line workers have a good idea what Sarah wants, since her views come to them nearly directly, not through half a dozen middle managers. And because of familiarity and nearly direct contact, employees develop a stronger loyalty to Sarah and the company. Morale is high; so is productivity.

Since the advantages of flat organization are obvious, you might wonder why all businesses (also, governments, armies, and so on) don't follow this pattern. It's because flat, broad structures are less able to supervise and control their workers than tall, narrow structures. At Sarah's, each superior has eleven workers to watch, supervise, and control. At Johnny's, each superior has only two workers to watch, supervise, and control. (Reader, you may not be able to find any real organizations where the span of control is two any more. The numbers are selected here for computational ease.) At a rough estimate, each worker receives five times as much supervision at Johnny's as at Sarah's. But is so much supervision necessary?

The conditions permitting a flat structure A flat structure—with little supervision of the workers—is fine under some conditions, especially when subordinates are highly competent, when they are highly motivated to succeed and please their boss, and when they identify with the goals of the organization. Then workers can be trusted to work hard and well, without much supervision.

The conditions that make this possible include clear rules and expectations, lots of money spent on selecting and training good workers, job security, a career ladder to reward good service, and a corporate stability that justifies workers' investment of loyalty in the company. These are all features of what economist Richard Edwards, in his book *Contested Terrain*, has called the "bureaucratic control" of workers. Under this bureaucratic system, control is internalized. Workers obey the rules without much supervision because they believe in the rules and expect obedience to pay off in future rewards. Since control is internalized, it doesn't have to be externalized in the form of close supervision. This permits a flat structure and all the benefits of a flat structure.

However, bosses who favor "lean and mean" organization have largely destroyed the possibility of flat structuring. More and more organizations have *downsized*—that is, fired and laid off workers or cut their pay and benefits. Many organizations have also eliminated job security. These acts have reduced workers' willingness to invest their loyalty in the company in return for future rewards. Workers have a hard time imagining a career there, or even—given the rise in mergers and bankruptcies—imagining that the company will survive.

SUMMING UP

Do large organizations turn people into robots? Yes, there's lots of evidence that they do, at least in the metaphorical sense that they rob people of much of their creativity, honesty, openness, and individuality. But despite the common sentiment that "small is beautiful," and the growing success of small and medium-sized businesses, there is little chance that large organizations will ever disappear. The advantages of large size—a detailed division of labor, funds for research and development, ability to control the market and wield political influence (among others)—are too important to pass up. And as long as there are large organizations, there will be bureaucracies. Despite the obvious failings, complex structures of rules, roles, and rewards get work done predictably and

efficiently. You cannot run a business with tens of thousands of employees the way you would run a family or a rock and roll band.

Having settled for large and bureaucratic organization, that leaves only one choice to make: flat or tall. Flat structures, as we have seen, avoid the worst problems we associate with large bureaucracy: unfamiliarity with and unresponsiveness to clients. However, as we have also seen, flat structures work well only under conditions of trust and stability. Lacking these, the result is increased fraud and reduced productivity.

For better or for worse, large and tall bureaucratic organizations have *not* outlived their usefulness. Conditions of uncertainty and distrust, like those prevailing today, demand tall, closely supervised structures. This means closing our eyes to the worst features of bureaucracy we noted earlier. Alternately, we can create organizations that provide job stability and stimulate corporate loyalty, like Japan's (until recently) fast-growing corporations. Flat-and-broad structuring gives organizations predictable and effective decision making without the features of bureaucracy that Kafka dreaded. The possibility exists; the choice is ours.

REVIEW EXERCISES

For Discussion and Debate

1. "The larger an organization, the more centralized decision making must be."

2. "For all their faults, bureaucracies are preferable to any other workplace."

3. "There is no reason a 'tall structure' has to be impersonal."

4. "Different cultural values would make equally large organizations work differently in different societies."

Writing Exercises

1. "Bureaucracy is likely to improve the job prospects of racial minorities and women."

2. "Places I've worked are awful, even though they're not 'tall structures.' "

3. "More women managers would make bureaucracies more humane."

4. "Large organizations are good at controlling people, not at getting things done."

Research Activities

1. Run an experiment with a dozen or more of your classmates to find out if flat organization (e.g., with a span of control of four or more) works better at accomplishing a task than a tall structure (e.g., with a span of control of two) can do.

2. If you can, spend a day in a large organization (as a participant observer), noting evidence of stress, cooperation or conflict, isolation, and communication. Keep detailed notes.

3. Read the history of one major organization to see how it changed its structure and mode of operation as it grew larger. What other factors played a part in the ways it changed?

4. Interview three or more people who hold supervisory or managerial positions in large organizations to find out what they view as the strengths and weaknesses of tall versus flat structures.

SELECTED REFERENCES

BOZEMAN, BARRY, PAMELA N. REED, and PATRICK SCOTT, Red tape and task delays in public and private organizations, *Administration and Society* (November 1992), 24, 3, 290–322.

BURKHARDT, MARLENE E., and DANIEL J. BRASS, Changing patterns or pattern of change: The effects of a change in technology on social network structure and power, *Administrative Science Quarterly* (March 1990), 35, 1, 104–127.

BURRIS, BEVERLY H., Technocratic organization and control, *Organization Studies* (1989), 10, 1, 1–22.

CARROLL, BARBARA WAKE, Systemic conservatism in North American organizations, *Organization Studies* (1990), 11, 3, 413–433.

CHANDLER, ALFRED D., JR., Corporate strategy and structure: Some current considerations, *Society* (March–April 1991), 28, 3(191), 35–38.

EDWARDS, RICHARD, *Contested terrain: The transformation of the workplace in the twentieth century* (New York: Basic Books, 1979).

HALL, RICHARD, SHANHE JIANG, KARYN LOSCOCCO, and JOHN K. ALLEN, Ownership patterns and centralization: A China and U.S. comparison, *Sociological Forum* (December 1993), 8, 4, 595–608.

HECKSCHER, CHARLES, Can business beat bureaucracy? *American Prospect* (Spring 1991), 5, 114–128.

HUBER, GEORGE P., C. CHET MILLER, and WILLIAM H. GLICK, Developing more encompassing theories about organizations: The centralization-effectiveness relationship as an example, *Organization Science* (February 1990), 1, 1, 11–40.

HUGMAN, RICHARD, and ROGER HADLEY, Involvement, motivation, and reorganization in a social services department, *Human Relations* (November 1993), 46, 11, 1319–1348.

KERBO, HAROLD R., and KEIKO NAKAO, Corporate structure and modernization: A comparative analysis of Japan and the United States, *International Review of Sociology*, new series (1991), 3, 149–173.

LANE, CHRISTEL, Industrial reorganization in Europe: Patterns of convergence and divergence in Germany, France and Britain, *Work, Employment and Society* (December 1991), 5, 4, 515–539.

LAPORTE, TODD R., and PAULA M. CONSOLINI, Working in practice but not in theory: Theoretical challenges of "high-reliability organizations," *Journal of Public Administration Research and Theory* (January 1991), 1, 1, 19–47.

LEGRAND, CARL, RYSZARD SZULKIN, and MICHAEL TAHLIN, Organizational structures and job rewards in Sweden, *Acta Sociologica* (1994), 37, 3, 231–251.

LEICHT, KEVIN T., and MICHAEL WALLACE, Work organization, business culture and job entitlement in the United States and Japan, *Comparative Social Research* (1990), 12, 177–208.

MARSH, ROBERT M., A research note: Centralization of decision-making in Japanese factories, *Organization Studies* (1992), 13, 2, 261–274.

MILLER, DANNY, Organizational configurations: Cohesion, change, and prediction, *Human Relations* (August 1990), 43, 8, 771–789.

O'Reilly, Charles A. III, Organization behavior: Where we've been where we're going, *Annual Review of Psychology* (1991), 42, 427–458.

Prechel, Harland, Economic crisis and the centralization of control over the managerial process: Corporate restructuring and neo-Fordist decision-making, *American Sociological Review* (October 1994), 59, 5, 723–745.

Sabel, Charles F., Bootstrapping reform: Rebuilding firms, the welfare state, and unions, *Politics and Society* (March 1995), 23, 1, 5–48.

Sosin, Michael R., Decentralizing the social service system: A reassessment, *Social Service Review* (December 1990), 64, 4, 617–636.

9. Education

In recent years there has been a great deal of debate about the goals and outcome of **education**. By one definition, the purpose of education is to "draw forth" or "lead out"—to stimulate a love of questioning and promote self-reliance and risk taking. Included in this is the teaching of general skills and knowledge. But since personal growth is the goal, success is to be measured differently for each student. There is no universal norm for judging success.

By another definition, education and schools are to train—to drag, direct, or discipline—their students to function effectively in the real world. This would include familiarizing the students with stock answers, promoting obedience and orderliness, and teaching in skilled activity. By this criterion, the proper outcomes of education are standardized tests and credentials to those who earn them.

Increasingly it is clear that these two ideas of education are different and possibly incompatible. They reflect different concepts of human nature and lead to different organizational strategies that may produce one outcome but rarely (if ever) both.

In this chapter we examine three issues that are related to this polarization. The first section considers whether the streaming of unequally talented children provides them all with good education and/or perpetuates social inequality. The second section asks whether boys and girls have different types of educational needs and, perhaps, the need for separate schools. Finally, the third section analyzes home schooling to determine why some parents don't want their children educated in institutions designed for that purpose.

9.1

Does school streaming keep poor people poor?

The issue: *Whether public schools, which many hoped would reduce inequality in modern societies, actually perpetuate and legitimate inequality. Some believe that one way schools may do this is by segregating the so-called "better" students from the "worse" ones.*

Introduction In public school systems in the United States and Canada, a debate has raged over whether students, particularly at the secondary level (junior and senior high school), should be "streamed," or "tracked" into classes according to their abilities. This is part of a larger debate around *ability grouping.*

There are three main types of ability grouping. Under the first, very common in elementary classrooms, students may be divided according to *differential ability* to handle materials: for instance, as "slow," "average," and "advanced" readers. Often, especially in elementary school, such groupings are disguised by the use of animal or bird names, on the principle that students should not be discouraged by being told they are in the slow group. However, students who have experienced this during their schooling say that they generally knew which group was which, so that if slow readers picked the name "cheetahs" a ripple of unkind laughter would go around the class.

The second type of grouping is termed *setting* in Britain. Different classes exist in each subject, and students are assigned to classes that cover the ground more or less rapidly, according to ability in that particular subject. This system is frequently found in North American high schools, where classes may be demarcated as "honors," "academic," or "general"—the level often indicated by the registration number assigned to the class. This class-by-class grouping is often referred to as "streaming." So, confusingly, is the third level.

In the third level—variously referred to as *tracking* or *streaming*—students move as a block from one class to another, so that they take all classes on a "general," "vocational," or "academic" level. In parts of Britain, particularly England, until the mid-1970s, they were not only on different streams but also attended different schools. Reading the British literature on this subject can therefore be confusing, because sometimes streaming refers to this older system of separate schools rather than to a system of tracks within one school. During the 1970s, there was a move toward comprehensive schooling, whereby students would attend one high school (similar to a North American combined junior and senior high), which might either include several streams or have classes or sets at different levels within each subject.

The following discussion will focus on the second and third levels of ability grouping, including both formal streaming and class-by-class streaming. On the one hand, proponents of types of ability grouping consider that, when children and young adults are carefully selected for streams or classes, each child can receive instruction at the level she or he requires. On the other, opponents claim that ability grouping, particularly tracking or streaming, perpetuates inequality by disadvantaging a majority of students, particularly those from poor and/or minority backgrounds, by the provision of different materials to different streams and by labeling students according to their streams.

STREAMING DOES NOT PERPETUATE INEQUALITY

Rather than perpetuating inequality, tracking or streaming and other forms of ability grouping can act to reduce it by providing children with an education that is suited to their abilities and thus allowing them to achieve to their maximum potential. In the past there was an association between tracking and race or social class. We can avoid this by means of a common curriculum throughout much of elementary school and providing remedial education where required to "level the playing field." When students reach secondary school or the upper elementary grades, they will develop differences in interest, skill, and ability, and it is right that they should have access to a system that will allow them to develop their individual talents to the fullest extent possible.

Results of intelligence and achievement tests and examination scores show clearly that not all children are the same in ability or performance. If all children have to deal with the same curriculum and the same teacher, all will suffer. In mixed classes, bright children become bored with the slow pace of instruction and progress of the class. Less able children fall behind, often irretrievably, becoming discouraged. Those in the middle will find that the teacher is busy with children requiring instruction to catch up, or with troublemakers, who are discouraged or bored. In uniform teaching, there are no winners.

Streaming and provision of enrichment classes in certain subjects mean that the bright students can be given material more suited to retaining their interest. When test scores from streamed and unstreamed classes are compared, controlling for ability or intelligence, bright students in streamed classes do better, according to findings by James Kulik and Chen-Jin C. Kulik.

The advantages of streaming have been known for years; indeed they were summarized as long ago as 1931 by Turney, and repeated in 1990 by Robert Slavin as:

- Streaming permits pupils to make progress commensurate with their abilities.
- It makes possible an adaptation of instructional technique to the needs of the group.
- It reduces failures.
- It helps to maintain interest and incentive, because bright students are not bored by the sluggish participation of the dull.
- Slower pupils participate more when not eclipsed by those much brighter.
- It makes teaching easier.
- It makes possible individual instruction to small slow groups.

All of these points, when investigated by present-day researchers, still hold. Teaching a class of mixed-ability students is regarded by many teachers as a nightmare. Bright children from any race or class deserve to be challenged with materials that will broaden their horizons and extend their abilities. This is not possible within mixed-ability class-

rooms. Therefore, not only does tracking not perpetuate inequality; if used properly it will actively reduce it.

STREAMING DOES PERPETUATE INEQUALITY

Not only have the arguments *for* tracking been current for some 67 years, so have those *against* it, although recently a few more have been added to the list. Robert Slavin, an avid opponent of tracking, lists both sets of arguments, as summarized by Turney in 1931. Here are the arguments against:

- Slow pupils need the presence of the able students to stimulate them and encourage them.
- A stigma is attached to low sections or classes, operating to discourage the pupils in these sections.
- Teachers are unable, or do not have time, to differentiate the work for different levels of ability. Often high-ability classes or groups simply receive more work, rather than a different level of work.
- Teachers object to the slower groups and do not want to teach them.

Some of these arguments have been confirmed and some refuted by research over the years. All, however, continue to be made. There are two recent additions to the list of disadvantages, and we will come to them shortly. But first, points three and four above require examination.

Often higher ability classes or groups simply receive more work rather than a different level of work, and the dislike of dealing with slow classes may contribute further to a lack of preparation of material for them. Where material for "slow" classes is available from publishers, it may be of such a low level that the students find it insulting and patronizing, further reducing any incentive to study.

The two points Slavin would add are:

- Ability grouping discriminates against minority and lower-class students.
- Low-stream students receive instruction that is slower paced and of lower quality than that available to higher-track students.

This last point bears expansion. The instruction of low-stream students is not only slower paced than, but indeed different in kind from, instruction aimed at college-entry-stream students. Students not only cover less material but do so with less concern for detailed analysis, including social analysis. Low-stream students, who are often disproportionately poor and from minority groups, leave school with fewer skills needed to obtain employment, with less knowledge of how their society works, and with less faith in their ability to effect changes in their own lives.

Students in low streams appear to spend more time off-task, and teachers spend more in trying to maintain order. Less material is covered, and it becomes rare to impossible for students to move up into a more academic stream, as they are permanently behind. Low-stream classes lead to other low-stream classes, and students who leave school with a "vocational" qualification are likely to find that employers regard this as equivalent to failure.

Conventional wisdom has it that while heterogeneity or homogeneity of grouping may have little effect on "average" students, the ends of the ability spectrum—very high or very low achievers—nevertheless benefit from homogenous group placement. While the Kuliks did claim a benefit for high achievers in streaming, other studies do not necessarily bear this out. Slavin found no benefit for high achievers. Neither the Kuliks nor Slavin found that low achievers bene-

fited in terms of outcome measures. Referring to very low mathematical-ability students, Canadian researcher Lorna Earl found homogeneous low-stream placement a hindrance.

> A study by Peterson of heterogeneous grouping considered the premise that students of low ability will achieve better when provided with additional opportunities for learning. The study demonstrated that remedial math students placed in an accelerated program made significantly more progress in areas of problem solving, math concepts, and computational skills compared with students in a remedial class. Perhaps these students had more opportunities for learning compared with their low-stream counterparts (Earl, 1989, 298).

There can be many reasons why students find themselves in low-stream classes. Sometimes it is not due to any lack of ability but rather to lack of interest in school and to active resistance toward it. Students are capable of summing up the school system and finding it lacking in what they need. Often working-class and minority youth, if asked, will explain that the school system has little that they want, particularly if it labels them as failures and puts them into low streams with uninteresting material. Where subjects that are relevant to students' own interests and communities are introduced—such as black history and community studies, labor history, or the math required to plan and operate a community market garden—teachers report not only that students are more interested but also that they start to perform at higher ability levels.

Some researchers have examined ways that students are allotted to streams. Their findings are worrying. Low streams are strongly associated with minority or lower-class youth. Gender is less evidently associated with placement overall, but girls who are not specifically identified as academically gifted may find themselves counseled at the high school level to take predominantly vocational or clerical courses. Teachers and counselors make assumptions about the needs of students, and often race, class, and gender are central to these assumptions.

Other researchers have been examining the nature of the counseling and choice/selection process operating at the high school level and its ambiguities and uncertainties. Michael Garet and Brian Delany write of "multiple, loosely connected standard operating procedures at the schools" that may result in discriminatory placement of students, not through deliberate intent but through myriad small decisions, adjustments, and tinkerings, driven by the ever-present need to create a manageable school timetable. Students may be assigned to classes in a sort of bureaucratic muddle of administrators and teachers trying to make do, fix schedules, and make ends meet. In the process, assumptions based on gender, race, class, and perceived future needs of the students easily creep into the decision making in ways that are difficult to uncover.

The rationale for streaming assumes that students can be categorized, based on dramatically different learning needs and learning capabilities. Yet within a particular stream there may be a very wide range of interests or talents and abilities, or even measured intelligence levels. A junior high extended achievement stream, for instance, may include students with measured IQs of from around 115 to upwards of 160—the measurement reflecting how well each student did on a test on one specific day. Yet streaming tends to encourage a view of these children as essentially similar to each other and essentially different from the "regular" children who scored 105 or 110 on the IQ test.

SUMMING UP

All in all, it is hard to see how streaming is justified, and easy to see how it can connect with the perpetuation of inequality. We can find little justification for streaming other than this one: that many teachers like it and say it helps them with class preparation and management. That is, teachers prefer to teach high- or middle-stream classes. In much of the literature, low-ability streams are associated with resistance to school, and teachers may seek to avoid such streams because they are discouraging to teach, hard to control, and even physically threatening. Destreaming is seen as having the benefit that "resistors" are no longer grouped together, but spread out, one or two to a class.

There has been some support for the view that destreaming not only can spread out potential troublemakers but also reduce the extent to which student attitudes become polarized as pro- or antischool. Destreaming has therefore been proposed as a partial antidote to antischool attitudes and to their ultimate expression with low-stream students—dropping out. A further component may be an ending of the social promotion of students from one grade to another, so that, for instance, students would expect either to achieve certain minimum requirements or to repeat a year.

Robert Upshaw, a social activist and member of the Black Learners Education Committee in Halifax, Nova Scotia, is strongly opposed to both streaming and social promotion. He sees many black youth going through the school system, which they find inimical to their interests, with the intention of leaving as early as possible and, therefore, with minimum qualifications.

Attention to what is meant by destreaming is necessary if it is to meet with teachers' approval. Robert Slavin points to a difficulty in reconciling destreaming with traditional teaching if students in a class are perceived as essentially similar to each other in ability and interests. Instead, he promotes cooperative teaching, in which students and teachers can draw on the strengths and talents of individual students, to the benefit of both individual and group.

REVIEW EXERCISES

For Discussion and Debate

1. "Athletics is the only way young black men can get ahead."
2. "Tracking is the only way people can be taught what they need to know for their jobs."
3. "These days, anybody can get a good education if they'll only put their mind to it."
4. "Tracking is the way that schools maintain social class divisions."

Writing Exercises

1. Associations you have observed between streaming and ethnicity.
2. "My own experience: Selecting classes in high school."
3. "When my children are in school, they'll be in the top stream."
4. "Enriched programs should be for everyone."

Research Activities

1. Interview six of your friends. How many of them were in streamed classes in high school or junior high? How were their streams selected? Are they in favor of streaming?
2. Interview six people of the same generation as your parents. How many of them were in streamed classes in high school or junior high? How were their streams selected? Are they in favor of streaming? Do they give the same reasons as people who were more recently in school?
3. Search the World Wide Web for arguments for or against tracking. What arguments are presented, and whose views are represented?
4. Work with a group of four to six students. List the courses each of you took in high school and the decisions represented by these course choices. How many choices were career-oriented? What differences in advice were you given? What have you learned from this exercise?

SELECTED REFERENCES

CONNELL, R. W., et al., *Making the difference: Schools, families and social division* (Sydney: Allen and Unwin, 1982).

CONTENTA, SANDRO, *Rituals of failure* (Toronto: Between the Lines, 1993).

DEI, GEORGE J. SEFA, *Anti-racism education: Theory and practice* (Halifax, NS: Fernwood, 1996).

DELPIT, LISA D., The silenced dialogue: Power and pedagogy in educating other people's children, *Harvard Educational Review* (August 1988), 58, 3, 280–298.

DENTI, LOUIS G., Walling students with disabilities out of the mainstream: Revealing the illusions of inclusion, *International Journal of Group Tensions* (Spring 1994), 24, 1, 69–78.

EARL, LORNA, *Streaming: Interpreting the literature* (Scarborough, ON: Scarborough Board of Education, 1989).

Francis, Kim C., Robert J. Bell, and Martha J. Bell, Language diversity in the university: Aspects of remediation, open admissions and multiculturalism, *Education* (Summer 1994), 114, 4, 525–529.

Gamoran, Adam, Alternative uses of ability grouping in secondary schools: Can we bring high-quality instruction to low-ability classes? *American Journal of Education* (November 1993), 102, 1, 1–22.

Garet, Michael, and Brian Delaney, Students, courses, and stratification, *Sociology of Education* (1988), 61, 2, 61–77.

Grey, Mark A., Immigrant students in the heartland: Ethnic relations in a Garden City, Kansas, high school, *Urban Anthropology* (Winter 1990), 19, 4, 409–427.

Hallinan, Maureen, School differences in tracking effects on achievement, *Social Forces* (March 1994), 72, 3, 799–820.

———, and Jeannie Oakes, Tracking: From theory to practice, *Sociology of Education* (April 1994), 67, 2, 79–84.

Howe, Kenneth R., Equality of educational opportunity and the criterion of equal educational worth, *Studies in Philosophy and Education* (1993), 11, 4, 329–337.

Kulik, James A., and Chen-Jin C. Kulik, Meta-analysis in education, *International Journal of Education Research* (1989), 13, 3, 221–340.

Madaus, George F., A technological and historical consideration of equity issues associated with proposals to change the nation's testing policy, *Harvard Educational Review* (Spring 1994), 64, 1, 76–95.

Oakes, Jeannie, *Keeping track: How schools structure inequality* (New Haven, CT: Yale University Press, 1985).

Reynolds, Arthur J., Roger P. Weissberg, and Wesley J. Kasprow, Prediction of early social and academic adjustment of children from the inner city, *American Journal of Community Psychology* (October 1992), 20, 5, 599–624.

Riddell, Sheila, The politics of disability: School experience, *British Journal of Sociology of Education* (December 1993), 14, 4, 445–455.

———, George O. B. Thomson, and Sarah Dyer, A key informant approach to the study of local policy-making in the field of special educational needs, *European Journal of Special Needs Education* (March 1992), 7, 1, 47–62.

Slavin, Robert E., *Achievement effects of ability grouping in secondary schools: A best evidence analysis* (Madison, WI: National Center on Effective Secondary Schools, Wisconsin Center for Education Research, 1990).

Thomson, George O. B., J. Ward, and L. Gow, The education of children with special needs: A cross-cultural perspective, *European Journal of Special Needs Education* (September 1988), 3, 3, 125–137.

Tomlinson, Sally, Why Johnny can't read: Critical theory and special education, *European Journal of Special Needs Education* (March 1988), 3, 1, 45–58.

Upshaw, Robert, personal communication. Also see Racism in Nova Scotia schools: Interviews with Tanya Hudson, Robert Upshaw, and Evangeline Cain Grant, by Ruth Gamberg and Ann Manicom, *Our Schools Our Selves* (1991), 3, 3, 20–56.

9.2

Do co-ed schools make sense?

The issue: Whether schools are educating girls adequately, given gender-based differences in school and in adult experiences outside the school. Would girls (and maybe even boys) be better off if they were educated separately?

Introduction The debate over whether boys and girls, or men and women, should attend different schools has changed greatly since it first became an issue. In the nineteenth and early twentieth centuries, different needs were assumed. Concepts of what boys and men were and how they should behave were very different from concepts applying to girls and women.

During the twentieth century, the understanding of "different needs" became problematic, as the provision of different schooling to girls and boys could be seen as responsible for girls' lack of qualifications in subjects they needed for obtaining good jobs, and hence for the ghettoization of women in fields for which math and science were not requirements.

Recently, the debate has been reopened with claims that boys and girls have different ways of processing the information given them about the world. Some researchers say this is because of different socialization received by girls and boys, almost from their first day of life, when proud relatives say of an infant girl, "Isn't she cute?" and of a boy, "Isn't he strong?" Others look to evidence of different brain organization, claiming that males are more left-brained and given to lineal thinking and problem solving, whereas females are more able to link the processing from each brain hemisphere and engage in lateral or global thinking. It is, however, unclear to what extent brain organization is linked with socialization.

BOYS AND GIRLS NEED THE SAME KIND OF SCHOOLING

In the past many people have considered that girls and boys indeed did have different educational needs. They would lead very different lives after school days were at an end. Men would be the breadwinners, engaging in a variety of jobs commensurate with their individual talents and skills to earn money for their households. Women, by contrast, would be destined for a life of caring for home and family. Much educational theory, therefore, focused on the need to provide different education for girls and for boys.

Boys would take courses such as drafting or physics, math or machining, whereas girls were taught the skills associated with homemaking. Of course, both would require instruction in the use of language and to some extent in history, although the details of political life were not thought necessary for girls to know. Some girls who were identified as extremely gifted might be interested in pursuing academic studies further but, thought some people in the nineteenth century, there were some subjects such as math or physics that would overtax their brains. This might, if the girls studied too hard, cause them to become biologically unfit for motherhood. Presumably, too much thinking would divert needed oxygen to their brains instead of their reproductive organs. Further, there were subjects such as biology which it might not be "proper" for girls to study.

During the twentieth century, most of these ideas about girls and boys having different requirements gradually disappeared. By the mid-twentieth century, girls studied almost the same curriculum as boys. Math, science, languages, history, and geography were seen as equally appropriate for both and equally required for both. Only in the areas of physical education and home economics versus shop did differences persist. There came to be a recognition that many women, like many men, had a need to study subjects they would later use in their employment, and also that both women and men required the same kinds of information about society and its workings in order to be good citizens. In the past few decades, many school districts have made new rulings on home economics and shop. Usually, now both girls and boys study cooking, sewing, leatherwork, and woodwork. This makes sense in terms of the work they will be expected to do, both inside and outside the home, when they leave school.

Girls leaving school today go into a competitive work world, where they will have to demonstrate skills in order to obtain a good job. Some will undertake traditionally female jobs such as secretary, nurse, or elementary school teacher. Others may be pilots, plumbers, police officers, or politicians, dancers or designers, machinists or musicians, editors or engineers. The range of jobs women do is as varied as that of men. Almost all occupations require further training after school, either through university or community college education or through courses run within the workplace. Many young women and young men will leave school not knowing what their profession will be, and they need to keep their options open during their school years, with some basis in sciences as well as arts, in order to be eligible for entry into good post-secondary programs.

Even where women engage in traditional occupations, they require a thorough grounding in science and technology. Secretarial work is highly computerized, and many secretaries require a good working knowledge of computers. Elementary school teachers have to teach math and sciences, so they must themselves be comfortable with these subjects. Nursing is coming to be viewed increasingly as a profession requiring study in the sciences.

Education not only prepares people for the workplace but enables them to add value to their lives within their homes and through recreation activities. More and more, women and men are undertaking the same tasks in their home. A single-parent father has to be able to cook, wash clothes, and take care of a home; so does a father in a two-parent home whose wife works long hours as a nurse or a reporter. Many women do home repairs.

As citizens women and men are equally part of their country's political process, so they need to have the same information and the same amount of access to gain skills in how to use this information, to assist their communities and their families. Both require knowledge of the law and legal procedures, of politics, elections and voting, of the procedures for running for office, so that they may become responsible citizens of their country.

BOYS AND GIRLS HAVE DIFFERENT EDUCATIONAL NEEDS

There are many reasons to think that boys and girls may need different kinds of schooling. First, some have observed that males and females appear to have different aptitudes, or at least different average mixes of aptitudes. Whether these differences are inborn, or a result of family childhood socialization, or both, is hard to say. But it has often been noted that females are less likely to study mathematics, science, or computers at any level of the co-ed school system.

What is also known from research is that females do better in these subjects—show more interest and achieve higher grades, for example—in all-girl schools, particularly where teachers strongly encourage such achievement by girls. Also, some research suggests that a key method of getting girls interested in these subjects is by emphasizing communication and creative problem solving, rather than the theoretical or technical aspects of the topic. Treating girls as if they had the same interests as boys doesn't work.

What this reminds us of is that people with different aptitudes and interests require different kinds of instruction. If boys and girls actually have different aptitudes and interests, they may do best at schools that aim at working with these particular "givens."

Second, we should bear in mind that both boys and girls bring different childhood experiences into the classroom; this is the backdrop against which teaching must take place. In our society, media images frequently demean females, and parents treat their sons and daughters differently; and in these and other ways, boys and girls develop different aspirations. Though girls normally get higher grades than boys—at least in primary school—typically, their self-esteem, self-confidence, and academic self-assessment are all lower than boys.' By the time they enter high school (and adolescence)—when plans are to be made and aspirations and confidence need to be highest—girls often set lower goals for themselves than do boys of the same intellectual ability. They need extra encouragement from teachers and parents to strengthen their self-esteem.

Perhaps they receive more encouragement in schools specifically aimed at meeting girls' needs. Research shows that girls in girls-only schools—whether secondary or college—are more likely to have higher academic achievement, participate more in school activities, enroll in more science courses, find female faculty role models, consider college supportive, and gain in self-esteem. No wonder the women-only "Seven Sisters" colleges have produced higher female achievers than the best coeducational colleges in the United States.

Beyond this, girls have different lives to prepare for, and this may be another reason why they need different and separate schooling—not different in terms of the subjects taught but in how to apply them and how to make their way through the world. These different lives may include domestic inequality, domestic violence, and workplace discrimination—all situations where awareness of a problem can help women combat it.

Girls need counseling on what to expect from an adult women's life, mentors and models of success in adulthood, strategies for coping with uniquely female concerns, and, at the least, planning to meet them with some awareness of what is in store. For example, research shows that in a traditional male career such as medicine or engineering, women run a higher risk of not marrying, having no children if they do marry, and divorcing if they marry. This is the kind of information everyone needs to have, particularly high-achieving girls. This is more likely to be discussed in a girls-only school than in a co-ed school. Let's now look at some of these issues in greater depth.

The co-ed playing field is not level   Very often in our society, women and men do the same jobs and compete for the same rewards. Therefore they require instruction in the same or similar areas. However, they are often unable to compete on equal grounds when they leave school or even during the school years. From this standpoint, provision of different kinds of *teaching* (as opposed to different kinds of *subjects*) might help to level the playing field. When girls and boys enter school, they come with five or six years of knowledge about women and men. Throughout their school years, they see men and women portrayed all around them. Very often these portrayals, especially outside school but sometimes in it also, emphasize men and women as different: in physical strength, in attitudes and preferences, in abilities, and in the type of brain they have. Scientists and educators debate and critique these portrayals, some finding them very inaccurate; however, they are what school-age children in North American society are exposed to on a daily basis.

In school, girls and boys are presented with the same subjects, in the same way. Sometimes an exception is made for physical education where, for instance, girls are told they should not expect to be able to compete with boys, despite, at elementary level, often being bigger and stronger. Yet in math class, science class, English, and music classes, they are expected to compete. Society tells girls and boys that they have different brains and different abilities "naturally," but the school subjects do not deal with these assumed "differences."

Yet some teachers have observed differences in the ways girls and boys relate to instruction. Boys, they say, demand more of the teacher's attention, talk more and make more noise, and are swifter to raise their hands to answer questions, sometimes raising them before they have formulated answers or even before they are sure they can construct an answer. Girls, they say, take a little longer to think of an answer before raising their hands, and therefore appear more passive in the classroom.

Taking a more critical approach, we can say that girls may be under some pressure to be seen to do less well than boys in the classroom, particularly when the traditionally male subjects of math and science are concerned. Girls may also be uncertain as to whether they actually can do well in these subjects, particularly if they have always learned to associate math and science with male employment. Some girls may assume that they cannot succeed in science, and so do not try, dropping these subjects at the earliest possible stages.

Similarly, some boys may assume that a knowledge of words and literature is something girls are born with and something they should not attempt to gain for themselves, thus becoming less than expert communicators. Indeed, they may consider it demeaning or sissy to attempt to excel in a "female" subject.

Research indicates that teachers may expect more of boys in the classroom, particularly when the stereotypically masculine subjects of math and science are being studied. Dale Spender and others have indicated that their research shows teachers are more likely to give boys clues or hints on how to do problems and praise them when they then figure them out. Teachers are also more likely to respond to boys' hand-raising or calling out in class and to select them to answer questions. Girls raising their hands are more likely to be overlooked.

Research also indicates, however, that when teaching techniques that are more in line with girls' learning strategies are used, the girls do well in traditionally male subjects. Seymour Papert, inventor of the computer language Logo, long ago pointed out that math was typically taught through a combination of lectures and individual problem solving. When math was presented as a group activity, providing a forum for interaction and discussion of problems, girls did well and became more involved with the subject.

Thus it appears that when attempts are made to treat girls and boys as the same, the attempts often fail. However when teaching techniques take into account differences in ways that girls and boys have learned to position themselves with respect to the subjects, the classroom, and other people within it, the attempts may succeed.

Equality in the classroom There are several ways in which equality in schooling can be viewed. Should educators aim for equality of opportunity, in which every child is given the same chance to enter school and to study subjects such as math, languages, and science? If so, what of boys who think they should avoid studying languages or music and girls who do not feel they should sign up for math courses?

Should educators aim, rather, for equality of treatment, so that girls and boys receive encouragement to enter nontraditional fields, but once in them must experience the subject in the same way? If so, what of the girls who feel insecure about answering math questions in a traditional classroom, in front of the boys who consider they know it all? Or those who enjoy science but are made uncomfortable by teaching that emphasizes science as an individual, usually male, enterprise? Or what of the boys who worry in case their peers laugh at them for displaying their poetic skills?

Should educators focus instead on equality of outcome? Here we assume that a goal of education is a society in which both women and men are skilled communicators, with a knowledge of science, math, music, and other disciplines that enables them to choose freely their occupations or further courses of study. If girls and boys enter school already positioned differently with respect to the subjects, and with different attitudes toward themselves and their own abilities to develop skills, it follows that they may require different forms of teaching. If so, then the educational needs of girls and boys are indeed different, and these differences must be taken into account by educators.

SUMMING UP

Do co-ed schools make sense? We favor the affirmative position here, but have some doubts about it. There seems to be some evidence that girls who study math, a traditionally male subject, separately from the boys are more likely to excel at it than girls in a coeducational classroom. However, it can be questioned whether this is a question of different educational needs or of the same educational needs, which for both groups include teachers who believe students capable and also classmates who do not poke fun or seek to interrupt their study.

It does, however, seem that girls may require more encouragement in some sub-jects—those traditionally considered male—and that boys may similarly require encouragement in studying the arts and music. Further, if both girls and boys are able to discuss and critique the assumptions that are made about them and their abilities, it seems that both will benefit.

We find it essential that girls receive instruction on dealing with adulthood in a sexist society. There is merit to having at least some critical discussions be female-only, so that girls and young women can speak their minds and search for their solutions. It is also essential that boys debate this material, so that they do not grow up to be perpetrators of another generation of sexism.

Some other considerations should also be raised. Is it fair or appropriate to consider that boys, as a group, and girls, as a group, have different educational needs? Or is there another position here, which states that various groups of children will have needs that should be served by responsible educators, but that membership in these groups will not always be based on gender? While it may be the case that girls as a group receive different messages about their capabilities than do boys, educators cannot therefore assume that all girls will act on their information in the same way. Or are these well-meaning educators sending yet another message to children and young adults about gender as the most salient factor in their educational and professional lives?

It seems to us that sensitive, critical attention to the educational needs of girls and boys is required, together with the recognition that children differ in their interests, and that these differences do stem, in part, from the social construction of gender. However, to conclude that the needs of boys and girls are essentially different, and to assume that this difference takes precedence over all others, does a great disservice to boys and girls alike.

REVIEW EXERCISES

For Discussion and Debate

1. "Home economics? That's for girls who can't do science."
2. "There's more to education than teaching job skills."
3. "Everyone should learn how to look after a baby."
4. "Separate schools are the way to equality."

Writing Exercises

1. "The importance of gender in my education."
2. "Language learning is a natural for girls."
3. "My own educational needs for an understanding of the social world I would later face." (Were these needs met?)
4. Describe a school, real or imagined, in which the promotion of equality comes first, and indicate steps educators can take to achieve this.

Research Activities

1. Canvass 6 to 10 students of your own age about their schooling. Were any of their classes or class choices gender-based? Would they have liked to attend different classes?
2. Canvass 6 to 10 members of your parents' generation about their schooling. Were any of their classes or class choices gender-based? Would they have liked to attend different classes? How do they see the educational choices available today for boys and/or girls compared with those of their own day?
3. Whose words are worth more in the classroom? Search for journal articles on how teachers react to contributions from girls or boys. Compare or contrast your findings with your own experiences.
4. With a group of 4 to 6 other students, discuss your school experiences and how these were influenced by attitudes about gender. What advice would you, as a group, give to students and teachers today about classroom behavior?

SELECTED REFERENCES

BURSTYN, JOAN N., "Has nothing changed in a hundred years?" The salience of gender to the undergraduate experience, *American Journal of Education* (February 1993), 101, 2, 196–202.

CARPENTER, PETER, Single-sex schooling and girls' academic achievements, *Australian and New Zealand Journal of Sociology* (November 1985), 21, 3, 456–472.

———, and MARTIN HAYDEN, Girls' academic achievements: Single-sex versus coeducational schools in Australia, *Sociology of Education* (July 1987), 60, 3, 156–167.

CRAWFORD, MARY, and MARGO MACLEOD, Gender in the college classroom: An assessment of the "chilly climate," *Sex Roles* (1990), 23, 3–4, 101–122.

CROSBY, FAYE, BRENDA ALLEN, and TONYA CULBERTSON, Taking selectivity into account, how much does gender composition matter? A re-analysis of M. E. Tidball's research, *National Women's Studies Association Journal* (Spring 1994), 6, 1, 107–118.

DEEM, ROSEMARY, *Co-education reconsidered* (Milton Keynes, U.K.: Open University Press, 1984).

HALLINAN, MAUREEN T., and AAGE B. SORENSON, Ability grouping and sex differences in mathematics achievement, *Sociology of Education* (April 1987), 60, 2, 63–72.

KRAMER, PAMELA E., and SHEILA LEHMAN, Mismeasuring women: A critique on computer ability and avoidance, *Signs* (Autumn 1990), 16, 1, 158–172.

LEE, VALERIE E., and ANTHONY S. BRYK, Effects of single-sex secondary schools on student achievement and attitudes, *Journal of Educational Psychology* (October 1986), 78, 5, 381–395.

LEE, VALERIE, HELEN M. MARKS, and TINA BYRD, Sexism in single-sex and coeducational independent secondary school classrooms, *Sociology of Education* (April 1994), 67, 2, 92–120.

MAHONY, PAT, How Alice's chin really came to be pressed against her foot: Sexist processes of interaction in mixed-sex classrooms, *Women's Studies International Forum* (1983), 6, 1, 107–115.

MILLER-BERNAL, LESLIE, Single-sex versus coeducational environments: A comparison of women students' experiences at four colleges, *American Journal of Education* (November 1993), 102, 1, 23–54.

MIXELL, DEBORAH J., An annotated bibliography of the research comparing academic achievement and attitudes of students in coeducational and single-sex schools, on microfiche via ERIC database (South Bend: University of Indiana, 1989).

NICHOLSON, LINDA J., Women and schooling, *Educational Theory* (Summer 1980), 30, 3, 225–233.

OATES, MARY J., and SUSAN WILLIAMSON, Women's colleges and women achievers, *Signs* (Summer 1978), 3, 4, 795–806.

RICE, JOY K., and ANNETTE HEMMINGS, Women's colleges and women achievers: An update, *Signs* (Spring 1988), 13, 3, 546–599.

RIESMAN, DAVID, Quixotic ideas for educational reform, *Society* (March/April 1993), 30, 3(203), 17–24.

RUSSELL, SUSAN, The hidden curriculum of school: Reproducing gender and class hierarchies. In *Feminism and political economy: Women's work, women's struggle*, ed. Heather Joan Maroney and Meg Luxton (Toronto: Methuen, 1987).

SPENDER, DALE, *Invisible women: The schooling scandal* (London and New York: Writers and Readers Pub. Cooperative Society, 1982).

TIDBALL, M. ELIZABETH, Women's colleges and women achievers revisited, *Signs* (Spring 1980), 5, 3, 504–517.

WILSON, KENNETH L., and JANET P. BOLDIZAR, Gender segregation in higher education: Effects of aspirations, mathematics achievement, and income, *Sociology of education* (January 1990), 63, 1, 62–74.

9.3

Why not stay home to learn?

The issue: Widespread dissatisfaction with the public school system and, perhaps, with professional educators as a whole. Some parents feel that they can do a better job of teaching their children than the schools can. This is the impetus behind a small but growing movement toward home schooling.

Introduction Home schooling has been increasing in the United States and Canada over the past decade. The term means that, rather than attending a state school or registered private school and receiving their schooling there, children remain at home and receive their schooling from a parent or another relative. Many states and provinces have adopted the position that children may legally receive instruction at home, as long as they are registered with the school system and their curriculum of study is approved. However, there remains much hostility toward home schooling, and some home-schooling parents report difficulties in having their curricula approved.

Compulsory schooling is a development of the late nineteenth and early twentieth centuries. By 1918, every state in the United States had compulsory education laws in effect; every child had to attend school. The rationale for compulsory schooling was to give children the skills they would require in the work force and to make them good citizens. The latter goal was particularly emphasized in areas where immigration made for a mix of cultural values and norms. Many of the nineteenth-century reformers who called for mass public education were concerned to produce an obedient work force that would be suitably deferential to factory owners and management. Conflict theories of education have emphasized this point, and it is worth remembering in the debate that follows that education has been used as a form of social control.

Home schoolers often see themselves as resisting this social control. However, this works two ways. Parents say they do not want their children "brainwashed," but want them to "think for themselves." Many people, including schoolteachers, would certainly agree with this sentiment. However, what if parents choose home schooling because they do not wish their children to be exposed to ideas of multiculturalism and the equality of all peoples? Would we still say the child would be brainwashed at school?

This is a complex subject. The two debates below take fairly extreme positions. In practice, many home-schooling parents do not feel that schools are out of date, but simply that, for a variety of reasons, they wish to take responsibility—or take back responsibility—for their children's education.

Some home schoolers favor the concept of *deschooling* or *unschooling*, the idea that formal education, whether it takes place at school or in a home classroom, is misplaced because it regiments children and stifles their natural creative instincts and motiva-

tion. John Holt has suggested that no child should be enrolled in formal school programs below age 8. Other theorists have built on the work of Ivan Illich, who theorized an educational system in which people would seek out teachers who could teach whatever they felt drawn to pursue at the time. Illich has since revised some of his ideas, and others have critiqued his work on the grounds that social divisions of class, race, and gender make his ideal system currently impossible. Only in a situation where all were truly equal could all take advantage of the opportunities so offered.

HOME SCHOOLING MAKES STATE SCHOOLS OUTDATED

In North American educational systems, an increasing number of parents are discontented with public schools, claiming they are outmoded, clumsy, slow to change, and unable to teach children the values and skills they require for life in a complex multicultural society. Within a multicultural society, each group has its own values. Public schools, by definition, must select a particular set of values to teach. This may cause conflict with many families whose culture and beliefs differ from those of the school. Some families or communities perceive the school as teaching values they do not support and neglecting areas they find important. Public schools arose initially to train children, as future workers in the factories of the nineteenth century, in obedience—to obey orders unthinkingly. Today for many children public schools encourage alienation and rebellion.

Home schooling gives families the opportunity to emphasize areas they consider important, not only in conventional subjects but in values education and in ideas of what education should include. Some families emphasize concentration and self-discipline, others flexibility and "theme study." With home schooling, children are not torn between the values and work habits of home and school but can instead focus on learning.

If we compare the outcomes of schooling versus home schooling, the claim is often made that the education of home-schooled children is spotty. Parents may have expertise in some areas but not in others, and few home-schooling parents have teacher training. Studies have shown that this perception is not accurate. Jennie and Donald Rakestraw state that "the Tennessee Education Department reported that home-schooled students in Grades 2, 3, 6, and 8 in that state scored higher in every major area of the Stanford Achievement Test than the statewide public school averages for the 1985–1986 school year" (p. 176). Similar findings come from New York, Washington State, and Alabama. There may be many reasons for this success of home-schooled students. Children who are in a relaxed home atmosphere, free from the distractions and competitive nature of the school, are more able to exercise their natural inclination to learn what is presented to them. Without the regimentation of a curriculum imposed by others, they can pursue their interests.

State schools are dependent on public funding, and many school boards are facing funding cuts. When a small number of households have children in the public system, governments see education as a target for cutting, thus depleting the resources available to students and resulting in bigger classes, fewer field trips, and so on.

It is hard to obtain reliable figures for the numbers of students who are home-schooled. Estimates for the United States vary from around 200,000 (in 1988), through 470,000 (1990), to 1 million (1988), though the latter figure should probably be regarded as high. Reporting requirements vary for different states, hence the uncertainty. Figures from states that require registration indicate that about 1% of children are home schooled, even though in these states some home-schooled children are not reported. Registered home-schooled children are seen as exempt from compulsory attendance laws in 31 states. In Canada, home schooling is legal in all provinces. In Britain, about 15,000 families home-school their children. All these figures are increasing rapidly (by 20 or 25% per year) according to home-schooling supporters.

Many universities will accept home-schooled students, although it remains common for home schoolers to attend high school for two or three years to qualify for university admittance.

Although many parents do not have formal teaching qualifications, they have access to a far wider array of resources than may be available to the classroom teacher. Prepackaged curriculums can be purchased or educational consulting sought, both from departments of education and from private consultants or organizations. Programs such as Hooked on Phonics are popular. Some parents purchase books on whole-language teaching and philosophies. Home-schooling parents have the advantage of not being forced to follow one educational method or philosophy simply because it is school board policy. Instead, they can shop around to find methods and curricula that best suit their child and their own values and beliefs. Home-schooling parents are not isolated, but have contact with other home schoolers through meetings, newsletters, and the Internet; and they constitute a community in which schooling techniques and philosophies are discussed.

In an era when public schools are underfunded, unwieldy institutions, slow to change, where teachers must attempt to assist children from a wide range of backgrounds and beliefs, home schooling is an indication of just how outdated the state schools are.

HOME SCHOOLING DOES NOT MAKE STATE SCHOOLS OUTDATED

In the preceding discussion many advantages of home schooling were raised. However, are there also disadvantages? Even if the advantages outweigh the disadvantages, does this mean public schooling is truly outdated? Further, what advantages and disadvantages accrue to the community rather than to individual families and their children?

Home schooling is not for everyone Not all parents can home-school. Not all have the time or the inclination. Even though advocates of home schooling state that it is no problem for single-parents or for full-time professional parents, realistic assessments of the time budget of parents suggest otherwise. A single parent who works a nine-to-five day, then comes home, tired, to spend time with her child—and make supper, wash clothes, and do all the other things involved in running a household—may certainly still engage in important and meaningful activities. But much of the opportunity is lost for engaging in the flexible and unhurried activities mentioned by home-schooling advocates, such as woodland walks and museum visits. Two parents who are each employed full time are in a position that is not much better.

Most people who are employed (whether or not they have a partner) need the salary from their employment to support themselves and their families; work is not a luxury. Although systems of small alternative schools, with parents from different families sharing the teaching, may be possible for these parents, total home schooling is not an option for many of them. Around 1% of school-aged children in U.S. school districts where registration is compulsory are registered as home-schooled. While this number has been increasing and may well increase further with the easing of restrictions on home schooling and greater understanding of what it is, it seems unlikely that home schoolers could ever be a majority of the population if the structure of employment remains as it currently is.

School sets the standards Parents who home-school do so for a variety of reasons. Some feel that they can do a better job than the schools. Often these are parents with university qualifications, including teacher training. They have support, as mentioned, from a home-schooling community through meetings, newsletters, and the Internet. Often they *do* do a better job, as indicated when their children's test scores are compared to average scores for public schools. They fear that their children's spontaneity and love of learning will be stifled in public schools.

Other parents come from strongly religious groups and wish their children to receive an education that emphasizes particular beliefs and values. They belong to communities of parents who provide support and, often, educational materials. Another group are parents whose children cannot be in school for health reasons. Some of these parents receive materials from the school, so that their children are working at the same level and pace as school students. Others use materials found by themselves or by other home schoolers.

However, the programs of study of most of the children must be approved and the children's progress monitored by the school board or local education authority. Many jurisdictions have rulings that if a child regularly fails to progress in schoolwork—in other words, if the parents cannot demonstrate that they are doing a good job—the authority can require that the child attend school. It is hard, therefore, to see how the school system is outdated when it is the school system that provides the standards against which progress is evaluated and many of the resource materials for teaching. Home-schooling parents rely on, and measure themselves by, the state system.

Socialization does take place A claim often made is that home schooling leads to problems with children's "socialization," taken here to have the popular meaning of interaction with peers rather than the sociological sense of learning how to function in society and become a social being. Home-schooling parents point out, quite correctly, that their children do spend time interacting with other children, including the children of other home schoolers and schoolchildren who engage in the same community-based pursuits and leisure activities as they do. They see as an advantage that information about living in society comes from the parents, rather than from other children, and that their children do not "run with the herd"—in other words, do not spend most of their time with the same group of peers. This argument returns to the concept of children learning values from their family.

However, children of home-schooling advocates often socialize only with other children who are, in many ways, very like them. This is particularly the case for children who are home-schooled for reasons of culture or religion. They may meet with children of other home-schooling families within the cultural group and with neighboring children who have been "approved" by their parents as belonging to families who share the same or similar values. How are

these children to learn to get along with those who are very different from themselves, in terms of culture and belief, if they do not meet them and have no exposure to their beliefs and ideologies?

A reality of life is that as adults they will not only have to get along with others but also to work with them. Few pursuits are totally individual. Most occupations are social, people working in a team with other people. Whether the team is called an "office" or an "orchestra," the work is done with other people, usually unrelated and coming from very different backgrounds. Schools, taking account of this reality, are moving more and more in the direction of group learning. Can home schooling compete?

What is the school's job? Finally, we should consider what the school system has to do, and whether this is truly the same as the home-schooling parent's job. Parents tend to evaluate the situation, educationally, in terms of advantages for their particular children. School boards and departments of education have to look to the benefit of the community and of all children. In recent years, school curricula in many jurisdictions of North America have emphasized tolerance and learning about cultures of other students and community members. Thanks to the work of community activists, teachers included, many school districts have adopted antiracist teaching, and teachers are becoming more sensitive to gender issues and cultural diversity.

Schools may indeed be inflexible and slow to change. Many people, including some home-schooling parents, say that the rate of progress toward antiracist teaching has been slow. At the same time, much leadership on issues of social justice and civil rights is coming from within the educational community. Teachers and administrators see themselves as carrying responsibility for a whole population. They do not all agree on how this responsibility is to be handled, and schools vary in their methods and their philosophies. But in state-run schools, children are likely to experience a sampling of the diversity of North American culture.

Certainly, the values of home and school, or of home and some groups within the school, may conflict, but this gives children a sense of how society is constituted and the social problems it faces. Not much is gained by protecting children, particularly older children, from the realities of society. Much is gained, rather, by letting them meet to debate these problems and their solutions. Schools, by their nature, are much better positioned to facilitate this than are those parents who choose to school from the home base. No, schools are not outdated. Instead, some home schoolers may have a view of society—and schools—that is far behind the times.

SUMMING UP

Why not stay home to learn? The idea makes a lot of sense, but we think schools still have a part to play in people's education. Schools are not rendered out of date by home schooling, but the opposition between public schools and home schoolers that is frequently expressed by each side calling down the other, is hardly productive. Many parents choose to home-school because of deficiencies they see within the school system or simply because they find pleasure and fulfillment in teaching their children. This is their right, but by exercising it they deprive the school system and other children of their expertise, knowledge, and critical thinking.

Parents who cannot send their child to school (perhaps because of environmental illness), as well as those for whom home schooling is a first choice, may find themselves regarded with great suspicion by school authorities and by parents of neighboring schoolchildren. They report being treated as if they are enemies of the school.

Rather than an opposition between home and school, many educators and parents would like to see the development of partnerships. Yes, schools can be inflexible, slow to take up new ideas and methods. Home schoolers who try out new methods can share with the schools the knowledge and expertise they gain. Yes, schools are places where students can share knowledge, skills, culture, and ideas. So is it possible for home-schooled children to have some access to the schools, to be able to take part in the orchestras and jazz bands, the multicultural evenings, the sports teams, the debates, and the model parliaments? All in all, is it possible, given partnerships between home and school, to broaden the range of what education is? This is the real challenge posed by the home-schooling movement.

REVIEW EXERCISES

For Discussion and Debate

1. "Teachers are the best people to educate children. Parents are too biased."

2. "Values are best learned in the home."

3. "Home-schooled students are isolated from the real world."

4. "Parents should have the right to choose any education they want for their kids."

Writing Exercises

1. Unschooling (also known as deschooling).
2. How values can be taught in the classroom.
3. "The education I would choose for my children."
4. "How I would have benefited (or how I did benefit) from home schooling."

Research Activities

1. Devise a questionnaire on types of school attended and preferred: public school, private school, boarding school, home school. Include questions on strengths and weaknesses of each type. Administer the questionnaire to a sample of 15 to 20 college students, and tabulate your results. What is the range of diversity in your sample, and what have you learned about attitudes toward different types of schooling?

2. Work with a group of four to six other students to draw up a plan for values education within public schools. How do you determine whose values are to be taught? What problems would you foresee in the implementation of such a plan?

3. Conduct an Internet search for home-schooling pages. What arguments are expressed? Note the religious or other group membership of the proponents, and investigate how the rationale for home schooling links with group membership.

4. Locate at least one person who either has home-schooled his or her children or plans to do so. Conduct an extended interview, giving the person the opportunity to state the reasons for home schooling.

SELECTED REFERENCES

ADAMS, DAVID S., Home schooling in Kansas: Friend or foe, *Children's Legal Rights Journal* (Winter/Spring 1994/5), 15, 11–21.

ARONS, STEPHEN, *Compelling belief: The culture of American schooling* (Amherst: University of Massachusetts Press, 1983).

BATES, VERNON L., Lobbying for the Lord: The new Christian Right home-schooling movement and grassroots lobbying, *Review of Religious Research* (September 1991), 33, 1, 3–17.

BECK, CLIVE, *Better schools: A values perspective* (New York: Falmer, 1990).

BUCKMAN, PETER, ed., *Education without schools* (London: Souvenir Press, 1973).

CLARK, BARBARA, *Growing up gifted: Developing the potential of children at home and at school*, 2nd ed. (Columbus, OH: Merrill, 1983).

DATCHER-LOURY, LINDA, Effects of mother's home time on children's schooling, *Review of Economics and Statistics* (August 1988), 70, 367–373.

DOUGHERTY, KEVIN J., Opportunity-to-learn standards: A sociological critique, *Sociology of Education*, special issue (1996), 40–65.

FINN, CHESTER E., Can the schools be saved? *Commentary* (September 1996), 102, 41–45.

GROLNICK, WENDY S., Parents' involvement in children's schooling: A multidimensional conceptualization and motivational model, *Child Development* (February 1994), 65, 237–252.

HOLT, JOHN CALDWELL, *How children learn*, rev. ed. (New York: Delta/Seymour Lawrence, 1989).

———, *Teach your own: A hopeful path for education* (New York: Delta/Seymour Lawrence, 1981).

ILLICH, IVAN, *Deschooling society* (New York: Harper & Row, 1971).

KINCH, HOLLY, A day in a home school, *The American Enterprise* (November/December 1995), 6, 82–83.

MCGRAW, JENNIFER, An exploratory study of homeschooling in Kansas, *Psychological Reports* (August 1993), 73, 79–82.

PITMAN, MARY-ANNE, Compulsory education and home-schooling: Truancy or prophecy? *Education and Urban Society* (1987), 19, 3, 280–289.

RAKESTRAW, JENNIE, and DONALD A. RAKESTRAW, Home schooling: A question of quality, an issue of rights. In *Social Problems*, ed. Frank R. Scarpitti and F. Kurt Cylke, Jr. (Los Angeles: Roxbury, 1995).

SCHUMM, WALTER R., Homeschooling in Kansas: A further exploratory study, *Psychological Reports* (June 1994), 74, pt. 1, 923–926.

SMOCK, SUE MARX, Assessing parents' involvement in their children's schooling, *Journal of Urban Affairs* (1995), 17, 4, 395–411.

VAN GALEN, JANE A., Explaining home education: Parents' authority of their decisions to teach their own children, *Urban Review* (1987), 161–177.

———, *Home schooling: Political, historical, and pedagogical perspectives* (Norwood, NJ: Ablex, 1991).

———, Ideology, curriculum, and pedagogy in home education, *Education and Urban Society* (1988), 21, 1, 52–68.

WHITEHEAD, JOHN W., and ALEXIS IRENE CROWE, *Home education: Rights and reasons* (Crossway Books, 1993).

WILLIAMSON, KERRI BENNETT, *Home schooling: Answering questions* (Springfield, IL: C. C. Thomas, 1989).

10. Politics and the State

Politics is not limited to the state. It is an activity in which people and groups struggle for control over resources, such as wealth, status, and power. Schools, businesses, and even families are governed by politics, and within these institutions, people vie for control. One of sociology's goals is to reveal the hidden politics of everyday life and develop political theories that apply to all social institutions.

But among social units, the state has a special part to play, for it always monitors and attempts to control the ways groups compete. The **state** is that set of public organizations that makes and enforces decisions that are binding upon every member of a society. It includes the elected government, civil service, courts, police, and military. The right to use violence puts muscle behind state decisions, and only a member of the police or military has the legitimate "right" to use violence without fear of punishment. In many societies, politics converts the struggle for state power into a competition for electoral votes. Both the need to gain electoral popularity and constitutional rules limit the state's use of raw force.

In this chapter we consider several of the many issues that are connected to politics and the state. The first section asks whether a global economy destroys national societies and largely eliminates the need for national governments. The second section considers whether privatization of important social and economic functions previously carried out by the state is good for society. Finally, the third section tries to find out who runs this country and whether it may be an economic elite.

10.1

Who needs countries when there's MTV, the Internet, and McDonalds?

The issue: Evidence that nations are becoming less independent and governments are giving up more of their activities to private industry, within the context of a global economy. Is this something we need to worry about? Will we all end up part of one big world society? And if so, does it really matter?

Introduction At various places in this book, we have discussed the effects of globalization. **Globalization** is the increasing interdependence among the economies and societies of the world. It is the highest stage of what Emile Durkheim viewed as the growth of "organic solidarity," or interdependence based on difference. Here we consider the effect of a global economy on the future of nation-states (polities or governments). Specifically, we ask whether globalization—the creation of a world economy—reduces the importance of nation-states—national societies and cultures. In effect, does it destroy them?

The global economy is a form of world social organization with six defining features. First, as noted, there is global economic interdependence. This means that most societies trade goods and services with one another; people are all buyers and sellers in a single world market. The availability and price of goods and services are determined simultaneously in hundreds of countries. Second, in the global economy a driving force for change is scientific and technological innovation. New methods for producing goods and services develop continuously. New technologies, such as computerized information storage, computer-assisted design, and telecommunication, spread rapidly to all parts of the world.

Third, the key actors in a global economy are "constructed" or corporate entities, especially multinational corporations (like General Motors, IBM, Toyota, and Exxon). Individuals, small local firms, and even national businesses lose out in the competition for international markets. They usually lack the capital and marketing network to compete effectively. In the end, multinational companies provide a growing fraction of all products and services in the world. Fourth, in the global economy, cultures and polities are *polycentric*; that is, they are located in, and influenced by, activities in many nations. More and more cultures today are everywhere, with centers of activity throughout the world. Fifth, an evolving "world culture" homogenizes human aspirations, narrowing the variety of desires and lifestyles. More and more, Europeans think and act like the French, English, and Germans—the dominant actors in the European Union.

Sixth, and most relevant to this debate, economic globalization forces nation-states to change. With less influence over the culture and economy, governments have less influence over the people they rule. What, if any, is to be the new role of nation-states in a global age? Does globalization do away entirely with the need for nation-states and national societies? Can we expect that by the end of the next century nations will no longer exist?

GLOBALIZATION DESTROYS NATION-STATES

Three main arguments support the view that economic globalization destroys nation-states and national societies. First, as we have noted, a global economy weakens the independence of national economies. Second, it weakens the distinctiveness of national cultures. Finally, when transnational organizations prevail, there is little role for national governments to play.

Globalization weakens economic autonomy The key actors in a global economy are multinational corporations. Currently, multinational corporations control half the world's total economic production. This fraction will continue to increase as more companies go international and destroy smaller local competitors with their huge size and competitiveness.

The political significance of multinationals cannot be overstated. Some have budgets larger than most countries. They gather and spend huge amounts of money and create and eliminate huge numbers of jobs. As a result, multinationals are important members of every economic community, yet they are loyal to none. They move their operations wherever they can increase their profits, whatever the consequence for countries in which they do business.

Because of their capital and control of jobs, multinationals exercise a great deal of political influence. Though never elected to office, they influence national politics by supporting some political candidates against others or by threatening to take away jobs or investment if a government fails to enact favorable policies. In some cases, simple bribery is enough to gain the desired political results. Poor nations are the most vulnerable to these influences. However, no nation can ignore them; the stakes are too high.

The growth of a global economy in the last two decades has coincided with governments playing a smaller role in the economy. Through most of the world, governments have deregulated business, reduced taxes, and weakened their labor and occupational health and safety laws. In doing so, they have hoped to persuade multinationals to open up shop and bring in jobs. Thus nation-states have willingly reduced the scope of government, largely putting themselves out of business.

Globalization weakens local cultures   Like other goods and services in a global economy, culture is traded on the world market. Sooner or later, the cultural products of any society—its music, art, literature, philosophy, foods, and folkways—are available for consumption in every society.

As major consumers, Americans enjoy easy access to this cultural smorgasbord— Latin American music, South Asian food, Western European art, and Pacific Rim hardware, for example. But despite their cultural imports, Americans are net exporters of culture. The worldwide cultural trade is largely one-sided and one-dimensional Disneyfication. Most cultural products that travel come from the West, especially the United States.

Mass media are a prime example. The world gobbles up American movies, pop music, and television programs. No sector of the American economy has succeeded in exporting its product worldwide as well as the entertainment industry. This fact sup-

ports Daniel Bell's claim that as manufacturing jobs leave America in search of cheaper workers, information-based industries (like entertainment) provide new jobs in the job market.

Some have criticized the export of American culture as a form of cultural imperialism. The American media convey a worldview that is nontraditional, secular, competitive, individualistic, and focused on material consumption. In many societies, Hollywood's implied support for capitalism and the American Dream promotes nontraditional lifestyles. The individualist ethic portrayed in the American media undermines group loyalties at the level of family, community, tribe, and nation. The nation-state plays little role in creating or preserving these worldwide cultures. It can hardly withstand them.

Transnational organizations prevail   As governments put themselves out of business chasing multinational dollars, and as the American media erode people's loyalty to their national cultures, civil society—the network of voluntary associations and small-scale local activities—also breaks down. Countries that have experienced war or authoritarian rule have little civil society to start with. Families, communities, churches, unions, and local service associations are already weak. Globalization is just the straw that breaks the camel's back. In other countries, globalization weakens a healthy civil culture. Local organizations are no more able to compete with transnational ones than are local businesses with multinationals.

As we have noted, globalization increases the number and influence of transnational organizations. First in importance among these are multinational businesses. Other important transnationals are quasi-governmental, like the European Union, NATO,

NAFTA, SEATO, the United Nations, and the World Bank. Others still, like the Red Cross and Amnesty International, are nongovernmental organizations, or they are social or religious movements, like Islamic fundamentalism.

All of these organizations satisfy an important need. Many local and national problems are international in scope and origin. International cooperation is needed to deal with global issues like pollution, genocide, the flow of refugees, the spread of disease, illegal traffic in human beings, and sales of drugs and nuclear weapons, among other things. Many transnationals—in particular, peace movements, human rights organizations (like Amnesty International), and environmental organizations (like Greenpeace)—reflect a new global outlook. Many new social movements are concerned with worldwide issues like peace, equality, and environmental protection. In time, these movements and organizations may take the place of local organizations and become the roots of a new global civil society.

GLOBALIZATION DOES NOT DESTROY NATION-STATES

Opposing arguments make three main points: despite globalization, nation-states are still important, national cultures are alive and well, and signs of change point to a hybridization, not replacement, of national societies.

Nation-states are still important Throughout the world, governments continue to play an important role. In many countries, they play a key role in the local economy. Take Japan, the economic success story of the last 30 years. In many countries, labor, management, and government all planned for the

short term, and often opposed one another. In Japan, government took the lead in planning for the future. It mediated between capital and labor and coordinated industrial investment for the best long-term results. Other newly industrial countries, especially those on the Pacific Rim (like South Korea, Singapore, and Taiwan), have followed Japan's example, with similar results. Using the state to design and coordinate development pays off, especially for countries with resources and room to grow economically.

Other states play an administrative role on behalf of foreign multinationals. Big businesses prefer to locate in countries that are stable and have good infrastructure: good communications and transportation, good schools and hospitals, and a peaceful population. In many developed societies the state ensures peace, order, and good government. It controls the work force, provides welfare to the poor, and educates the middle class. In short, it makes the country attractive to investors.

And a few industrial countries (like the United States) use state power to fight, militarily and diplomatically, for the interests of favorite industries or multinationals. Operation Desert Storm, for example, was fought ostensibly because of invasion of another state, but a concern with the oil industry is what really brought U.S. troops to Kuwait. No compelling economic interest brought the same number of troops to Bosnia, Rwanda, or Somalia, where threats to democracy and physical survival were more pressing.

National cultures are alive and well By now, Disney movies and rap videos have smothered the world's entertainment market like a thick, fluffy blanket. And there is probably no place on earth where young people don't wear Levis, Nike running shoes, and Harvard sweatshirts. But consumer-oriented lifestyles do not hold a meaning for everyone. In many parts of the world, people still require the sense of something in life that is deeper and bigger than a Big Mac. They resist the intrusion of a foreign culture. For example, fundamentalist Islamic groups oppose the homogenizing and secularizing tendencies of Western culture. Their actions keep local and national identities strong.

As a result, cultural differences continue throughout the world in every area—in religion, sports, the arts, even in sociology. States play a part in stimulating local distinctiveness. It is only in English-speaking countries, where the language barrier to American cultural influence is lowest, that one finds national cultures deteriorating. There, the state must play an even larger role if local culture is to survive. Nothing will prevent the intrusion of foreign culture nor erase its effects.

Even more amazing than an apparently universal desire to watch American sit-coms is an equally universal desire to maintain tribal loyalties that date back thousands of years. Though consumerism is a dominant theme of the twentieth century all around the world, so is tribalism. Every year sees new atrocities committed in the name of racial, ethnic, religious, or national self-determination. This violence is merely the tip of the iceberg. It tells us that people everywhere still have a strong commitment to local, traditional identities.

The reception of foreign cultural products is active, not passive. With regularity, new uses are found and new meanings are attributed to foreign culture. Some believe that the survival of traditional identities and the selective use or adaptation of Western culture reflect a continuing need.

Hybridization is occurring   As states and local cultures influence the uses made of foreign cultural products, the result is a hybrid or cross-breed of the two cultures—something entirely new. Despite the American media, there will probably never be a single world culture. Running against the trend to homogeneity *across* societies is a trend to heterogeneity *within* societies—a result of mass migrations and individualized lifestyles (we have discussed these in earlier chapters). These two opposing processes create *megacultures* that cross geographic boundaries.

For example, we find the Hispanic megaculture all over the world. The version of it we see in Spain is different from, though related to, Hispanic cultures in Argentina and California. At the same time, the country of Spain contains samples of other megacultures. This shows us that the boundaries of cultures and states do not coincide any more. Fewer cultures survive than in the past but, increasingly, the cultures that survive are bigger than states. In the future, there may be fewer than a dozen such worldwide multinational cultures but thousands of local ones.

Hybrid cultures—new mixes of local and international elements—come about through both local resistance and new forms of cooperation. The new transnational organizations are instruments for cultural cross-breeding as much as instruments for domination. Hybrid results feed back and forth, endlessly modifying the world's arts, culture, politics, and even economies.

This process is also dialectical, a result of opposing currents. According to political scientist Benjamin Barber, on the one hand there is a "McWorld" influence—Western cultural domination and homogenization. This brings uniformity and also cultural detachment from a nation's own history and identity. On the other hand there is a "Jihad" influence—a frustrated cultural imperialism confronted with another cultural imperialism, Euro-Americanism. Named after the Islamic "holy war against infidels," the Jihad influence is a form of exclusionism that brings conflict, even war. The influence of neither McWorld or Jihad can prevail, because each reflects a genuine, universal desire. The continuing conflict produces new, evolving cultural forms.

SUMMING UP

Who needs countries when there's MTV, the Internet, and McDonald's? It looks like we all do, to some degree. The evidence we have examined suggests that even these massive global enterprises do not do away with the need for, or existence of, nation-states. Nation-states continue to exist because they perform an important role, even in a global economy. States plan local economic development and provide stability for multinational investors. They protect local cultures and provide a source of identity that is sometimes ideologically close to tribal.

Yet there is no doubt that nation-states will play a smaller role in the future than they have in the past. The age of the nation-state, roughly 1750–1950, is over. In the future, the important actors in history will be either larger than states (multinational businesses, transnational organizations, and mega-cultures) or smaller than states (regional or ethnic tribes and social movements). Units larger than states command more capital and international influence. However, in many countries, units smaller than states command more loyalty. The state will not wither quickly (witness Russia after the Revolution of 1917) and, to be sure, the process will be interrupted by migrations, economic shifts, wars, and cultural changes. Yet the state will decline.

The nation-state was a construct—a corporate entity—that served many people well at a particular moment in history. Lest we shed too many tears over the decline of nation-states, we should remember the role they also played in colonialism, imperialism, two world wars, and the repression of minorities. Whatever history's verdict, the nation-states we grew up in were just another stage in the movement toward global integration.

REVIEW EXERCISES

For Discussion and Debate

1. In what sense is globalization something new? In what sense is it very old?

2. Do multinationals take the place of nation-states, or do they rely on nation-states to make them work effectively?

3. Why are transnational organizations like the Red Cross becoming more important?

4. What is the evidence that, despite globalization, national cultures still remain distinctive?

Writing Exercises

1. "The Jihad cannot prevail over McWorld, nor can McWorld hope to prevail over the Jihad."

2. "Tribal identities become more important as the world becomes more impersonal."

3. "National differences were never as distinctive as people made them out to be."

4. "The West, especially the United States, will continue to teach the world how to live."

Research Activities

1. Collect information on which American movies and television programs are most popular outside the Western world. What do you learn from this about cultural change in these societies?

2. Collect information on which foreign movies and television programs are most popular in North America. What do you learn from this about culture change in North America?

3. How has the importation of Western consumer products changed everyday life in one non-Western country (you choose which one). Use published materials to compare life in that country today and 30 years ago.

4. Devise a list of things you might measure to determine whether the world powers of 50 years ago (the United States, Britain, the U.S.S.R., France) have less clout today than they did then. Measure one of these things to see how it has changed over the last 50 years.

SELECTED REFERENCES

AMIN, SAMIR, and BEATRICE WALLERSTEIN, The future of global polarization, *Review* (Summer 1994), 17, 3, 337–347.

BARBER, BENJAMIN, *Jihad vs. McWorld* (New York: Times Books, 1995).

BELL, DANIEL, *The coming of post-industrial society* (New York: Basic Books, 1973).

CHASE-DUNN, CHRISTOPHER, and THOMAS D. HALL, World-systems and modes of production: Toward the comparative study of transformations, *Humboldt Journal of Social Relations* (1992), 18, 1, 81–117.

FRANK, ANDRE GUNDER, and BARRY K. GILLS, The five thousand year world system: An interdisciplinary introduction, *Humboldt Journal of Social Relations* (1992), 18, 1, 1–79.

FRIEDMAN, JONATHAN, Order and disorder in global systems: A sketch, *Social Research* (Summer 1993), 60, 2, 205–234.

FUKUYAMA, FRANCIS, *The end of history and the last man* (New York: Free Press, 1992).

GEREFFI, GARY, Development strategies and the global factory, *Annals of the American Academy of Political and Social Science* (September 1989), 505, 92–104.

GOLDFRANK, WALTER, Current issues in world-systems theory, *Review* (Spring 1990), 13, 2, 251–254.

HALL, STUART, Culture, community, nation, *Cultural Studies* (October 1993), 7, 3, 349–363.

HELD, DAVID, and ANTHONY MCGREW, Globalization and the liberal democratic state, *Government and Opposition* (Spring 1993), 28, 2, 261–285.

KARNOUH, CLAUDE, WAYNE HAYES, and VALERIE MARCHAL, The end of national culture in Eastern Europe, *Telos* (Fall 1991), 89, 132–137.

MELOSSI, DARIO, Weak Leviathan and strong democracy, or two styles of social control, *International Journal of Contemporary Sociology* (April 1994), 31, 1, 1–15.

MORSE, ELLIOTT R., The new global players: How they compete and collaborate, *World Development* (January 1991), 19, 1, 55–64.

OOMMEN, T. K., Reconciling pluralism and equality: The dilemma of "advanced" societies, *International Review of Sociology*, new series (1992), 1, 141–172.

PICCIOTTO, SOL, The internationalisation of the state, *Capital and Class* (Spring 1991), 43, 43–63.

REICH, ROBERT, *The work of nations* (New York: Vintage, 1992).

RIEFF, DAVID, A global culture? *World Policy Journal* (Winter 1993–94), 10, 4, 73–81.

ROBERTSON, ROLAND, Mapping the global condition: Globalization as the central concept, *Theory, Culture and Society* (June 1990), 7, 2–3, 15–30.

SMITH, DAVID A., Technology and the modern world-system: Some reflections, *Science, Technology, and Human Values* (Spring 1993), 18, 2, 186–195.

SOEDJATMOKO, Toward a world development strategy based on growth, sustainability, and solidarity: Policy options for the 1990s,

Technological Forecasting and Social Change (December 1990), 38, 4, 313–322.

SWEEZY, PAUL M., HARRY MAGDOFF, and LEO HUBERMAN, Globalization—To what end? Pt. I, *Monthly Review* (February 1992), 43, 9, 1–18.

SWEEZY, PAUL M., and HARRY MAGDOFF, Globalization—To what end? Pt. II, *Monthly Review* (March 1992), 43, 10, 1–19.

WALLERSTEIN, IMMANUEL, World-systems analysis: The second phase, *Review* (Spring 1990), 13, 2, 287–293.

10.2
Does it really matter who runs the jail?

The issue: Governments are reducing their role in society, leaving more to the marketplace and private initiative. Is this a change for the better, heralding a more efficient use of society's resources? Or is it simply a way of turning our backs on society's most vulnerable members? And does private industry really do a better job?

Introduction The last section noted that economic globalization reduces the role of governments in national and international affairs. More and more governments are reducing their activities, giving up some entirely, in hopes of reducing public spending. Their goal is to lower taxes and attract jobs. One method for doing this is through **privatization**—placing what were once state activities in private hands.

Many services provided by the state today were once provided by private businesses. In some states, even national defense, which we think of as a task that must belong to the state, was once provided by mercenary forces. Yet in many countries in the last few years, functions customarily performed by the state have been taken over by the private sector—even in the United States, where public control has never developed as highly as in many European countries or in Canada.

Since responsibilities vary from one state to another, what gets privatized varies from one state to another. In formerly communist societies like Hungary and East Germany, heavy industry, transportation, communication, and energy production—once all public—may be privatized. In social democratic societies like Sweden and New Zealand, health care, education, public housing, and public broadcasting may be privatized. In capitalist societies like the United States, in some states, even courts and the building, maintenance, and running of prisons occasionally pass into private hands. Jails have already been privatized in some states of the United States as well as in the United Kingdom. What are the likely consequences of privatization for the state and society?

THE STATE DOES BETTER THAN THE PRIVATE SECTOR

Education Many argue that the state is better than the private sector at providing its citizens with a good education, including college education. As proof, they note that in countries where the government subsidizes postsecondary education, no one misses out on a college education for reasons of financial need. In Germany and France, for example, all students who pass the entrance exams can attend college free. Some of the best colleges in the United States are public, state-funded schools. They are inexpensive for state residents, many of whom could not otherwise afford a higher education, and there are tuition breaks for excellent students who cannot afford a private university education.

Health care   Many also believe that health care is better taken care of by the government. For example, per capita health care costs are lower in Canada, where health care is universal, than they are in the United States, where a near majority of individuals have little or no health care insurance. More people have good health when health care is in the government's hands. Then, people's health improves. Differential access to health care results in huge variations in life expectancy, infant mortality, and illness among communities with different average incomes. If all health care were left to the private sector, only people rich enough to afford quality health care would get it. The health differentials would be even greater.

The economy   Many argue that without considerable state regulation of the economy, people would be at the mercy of a small business elite (see the next section for more discussion on this topic).

Competition and consumer protection are two separate public goods. Self-interested competition is vital to capitalism, and competition between self-interested sellers is supposed to yield lower prices and better products. However, over the twentieth century, self-interest has led to a high degree of corporate concentration. This concentration of wealth and economic power stifles competition, leading to higher prices and worse products. So the government must step in to protect consumers against the self-interest of others more powerful than they. For example, it must ensure safe food and medical products and safe means of transportation.

Welfare   Many believe it is the government's responsibility to ensure that the needy have adequate shelter and enough food. As we saw in an earlier section, people in most modern societies believe the government has an obligation to take care of its poor, elderly, and disabled. This is the meaning of *social citizenship*. Until recently, the state has also had the resources to ensure that people who need help receive it.

Child care   Most parents have to work for a living. Many, though far fewer in the United States than in other countries, believe that the state has a responsibility to ensure that children are properly cared for while their parents are at work. Publicly funded child-care programs make it possible for parents to continue working when they have small children at home. This saves parents from having to choose between working for pay and having a family. And these programs make fiscal sense. By enabling mothers to work, they free many women from reliance on government unemployment insurance or welfare.

Infrastructure   Many argue that it is the responsibility of the government to maintain the society's infrastructure—its roads, bridges, sanitation, communications systems, garbage disposal, and so on. Without these facilities, people's health suffers and business grinds to a halt. So, even if the state does nothing else, it must maintain the infrastructure.

THE PRIVATE SECTOR DOES BETTER THAN THE STATE

Education   Some point out that most states already have a dual educational structure: a public school system and a private school system. They claim that the private system has always been better than the public system. Occasionally this is because the private schools can afford better teachers, better administrators, and more and better facilities. This difference in quality widens as fewer government funds are available for even the most basic public educational expenses. More often the difference is due to the students; private schools get the better students, who bring cultural capital and strong parental support for education.

So the growing popularity of private schools does not prove that private schooling produces better graduates than equally well-endowed public schools. We cannot justify further privatizing education until we have shown that, other things being equal, private schools actually teach students better.

Health care Some, especially health insurers and professionals in the United States, argue that private health care is better than public health care. At best, consumers of private health care are treated faster, with newer technologies, by better qualified doctors. At worst, consumers of public health care are treated in underfunded health centers staffed by overworked, underpaid, and less qualified medical personnel.

Again, as with education, the apparent superiority of the private sector does not prove that private treatment produces better outcomes than equally funded public treatment. No modern country has gone as far as the United States in privatizing health care. However, most health and economic researchers believe that other, equally prosperous societies do a better job than the United States of providing high-quality and affordable (i.e., public or subsidized) treatment.

The economy Underlying economic liberalism is an assumption that a self-interested pursuit of gain produces the healthiest economy: the best supply of goods at the right price. Thus open competition is the fairest, most efficient way to organize economic life. If so, the government has no business regulating the economy. More important, it lacks the ability to do so in a way that satisfies its citizens' best interests. Attempts by communist governments to create "command economies," which set production goals and prices, proved to be a disaster. Publicly, the most desired consumer goods are always in short supply, but a black market in these goods thrives. For the right price, people can still get anything they want. This shows that markets that supply people's wants must be consumer driven, not government driven.

However, critics of this view argue that few markets are truly competitive; most are monopolized and controlled by large producers. As well, advertising creates artificial desires. So in capitalist societies, large manufacturers, not consumers, manipulate both the demand and supply. The market is neither free nor competitive. Finally, even if free markets are the best way to distribute discretionary or luxury goods, they may not be a good way to distribute necessities like food and shelter.

Welfare As we saw in an earlier section, some people want to get rid of welfare. You will recall at least three reasons for this view: First, government no longer has the resources it requires to take proper care of its needy. Second, government aid fosters dependency among the able poor and saps their initiative to take care of themselves. Third, welfare breaks up families by eroding the sense of family responsibility and obligation. Yet, as we saw earlier, there is no evidence that people retain a culture of dependence once they have the chance to earn a decent income. For most, welfare is just a short-term protection and a benefit of social citizenship. The provision of jobs and job-related education gets most people off welfare right away.

Welfare is not likely to disappear from modern nation-states, and the question is who is best equipped to provide it: government or private sources? As with health care, it can be argued that bringing the profit motive into the picture will make efficiency more important than quality, and standardization more important than compassion. In these ways, privatization risks the very goals that welfare was established to achieve.

Child care Some believe that the care of children is, first and foremost, a parental responsibility. According to this view, the state is not responsible for raising children. If it took on that obligation, it would be unable to fulfil it. Further, critics argue that day care does not give children the kind of love and attention that they need to grow into well-adjusted adults. Moreover, providing free day care to working parents reinforces the idea that the government will take care of our family responsibilities if we neglect them. However, the evidence does not support either of these views. First, neglect is typically a result of depression induced by uncontrollable stresses (often income-related). Second, high quality day care does no demonstrated harm to child development. Unfortunately, many working parents cannot afford high quality day care. This argues in favor of improving and extending public day care, not leaving it in private hands.

Infrastructure Some argue that the private sector can build roads and bridges, take care of garbage disposal, and so on far more efficiently than the state. It can hire workers for less money, buy supplies more cheaply, and produce less bureaucratic red tape than governments. Rather than pay for these services out of a universal tax, such products and services should be offered on a per user basis. For example, you use the road, you pay for it; you put garbage out to be picked up, you pay for it; you ride the bus or subway, you pay for it.

However, others argue that user fees such as these are regressive taxes. The same service costs poor people a higher proportion of their income than it costs rich people. All regressive taxes hurt the poor and reduce the quality of social citizenship. Further, private industry cannot provide the same services more cheaply. Since private businesses have to make a profit, usually they provide a worse service more cheaply and we must decide whether this service is adequate. Or they provide the same service at a higher rate. To escape this added cost is one reason why states provided the service in the first place.

THE EFFECTS OF RAPID PRIVATIZATION

Despite evidence that the public sector provides many services better and cheaper, privatization is proceeding rapidly in many countries. Privatization can follow either of two patterns: call them the economic (faster) and political (slower) imperative models. What are the likely consequences for the state of faster versus slower privatization?

Privatization that follows the *economic imperative* model tries to increase economic growth as quickly as possible, whatever the political risk. Rapid privatization of key state activities quickly produces large financial benefits for a few, but layoffs and unemployment for many others. This increases economic inequality. It also leads to widespread public dissatisfaction and pessimism about the economy. Support for the government, the free market, and liberal democracy decline. Governments take this path in hopes that the economy quickly improves and begins to benefit the majority. Otherwise, the state loses its legitimacy, civil society disintegrates, and political unrest emerges.

On the other hand, a state that follows the *political imperative* model privatizes key sectors of the economy slowly and cautiously. It maintains high employment levels, even if the public debt increases and incomes rise faster than productivity. Here, income equality is unchanged and most people are optimistic about the economy. Public satisfaction is reflected in a high degree of support for the government, the free market, and liberal democracy. However, economic growth is slow. Governments take this path in hopes that the economy starts to grow before inflation and indebtedness cause an economic crash. Economic growth takes longer in this scenario. Meanwhile, the government remains stable and popular.

For example, two formerly communist countries, Hungary and East Germany, recently began to privatize their economies. Hungary has followed the economic imperative model of rapid privatization. East Germany, now part of a unified Germany, has followed the political imperative model. Cushioned by help from West Germany, it has been able to change at a more moderate pace. Survey researchers sampled public opinion in both countries, asking people to evaluate the political and economic systems under communism, at the time of the survey, and (as they imagine it will be) in 5 years.

The results show that in both countries, people give low ratings to both the economy and the government—past, present, and future. And in both countries, people expect the government and the economy to perform better in 5 years. But there the similarity between the two countries ends. In slow-privatizing East Germany, people have a sense they are making progress. They feel that, both politically and economically, the capitalist present is better than the communist past, and the future is more promising still. In fast-privatizing Hungary on the other hand, people glorify the communist past. To Hungarians, the political and economic past looks better than the present or future.

Often, glorification of the past is a warning sign of fascism. It indicates a willingness to look for and accept simple solutions to society's economic and political problems, even at the expense of freedom. This reminds us that faster economic change is riskier change. Unless Hungary's economy improves rapidly, Hungarians may turn their backs on liberal democracy. This is what Germans did to the liberal Weimar Republic in 1933, bringing about Adolf Hitler's rise to power.

SUMMING UP

Does it really matter who runs the jail? Yes it does, if we view jails and other social institutions as having goals other than profit making. Moreover, the rate at which a society moves in the direction of privatization also matters.

The line dividing the functions under state control from those left to the private sector is drawn differently in different countries. It also varies over time in the same country. Expanding the American welfare state in the 1930s meant redrawing the line, with the government assuming more responsibilities. The recent and gradual shrinkage of public spending reflects another redrawing of this line.

Whatever the reasons, evidence suggests that too-rapid privatization runs a serious risk of destabilizing the state. The amount of risk is proportional to: (1) the degree and type, and (2) the speed of privatization. Privatizing government activity in a formerly communist or social democratic country is riskier than in a highly privatized society like the United States. Privatizing a government activity closely tied to personal survival (e.g., food, shelter, health care, personal income) is riskier than privatizing other functions (e.g., communication, transportation). And privatizing all state activities at once is extremely risky.

The answer to the question we originally asked is, yes, rapid privatization does weaken the state. Too-rapid or too-extreme change in one part leads to unpredictable, even violent reactions in other parts. Given the already dis-tressing effects of globalization, too-rapid privatization may spell the end for some nation-states. Like the plunge into a cold mountain stream, what is bracing for some is fatal for others.

REVIEW EXERCISES

For Discussion and Debate

1. What reasons are usually given for privatizing public services? Which of these reasons seem most sensible to you?

2. Why is government regulation of the economy thought likely to have negative effects?

3. Why do some expect health care to improve if it is less regulated by the government?

4. In what respects is fast privatization likely to be better than slow privatization? In what respects is the opposite likely to be true?

Writing Exercises

1. "We learn little about privatization in capitalist countries by studying privatization in formerly communist countries."

2. "Public education is bound to be better than private education, providing the same amount is spent on each student in each case."

3. "Private prisons are even less likely than public prisons to rehabilitate criminals."

4. "Putting welfare in private corporate hands is like asking a wolf to watch the sheep."

Research Activities

1. Collect data from your own country and any Scandinavian country and compare the degree of privatization in one of the social or health services discussed here.

2. Collect measures of outcome quality—for example, quality of education, quality of health—from your own country and from another country where social or health services are less privatized. What differences do you find?

3. Devise a brief questionnaire to measure public support for public provision of a social or health service that is currently private. Administer this questionnaire to six people and tabulate the results. What "kinds" of people are most supportive of the change?

4. Do some reading on the former communist countries to learn why they have started to privatize what were once public services.

SELECTED REFERENCES

AULETTE, JUDY, The privatization of housing in a declining economy: The case of Stepping Stone Housing, *Journal of Sociology and Social Welfare* (March 1991), 18, 1, 151–164.

BROTMAN, ANDREW, Privatization of mental health services: The Massachusetts experiment, *Journal of Health Politics, Policy and Law* (Fall 1992), 17, 3, 541–551.

ESTES, CAROLL, and JAMES H. SWAN, Privatization, system membership, and access to home health care for the elderly, *Milbank Quarterly* (June 1994), 72, 2, 277–298.

FAIRBROTHER, PETER, Privatisation and local trade unionism, *Work, Employment and Society* (September 1994), 8, 3, 339–356.

KALYVAS, STATHIS N., Hegemony breakdown: The collapse of nationalization in Britain and France, *Politics and Society* (September 1994), 22, 3, 316–348.

LEHMANN, SUSAN GOODRICH, Costs and opportunities of marketization: An analysis of Russian employment and unemployment, *Research in the Sociology of Work* (1995), 5, 205–233.

LILLY, J. ROBERT, and PAUL KNEPPER, An international perspective on the privatisation of corrections, *Howard Journal of Criminal Justice* (August 1992), 31, 3, 174–191.

McDONALD, DOUGLAS C., Public imprisonment by private means: The re-emergence of private prisons and jails in the United States, United Kingdom, and Australia, *British Journal of Criminology*, special issue (1994), 34, 1, 29–48.

McINTOSH, CHRISTOPHER, To market, to market: Navigating the road to privatization, *Futurist* (January–February 1994), 28, 1, 24–28.

NELSON, JOEL I., Social welfare and the market economy, *Social Science Quarterly* (December 1992), 73, 4, 815–828.

ODLE, MAURICE, Towards a stages theory approach to privatization, *Public Administration and Development* (February 1993), 13, 1, 17–35.

O'LOONEY, JOHN, Privatization and service integration: Organizational models for service delivery, *Social Service Review* (December 1993), 67, 4, 501–534.

PICKVANCE, C. G., Housing privatization and housing protest in the transition from state socialism: A comparative study of Budapest and Moscow, *International Journal of Urban and Regional Research* (1994), 18, 3, 433–450.

PRAGER, JONAS, Is privatization a panacea for LDCs? Market failure versus public sector failure, *Journal of Developing Areas* (April 1992), 26, 3, 301–322.

RELMAN, ARNOLD S., What market values are doing to medicine, *National Forum* (Summer 1993), 73, 3, 17–21.

RYAN, MICK, Evaluating and responding to private prisons in the United Kingdom, *International Journal of the Sociology of Law* (December 1993), 21, 4, 319–333.

SAMSON, COLIN, The three faces of privatisation, *Sociology* (February 1994), 28, 1, 79–97.

SMITH, STEVEN RATHGEB, and MICHAEL LIPSKY, Privatization in health and human services: A critique, *Journal of Health Politics, Policy and Law* (Summer 1992), 17, 2, 233–253.

SOUTH, NIGEL, Privatizing policing in the European Market: Some issues for theory, policy, and research, *European Sociological Review* (December 1994), 10, 3, 219–233.

VARESE, FEDERICO, Is Sicily the future of Russia? Private protection and the rise of the Russian Mafia, *Archives Europeenes de Sociologie* (1994), 35, 2, 224–258.

WILSON, ERNEST J. III, A mesolevel comparative approach to maxi and mini strategies of public enterprise reform, *Studies in Comparative International Development* (Summer 1993), 28, 2, 22–60.

10.3

Who's in charge of this country anyway?

The issue: The future of democracy in modern industrial societies. With government playing a smaller role in running the country, we have to wonder who is running the shop. Maybe nobody is running the country, and it's in free-fall. Or maybe the same people as always are running it from behind the scenes. But who might they be?

Introduction Debate about this seemingly simple question is maddeningly complicated, yet the answer is important to everyone. In some societies, the question "Who rules?" is much easier to answer. In small Native American societies no one rules in the sense we mean today. A chief or headman is elected by band members. Typically, he or she coordinates group discussions and speaks on behalf of the group. Or, in larger tribal systems, chieftainship is hereditary but still limited in power, by our standards.

In feudal societies, rulers do exist and they are easy to identify. Often, there is a noble class, including a king, queen, princes and princesses, and a circle of aristocrats (dukes and duchesses, barons and baronesses, earls, countesses, marquises, esquires, and the like). They control the chief source of wealth—land—and use their control of the land to demand rents, taxes, and obedience from the peasants. This control is generally—not always—exercised by male members of the aristocratic classes. The church is also important in maintaining order on behalf of the ruling class.

In commercial states merchants and bankers have the most influence, in direct proportion to a merchant's or banker's wealth. Since the political ruler, often a duke, needs cooperation and taxes from the wealthy, political power is shared in these states. With the growth of commerce and a powerful commercial class comes what we think of today as republican democracy.

In industrial societies, a class of industrial owners—what Karl Marx called the bourgeoisie—has the most influence. It owns the factories that produce manufactured goods. By making profits on these goods, the bourgeoisie amasses wealth and controls the wages of a large working class. Often the industrial ruling class has connections with the older commercial and banking class. In the long run the owners of industry become financially and politically supreme, by investing heavily in resources (oil and mines), transportation (railways), and utilities (electric power).

As you can see from this brief, simplified history of political rule, different kinds of societies with different kinds of economies have different ruling groups. So who rules globalized, post-industrial America at the end of the twentieth century?

AN ECONOMIC ELITE DOES NOT RULE AMERICA

By "economic elite," we mean a few thousand people who possess great wealth (often through inheritance) or otherwise control the largest American banks and businesses. They include, for example, the chief executive officers of the Fortune 500 companies, who are mainly white, middle-aged men. By "rule," we mean these people influence the making of laws and state policies, with an interest in seeing that their organizations benefit. Arguments that support the view that an economic elite does *not* rule America include the following: an elected government rules the country; many competing elites share control; the economic elite is not united; economic elites have less influence in good times than in bad; and it is the upper class that rules.

An elected government rules   In principle, the people rule in a democracy. That means they get to elect political representatives every 4 years. However, average citizens have little direct impact on the political decision-making process once their representatives are elected. Among other reasons, they lack the time and information to exercise influence. And few states allow the exercise of direct democracy in the form of referendums on particular issues. As a result, we usually find little similarity between laws that are made and public opinion that is expressed in opinion polls. (For example, the public is far more sympathetic to capital punishment than elected representatives.) Elected representatives do have time and access to information to influence the political process. That is their job, what we elect them to do.

Competing elites exercise control   Economic elites have a great deal of influence over political decisions—in many cases even a decisive influence. However, other elites in society also exercise influence. They include labor leaders, church leaders, military leaders, senior elected officials, senior civil servants, high court judges, and appointed political officials. Each elite group promotes the advancement of its own interests, using the group's institutional resources and media appeals to popular opinion. These interests often conflict with those of the economic elite.

As a result, many laws and government programs do not obviously and immediately serve the interests of the economic elite. For example, laws protecting the environment against pollution, guaranteeing a minimum wage, or regulating the quality of foods and drugs do not help the economic elite profit. Usually they do the opposite. The enactment of such laws shows that other elites have influence too.

The economic elite is not united   The premise that an economic elite rules the country supposes that all members of the economic elite think the same way. This is far from true. Different economic organizations and their elite leaders often have different goals. For example, industrial elites often favor tariffs and quotas to keep out cheap imported goods. Banking elites are indifferent to this concern, or they may even oppose tariffs or quotas, since they fear a counterattack by other countries where they want to invest money. Thus free trade—which reduces tariffs and quotas between trading part-

ners—benefits investors more than it benefits manufacturers. Because bankers prevail, more cheap manufactured goods are flowing into America than ever before.

Along similar lines, the leaders of the big business community hold different views from the leaders of the small business community. Big businesses have less trouble accepting unionization, minimum wage laws, health and safety regulations, and affirmative action rules. They simply pass along to consumers the cost of obeying these rules. By contrast, small businesses, with fewer consumers and a smaller profit margin, have more trouble passing new costs on to customers, so they are more likely to oppose these rules.

The economic elite has less influence in good times   In good times, the economic elite has less influence. Economic performance is taken for granted, so it is of less concern to the public and the government. In bad times, people will do just about anything, say just about anything, believe just about anything. They are easily manipulated by people who are economically secure. In good times—or at least, in times that look good compared to the recent past—people are more cautious and less gullible. Then, the elite has less hold over their thoughts and actions. (Quiz: What kind of times are we in now? What makes you so certain?)

The upper class rules   Every agricultural society has an upper class that enjoys considerable wealth, power, and prestige. The wealth that passes from generation to generation is based on land ownership. Since most people are poor and landless, wealth and control of the land translate into power. Over generations, wealth and power are translated into prestige or social standing in the community. But in a commercial or industrial society an upper class is less visible, and fortunes are made and lost at a much faster rate. Some analysts claim there is an American upper class comprising families that have held wealth and power for several generations: the Vanderbilts, Astors, Rockefellers, DuPonts, Roosevelts, Dukes, and perhaps the Kennedys.

Class theorists argue that the power of the economic elite is largely an illusion. In truth, it is the upper class that rules because it owns the dominant banks and industries. As owners, upper-class people dominate the boards of directors that control the banks and industries. There is little chance of outsiders entering the economic elite—gaining a seat on the board of directors, for example—but it sometimes happens. Thus upper-class rule of the economy and the country looks like rule by an elite, but it isn't.

AN ECONOMIC ELITE DOES RULE AMERICA

Arguments on the other side address all of these views and put forward additional evidence. Let's proceed by considering *why* those who disagree hold that an economic elite rules the country and then *how* they believe an economic elite goes about ruling.

Why an economic elite rules There are several reasons why an economic elite rules the country. As we noted in a previous section, nations and their governments have been mortally weakened by economic globalization. By privatizing public services and deregulating business, many have shrunk the job of governing. Thus political elites are less important than in the past.

A worsened economy combined with weak government have diminished the strength of other competing elites too. As the labor movement has lost members, its

leaders have been less able to exercise influence in public life. As government has lost strength, all of its elites—elected, appointed, and civil service—have exercised less influence. Other elites dependent on public spending—for example the military, scientific, and intellectual elites—have also lost influence. With the decline of competing elites, the economic elite has gained power. At the same time, corporate concentration has continued to increase. The last decade of this century has seen a rash of mergers and acquisitions (takeovers). Today, more wealth and more jobs are controlled by fewer people—namely, the economic elite.

Why not the upper class? Contrary to the claims of class theorists, many (most?) dominant corporations are owned by thousands of small stockholders, not individuals or families. But these owners are too numerous and disconnected to run the company. As a result, top managers run the company, and as members of the board of directors, they control the owners' property. Top managers also buy shares in the company and become owners themselves. However, these top managers are not upper-class people, nor does the upper class play a big role in controlling the company. So the upper class does not use its economic power to rule America.

How the economic elite rules The economic elite rules America through a combination of methods that include cooperation, corporate interlocks, informal connections, and mechanisms of influence.

◆ *Cooperation:* Though economic elites disagree about many things, they share a common interest in free markets and political stability. These goals are best achieved by sharing control of the country through a collegial relationship with other elites. What Robert Presthus called "elite accommodation" really is just a form of cooperation. Give way on issues that do not harm your own immediate interests, and expect your fellow elites to do the same for you. The result is a high degree of cohesion within the elite.

- *Corporate interlocks*: Communication and familiarity among elite members are achieved, in part, through "corporate interlocks" or interlocking directorships. A major corporation may have 20 directors or more, and a given director may sit on as many as five to ten other boards. Generally, the more important the organization an individual controls, the more boards he will be asked to sit on. Through their memberships on many boards, elite individuals get to know scores of other powerful elites. Their contact and familiarity increase elite cooperation. They also tie together major organizations, for example, major industries with major banks or major banks with major insurance or investment companies.

- *Informal connections*: The study of biographies uncovers a range of informal ties between economic elites. Many grew up in the same neighborhood and attended the same churches and summer camps. Many met as members in the same private clubs. In these ways, they became friends, and some even married into one another's families. Many also attended elite elementary and secondary schools, elite colleges, elite business and law schools. There they were socialized into the American elite subculture long before actually becoming members of the elite. Along with friendships and other informal ties, this common cultural background strengthens the elite's cohesion.

- *Mechanisms of influence*: The economic elite rules the country by means that include political contributions, informal discussions, and media coverage.

First, contributions of money to both major parties and all the major candidates ensure that elites and their organizations receive an attentive hearing when they have a political problem. (It costs millions of dollars to run a successful campaign for office; politicians appreciate large donors.) Fear of losing financial support influences the judgment of all but the bravest, or richest, officeholders.

Second, however, informal discussions are often enough to gain elites the desired result. Many politicians may already share the elite's belief in free markets, political stability, and the social value of big business. This aside, they may come into office from elite backgrounds or hope to enter the economic elite after leaving politics.

Third, the mass media, large enterprises themselves, are controlled by the economic elite. With a weak public broadcasting sector in the United States, the media are very susceptible to pressures by owners and advertisers. And with rare exceptions, politicians who fail to cooperate with the elite's interests are flayed by the media. This makes it harder for them to pass their legislation or get reelected. The mass media can turn a failure to cooperate with economic elites into a terminal political illness.

SUMMING UP

Who's in charge of this country anyway? Well, it's not you and me. We agree with those who argue that the economic elite rules America, but we say so with hesitation. There are two good reasons for a qualified or mixed answer.

First, studies of political power and influence have always been fraught with methodological problems. Groups that dominate on one issue may not be able to dominate on another. Groups that dominate under one set of conditions may not be able to dominate under another set. And groups that appear to dominate when domination is measured in one particular way may not appear to dominate when domination is measured in another way. This tells us that in a modern democracy, political rule is domination with exceptions. Political influence is unpredictable, dispersed, and often nearly invisible. Because of the difficulty we have seeing and predicting political acts, we cannot say precisely who rules America. We can only say who doesn't.

Second, this problem is compounded by the globalization of wealth and power. The influences on political decision makers used to come mainly from inside the country—from other American politicians and from economic and other elites. Today they come from outside the country too. To get reelected, the president (and any other aspiring statesman) has to be on good terms with the prime minister of Israel, the head of the European Union, the president of the World Bank, the premier of China, and countless offshore billionaires and millionaires. They can all do America harm or good; the president will want to avert the harm and take credit for the good.

Today, the geographic boundaries of the American political system are just about as permeable, and blurred, as the boundaries of the economic system. It is impossible to see all of the major influences on American politics. Some of the most important ones may be located outside U.S. borders. Thus the right answer to our question, "Does an economic elite rule America?" may turn out to be "Yes, but only part of that elite is American."

REVIEW EXERCISES

For Discussion and Debate

1. Is it possible that no one is in charge of the United States, and that the system that has been established simply runs itself?

2. What are the mechanisms that bring about cooperation among elites with competing interests?

3. What do we mean by an "upper class," and how is it connected with the "elites"?

4. Is it possible for someone like you to get into the ruling elite? How?

Writing Exercises

1. "The globalization of wealth and power means that foreigners run our country."

2. "Today, the truly powerful are more and more likely to hide their power."

3. "One should not underestimate the political importance of the military elite."

4. "Power is more likely to be shared democratically when the economy is growing."

Research Activities

1. Collect data on the five most powerful people in your own community. Who are they? How did they become powerful?
2. Collect information about a recent political controversy in your community. What was the conflict about, and who supported each side? How did the winning side win?
3. Compare news reports on a recent public controversy to see how differently newspapers and radio and television commentators analyzed the same issues. Who owns these newspapers and radio and television stations? How might owners have affected the position these commentators took?
4. Collect social and biographical information about the "leading families" in your community, and see if you can connect them through marriage, friendship, club membership, board directorships, and the like.

SELECTED REFERENCES

ALLEN, MICHAEL PATRICK, Elite social movement organizations and the state: The rise of the conservative policy-planning network, *Research in Politics and Society* (1992), 4, 87–107.

BALTZELL, E. DIGBY, *The Protestant establishment: Aristocracy and caste in America* (New York: Random House, 1964).

BEALEY, FRANK, Democratic elitism and the autonomy of elites, *International Political Science Review* (July 1996), 17, 319–331.

BEYME, KLAUS VON, The concept of political class: A new dimension, *West European Politics* (January 1996), 19, 68–87.

BOWLES, SAMUEL, and HERBERT GINTIS, Power and wealth in a competitive capitalist economy, *Philosophy and Public Affairs* (Fall 1992), 21, 4, 324–353.

BURRIS, VAL, and JAMES SALT, The politics of capitalist class segments, A test of corporate liberalism theory, *Social Problems* (August 1990), 37, 3, 341–359.

CLEMENT, WALLACE, *The Canadian corporate elite: Economic power in Canada* (Toronto: McClelland and Stewart, 1975).

———, *Continental corporate power: An analysis of economic power* (Toronto: McClelland and Stewart, 1977).

DAVIS, GERALD F., The corporate elite and the politics of corporate control, *Current Perspectives in Social Theory* (1994), supplement 1, 215–238.

DOMHOFF, G. WILLIAM, *The higher circles: The governing class in America* (New York: Random House, 1970).

———, *State autonomy or class dominance? Case studies on policy making in America* (New York: Aldine de Gruyter, 1996).

ETZIONI, AMITAI, Status-separation and status-fusion: The role of PACs in contemporary American democracy, *Research in Political Sociology* (1989), 4, 145–165.

GIDDENS, ANTHONY, An anatomy of the British ruling class, *New Society* (October 1979), 50, 887, 4, 8–10.

HOLLINGER, ROBERT, *The dark side of liberalism: Elitism vs. democracy* (Westport, CT: Praeger, 1996).

KADUSHIN, CHARLES, Friendship among the French financial elite, *American Sociological Review* (April 1995), 60, 2, 202–221.

KERBO, HAROLD R., *Who rules Japan? The inner circles of economic and political power* (Westport, CT: Praeger, 1995).

MCADAMS, JOHN, Testing the theory of the new class, *Sociological Quarterly* (1987), 28, 1, 23–49.

PARENTI, MICHAEL, *Democracy for the few*, 6th ed. (New York: St. Martin's Press, 1995).

PECK, JAMIE, Moving and shaking: Business elites, state localism and urban privatism, *Progress in Human Geography* (March 1995), 19, 1, 16–46.

PORTER, JOHN, *The vertical mosaic* (Toronto: University of Toronto Press, 1965).

PRESTHUS, ROBERT VANCE, *Elites in the policy process* (New York: Cambridge University Press, 1972).

REINHARD, WOLFGANG, ed., *Power elites and state building* (New York: Oxford University Press, 1996).

Scott, John, Networks of corporate power: A comparative assessment, *Annual Review of Sociology* (1991), 17, 181–203.

Teles, Steven Michael, *Whose welfare? AFDC and elite politics* (Lawrence: University Press of Kansas).

Williams, A. Paul, Access and accommodation in the Canadian welfare state: The political significance of contacts between state, labor and business leaders, *Canadian Review of Sociology and Anthropology* (May 1989), 26, 2, 217–239.

Wright, Erik Olin, and Bill Martin, The transformation of the American class structure, 1960–1980, *American Journal of Sociology* (July 1987), 93, 1, 1–29.

11. Health

Good **health** is something we take for granted until we lose it. Research has shown that the absence of good health—especially when it limits our daily activities—has a large impact on our sense of well-being. It also affects our social relations and economic earning power. Good health is extremely important.

But given its importance, it seems odd that people, groups, and cultures disagree on what constitutes good health, what produces it, and what restores it when it is lost. It is also odd that people appear to have different risks of losing their good health, which is to say that good health is socially variable and, perhaps, socially structured. The question is not whether this is so; epidemiologists know it and insurance companies rely on it. The question is why. Finally, given the gradual reduction in public spending, discussed in the last chapter, there is a move toward making people more responsible for their own health. Nowhere is this more evident than in the gradual deinstitutionalization of people with long-term health problems. As sociologists, we have to ask whether this policy has the effect of making people healthier or simply allows us to ignore their sickness.

This chapter addresses all three of these issues. The first section asks whether we can reach any agreement on what constitutes good health. If not, we cannot hope to determine whether good health varies from one social group to another or is improving overall. In the second section we ask why poor people appear to lack equal access to good health, and we consider alternative explanations. Finally, in the third section we look at the trend toward releasing mental patients from long-term hospitalization and ask why was this done and what was its effect.

11.1
How do we know who's sick?

The issue: Life and death and everything in between. As we shall see, poor health is more common in some social groups than in others. But before we can see these patterns and make sense of them, we need to be clear on what constitutes good health and its opposite, illness. Is there much agreement on what sickness actually is?

Introduction We all know when we feel healthy and when we feel ill. The trouble is, under similar conditions some people feel healthy and others feel ill. It is difficult to predict people's *feeling* of health or illness. As individuals, people experience illness differently, and, to compound the problem, cultures differ in how they view health and illness, even pain.

Part of the problem originates in the mysterious relationship between the mind and the body. Some cultures (like ours) see a radical distinction between mind and body—even a competition between them for supremacy. Except in the case of mental illnesses, they view sickness as something that happens to the body, which is then reported to the mind. Good health, then, is an absence of bodily sickness, although, as we shall see, even in our culture, some have defined health more comprehensively.

Other cultures make less distinction between the body, mind, and spirit, or soul. They see a continuing subtle interplay among them. A malfunction in one area—body, mind, or spirit—can produce a malfunction in the others. The cure for malfunctions in one domain must be sought in another. The idea of treating bodily symptoms rather than the underlying mental or spiritual causes is utterly foreign to this thinking.

If our goal is to improve the health of the world's population, or even our own, for that matter, we must first establish a minimal consensus on what constitutes health and illness. Some believe this is possible; others do not.

THERE IS NO GENERAL AGREEMENT

People who argue that there is no general agreement over what constitute health and illness point to differences among societies in terms of how each approaches these issues, as well as differences within societies and changes over time. They also note that conceptions of health and illness are socially constructed and constantly being negotiated.

Differences between societies Supporters of the view that there is no general agreement about health and illness point out that these concepts can take on different meanings, depending on the cultural context and his-

torical period. So, for example, these concepts are defined differently in the East than in the West. They are also defined differently in modern societies than in more traditional societies. As we have noted, in the West, health is largely defined as an absence of illness. If you are not sick, you are, for all intents and purposes, considered healthy. But in the East, health is considered to be more than a lack of illness. It is a state of harmonious balance among all the aspects of an individual's life. This includes a person's emotional and psychological states of being, as well as the physical condition of the body.

In the West, an illness is defined by the scientific-medical establishment as a disturbance in the functioning of the body. You are ill when something in your body is not working properly. This may be due to the intrusion of a germ or virus, an internal, genetically based malfunction, a result of insidious physical forces—like the icy road upon the accelerating elbow—or all of these. Whatever the cause, an illness is a physical condition that causes some part of the body to malfunction.

Only during this century have malfunctions of the mind also come to be defined as illnesses. This occurred because the increasingly powerful medical profession has concluded—through Freud's ground-breaking work on hysteria—that mental or psychological malfunctions can produce physical symptoms. And today the profession also recognizes that even when there are no physical symptoms, mental anguish can be just as real and painful as physical pain.

In the East, on the other hand, illnesses have long been defined as imbalances in a person's life brought about by various causes. Many causes may be primarily emotional or psychological in nature. Something considered an illness in the East does not have to affect the physical body primarily, or even at all. Accordingly, diagnosis of the illness is often left to spiritual leaders and not, strictly speaking, to medical practitioners.

Eastern and Western societies also differ in how illnesses are treated. In the West an illness is a physical problem, to be overcome with the patient's cooperation if possible, or without it if necessary. The object of scientific attention is the illness, not the patient. The illness is seen as an isolated feature of the patient. For this reason, little attention is paid to how treatment of the physical problem affects the patient emotionally or psychologically. (Sometimes, little attention is even paid to how treatment affects other parts of the body!) This outlook fits well with a highly specialized approach to medicine.

As we have noted, in the East an illness, even when it is primarily physical, is viewed as an imbalance that needs correcting. The unit of analysis is always the patient, not the illness. Accordingly, the patient's involvement is central to the treatment process. Though made up of distinct parts, the patient is treated as a whole. Healers could not imagine trying to fix an isolated part, when the problem is an imbalance between the parts. So for treatment to have any success, it must include the emotional and psychological dimensions of the patient, as well as the physical one.

The same dichotomy that marks differences in Eastern and Western approaches to illness also marks differences between more and less developed (or modernized) societies. Modern societies, dominated as they are by scientific rationality, see illnesses as having empirically measurable symptoms and empirically measurable causes. On the other hand, traditional societies lack scientific rationality and place more emphasis on spiritual (nonempirical) causes. Illnesses for them carry heavy moral and spiritual weight. So it is not surprising if they locate the cause of an individual's pain in a failure to properly worship ancestral shrines or in the spells and curses of another group member believed to possess supernatural powers (such as those of a witch). In Western eyes, such an approach to illness is the result of superstition. It demonstrates an ignorance of scientifically verifiable causes and effects and cannot possibly provide successful treatment.

Differences within societies People who argue that there is no general agreement about health and illness also point out that even in modern Western societies, the scientific-medical establishment defines health and illness differently—some would say more narrowly—than do practitioners of alternative medicine and public health people. This may particularly be the case when we look at how women's bodies and reproductive systems are defined by the medical establishment. Pregnancy, childbirth, menopause, even menstruation may be discussed in medical literature as "conditions" during which women are in need of "treatment." By contrast, holistic practitioners and womens' health advocates say that these times should be viewed as part of health, not illness.

Increasingly, people dissatisfied by the way the medical establishment treats illness have turned to other ways of achieving good health. Many of these ways are preventive as much as remedial. Alternative approaches vary widely; they include yoga and other bodily exercises, meditation and other mental exercises, macrobiotic or vegetarian diets, herbal remedies, acupuncture, and an array of spiritual approaches.

What they have in common is an emphasis on principles that are key to the Eastern approach. They are all holistic perspectives that take into account a person's emotional, psychological, and spiritual needs. Over the last few decades, these alternate approaches have gained popular acceptance—so much so that they have begun to influence the medical profession itself.

Changes over time People who argue that there is no general agreement about health and illness point out that popular thinking about health and illness changes over time. Some things that were once considered to be illnesses—homosexuality, for example—gradually come to be seen as normal or healthy. Other things that used to be considered normal—for example, heavy drinking—become medicalized and treated as an illness. We consider certain conditions to be illnesses that once were ignored completely or treated as crimes. Eighteenth- and nineteenth-century Western criminal history is full of examples of people being imprisoned for acts that we would now consider to be the result of mental illnesses.

One condition now recognized to constitute an illness did not even have a name a few years ago. Posttraumatic stress disorder is generally accepted by the medical community as a type of suffering caused by the emotional and psychic consequences of a traumatic event. (The event may even have been forgotten or repressed, with consequences coming long afterward.) Another example is postpartum depression.

Socially constructed concepts Finally, people taking this position note that conceptions of health and illness are socially constructed. What we consider to be health or illness is shaped by society and social relations. They are real enough, but the way people experience and understand them has a subjective dimension that is influenced by the culture in which they live.

Changes in attitudes and social institutions, even economic conditions, affect the ways people view health and illness. This is

equally true of health care practitioners and the public at large. Negotiations and renegotiations of meaning, through repeated interactions among health care practitioners, patients, government bureaucracies, and hospital administrations, affect how people ultimately come to view health and particular illnesses, as well as illness in general. So, for example, people consider some illnesses to be more disreputable, blameworthy, and preventable than others. For many people, AIDS and drug addiction fall into this category. By contrast, congenital heart weakness or the common cold do not. However, even here we see changes in public thinking. Such changes reflect a growth in understanding about the causes of different diseases. They also show the effects of medicalization, whereby the medical profession relabels the disease as a health problem rather than a moral one.

As social constructs, notions of health and illness are largely shaped by cultural factors. For example, Westerners (more than people in the East) tend to somatize distress; that is, they express anxiety, stress, unhappiness, and psychic trauma in physical symptoms. This is perhaps because, as we pointed out earlier, Western societies view illness as something that takes place in the body and is identifiably wrong with the functioning of the body.

The way in which health and illness are experienced and expressed—the way in which people take on what sociologists have called "the sick role"—also varies by gender, class, ethnicity, and age. This lends further credence to the argument that these are social constructs. Some people are more willing patients than others. It is by willingly taking on the patient role that they escape blame for their inactivity or disability, forcing us to accept medical explanations instead of moral ones.

THERE IS A GENERAL AGREEMENT

Most of us can identify sick people Those who argue that there is a general consensus about health and illness point out that most people can distinguish between healthy and sick people. This is particularly true in respect to physical health. Most people have a basic, intuitive understanding of health as the ability to function in daily life. By this standard, illness is an impairment of that functioning and must be open to redefinition as daily life changes. This basic understanding is what allows the World Health Organization to determine, according to universally agreed upon minimum criteria, who is healthy and who needs care.

Since 1946, the World Health Organization has used a multidimensional definition of health that runs as follows: "A state of complete physical, mental and social well-being and not merely the absence of disease or infirmity." This definition shows that at least this organization has incorporated both Eastern and Western concepts of health. What remains unclear is how much agreement there is on what counts as "physical, mental and social well-being."

What people usually mean when they say someone is ill is that he or she is not acting in ways considered normal or desirable, for reasons beyond personal control. Thus the label "ill" is a way to avoid making moral judgments of nonnormative or deviant behavior. Since societies differ in the behaviors they consider deviant and the explanations they give for this deviance, they also differ in what they consider to be good or bad health. However these differences are not limitless. And at the extremes—for example, with measures of life expectancy or infant mortality— there is general agreement about the meaning and value of these health outcomes.

Eastern and Western conceptions are similar A second argument by people on this side of the debate is that differences between Eastern and Western conceptions of health and illness have been exaggerated. And, increasingly, there has been a mutual influence between East and West with respect to how health and illness are understood.

The differences between Eastern and Western conceptions of health and illness have diminished in recent years. On the one hand, Western medical techniques have been adopted throughout the world. On the other hand, Western medical practice has incorporated many Eastern principles in its approach. Particularly, it has taken nonphysical symptoms far more seriously in treating illnesses, and has come closer to viewing the patient from a holistic perspective. Women's health advocates in particular have emphasized the importance of holistic understanding.

Other examples of the incorporation of Eastern principles include a greater emphasis on emotional and psychological problems as either sources of illness or as illnesses themselves, and more focus on nonphysical aspects of the patient in the treatment process. Eastern influence is also evident in the growing recognition that stress and other emotional or psychological disturbances can be major contributors to the onset, severity, and duration of illness. This comes close to accepting the Eastern premise that individuals need to achieve inner harmony or balance.

Health and illness are not social constructs Third, proponents of this view argue that health and illness are not entirely social constructs. Rather, they are objective descriptions of valid, empirically verifiable states of being. Our descriptions may vary over time with advances in scientific knowledge, but this variation shows that we are gaining an ever more accurate picture of phenomena as they actually are. It does not mean that the concepts health and illness are merely words that can mean whatever we want them to mean.

Thus, for example, societies may differ in whether they consider recurrent sleeplessness to be a problem. They may even differ in whether they consider it to be a health problem. And they may differ in whether they look for the explanation in a physical, mental, or spiritual source. But in any society that views sleeplessness as a health problem, some treatments will "work" and others will not. The test is whether the patient can get a good night's sleep. Ultimately, the test of any science is whether it makes valid predictions and provides solutions to acknowledged problems. In the end, it is scientific evidence based on systematic treatment that will settle this debate.

SUMMING UP

Who is sick? It's harder to say than you might think. On one side of this debate are people who argue that there is no general agreement about what constitutes health and illness. They point to broad cultural differences, as well as changes over time, in how people understand these concepts. They also argue that ideas about health and

illness are social constructs and as such are in a constant process of redefinition.

On the other side of the debate are people who argue that, in spite of superficial differences in the ways people understand health and illness, there is basic, underlying agreement about what these concepts mean. Moreover, such agreement is necessary if we, as an international community, are to determine who is healthy, who needs care, and what kind of care to provide. We need to assume agreement about health and illness, to be able to determine which health policy objectives to pursue, and how to judge their relative effectiveness.

For those who continue to believe that there is no consensus, a worldwide health policy may prove impossible. However, it does not have to result in inaction. Instead, it points to a need to tailor health policies to local understandings of health and illness.

In the end, evidence supports both sides of the debate. Some treatments of some illnesses work well across cultures, but many do not. It is in the latter gray area of treatments that do not work, or do not work as well as expected, that all of us must look for culturally variant solutions to health problems, or even for new thinking about whether they are health problems at all.

REVIEW EXERCISES

For Discussion and Debate

1. Which notion of good health—the Eastern or the Western—makes most sense to you? Why?

2. Why has the West paid so much more attention to physical health than it has to spiritual health?

3. "What seems like good health to one person may be bad health to another. It's all relative."

4. Could there be health professions as we know them if we adopted Eastern conceptions of health?

Writing Exercises

1. "Chanting and chewing on weeds is not my idea of a cure."

2. "Just because some guy uses equipment that cost $2 million doesn't mean he knows anything about human health."

3. "It took ten thousand years for humanity to reach its present understanding of the human body, and alternate health practitioners want to undo that progress overnight."

4. "The main achievement of Western medicine has been to help people live in pain for decades longer."

Research Activities

1. Read up on the history of one of the alternative health professions. How is it organized as a profession, and how is that organization different from, say, the American Medical Association?

2. See if you can find evidence that, by Western standards of scientific proof, Eastern health practices (e.g., local plants, shamans) cure people.

3. See if you can find evidence that, by Eastern standards of knowing, Western health practices (e.g., expensive drugs, technology) cure people.

4. Interview six people who are physically ill to see if you can find any evidence of a mental or spiritual malaise that is at the root of that illness. Report your findings.

SELECTED REFERENCES

AMAYA, VICTOR, and MARIA BLACK, Tradition for revolution: Traditional medicine in El Salvador, *Community Development Journal* (July 1993), 28, 3, 228–236.

ATWOOD, JOAN D., and LAWRENCE MALTIN, Putting Eastern philosophies into Western psychotherapies, *American Journal of Psychotherapy* (July 1991), 45, 3, 368–382.

BAILEY, CAROL A., Equality with a difference: On androcentrism and menstruation, *Teaching Sociology* (1993), 21, 2, 121–129.

EASTHOPE, GARY, The response of orthodox medicine to the challenge of alternative medicine in Australia, *Australian and New Zealand Journal of Sociology* (November 1993), 29, 3, 289–301.

FRANKISH, C. JAMES, and LAWRENCE W. GREEN, Organizational and community change as the social scientific basis for disease prevention and health promotion policy, *Advances in Medical Sociology* (1994), 4, 209–233.

FRASER, J. DUNFIELD, Consumer perceptions of health care quality and the utilization of nonconventional therapy, *Social Science and Medicine* (July 1996), 43, 2, 149–161.

GALLAGHER, EUGENE B., A typology of health rationality applied to third world health, *Advances in Medical Sociology* (1994), 4, 257–280.

GILLETT, GRANT, Beyond the orthodox: Heresy in medicine and social science, *Social Science and Medicine* (November 1994), 39, 9, 1125–1131.

GRECO, MONICA, Psychosomatic subjects and the "duty to be well": Personal agency within medical rationality, *Economy and Society* (August 1993), 22, 3, 357–372.

HARE, RAVINDRA S., Dava, daktar and dua: Anthropology of practiced medicine in India, *Social Science and Medicine* (September 1996), 43, 5, 837–848.

HEITZER-ALLEN, DEBORAH L., CARL KENDALL, and JACK J. WIRIMA, The role of ethnographic research in malaria control: An example from Malawi, *Research in the Sociology of Health Care* (1993), 10, 269–286.

HUDSON, TERESE, Measuring the results of faith, *Hospitals and Health Networks* (September 1996), 70, 22–24.

IDE, BETTE A., and TURKAN SANLI, Health beliefs and behaviors of Saudi women, *Women and Health* (1992), 19, 1, 97–113.

JENKINS, CHRISTOPHER N. H., Health care access and preventive care among Vietnamese immigrants: Do traditional beliefs and practices pose barriers? *Social Science and Medicine* (October 1996), 43, 7, 1049–1056.

JOHNSON, KIRSTEN K., and MARY ANNE KANDRACK, On the medico-legal appropriation of menstrual discourse: The syndromization of women's experiences, *Resources for Feminist Research* (1995), 24, 1–2, 23–27.

KIRBY, JON P., The Islamic dialogue with African traditional religion: Divination and health care, *Social Science and Medicine* (February 1993), 36, 3, 237–247.

LANIER, GINA S., Constructing empowerment and validation in birth: Direct-entry midwives and home birth, *Social Problems* (1995).

MCLEROY, KENNETH R., and CAROLYN E. CRUMP, Health promotion and disease prevention: A historical perspective, *Generations* (Spring 1994), 18, 1, 9–17.

NGOKWEY, NODLAMB, On the specificity of healing functions: A study of diagnosis in three faith healing institutions in Feira (Bahia, Brazil), *Social Science and Medicine* (1989), 29, 4, 515–526.

PHILLIPS, DAPHNE, Fatalism and health in the Brazilian state of Sao Paulo, *International Sociology* (September 1994), 9, 3, 363–375.

PITTS, MARIAN, Lay beliefs about diarrhoeal diseases: Their role in health education in a developing country, *Social Science and Medicine* (October 1996), 43, 8, 1223–1228.

POPAY, JENNIE, Public health research and lay knowledge, *Social Science and Medicine* (March 1996), 42, 5, 759–768.

SENTURIA, KIRSTEN D., Maternal and child health in Albania, *Social Science and Medicine* (1996), 43, 7, 1097–1107.

SOKOLOSKI, ELIZABETH H., Canadian First Nations Women's beliefs about pregnancy and prenatal care, *Canadian Journal of Nursing Research* (1995), 27, 1, 89–100.

WALLERSTEIN, NINA, Empowerment and health: The theory and practice of community change, *Community Development Journal* (July 1993), 28, 3, 218–227.

WIRTH, DANIEL P., The significance of belief and expectancy within the spiritual healing encounter, *Social Science and Medicine* (July 1995), 41, 2, 249–260.

11.2

Do people everywhere have the same chance of good health?

The issue: *What explains the patterns of poor health mentioned in the last section? In particular, are they of sociological interest? That is, do they tell us something about the way our society is organized? And is there anything we—whether as citizens or sociologists— can do to equalize people's chances of good health?*

Introduction In the last section we debated whether people agree on what constitutes good health. Ultimately, bad health means pain, frequent illness, limited activity, and a shortened life span. Do people everywhere have the same chance of good health? Or is health socially structured? For example, do poor people have less chance of good health—of a long life and little activity limitation—than wealthy people do? The answer is that class variations in health are clearly evident. Poor people lead shorter lives, on average, and run higher risks of physical and mental illness and limited activity. Can such variations be avoided? Are poor people "choosing" bad health, and could they be healthier if they chose to? As usual, there are debates on both sides of this issue.

POOR PEOPLE HAVE THE SAME CHANCE OF GOOD HEALTH

Although some argue that poor health is a matter of people's life chances, that people in different social classes have different opportunities to lead happy, healthy lives, precisely because of their position in the social hierarchy, not everyone agrees. Others argue that good health is a matter of choice, not socially defined life chances. This view is based on the belief that all people have a good chance to lead happy, healthy lives. But they have to take advantage of the opportunities that are available to them.

The poor cause their own problems In particular, those who argue that good health is a matter of choice point to social variations in health-enhancing behavior. For example, they note that poor people are more likely to have a bad diet. Some of this is unavoidable, due to a shortage of money, but some of it is not. The poor eat too many carbohydrates and fatty foods. They smoke too many cigarettes and drink too much alcohol. Use of hard drugs is also more common among the poor, especially, the urban underclass we discussed in an earlier chapter. And this group—especially young men in this group—are likely to engage in violent or risky behavior, such as fighting, shooting guns, or driving too fast, all of which are bad for one's health in the long run. Finally, poor people are less likely to exercise regularly. More exercise would prolong their lives and improve their physical health.

The poor don't use available services Along similar lines, the poor are less likely than middle-class people to use available health services. It is true that many poor people lack health insurance. However, in the United States, even poor people who have health insurance and other access to professional health care are less likely to use these services. Various explanations have been put forward to explain this self-destructive behavior. Some claim that reluctance to use health professionals is due to discomfort when interacting with middle-class physicians. The poor may feel out of place in doctors' offices, for example. Others claim that poor people are more fatalistic about their health, feeling that they have little control over their lives (including their health). And some claim poverty is bred from irresponsibility and that the poor are likely to be ill because they don't care about health as much as they do about pleasure and self-indulgence. In the view of these observers, it is folly for the government to spend money trying to help those who would not help themselves.

There is little emphasis on illness prevention More generally, poor people put little emphasis on good health or on preventing illness. Perhaps poor people have too many other worries—like unemployment, bad jobs, or poor housing—on their minds. Good health may occupy a low position on their list of worries. Or perhaps they have low self-esteem, due to the low regard in which society holds them. This would explain why they give little importance to their own physical health. Unfortunate as this is, no one but the poor can ensure their own health, some would say. People need to take care of themselves.

Too little health information is available Finally, just as good health varies with income and social class, it also varies with people's education. Generally, well-educated people are wealthier, more secure, have higher social status, and are healthier too. Perhaps education, not income, is the key to good health. Well-educated people get and use more information about health care and make use of this information in personally beneficial ways. If true, the key to improving people's health and narrowing the unequal chance of good health is through public education. Governments should ensure that all citizens have complete information about their health needs. After that, it is up to individuals to use this information in their own best interest.

POOR PEOPLE HAVE LESS CHANCE OF GOOD HEALTH

Arguments to the contrary address many of the views just put forward.

The poor have too little income Economic recessions and mass layoffs have plunged people of all educational levels into poverty.

For women and children, divorce also has economically disastrous consequences. What we find in these instances of sudden disaster is that poverty—and the consequences of poverty, such as stress and depression—produce many health problems of the poor. Typically, young and middle-aged people with bad health have one or more of the following characteristics: (1) they live in low-income households—indeed, below the poverty line; (2) if they have a job, they do unpaid or poorly paid work; (3) many live in one-parent families; of these, many receive welfare and live in subsidized housing.

The situation is beyond their control What is the connection between poverty and ill health? Researchers have considered this question from various angles and come up with various answers. Some studies find that poverty increases stress and anxiety, with harmful consequences. Other studies find that stress is associated with higher incomes, but depression is associated with poverty. Stress weakens the immune system, leaving stressed people more likely to contract infectious diseases. Stressed people are also more likely to suffer long-term, disabling depression, which makes it impossible to work or care for their children and themselves.

Poor people who work tend to have worse jobs, from a health standpoint. Working conditions are likelier to be unsafe, unhealthy, or stressful. For the poor, food and living conditions are also inferior, so they suffer from poor nutrition and too little sleep. At home and work, their environment is also less safe. For this reason, poor people run a higher risk of accidents and violence beyond their own control.

In general, analysts who relate social class to health note that cleanliness, avoidance of infectious environments, sanitation, and health care all cost money; so that some are less likely to be able to control the environments in which they work and live than others.

People cannot afford good care Today, nearly one American in three lacks health insurance. This means that any visit to a hospital, doctor, dentist, or other health professional must be paid for out of pocket. Given the cost of professional services, many people cannot afford to take care of their health, unless an illness is directly threatening their lives. Poor and rich people may differ slightly in their willingness to use insured (or "free") health services. However, insured and uninsured people differ far more in their willingness to seek health services. Thus it is income, not motivation or education, that accounts for most failures by poor people to seek professional health care.

Fewer services are available Furthermore, in many communities health professionals and health facilities are unavailable. Like most people, doctors, nurses, and other health professionals prefer to work in safe, prosperous communities. Life there is typically more pleasant and earnings for professional work are higher. As a result, there are fewer health professionals and health services (e.g., hospitals, hospital beds, clinics) per capita in poor than in rich states, rural than in urban areas, or poor than in wealthy parts of the city. In poor areas, the available services are likely to be crowded and overused, and it may take longer to get an appointment.

The poor cannot afford to be ill Aside from other shortcomings, poor people are more likely to lack private transportation. To get to a doctor at some distance from home, they may have to take the bus. This means more discomfort, delay, and time lost. Also, poor people usually work at jobs where they lose pay if they take time off to see a doctor or even to recover from illness. This is not true in most professional jobs. Professional workers have more autonomy—can come and go more easily—and suffer few, if any, penalties for losing work time due to illness. In short, poor people cannot afford to be sick, because they cannot afford to lose wages or risk their job. Many prefer to work while sick for these reasons. They know that taking time off to recover would be healthier, but they can't afford it.

The needs of the poor are ignored   Finally, we noted earlier a reluctance by the poor to use health professionals, due to their discomfort when interacting with middle-class physicians. Most doctors are middle-class people from middle-class backgrounds, accustomed to dealing with middle-class patients, and as long as medical education is very expensive they are likely to remain so. They may have as much difficulty dealing with poor people as with people from another culture. There are bound to be communication problems, including differences in the ways people experience and describe illness. Medical schools do not prepare doctors well for these kinds of cross-cultural encounters. As a result, both doctors and patients are uncomfortable.

So there is good evidence that too little income, not too little education or information, is the main cause of poor people's health problems. However, what remains uncertain is the link between poor health and social position, whether measured by income or socioeconomic class. Let us consider two studies that illustrate the complexity of this linkage.

The British Civil Service study   All health researchers and epidemiologists know that people's life chances vary with their posi-

tion in the social order, but they disagree about the reasons why. A British study tried to find the reason by collecting carefully detailed information over a 10-year period. To make the research manageable, researchers studied 10,000 British male civil servants, aged 40–64 at the time the study began. They limited themselves to men, since women's health risks and experiences are different in many respects. And they limited themselves to British civil servants, because good records are available on their health, and they all have free access to health care. Moreover, the researchers were British.

The researchers asked two questions: What proportion of the sample survives for 10 years (or more) from the start of the study? And how does a man's chance of survival vary with his position in the organization? They found that survival chances do vary with a man's rank in the hierarchy. At every age, the risks of dying during the 10-year study period were three and a half times higher among the bottom-ranking clerical and manual workers than among the top-ranking senior administrators. Researchers ruled out the possibility that good health leads to a higher rank. Instead, high rank produces better health.

It is easier to say what does not explain this finding than to say what does. First, higher mortality is not due to unemployment; all of the men sampled were employed. Second, it is not due to absolute poverty; none of those sampled was destitute. Third, it is not due to differences in lifestyle, such as smoking or fatty food intake. Researchers found the same gradient for causes of death that are unaffected by smoking. And they found the same gradient after controlling statistically for smoking, cholesterol level, and blood pressure.

These data lead to two conclusions. First, there is an unmistakable health gradient that varies according to people's socioeconomic position. Being lower down the ladder shortens one's life. This applies to the general population too; poorer people live shorter lives. And the British data show that the socioeconomic death gradient hasn't changed since 1911. Despite changes in society and in the field of medicine and an overall improvement in people's life chances, rich people today are just as far ahead of poor people in the struggle to stay alive as they were 85 years ago. Second, there is no single chain of events from low rank, through illness, to death. Diseases are merely pathways, not causes, of death. Everybody dies of something, and highly stressed people can die of almost anything.

What the British study tells us, first, is that in studying life chances we have to focus our attention on social inequality, not poverty per se. Second, we have to look for generally (not specifically) harmful effects connected with inequality. What Richard Sennett and Jonathan Cobb called the "hidden injuries of class" show up in any of a number of ways.

The "healthy work" study In their book on "healthy work," researchers Robert Karasek and Tores Theorell brought together evidence from a large variety of studies. The research they compiled is from all over the world—some by the authors themselves, some by other researchers. To make their work more manageable, Karasek and Theorell limited their investigation of the relationship between social inequality and health. The book's argument runs as follows: Heart disease is a major health problem deserving close attention and public concern. The psychological condition "stress" is a known major contributor to heart disease.

In turn, "job strain" is a major cause of stress and, therefore, a major cause of heart disease. Job strain is caused by the interaction of: (1) an excessive psychological job demand—too much work to do, too little time to do it, and/or conflicting job demands; and (2) low job control—few or unvarying skills required by the job and little autonomy in decision making. Jobs that cause the most strain combine a high level of job demand and a low level of job control. Such jobs are found at the bottom of the socioeconomic hierarchy. Thus, according to this theory, people at the bottom of the social ladder, with the most stress-producing jobs, run the highest risk of heart disease.

This theory and its predictions are supported by data from many studies of coronary heart disease. Low-level service workers—waitresses, for example—do indeed have higher than average risks of heart disease. Why? Because in any restaurant, waitresses hold the lowest status, well below the manager, chef, (male) waiters, and customers. Often, they have to wear demeaning uniforms and suffer sexual harassment. Always, waitresses are expected to be quick and accurate, yet pleasant and patient. At peak hours, the job demands are nearly impossible. The job is also repetitious and leaves little room for personal creativity or discretion.

Symphony musicians, compared with other kinds of artists, also have a higher than average risk of heart disease. And here, too, the explanation is similar. Symphonic musicians have more skills and a higher income than most waitresses. But they also suffer from heavy job demands—a grueling practice, rehearsal, and travel schedule, for example. And, compared to other artists, they have little control over their own performance. Symphony musicians are merely "instruments" of the conductor. It is the conductor who has job autonomy, deciding how the work is to be performed.

SUMMING UP

Do people everywhere have the same chance of good health? Certainly not. Poor people suffer from higher rates of illness and have a lower life expectancy than rich people. This section has focused on the factors that may explain these differences. We have considered whether the causal link is to be found in differential, class-based access to good health or in different lifestyles and attitudes that make the poor more prone to getting sick and to dying relatively young.

On one side of the debate are those who argue that poor people have higher rates of illness and die younger because of class barriers to adequate health care. On the other side are those who argue that access to good health care is equal, or at least equal enough. By this account, it is because poor people engage in risky or negligent behaviors that they run higher chances of sickness and early death.

But good health is far more complex than just a question of diseases and death. Likewise, important as poverty may be, social inequality means more than wealth or the lack of it; it also means control over one's work and one's life. In its various forms, social inequality stresses the mind, the spirit, and the immune system, resulting in any of a number of health problems. As we have noted, stresses on people at the bottom of the social ladder can show up in many forms.

What is clear is that bad health is not a matter of bad choice or incomplete information. The nation's health problems cannot be solved simply by providing more public health education. Rather, society and a great many of its members would be better off with less inequality.

REVIEW EXERCISES

For Discussion and Debate

1. Why would some people appear to choose poor health over good health?

2. What kind of health insurance is likely to provide good health care for the largest number of people?

3. What is it about low rank, or low social status, that might cause poor health?

4. How might a job like waitressing be changed to make it less of a health risk, and how likely is this to happen?

Writing Exercises

1. "Why I'd rather be a symphony musician than a rock musician."

2. "Here's how I would cope with the pressures of high job demand and low autonomy."

3. "Taking health concerns too seriously lets you live longer but worse."

4. "The unhealthiest job I ever had."

Research Activities

1. Devise a brief questionnaire to find out what information people actually have about real health risks. Then administer this questionnaire to six students at your college and report the results.

2. Choose one disease or health condition and find out whether its prevalence or seriousness varies among people of different social classes in your own community.

3. Choose one disease or health condition and find out whether its prevalence or seriousness varies among people in your own country and one other country (your choice).

4. Study health problems in your college to find out whether lower-ranking (first-year) students have more or different problems than higher-ranking (fourth-year) students.

SELECTED REFERENCES

BARTLEY, MEL, Unemployment and health: Selection or causation—a false antithesis? *Sociology of Health and Illness* (March 1988), 10, 1, 41–67.

CARR-HILL, ROY A., Time trends in inequalities in health, *Journal of Biosocial Science* (July 1988), 20, 3, 265–273.

COCKERHAM, WILLIAM C., GUENTHER LUESCHEN, GERHARD KUNZ, and JOE L. SPAETH, Social stratification and self-management of health, *Journal of Health and Social Behavior* (March 1986), 27, 1, 1–14.

DAVIS, KAREN, Inequality and access to health care, *Milbank Quarterly* (1991), 69, 2, 253–273.

FORD, GRAEME, RUSSELL ECOB, KATE HUNT, SALLY MACINTYRE, and PATRICK WEST, Patterns of class inequality in health through the lifespan: Class gradients at 15, 35 and 55 years in the west of Scotland, *Social Science and Medicine* (October 1994), 39, 8, 1037–1050.

FOSSETT, JAMES W. , JANET D. PERLOFF, PHILIP R. KLETKE, and JOHN A. PETERSON, Medicaid and access to child health care in Chicago, *Journal of Health Politics, Policy and Law* (Summer 1992), 17, 2, 273–298.

KARASEK, ROBERT, and TORES THEORELL, Healthy work: Stress, productivity, and the reconstruction of working life (New York: Basic Books, 1990).

KRIEGER, NANCY, and ELIZABETH FEE, Social class: The missing link in U.S. health data, *International Journal of the Health Services* (1994), 24, 1, 25–44.

LAVEIST, THOMAS A., Segregation, poverty and empowerment: Health consequences for African Americans, *Milbank Quarterly* (1993), 71, 1, 41–64.

LIA-HOAGBERG, BETTY, PETER RODE, CATHERINE J. SKOVHOLT, CHARLES N. OBERG, CYNTHIA BERG, SARA MULLETT, and THOMAS CHOI, Barriers and motivators to prenatal care among low-income women, *Social Science and Medicine* (1990), 30, 4, 487–495.

LUNDBERG, OLLE, Causal explanation for class inequality in health—an empirical analysis, *Social Science and Medicine* (1991), 32, 4, 385–393.

MCCORD, COLIN, and HAROLD P. FREEMAN, Excess mortality in Harlem, *New England Journal of Medicine* (January 1990), 322, 3, 18, 173–177.

NAJMAN, JAKE M., Health and poverty: Past, present, and prospect for the future, *Social Science and Medicine* (January 1993), 36, 2, 157–166.

NAVARRO, VICENTE, Class and race: Life and death situations, *Monthly Review* (September 1991), 43, 4, 1–13.

PATRICK, DONALD L., JANE STEIN, MIGUEL PORTA, CAROL Q. PORTER, and THOMAS C. RICKETTS, Poverty, health services, and health status in rural America, *Milbank Quarterly* (1988), 66, 1, 105–136.

PEREIRA, JOAO, The economics of inequality in health: A bibliography, *Social Science and Medicine* (1990), 31, 3, 413–420.

POWER, CHRIS, Social and economic background and class inequalities in health among young adults, *Social Science and Medicine* (1991), 32, 4, 411–417.

REICH, MICHAEL R., Technical fixes and other problems in saving lives in the world's poorest countries, *Journal of Public Health Policy* (Spring 1988), 9, 1, 92–103.

SENNETT, RICHARD, and JONATHAN COBB, *The hidden injuries of social class* (New York: Vintage Books, 1973).

TOWNSEND, PETER, Individual or social responsibility for premature death? Current controversies in the British debate about health, *International Journal of Health Services* (1990), 20, 3, 373–392.

WENNEMO, IRENE, Infant mortality, public policy and inequality—A comparison of 18 industrialised countries, *Sociology of Health and Illness* (September 1993), 15, 4, 429–446.

WILKINSON, RICHARD G., Class mortality, income distribution and trends in poverty 1921–1981,

Journal of Social Policy (July 1989), 18, 3, 307–335.

———, Income distribution and mortality: A "natural" experiment, *Sociology of Health and Illness* (December 1990), 12, 4, 391–412.

WILLIAMS, DAVID D., Barriers to achieving health, *Child and Adolescent Social Work Journal* (October 1993), 10, 5, 355–363.

WRIGHT, JAMES D., Poor people, poor health: The health status of the homeless, *Journal of Social Issues* (Winter 1990), 46, 4, 49–64.

11.3

Should mentally ill people be deinstitutionalized?

The issue: What is the proper way to deal with a group with a chronic health problem: institutionalize them, treat them in the community, or simply let them deal with the problem on their own? Historically, North American societies have tried all of these options; each has its own shortcomings.

Introduction *Question*: What do mental patients have in common with AIDS victims, homosexuals, recreational drug users, heavy drinkers, and ex-convicts? *Answer*: They are all socially stigmatized. For example, research shows that many people do not want to have them as neighbors. Many fewer people are unwilling to have as neighbors members of racial minorities, recent immigrants, or people with large families. The social rejection and exclusion of ethnic and racial minorities have diminished; however, the rejection and exclusion of social minorities, including mental patients, continue.

As we noted in an earlier section, applying the "illness" label typically excuses deviant behavior, rendering it blameless. However, for many people, the mentally ill remain an exception to this rule. They have been declared ill, their deviance has been medicalized, and they are receiving treatment. Yet many people fear or blame the mentally ill for their deviance. As a result, many people don't want them as neighbors.

In light of this, should the care for mental illness be deinstitutionalized and mental patients released to community-based care? Deinstitutionalization of mental patients has become common in the last few decades. The release of mental patients into the community has increased with the reduction and privatization of social services discussed in earlier chapters. But given the widespread stigmatization of mental patients, is deinstitutionalization a good idea? And if it is, how should we deal with the problem of social stigma?

CARE FOR MENTAL PATIENTS SHOULD BE DEINSTITUTIONALIZED

Early support for deinstitutionalization The argument in favor of deinstitutionalization goes back at least to the early 1960s. It represents the convergence of many trends in social thought, which themselves reflect major changes in American society. Thus views on the mentally ill are a good indication of changes in the larger society that occurred from the 1960s onward.

One major support for deinstitutionalization was the liberal revolt against total institutions, signified by interest in sociologist

Erving Goffman's book *Asylums*. We discussed Goffman's views on total institutions briefly in Section 3.2. Essentially, Goffman and others viewed total institutions, including mental hospitals, as fundamentally antitherapeutic and ineffective in helping patients. Instead of making inmates healthy and better adjusted to life in the outside world, total institutions made inmates worse and/or less well adjusted.

A second support for deinstitutionalization was provided by social scientists and social workers. They opposed the growing medicalization of social problems. For sociology's labeling theorists, the problem posed by mental illness was often a problem of labeling and secondary deviation. Left alone, many so-called "mentally ill" people could function effectively in society. By labeling them and treating them as sick people, doctors (especially psychiatrists) worsened the problem.

The fact that doctors were able to medicalize growing numbers of deviants indicated the growing popular acceptance of psychiatry and professional power of psychiatrists. Social scientists and social workers, holding different views of mental illness and professional goals of their own, challenged this medicalization process. Thus, in part, the fight against deinstitutionalization was a fight over the right to define the boundaries of mental illness and ways of dealing with it.

A third support for deinstitutionalization came from the legal community. From the 1950s onward, lawyers grew more and more active in fights for the civil liberties of minority groups. In the 1950s and afterward, lawyers fought for equal rights for American blacks; in the 1960s, they entered the fight for the rights of draft dodgers and protesters against the Vietnam War. Increasingly, lawyers fought for the rights of prisoners and against capital punishment. Then they turned their attention to the rights of other dependent or vulnerable people: children, women, the terminally ill, and the mentally ill. Though a fight for civil liberties, lawyers' actions on behalf of the mentally ill were also part of the war against the medicalization of social problems. From the 1960s onward, lawyers and doctors often clashed over people's rights, needs, and competencies.

A fourth support for deinstitutionalization came from community mental health professionals. With encouragement from less traditional physicians, psychiatrists, and social workers, their numbers had been growing since the 1950s. As their numbers grew even more rapidly in the decades that followed, it became possible to treat more mentally ill people released into the community.

A fifth support for deinstitutionalization came from pharmaceutical companies. By 1960, traditional treatments of depression and schizophrenia such as electroconvulsive therapy (ECT, or shock treatment) had acquired a bad name. Most people viewed ECT as harsh, excessive, and, except as a means of pacifying violent patients, ineffective. Increasingly, pharmaceutical drugs, especially tranquilizers, antidepressants, and lithium for schizophrenia, were substituted. They had the same pacifying effects but were less visible, cheaper, safer, and did less permanent damage than shock treatment. As these drugs came into general use and momentum gathered to release patients into community care, it became clear that chemical treatment worked just as well outside mental hospitals as it did inside them.

Finally, a sixth source of support came in the 1980s and 1990s with the so-called "taxpayers revolt." More and more citizens wanted lower taxes and less public spending, even if that meant fewer social services and more risk for vulnerable groups in society. Taxpayers wanted cheaper alternatives to institutional care for a variety of social deviants, including mentally ill people.

What supporters expected Generally, the fight to deinstitutionalize mental patients had a negative goal—the release of mental patients—but no positive goal. There was no clear plan about what to do with mental patients once they were in the community. However, there was widespread agreement about the likely benefits of releasing mental patients.

- First, supporters believed that deinstitutionalization would avoid the disruption of social ties and social roles that came with induction into total institutions—whether mental hospitals, prisons, convents, or military camps.

- Second, it would permit patients to exercise initiative and learn skills associated with independent living.

- Third, in both these ways deinstitutionalization would prevent the worsening of patients' original symptoms. In particular, it would prevent the development of institutional behaviors and attitudes connected with "prisonization" (discussed in an earlier section). It would also allow mental patients to escape dangers like physical and sexual assault associated with life in total institutions. Hence, outpatient care would be health preserving and health enhancing.

- Fourth, though there was no standard plan for outpatient care, many felt that community-based professionals in clinics and halfway houses would provide better care than what mental patients received in institutions. In addition, outpatient care would reduce the stigmatization of mental illness and foster the outpatients' integration back into society.

The supporters of deinstitutionalization hoped these things would happen and felt they had good reasons for supporting the plan. But things did not work out precisely as planned.

CARE FOR MENTAL PATIENTS SHOULD NOT BE DEINSTITUTIONALIZED

Unfortunately, the fine ideals and high hopes of deinstitutionalization were rarely achieved. Mental patients without friends or family to care for them had to live in rundown, unregulated rooming houses in poor parts of the city. Thus, the most immediate result of deinstitutionalization was to deprive many ex-patients of the community life available within the mental hospital. Whatever its faults, the mental hospital had provided patients with familiar faces and people to talk to. By contrast, life on the outside was often isolated and lonely.

The problem was largely economic. The move to deinstitutionalize mental patients coincided with major cuts in spending on health care and social services. Though community-based health care is cheaper than institutional care, it still costs more than many governments were prepared to pay. So many mental patients released into the community were given less professional care than supporters of deinstitutionalization had expected. The results were predictably harmful.

A shortage of funds meant too few resources for outpatient care, including too few professional therapists and support groups. Too few day programs were provided in the community, and there was not enough adequate, affordable housing, whether in halfway houses or through subsidies to private landlords.

Now just imagine what would happen if troubled, vulnerable people left a sheltered environment and came to live in the middle of a big city in poor housing, with little professional help, little to do, and little money to spend. Many, you predict, would become street people, spending most of their time in public, highly visible places. Some would get into trouble, or at least attract the attention of the police. As a result, homelessness and public deviance by ex-mental patients would increase. With no one else to handle it, the police would step in. With nowhere else to go, many ex-patients would end up in jail. There, they would get even less treatment than they did in the mental hospital. And with more ex-patients on the streets and less treatment provided them, public attitudes would harden against the mentally ill. Middle-class people in particular would oppose the location of shelters, clinics, or group homes for the mentally ill in their neighborhoods. The resulting sentiment toward mental patients would be captured in the acronym NIMBY: "I have nothing against them but, please, **Not In My Back Yard.**"

Did you predict all of these things? Yes, they did all happen, and they were perfectly predictable. Governments and taxpayers did not want to spend enough to make the programs work. Spending enough is the key. We can solve most of the problems associated with deinstitutionalization by spending more money to care for released patients. But what about the NIMBY problem that's been created? Can it be solved too, and if so, how?

The NIMBY problem can be solved   In the last 10 years, there has been enough sociological research on the NIMBY problem to give us the answer. Where mental patients are concerned, researchers find that few people oppose nonresidential facilities. Few people mind outpatients coming into their community for treatment or day programs. However, some do oppose residential facilities (shelters or halfway houses) for the mentally ill in their "backyard." Fortunately, people who oppose a residence in their neighborhood prove to be less politically active than people who support

the location. In the end, they are incapable of mounting effective opposition.

Liberal, nontraditional neighborhoods—often working-class neighborhoods—are the most likely to accept and even welcome residential facilities. Opposition is least if people are informed individually about the plan to locate a shelter or halfway house in their neighborhood. However, a community meeting on the topic is likely to mobilize opposition. Surprisingly, for the best integration of patients, a moderate community reaction is better than none at all. Once established, a facility for mental patients poses no problems for the neighborhood. Research shows that, if uninformed of its presence, most residents do not even know the facility is there. Since no problems arise, opposition to the residence declines in time. There is no adverse effect on property values and no effect—positive or negative—on attitudes to mental illness.

SUMMING UP

Should mentally ill people be deinstitutionalized? Yes, but not if it's only to ignore them more effectively. The deinstitutionalization of mental patients was one of many civil liberties fights that gained momentum in the 1960s. Then, like other progressive movements of the 1960s, it ran out of steam.

In the 1990s, deinstitutionalized mental patients make up a large share of the homeless and jail population, since there is nowhere else for them to go. It is hard to say whether these mentally ill people are worse off than residents of total institutions had been in the 1950s. Many would say they are better off in some ways but worse off in others.

As we saw, the plan to deinstitutionalize the mentally ill faltered on the hidden shoals of tax cuts and insufficient spending. As homeless people, the mentally ill were even more stigmatized than they had been before. In an age of middle-class backlash, NIMBY was a predictable response to the needs of the mentally ill. However, the basic thinking behind deinstitutionalization was right, and the NIMBY problem is surmountable. With enough public spending and commitment to finding good locations for outpatient facilities, deinstitutionalized mental patients will make the best possible recovery. We will not likely return to large-scale institutionalization of the mentally ill in the future. To a greater degree than in the past, our approach will depend on the type of mental illness and its severity.

We ended the last section by noting that in our society, bad health is not a matter of bad choice or incomplete information. The nation's health problems cannot be solved by providing more public health education. Nor, in the case of mental health, can it be solved just by removing people from health-worsening custodial institutions. A more positive input is needed. Mentally ill people need programs of treatment and professionally trained people to provide them.

We also noted that social inequality may be inevitable, yet in some societies too much social inequality is unnecessary and harmful. Inequality hurts people's health in countless ways—for example, making them sick and shortening their lives.

As we have seen at other points in this book, strains associated with poverty, unemployment, and economic uncertainty disrupt social relations. For example, they raise the risk of domestic violence and negligent parenting. More relevant to this present debate, social strains hurt people's mental health. No one can deny the importance of genetically determined influences. At one level, mental illness is nothing more than a chemical imbalance. However, this imbalance is often associated with, and triggered by, traumatic or stressful social conditions.

So even something so chemical and "psychological" as mental illness is well within the realm of sociological interest. This section has shown that mental illness is socially defined, and that people defined as mentally ill are socially stigmatized. Social strains increase the risk of mental illness. Competing social groups, usually competing professions, dispute the best treatments for mental illness. Competing social groups determine the availability of funds to treat mental illness. The failure to treat mental illness adequately produces new social problems, like homelessness. A socially sensible approach to neighbors leads to acceptance of treatment facilities in the neighborhood.

REVIEW EXERCISES

For Discussion and Debate

1. Why are mentally ill people so often stigmatized and excluded?

2. In your opinion, what is the best single argument in favor of deinstitutionalizing mental patients? Why do you think so?

3. Would your neighbors object to having a halfway house for former mental patients on your own street? If so, why?

4. What is the best way to ensure acceptance of a halfway house for former mental patients in a middle-class neighborhood?

Writing Exercises

1. "Fears of mental illness reflect nothing more than prejudice and ignorance."

2. "Cost aside, it would be better to have mental patients back in mental hospitals."

3. "Here's how I would reintegrate a former mental patient back into the community."

4. "The legal rights of mental patients are still being ignored. For example, . . ."

Research Activities

1. Collect some information on mental hospitals and prisons that would allow you to compare them to determine whether mental hospitals also "prisonize" their inmates.

2. Develop a questionnaire that measures people's attitudes toward, and beliefs about, mental illness. Administer this questionnaire to six people and report on the results.

3. Using published material, find out the degree of connection between homelessness and deinstitutionalization. What proportion of the homeless are mentally ill? What proportion of the mentally ill are homeless?

4. Find out about the pharmaceutical control of symptoms of mental illness. Focusing on one commonly used drug, what are its advantages over hospitalization? What are its negative side effects or other disadvantages?

SELECTED REFERENCES

ARENS, D. A., What do the neighbors think now? Community residences on Long Island, New York, *Community Mental Health Journal* (1993), 29, 3, 235–245.

AUBREY, T. D., B. TEFFT, and R. F. CURRIE, Public attitudes and intentions regarding tenants of community mental health residences who are neighbours, *Community Mental Health Journal* (1995), 31, 1, 39–52.

BORINSTEIN, A. B., Public attitudes toward persons with mental illness, *Health Affairs* (1992), 11, 3, 186–196.

BROKINGTON, I. F., et al., Tolerance of the mentally ill, *British Journal of Psychiatry* (1993), 162, 93–99.

CURRIE, R. R., et al., Maybe on my street: The politics of community placement of the mentally disabled, *Urban Affairs Quarterly* (1989), 25, 2, 298–321.

FISHER, GENE, PAUL R. BENSON, and RICHARD C. TESSLER, Family response to mental illness: Developments since deinstitutionalization, *Research in Community and Mental Health* (1990), 6, 203–236.

GOLDMAN, H. H., J. P. MORRISSEY,, and L. L. BACHRACH, Deinstitutionalization in international perspective: Variations on a theme, *International Journal of Mental Health* (1983), 11, 4, 153–165.

GRONFEIN, WILLIAM, Psychotropic drugs and the origins of deinstitutionalization, *Social Problems* (June 1985), 32, 5, 437–454.

HERMAN, NANCY J., "Mixed nutters" and "looney tuners": The emergence, development, nature and function of two informal deviant subcultures of chronic ex-psychiatric patients, *Deviant Behavior* (1987), 8, 3, 235–258.

ISAAC, RAEL JEAN, and VIRGINIA C. ARMAT, *Madness in the streets: How psychiatry and the law abandoned the mentally ill* (New York: Free Press, 1990).

MALLA, A., and T. SHAW, Attitudes towards mental illness: The influence of education and experience, *International Journal of Social Psychiatry* (1987), 33, 1, 33–41.

MECHANIC, D., and J. ROCHEFORT, Deinstitutionalization: An appraisal of reform, *Annual Review of Sociology* (1990), 16, 301–327.

MONOHAN, J., A terror to their neighbours: Beliefs about mental disorder and violence in historical and cultural perspective, *Bulletin of the American Academy of Psychiatry and the Law* (1992), 20, 2, 191–195.

MORRISSEY, JOSEPH P., and HOWARD H. GOLDMAN, Care and treatment of the mentally ill in the United States: Historical development and reforms, *Annals of the American Academy of*

Political and Social Science (March 1986), 484, 12–27.

NOH, SAMUEL, and WILLIAM R. AVISON, Spouses of discharged psychiatric patients: Factors associated with their experience, *Journal of Marriage and the Family* (May 1988), 50, 2, 377–389.

RIZZO, A. M., et al., Strategies for responding to community opposition to an existing group home, *Psychosocial Rehabilitation Journal* (1992), 15, 3, 85–95.

SCHEPER-HUGHES, NANCY, "Mental" in "Southie": Individual, family, and community responses to psychosis in South Boston, *Culture, Medicine and Psychiatry* (March 1987), 11, 1, 53–78.

SCULL, ANDREW, Deinstitutionalization and public policy, *Social Science and Medicine* (1985), 20, 5, 545–552.

TEFFT, B., A. SEGALL, and B. TRUTE, Neighbourhood response to community mental health facilities for the chronically mentally disabled, *Canadian Journal of Community Mental Health* (1987), 6, 2, 37–49.

WAHL, O. F., Community impact of group homes for mentally ill adults, *Community Mental Health Journal* (1993), 29, 3, 247–259.

WARNER, RICHARD , Deinstitutionalization: How did we get where we are? *Journal of Social Issues* (Fall 1989), 45, 3, 17–30.

WEGNER, E. L., Deinstitutionalization and community-based care for the chronic mentally ill, *Research in Community and Mental Health* (1990), 6, 295–324.

WILMOTH, G. H., S. SILVER, and L. J. SEVERY, Receptivity and planned change: Community attitudes and deinstitutionalization, *Journal of Applied Psychology* (1987), 72, 1, 138–145.

12. Population

A **population** can be defined as "the stock of a species with throughput"—which is to say, a set of people (or animals or even inanimate objects) that changes in size as members are added to or subtracted from the set. And the social science that provides sociologists with materials for the study of population is demography.

Sociology and demography are two separate disciplines, but they are intimately linked. **Demography** is the scientific study of the size, structure, distribution, and growth of the world's population. **Social demography**, the topic of this section, is concerned with the effects of population on the organization of societies, and vice versa. Demographers play a central role in collecting and analyzing population data such as census data. And sociologists rely on demographers for this information to help us understand population problems.

In this chapter we focus on three population problems that are causing concern in different parts of the world. First, we consider whether the world as a whole is becoming overpopulated—in effect, a population time bomb that will eventually use up the planetary resources we rely on to survive. In the second section we ask whether the attempt one society, China, has made to limit its population growth through forced family limitation is a good thing and worthy of imitation by other rapidly growing societies. Finally, the third section focuses on North America and other economically developed societies and asks whether it is time to limit immigration to prevent overcrowding, unemployment, or intercultural conflict.

12.1

Are there too many people around?

The issue: _Whether we are about to be swamped by too many humans. Some ignore the rapid population growth and, in ignoring it, see no problem. Others hunt for and find dire predictions of ecological disaster, famine, and war over scarce resources. Is there any way we can foresee the likely future consequences of our current population trends?_

Introduction The answer to this question begins with a theory proposed two centuries ago by the English economist Thomas Malthus. His slender and influential book, _An Essay on Population_, argued that populations grow _exponentially_, or _geometrically_. A population growing exponentially at a constant rate adds more people every year than the year before.

Consider a population of 1000 women and 1000 men. Each woman marries and has four children. If all survive, in the next generation there are roughly 2000 women and 2000 men. If all of those women have four children each, in the next generation there are roughly 4000 women and 4000 men, and in the generation after that, 8000 women and 8000 men. So, with a constant pattern of four births per woman, the population doubles every generation (roughly 30 years). In 300 years, the original population of 2000 exceeds a million people! This is the power of exponential growth.

On the other hand, increases in the food supply are only *additive*, or *arithmetic*. The growth in food supplies is limited by available land, soil quality, and the level of technology. Malthus believed that there is a real risk of populations outgrowing increases in the food supply. The chance of running out of food thus poses a real threat to humanity. For that reason, checks or limits are needed to keep population growth in line with the food supply. Welfare schemes to help the poor are futile, said Malthus. If we feed the hungry, they will increase their numbers until they are hungry again.

The only sure solutions are positive checks and preventive checks. *Positive checks* prevent overpopulation by increasing the death rate. They include war, famine, pestilence, and disease. *Preventive checks* prevent overpopulation by limiting the number of live births. They include abortion, infanticide, sexual abstinence, delayed marriage, and contraceptive use.

Malthus painted a grim picture of the world's future. But was he right? Is the world a population time bomb, as Malthus believed? As usual, views on this matter vary.

THE WORLD IS STILL A POPULATION TIME BOMB

Those who argue today that there is still a population problem, that the world is becoming overpopulated, or that the world is a population time bomb make some of the same arguments Malthus did nearly two centuries ago.

World population is still growing Today, in central Africa, women average six children or more, not the four we cited in our example. However, even the more modest four children per mother is common in Southeast Asia, the Islamic world, parts of Africa, and Latin America. In short, hundreds of millions of mothers are still producing children at this rate. As we have seen, with four children per mother a population doubles every 30 years or so. Even allowing for slower growth, experts predict that in 30 years the current world population of just under 6 billion people will be 3 billion larger. Will the world be able to feed 50% more people, let alone 100% more, in 30 years?

Population is growing faster than food Here, expert estimates vary. However, statistics collected by Worldwatch indicate that the world's grain production is falling. The store of available food is only enough to last for a short time, in the event of widespread crop failures. Other ecologists conclude that the number of people on earth will have to drop to at least one-third the current level by 2100 in order to survive in relative prosperity. Though an optimum population is between 1 and 2 billion people, the current population is near 6 billion, and predictions using current growth rates put it at between 12 billion and 15 billion people in 2100.

At the current growth rate of 1.1% a year, the population of the United States in 2100 could be 1.2 billion people, the current population of China. Today, each American consumes about 23 times more goods and services than the average person in the third world and 53 times more than someone in China. A future America, with as many people as China today, might have to settle for something close to a Chinese standard of living.

Population growth strains resources One of the problems hinted at above is a growing shortage of nonrenewable resources, which include land, fresh water, petroleum fuel, and minerals needed for manufacturing. It is not always clear which problems are caused by overpopulation. However, some observers link growing shortages of nonrenewable resources—even shortages of water—in the developed world to the problem of overpopulation.

In recent decades, humans have dramatically transformed the environment. The entire global ecology is affected, especially the equilibrium of the biosphere and the interdependence between living systems. This raises doubts about the survival chances of humanity. The ultimate source of concern for environmental change is its potential effect on the livability of the globe and its ability to support the variety and complexity of ongoing human activities.

Too rapid population growth threatens human self-regulating systems as well as natural ecosystems. Even if rapid population growth does not cause all these problems, it makes them harder to solve.

Population growth slows economic development

One major consequence of rapid growth is a population in which a large proportion are school-aged or younger. And since people need education, rapidly growing societies must spend a large portion of their budget on schools and schooling. In such societies, childbearing women are less likely to be economically active. Along with old people, children, and the infirm, they require much public spending on health and welfare. So in a rapidly growing society, health, education, and welfare spending consume a large part of the national budget. The expense has to be paid by relatively few economically active adults.

Several consequences flow from this. First, high-fertility societies are often unable to afford good health, education, and welfare programs. Money spent on these

programs takes money away from programs to develop manufacturing or export industries. This limits the country's ability to develop economically; at best, it slows the process dramatically.

Technology cannot solve the problem

In nineteenth-century England the population problem Malthus had predicted seemed to solve itself. Mortality began to fall, and soon so did childbearing. Food production increased and people's standard of living began to improve. All of these changes were due, in one way or another, to the development of new technology. Will technology come to our rescue again in the twentieth century?

Not necessarily, for several reasons. There are limits to what we can expect technology to do. Given present levels of technology, all the world's people cannot possibly enjoy the level of affluence North Americans enjoy today. There is just not enough wealth to go around. Beyond that, technology is costly and uncertain. As well as population size and consumption (lifestyle) patterns, technology determines the amount of pollution generated, so it plays a part in destroying the ecosystem. Technology depletes natural resources, contributing to environmental problems and even perpetuating social inequality. Evidence suggests that technology will continue to improve, yet technology also has harmful side effects. Also, if our consumer culture is not checked, gains from technology will be offset.

Positive checks replace preventive checks

Malthus noted that in a population that failed to take preventive measures, positive checks would come into play. Plagues, famines, epidemics, wars, and other causes of death would increase. Eventually, a rise in the death rate would bring the population down to a manageable level. Malthus did not realize that technological advances in agriculture would make it possible to vastly increase the food supply. Today, even in less developed countries, most people have *some* food to eat. However, famines and epidemics continue to rage throughout the world—especially in the countries where the population is growing most rapidly.

Note also that the twentieth century is remarkable for two major shifts in human experience. One is an explosion of population growth that is still continuing. The other is an explosion of "mega-murders"—deaths by war, civil war, and internal terror—that by one estimate have consumed 188 million lives. Some scholars have estimated that more people died from genocide than from all wars combined in the twentieth century! Malthus would not be surprised by these facts. Probably, rapid population growth increases conflict, brings pressure for rapid solutions, and reduces our ability to solve problems peacefully.

THE WORLD IS NOT A POPULATION TIME BOMB

Those who take the opposing view challenge Malthusians on many points of evidence.

Famines are political, not agricultural Today, few demographers support all of Malthus's gloomy views. They realize that claims of overpopulation are sometimes used to mask issues of powerlessness and social inequality. For example, the famines that have plagued Ethiopia and Somalia in recent years are not a result of overpopulation. The World Bank has pushed for cash crops there, destroying local means of sustenance. Further, protectionism in agriculture by first world nations has closed markets to third world nations, thus hurting their economies. Famines are also a result of improper land use, civil wars, and other social and political

factors, such as low prices set on foods by the state. For strategic reasons, governments sometimes put a low priority on shipping food to regions of the country where rebel supporters are most numerous. In this way they try to starve the rebels into submission. This use of strategic famine has a long history. So we cannot take famines in themselves as proof of overpopulation. Beyond that, many developed societies pay their farmers not to grow crops, even if this means a shortage somewhere else in the world. So we cannot take low rates of food production to indicate the maximum amount of food that can be produced in the world today.

World food production is growing Some estimates show food production falling behind population growth. However, other estimates show food production growing faster than world population—that is to say, at more than 4% per year. It is hard to account for the discrepancy between these estimates. Perhaps experts assess the trustworthiness of data sources differently or count different kinds of foods into their calculation.

Population growth is not to blame for slow development It is likely that rapid population growth slows down economic development. However, at issue is *how much* it slows development, compared with other factors. Note, for example, that economic growth has been extremely slow in much of the Western world for the last decade or so. That cannot be blamed on rapid population growth.

There are many possible reasons for slow economic growth: global competition, a shortage of capital, competing economic or social goals, poor corporate planning, poor economic planning, poor political leadership, exploitation by foreign investors, internal strife, even a low level of commitment to economic growth. How much each of these factors contributes to explaining slow growth in a developing country is an empirical question. To answer it we need to study countries carefully, one at a time. We cannot assume that rapid population growth is the most important influence in each, or any, case.

Population growth is not to blame for conflict and stress Likewise, we cannot assume that rapid population growth is the most important influence on social conflict or environmental stress. It is true that social conflict, rapid population growth, and environmental stress are often found together. But showing a correlation is not the same as establishing causation. All three may be caused by yet another factor, and at least two possible candidates suggest themselves: national poverty and global inequality.

National poverty and a low position in the global hierarchy of nations are correlated with each other. As well, each and both promote social conflict, rapid population growth, and environmental stress. Take poverty: Compared to rich people, poor people are more likely to invest heavily in children (their only insurance against impoverished old age). They are also more likely to overuse their land in order to get the maximum short-term productivity. And they are more likely to engage in violent conflict with members of other groups or tribes, against whom they compete for scarce land, jobs, or housing.

To repeat, rapid population growth is part of each scenario, but it does not necessarily cause the other problems. Poverty and inequality often cause problems that are similar to those caused by overpopulation and may contribute to overpopulation too.

Technology will triumph again Taking a long view of human history, you have to put your money on humanity coming through once again. Many civilizations have fallen in the past—Babylonian, Egyptian, Greek, Roman, and so on—yet here we are today, still alive and able to talk about it. History is full of wars, plagues, epidemics, challenges, and crises. Yet the human race is still here—larger and more prosperous than ever. The human ability to hatch new ideas and technologies—to be creative—has carried us through, and it can do so again. We may not be able to say precisely which technology will help us out of our present difficulty, nor who will invent it or when, but we can feel certain that it will happen sooner or later.

Economic growth will slow population growth And with the arrival of new ideas and new technology, economic development will explode once again. When that happens, we can expect rapidly growing populations to enter the demographic transition toward lower death and birth rates. History shows that people have much to gain by doing so and too much to lose by failing to do so. With low death rates, they will have little need for many children, especially once old age security and middle-class lifestyles become available.

SUMMING UP

Are there too many people around? Well, that really depends on what you mean by "too many." More than that, the issue is how quickly people are increasing, not simply how many heads there are to count. In his book *How Many People Can the Earth Support?*, population expert Joel Cohen recognizes that the population time bomb question cannot be answered as posed. The earth can support many more people than currently live on it, but it supports them with more or less ease under different conditions. Cohen notes a number of factors that determine when more or fewer people are feasible:

Equality of well-being With more equal global resources, the earth can support many more people than it does today.

Technological development With more time to prepare technologically for their arrival, the earth can support many more people.

Political institutions With governments that are more honest, effective, and peaceful, the earth can support many more people. (But more people might limit our liberty and political participation.)

Economic institutions With safer, better organized work and healthier, better educated workers, the earth can support many more people.

Demographic arrangements With a higher death rate and shorter life span, the earth can support many more people. (Also, with better child-care arrangements, can allow more women to work.)

Level of well-being If we can tolerate a lower level of material well-being, the earth can support many more people than today.

Environmental conditions If we can tolerate more physical and biological degradation of the environment, the earth can support many more people.

What range of variation? If we can tolerate more fluctuation in death rates and material conditions, the earth can support many more people.

What risk of catastrophe? If we can tolerate more uncertainty about the occurrence and outcome of disasters—famines, epidemics, wars, and so on—the earth can support many more people.

Two things are to be noted about this list. First, we cannot bank on the occurrence of changes—for example, more equality, better government, or new technology—that will make the earth able to support many more people. Second, most of us would be unwilling to give up many goods—material prosperity, long life, political liberty, a low-risk future—merely to have more people. Putting these two observations together, Cohen is telling us the world *is not* a population time bomb if we can accept accommodating more people and adjust ourselves to doing without things we like and value. If we cannot or will not make these changes, then there are limits to how many people the earth can support, and the world *is* a population time bomb.

REVIEW EXERCISES

For Discussion and Debate

1. Would it be fair to say that the world's population problem is just as Malthus described it two centuries ago?

2. Hasn't the continuing invention of new materials and new technologies shown that it is unnecessary to worry about nonrenewable resources?

3. Would Malthus likely view twentieth-century wars and genocides as positive checks?

4. "The problem is not population *size* so much as it is rate of population *growth*."

Writing Exercises

1. "The most important thing I would be unwilling to give up to have more people on earth."

2. "Technology cannot come to the rescue this time."

3. "The real problem is not that there are too many people but that our political

institutions cannot take care of the people who already exist."

4. "How I would try to persuade people in less developed countries to have fewer children."

Research Activities

1. Find out how long it takes the population to double in three countries of your choosing: one highly developed, one moderately developed, one largely undeveloped.

2. For the three countries you choose in research activity 1, find out how the doubling time has changed in the last 50 years. What accounts for these changes?

3. Again, for the same three countries, collect data on the age distribution of each population and draw an age-sex pyramid to depict each one. What is the observable connection between doubling time and the shape of the age distribution?

4. For any of the age-sex pyramids you drew in research activity 3, examine irregularities in the shape (i.e., indentions or bulges at various points). What historical events account for these irregularities?

SELECTED REFERENCES

AMALRIC, FRANCK, and TARIQ BANURI, Population: Malady or symptom? *Third World Quarterly* (December 1994), 15, 4, 691–706.

BECKERMAN, WILFRED, "Sustainable development": Is it a useful concept? *Environmental Values* (Autumn 1994), 3, 3, 191–209.

BILSBORROW, RICHARD E., Population growth, internal migration, and environmental degradation in rural areas of developing countries, *European Journal of Population* (1992), 8, 2, 125–148.

BOER, LEEN, and AD KOEKKOEK, Development and human security, *Third World Quarterly* (September 1994), 15, 519–522.

CATTON, WILLIAM R., JR., Carrying capacity and the death of a culture: A tale of two autopsies, *Sociological Enquiry* (Spring 1993), 63, 2, 202–223.

DYSON, TIM, World population growth and food supplies, *International Social Science Journal* (September 1994), 46, 3(141), 361–385.

EHRLICH, PAUL R., and ANNE H. EHRLICH, *The population explosion* (New York: Simon and Schuster, 1990).

GILLAND, BERNARD, Considerations on world population and food supply, *Population and Development Review* (June 1983), 9, 2, 203–211.

GREBENIK, E., Demography, democracy, and demonology, *Population and Development Review* (March 1989), 15, 1, 1–22.

HENDERSON, CONWAY W., Population pressures and political repression, *Social Science Quarterly* (June 1993), 74, 2, 322–333.

HERN, WARREN M., Has the human species become a cancer on the planet? A theoretical view of population growth as a sign of pathology, *Current World Leaders* (December 1993), 36, 6, 1089–1124.

KEYFITZ, NATHAN, The growing human population, *Scientific American* (September 1989), 261, 3, 119–126.

———, Seven ways of causing the less developed countries' population problem to disappear— In theory, *European Journal of Population* (1992), 8, 2, 149–167.

———, Tomorrow's cold war, *Queen's Quarterly* (Spring 1994), 101, 1, 15–23.

LIVI-BACCI, MASSIMO, Population policies: A comparative perspective, *International Social Science Journal* (September 1994), 46, 3(141), 317–330.

McNICOLL, GEOFFREY, Population and institutional change, *International Social Science Journal* (September 1994), 46, 3(141), 307–315.

PETERSEN, WILLIAM, The social roots of hunger and overpopulation, *Public Interest* (Summer 1982), 68, 37–52.

PIMENTEL, DAVID, Global warming, population growth, and natural resources for food production, *Society and Natural Resources* (October–December 1991), 4, 4, 347–363.

Sen, Amartya, Population: Delusion and reality, *New York Review of Books* (September 1994), 41, 15, 22, 62–71.

Simon, Julian L., Population growth is not bad for humanity, *National Forum* (Winter 1990), 70, 1, 12–16.

Skinner, Curtis, Population myth and the third world, *Social Policy* (Summer 1988), 19, 1, 57–62.

Waddell, Craig, et al., Perils of a modern Cassandra: Rhetorical aspects of public indifference to the population explosion, *Social Epistemology* (July–September 1994), 8, 3, 221–237.

Wilmoth, John R., and Patrick Ball, The population debate in American popular magazines, 1946–90, *Population and Development Review* (December 1992), 18, 4, 631–668.

12.2
Should people be allowed to have as many children as they want?

The issue: How to reduce the current rate of childbearing in countries that are contributing most to the world's rapid population growth. Should childbearing—historically, a very private choice—be limited in the public interest? If so, how should governments and other interested parties impose those limits?

Introduction The last section showed how important it is to reduce the world's rate of childbearing. But how should people go about reducing their birth rates? Often, a country's leaders have tried to get women to bear fewer children, but without much success. This has been especially true in central Africa, where childbearing continues at extremely high levels. Leaders would do well to follow the example of a country that succeeded in reducing its fertility. Two examples of success suggest themselves: England and China.

England represents a *voluntary model* of fertility reduction. There, without government interference, fertility fell slowly but steadily from about 1870. Today, fertility is below the replacement level. In the long run, the English population will even shrink further. This is all part of the demographic transition mentioned in the last section. Once improvements in medicine and public sanitation brought down the death rates and economic growth offered a middle-class lifestyle, people decided to have fewer children. No special effort by the state was needed to bring about smaller families.

The same transition has occurred throughout Western Europe, North America, and Australia, but in the developing world, it hasn't happened as quickly. In the last 30 years, mortality rates came down rapidly in many of these countries, owing to Western medicine and sanitary engineering. But because people take a while to respond to drops in mortality, fertility has continued at high levels. The result was, and is, a continuing population explosion.

China, by contrast, represents what we might call a *coercive, (involuntary) model* of fertility reduction. Sixty years ago, China was in the same condition as the central African countries are today. It was poor, mainly rural, and periodically ravaged by famines, epidemics, and civil war. Most important, it had a huge population, and with a high fertility rate, the Chinese population was growing every day.

What China did   Through the 1930s and early 1940s, Chinese communists and nationalists cooperated to drive out the Japanese invaders. Once the Japanese were gone, the rival groups fell to fighting each other. The communists, led by Mao Tse-tung, won, and in 1949 they took control of the mainland government. The nationalists, led by Chiang Kai-shek, retreated to the island of Taiwan.

The government realized the need to modernize and industrialize China as quickly as possible. But even with help from the Soviet Union, they could modernize only very slowly. There was too much to do and too many people to do it with. The government realized they would have to make policies to bring down the rate of population growth. This included laws establishing the equal rights of women and changing women's conditions of work and marriage. Beyond that, the Chinese government addressed childbearing as directly as possible, by obliging people to get marriage permits and permits to bear children. In 1971, it began its *wan, xi, shao* ("later, longer, fewer") campaign. This asked people to marry later, leave a longer space between births, and bear fewer children in total. Then, in 1980, it legislated the one-child-per-couple policy. Couples who disobeyed this policy were likely to suffer community disapproval; more important, they would have trouble getting work, housing, and social services.

A survey carried out in 1983 showed that these policies had achieved rapid and dramatic success. By the time of the survey, the mean age of marriage had risen from 19 (in 1949) to 23. In 1949, only 7% had married after the age of 22, but 51% had done so in 1981. Conclusion: The Chinese had quickly

become used to late marriage. More dramatic still was the recorded drop in fertility. In 1965, the average Chinese woman was bearing an estimated 6.1 children in her lifetime—the same level of childbearing we see in central Africa today. By 1980, 15 years later, total fertility was down to 2.2 children, roughly the level of population replacement (or zero growth). Conclusion: the Chinese had quickly become used to less childbearing.

City people—especially highly educated people and "cadres," (administrative, professional, and managerial people)—obeyed the policy most closely. They had the most to lose by failing to obey. Peasants also reduced their childbearing from earlier levels, but they were still bearing more than an estimated 4 children per woman in 1981.

In a single generation, Chinese marriage and fertility patterns changed from those of a desperately poor third world country to those of a Western industrial country. Population growth slowed dramatically and the economy grew, as expected. China was the demographic success story of the world. But, on balance, are such coercive policies a good way to bring about population change? Here, opinions differ.

A COERCIVE PROGRAM IS GOOD

The arguments favoring a coercive policy, as practiced in China, are clear-cut: A coercive policy reduces fertility quickly, and as a result, the standard of living rises quickly. The alternative approach is too slow and costly. Further, a coercive program is a form of preventive health care.

Fast fertility reduction   As we have noted, the coercive Chinese program brought about a rapid fall in fertility by urging women to marry later, wait longer between births, and bear fewer children. The one-child policy, implemented after two decades of earlier efforts to reduce fertility, merely took away the final choice of how many children to have in total. The statistics show that under the new policy, childbearing rates drop at every age, but especially at the youngest and oldest ages. There are few births to teenagers or women in their 30s and 40s. Most childbearing is completed in women's early to mid-20s.

Combined with other policies, this fertility policy changed Chinese women's lives. Women born in the 1920s, for example, had received little or no education, married young, produced baby after baby, and worked in the fields when not bearing children. They experienced a rigid division of labor and authority between men and women. By contrast, women born in the 1950s received a primary, secondary, and even postsecondary education, married in their 20s, had one or two children immediately, put their children into day care, then went to work in the fields, factories, or offices. There was no longer any division of labor or authority between men and women.

A rapid rise in standard of living By giving women more education and reducing the time they spent bearing and raising children, a higher proportion of the Chinese people became available for other work. More people were of working age, and working-age people could spend more of their time in paid work.

This revolution in the labor force, combined with state plans for industrialization and export, produced an economic miracle. Today, China is rapidly taking its place among the Pacific Rim "tigers"—Japan, Taiwan, Hong Kong, Korea, and Singapore—as a leading exporter of manufactured products. China has a long way to

go to catch up with Japan in terms of industrial production and standard of living, but it is improving at an unparalleled rate. Some of the improvement is due to China's coercive family planning policy.

The alternative is too slow As we mentioned, Western nations also industrialized and reduced their fertility, and they did so without coercion. However, it took about a century to do each, and industrialization had to be well under way before fertility began to drop. Today, less developed countries cannot afford to wait so long. Without clear evidence of falling mortality, old-age security, and new economic opportunities, few people in less developed countries voluntarily reduce childbearing. Yet every dollar spent on children is a dollar unavailable for industrialization. Every day that passes without industrialization is a day when people import foreign manufactured goods and increase their indebtedness, poverty, and underdevelopment.

In some respects, industrialization today is more difficult than it was a century ago. True, the technology already exists, but finding the money to buy technology and compete successfully in the global market is much more difficult. Less developed countries need to hurry if they are to have a place in the competition. Coercive family planning is an effective way to hurry.

Part of a preventive health program Many less developed countries recognize the need for public health programs and, especially, for preventive health care. Such programs bring rapid and dramatic improvements in people's health. It is only later, with more prosperity, that a society can afford high-cost technology and highly paid specialists to provide remedial health care. So a developing society is wise to focus on preventive health measures to quickly and equally increase people's lifespan and free them from illness. It does this with the least possible reliance on medical and other health professionals, at the lowest possible cost.

Coercive family planning can be viewed as one of many preventive health programs. Fertility reduction reduces the health risks and costs associated with pregnancy and childbirth. And by reducing the number of children, it also reduces the number of parenthood experiences (or years spent in parenthood). Since parenthood is a source of stress and conflict, this improves people's mental health. All this reduces the need for health professionals.

COERCIVE PROGRAMS ARE BAD

Those arguing against coercive programs accept the arguments made by people who favor them. However, they identify shortcomings of a coercive policy that we have not mentioned yet. First, they argue, coercive policies are possible only within an authoritarian state, and no one wants to live in such a state. Second, coercive policies carry harmful unintended consequences: the proliferation of rules, new opportunities for conflict, costs of selective child prevention, and an old-age security problem.

An authoritarian state A successful coercive program is possible only in an authoritarian state. An authoritarian state represses civil society and political dissent. It is easy to confuse authoritarianism with militarism and fascism because all three weaken popular or collective social protest. Each creates an all-powerful state that intervenes in the economy and social life. This state penetrates everyday life fully, even influencing the dress and hairstyle of ordinary citizens. Far more chilling is the way government violently represses opposing polit-

ical views, often dealing with political opponents by kidnapping, torturing, imprisoning, and even murdering them. All of this has happened in China.

Is this price worth paying in order to ensure rapid industrialization via rapid fertility decline? Most people would say it is not. From the authoritarianism needed to carry out this policy flow a number of harmful social consequences.

Too many rules Enforcing rules that regulate the marriage and childbearing of hundreds of millions of people means creating a bureaucratic organization. This bureaucracy is sure to be costly. Without proper oversight, it is also likely to be oppressive and discriminatory. Bureaucracies always create more rules to clarify existing rules. Eventually, no one knows all the rules, leaving the door open to regional variations and to abuses: bribery, corruption, prejudice, and particularism. In workplaces and small communities, such uncertainty puts even more power in the hands of already powerful party and community officials.

New opportunities for conflict Where there are rules, there are conflicts of interpretation, rule violations, and blackmail over rules violated. The marriage and childbearing rules have already opened up a wide gap between rural and urban ways of life. Urban people are more likely to obey the rules and more likely to gain by doing so. This creates inequality and envy between rural and urban people.

The greatest problems occur when it is most difficult to tell whether a rule has been violated, especially whether it has been violated without penalty. In China, one cannot easily bear and raise a child without someone noticing. Nor is it easy to marry, or live as though married, without people noticing. But it *is* easy to become pregnant without someone noticing. What happens then?

Costs of selective child prevention First, a bit of information about Chinese culture. The Chinese shun daughters because China is traditionally a *patrilocal* society. After marrying, sons stay home and take care of their parents. Daughters move out to join their husband's parents. Thus daughters are "lost" to their own parents, while sons are not. For this reason, if only one child is permitted, a son is better.

Many Chinese women who become pregnant are under pressure to abort their child: first, if they are not married or not permitted to be married; second, if they are married but not permitted to have a child; and third, if they are permitted to have a child but don't want to have a daughter. In China as elsewhere, ultrasound technology makes it possible for women to know the sex of their unborn child.

A high rate of abortions, under still primitive health care conditions, increases women's health risks and health costs for the society. Infanticide—the killing of unwanted babies—is another practice common in China when daughters are concerned. Estimates of murdered children, especially daughters, run into the millions. The one-child policy is likely to increase both abortion and infanticide, especially when female fetuses are involved. So aside from the health risks associated with abortion and infanticide, there are the moral and emotional issues. And even leaving those aside, there are the opportunities for blackmail. People who have secrets can always be blackmailed, and infanticide, though common, is illegal.

The excessive abortion and murder of female children also shift the sex ratio. Twenty years from now, this means a shortage of brides for marriage-ready bachelors. Where and how will Chinese men get their wives? Historically, many Chinese girls were sold to their husbands as property. This is now illegal, but not everyone rejects the practice of buying a bride. Already there is evidence of girls and women being abducted for sale as brides in another part of the country. This problem will worsen as brides become even scarcer. And, like any traffic in illegal goods (e.g., drug traffic) or people (e.g., prostitutes), bride traffic is likely to attract and stimulate organized crime.

An old-age security problem Much less dramatic but equally important, a one-child policy leaves parents fearing that they will have no children or only one child to take care of them in their old age. As mentioned, the concern is greatest among parents with only a daughter.

SUMMING UP

Should people be allowed to have as many children as they want? Probably not, if you reached the same conclusion about the population time bomb that we did. The real issue is, how do we get people to have fewer children? Here opinion is sharply divided. China's one-child policy has been an enormous success, viewed from one angle. But like many rapid social changes, the one-child policy carries harmful, uncalculated side effects.

A voluntary program of family limitation, like one finds in Brazil or India (e.g., the sterilization program initiated by Indira Gandhi), works more slowly but it may have longer-lasting effects. To repeat, the key is to lower the infant mortality rate, reduce the economic value of children, and make available a middle-class lifestyle to people who consume less of their income raising children. Gradually, everyone accepts a voluntary program pursued in that way. It causes less disruption, less conflict—even less crime. It has slower but just as good effects, and in the long run it produces fewer harmful side effects.

To bring about voluntary family limitation, less developed societies make contraceptive technology easily and cheaply available; promote a smaller-is-better public education campaign; use taxes and pensions to reward small families or punish large ones; provide old-age security to protect the childless; and stimulate economic development. Successful experiences in Kerala, India, and elsewhere show that improving the social and economic status of women also reduces fertility. And we emphasize that they must reduce the social, cultural, and economic incentives of childbearing.

REVIEW EXERCISES

For Discussion and Debate

1. In what sense is childbearing a private responsibility? In what sense a public responsibility?

2. What connections might the Chinese government have assumed among fertility reduction, family and gender reform, and broader social and political reform?

3. Why have so many less developed countries taken a much longer time than China to reduce their fertility rates?

4. How might the Chinese plan to deal with their rapidly aging population, especially, with the need to care for old people without children?

Writing Exercises

1. "Telling people how many children they can have is the ultimate authoritarian act."

2. "If people decide to have large families, that's their business; but they should pay the cost."

3. "Here's how I would deal with the problem of infanticide and selective abortion (of females) in China, if I were in charge."

4. "This is how the one-child policy is different from other preventive health programs."

Research Activities

1. Collect statistics on birth rates in China and one other less developed country (e.g., India, Nigeria, Syria), starting, if possible, in the 1940s and ending in the 1990s. Plot the data on graph paper and report what you have found.

2. Excluding China, learn all you can about birth control policies in one less developed country. What reasons do analysts give for the success, or lack of success, of these policies?

3. Collect statistics on differences in fertility in your own community. What "kinds" of people have large versus small numbers of children? How do you explain this finding?

4. Devise a brief questionnaire to find out how many children students at your college intend to have after they settle down, and what "kinds" of people intend to have large versus small numbers of children.

SELECTED REFERENCES

ADLAKHA, ARJUN, and JUDITH BANISTER, Demographic perspectives on China and India, *Journal of Biosocial Science* (April 1995), 27, 2, 163–178.

BIRDSALL, NANCY M., and CHARLES C. GRIFFIN, Fertility and poverty in developing countries, *Journal of Policy Modelling* (April 1988), 10, 1, 29–55.

CALDWELL, JOHN C., I. O. ORUBULOYE, and PAT CALDWELL, Fertility decline in Africa: A new type of transition? *Population and Development Review* (June 1992), 18, 2, 211–242.

COONEY, ROSEMARY SANTANA, JIN WEI, and MARY G. POWERS, The one child certificate in Hebei Province, China: Acceptance and consequence, 1979–1988, *Population Research and Policy Review* (1991), 10, 2, 137–155.

CROSS, ANNE R., WALTER OBUNGU, and PAUL KIZITO, Evidence of a transition to lower fertility in Kenya, *International Family Planning Perspectives* (March 1991), 17, 1, 4–7.

FAUST, KIMBERLY, REBECCA BACH, SAAD GADALLA, HIND KHATTAB, and JOHN GULICK, Mass education, Islamic revival, and the population problem in Egypt, *Journal of Comparative Family Studies* (Autumn 1991), 22, 3, 329–341.

FEENEY, GRIFFITH, and YUAN JIANHUA, Below replacement fertility in China? A close look at recent evidence, *Population Studies* (November 1994), 48, 3, 381–394.

FREEDMAN, RONALD, MING CHENG CHANG, and TE HSIUNG SUN, Taiwan's transition from high fertility to below-replacement levels, *Studies in Family Planning* (November–December 1994), 25, 6, 317–331.

LEETE, RICHARD, and GAVIN JONES, South Asia's future population: Are there really grounds for optimism? *International Family Planning Perspectives* (September 1991), 17, 3, 108–113.

MAULDIN, W. PARKER, and JOHN A. ROSS, Prospects and programs for fertility reduction, 1990–2015, *Studies in Family Planning* (March–April 1994), 25, 2, 77–95.

MENKEN, JANE, and JAMES F. PHILLIPS, Population change in a rural area of Bangladesh 1967–87, *Annals of the American Academy of Political and Social Science* (July 1990), 510, 87–101.

MEREDITH, WILLIAM H., China's family planning policy today, *International Journal of Sociology of the Family* (Autumn 1993), 23, 2, 35–50.

MIAH, M., MIZANUR RAHMAN, and AINON NAHAR MIZAN, Labor force participation and fertility: A study of married women in Bangladesh, *International Journal of Sociology of the Family* (Autumn 1992), 22, 2, 69–82.

RAJAN, S. IRUDYA, U. S. MISHRA, and MALA RAMANATHAN, The two child family in India? Is it realistic? *International Family Planning Perspectives* (December 1993), 19, 4, 125–128, 154.

RILEY, NANCY, and ROBERT W. GARDNER, *China's population: A review of the literature* (Liége, Belgium: International Union for the Scientific Study of Population, 1997).

RUXIAN, YAN, Marriage and family among China's minority nationalities as viewed from Beijing, *Mankind Quarterly* (Summer 1991), 31, 4, 345–355.

SHARPLESS, JOHN, World population growth, family planning, and American foreign policy, *Journal of Policy History* (1995), 7, 1, 72–102.

SONKO, SHERIFF, Fertility and culture in sub-Saharan Africa: A review, *International Social Science Journal* (September 1994), 46, 3(141), 397–411.

VLASSOFF, CAROL, Progress and stagnation: Changes in fertility and women's position in an Indian village, *Population Studies* (July 1992), 46, 2, 195–212.

WARD, VICTORIA M., JANE T. BERTRAND, and FRANCISCO PUAC, Exploring sociocultural barriers to family planning among Mayans in Guatemala, *International Family Planning Perspectives* (June 1992), 18, 2, 59–65.

ZANG, XIAOWEI, Household structure and marriage in urban China: 1900–1982, *Journal of Comparative Family Studies* (Spring 1993), 24, 1, 35–44.

12.3
Is it time to raise the drawbridge on immigration?

The issue: Throughout the West, high rates of unemployment combined with large numbers of people who want to immigrate, despite the unemployment. One result is a backlash against immigrants (especially ethnic or racial minorities among them). Is there any way to decide how many and which kinds of immigrants are needed—if any?

Introduction The United States does not have a population problem of the kind we discussed in the last two sections. By any standard, there are not too many people for the land to support. Nor is the American population growing too quickly through high rates of fertility. Yet some people view high rates of immigration as a population problem and a social problem.

Recently, immigration has become an explosive political issue. Many people inside the country want the chance to bring their relatives over to the United States. Many outside the country want a chance to get in. But industrial downsizing makes many native-born Americans resist the push for an increased number of immigrants. Some even want the immigration rate cut back.

Postwar immigrants have been drawn to America primarily from southern Europe, Latin America, Asia, and Africa. These immigrants settled mainly in large metropolitan centers. In this respect they follow the general trend in which more and more Americans live near large cities. And in the largest cities, immigrants form a large and growing part of the total population. But even though they follow the general pattern of settlement (westward and to large cities), immigrants are often singled out for criticism and exclusion. Many are easily identified by their speech, skin color, or manner of dress, which make them easy targets. Is immigration becoming a problem in America? If so, should immigration be more limited?

IMMIGRATION SHOULD BE MORE LIMITED

People who argue that immigration should be more limited make three main points that focus on economic, cultural, and social issues, respectively. (In Australia, many now also make the case against immigration on ecological grounds, arguing that it speeds population growth, in turn spurring environmental degradation.) First, they claim that immigration poses an economic problem in a slow-growing economy. Second, they say that immigrants pose a problem of assimilation and cultural unity (an issue we discussed in an earlier section). Third, they raise the concern that high rates of immigration produce problems of social cohesion and conflict.

Immigrants are an economic problem People who want to limit or reduce immigration on economic grounds argue that immigrants use too many public services. Health care is particularly important for older immigrants, educational services for younger immigrants, and welfare for unemployed immigrants. On the one hand, critics complain that too many immigrants fail to get or keep jobs, so they increase the unemployment rate. On the other hand, they complain that too many immigrants take jobs away from native-born Americans in a tight job market. This increases unemployment and the welfare needs of native-borns. Given that the economy is uncertain, it seems foolish to import people who put new demands on public spending.

Immigrants are a cultural problem Increasingly, immigrants come from countries and cultures that are different from the dominant white American culture. This poses the problem of cultural assimilation. In an earlier section we discussed the pros and cons of multiculturalism. Whatever your view on this issue, a high rate of immigration puts more pressure on the society to come up with a solution. As with rapid population change due to high rates of fertility, rapid change due to high rates of immigration strains a society's capacity to adapt. Quick solutions to pressing social problems are rarely good or long lasting. By increasing immigration and the pressure for solutions, we increase the risk of making mistakes.

Immigrants are a social problem High rates press society to rapidly assimilate and acculturate the new immigrants or, alternately, to rapidly adopt multicultural policies that many reject. In the meantime, there is a chance that social conflict between immigrants and the host society will increase. For example, some have used this argument to help explain the Los Angeles riots: immigrants squeezed blacks out of jobs and neighborhoods, and the blacks fought back.

The type of problem will vary with the kind of immigrant. Thus highly educated immigrants from Hong Kong and other parts of Southeast Asia may place different demands on the system than less educated immigrants from Latin America or the Mediterranean region. In either case the possibility of conflict is increased by what some people consider the clannishness or self-segregation of immigrants. Often, immigrants develop a self-protective strategy that the sociologist Raymond Breton has called "institutional completeness"; it is this which gives the impression of clannishness.

Institutional completeness is a measure of the degree to which an immigrant ethnic group provides its own members with the services they need through their own institutions. These institutions include churches, schools, banks, and media that are separate from those of the larger society. Often it accompanies residential segregation. In a group with strong institutional (or community) completeness, members do not need to depend on the host society.

The kinds of problems immigrants face on arrival in America influence the degree of completeness a group develops. Immigrants may be unable to speak English. They may be unaccustomed to city life or lack marketable skills and job contacts outside their own community. On the positive side, they may have brought social contacts from their homeland that they can use to develop business and friendship ties here. So new immigrants create a community that plays to their strengths and hides their weaknesses.

This is important for groups that face serious prejudice. Living in a community with institutional completeness protects immigrants from a hostile social environment. Moreover, the institutionally complete community is self-perpetuating; institutions formed within it create a demand for the services they provide. Often, ethnic groups keep to themselves in separate communities even after the discrimination has diminished or disappeared. The group continues to defend its members against discrimination and pressures to assimilate. It also maintains group cohesion by creating institutions, gaining control of resources, and providing a variety of cultural and social services.

This pattern of self-segregation, aided by institutional completeness, is particularly typical of America's recent immigrants. Many display a pattern that has characterized trading peoples in many periods of history and countries of the world. We see the same pattern among Jewish, Armenian, and Turkish immigrants in Europe; Chinese immigrants in Southeast Asia; East Indian immigrants in the West Indies; Arab immigrants in East Africa; and Korean and Vietnamese immigrants in the United States.

In each case, the group immigrates to escape poverty or oppression. On arriving in their new homeland, these culturally and racially distinct people experience discrimination and exploitation by the local people. Seeing themselves as strangers in the country, they settle in particular parts of towns and cities among others of their own kind. They become self-employed (often merchants) and keep apart from other groups socially.

For self-protection, these trading peoples, or *middlemen*, form strong intraethnic organizations, eventually producing institutional completeness. They compete with local businesses and, by taking advantage of family and community ties, their businesses prosper. Gradually, a large proportion achieve a middle-class standard of living. The most successful even form business alliances with rich and powerful members of the dominant community. Individually and in groups, they become politically active.

Their success excites the hostility and envy of poor or downwardly mobile native-borns. In turn, this hostility renews the sense of danger this group felt upon immigrating and strengthens their self-protective actions. In this way, institutional complete-

ness, the appearance of clannishness, is maintained.

So there is truth in the assertion that immigrants are often clannish, but the clannishness is not due to immigration, per se, nor to high rates of immigration. It is largely due to the reaction of the host society, and as we will see, it is an avoidable reaction.

IMMIGRATION SHOULD NOT BE MORE LIMITED

People who argue against a limitation on immigrants, or even favor higher rates of immigration, counter each of the arguments we have examined with opposing evidence.

Immigrants are not an economic problem   Those opposing the view that immigrants are an economic problem note that immigrants generally help the economy grow. In the United States, the agricultural lobby is strongly in favor of immigration, since it supplies cheap labor to harvest crops. But because of selective immigration policies many immigrants are highly skilled or highly educated; they provide a cheap source of talented people that this country has not had to pay a cent to train. Many are also ambitious; just think how much courage and energy it takes to travel to another country and culture and start life all over again.

Since many, even most, are young and skilled, immigrants tend to enter the work force and remain in it. They do not increase the general unemployment rate; they often take jobs that native-born people are unwilling to do. (There is evidence of local or sectoral unemployment due to migrant workers, but the effect is limited.) On balance, the evidence shows that immigrants pay more in taxes than they draw in public services and benefits.

Immigrants are not a cultural problem It is true that high rates of immigration increase cultural diversity, and this puts pressure on the country to come to terms with the multiculturalism issue. However, as we concluded in the earlier chapter on this topic, multiculturalism is inevitable. Further, it may be the best way for a country to participate in today's globalized economy.

Immigrants are not a social problem We have discussed the self-protective immigrant strategies that lead to institutional completeness and an appearance of clannishness. However, these boundaries and barriers break down whenever the dominant population behaves in a cordial, hospitable manner. This is evident in soaring rates of intermarriage. Increasing numbers of young people cross ethnic, religious, and racial lines to date and marry "different" kinds of people. And the sociological evidence shows that intermarriage poses no difficulty for the couples concerned.

More generally, measures of ethnic and race relations in use since the 1920s show that social distance between groups is shrinking. More people accept "different" kinds of people as neighbors, workmates, and friends—as well as spouses—than ever before. In short, ethnic diversity does not become a problem unless we let it.

Research shows that familiarity reduces fear and hostility between groups, especially when interactions between different kinds of people are: (1) gradual, relaxed, and repeated; (2) cooperative, not competitive; (3) guided by norms of friendliness; (4) between people of equal status; and (5) supported by legitimate authorities (e.g., government officials, teachers, ministers). Such interactions are particularly beneficial when they contradict the stereotyped notions groups hold about each other.

The worst intergroup problems are likely to arise in fundamentally competitive situations—for example, work settings. Problems are more easily avoided among young people in social or educational settings. This puts a special responsibility on teachers and others in contact with young people to create the best possible conditions for intergroup understanding and cooperation.

Immigrants are a demographic benefit We have saved one of the most important benefits of a high immigration rate for last. This is the demographic benefit. In America and the rest of the Western world, fertility rates are near or below replacement. That means there is no danger of too many people. In fact, even with 5 to 10% unemployment there may be a danger of too few people. Among other things, a shrinking population means a shrinking work force and, therefore, a shrinking economic base. Immigration provides more people to consume, as well as make the economy's goods and services.

More important still, a population with fertility near or below replacement is an aging population. Low fertility, not increased longevity, is mainly what increases the average (or median) age of the population. Currently, the median American is nearly 40 years old (half the population is older, half younger). While fertility remains low or even shrinks, the median age rises even more. This means a large and growing fraction of old and retired people and a shortage of young people.

A society can have too many young people, as we saw in an earlier section, but it can also have too few. Population aging can be a bad thing. First, older people are less productive economically than younger people. A large proportion are retired, though some not by choice. Many require costly services, especially health care, in the last years of their lives. Most draw old-age pensions. We need young workers to pay for these pensions and other services. The fewer the young people, the more each one has to pay to cover the costs of the old people.

There is evidence as well that older people are more rigid in their ways and less innovative than younger people. This is bound to affect the economic, social, and cultural life of the country. Increasingly, as we noted in earlier sections, the country and world need flexibility and adaptiveness: new ideas, new technologies, new ways of relating to other kinds of people, and so on. Young people adapt in these ways more easily than do older people.

High rates of immigration supply the needed young people in two ways. First, as we have noted, a high proportion of immigrants are young, often in their teens or twenties. Second, immigrants from less developed societies tend to have higher rates of fertility than native-born Americans or other Western peoples. This means the immigrants will supply more babies per capita, and this too will keep the country's median age from rising at a rapid rate, though it is likely to rise nonetheless.

SUMMING UP

Is it time to raise the drawbridge on immigrants? Definitely not. By this we mean that there should be no fewer immigrants than there are at present. We do not necessarily mean immigration should be unlimited. Nor do we mean that immigration should be set arbitrarily at some particular level— for example, at a level twice as high, three times as high, or ten times as high as it is at present. Remember what we learned in the section on the population time bomb. There are no absolute answers to any population question. There is no absolute level at which a country is overpopulated or underpopulated, nor a point at which there are too many immigrants or too few immigrants.

Partly, there are too many unknowns: How many immigrants want to come, and with what skills? What is the state of language training, social services, and local school systems that must receive immigrants? What is the likely state of the economy when they arrive? Five years later? What is the state of public thinking towards immigration, multiculturalism, and intergroup cooperation today? (Usually, public opinion mainly opposes immigration at current or higher levels.)

More important still, as Joel Cohen showed us, all answers to population questions are conditional on the kind of society we want to have and the effort we are willing to make to have it. What changes are needed to accommodate twice as many immigrants, or ten times as many each year; and what would it take to make those changes? Can we afford to make those changes? Can we afford *not* to make those changes? How long can we put off making those changes before something bad happens? How bad would it be?

All our actions carry a danger and a cost. Inaction also carries a danger and a cost. The job of the sociologist is not to obscure that fact with pat answers; unfortunately, this is what politicians often do. Instead, the sociologist must uncover and dissect the question(s) so that we know exactly what is involved. Then the sociologist must supply evidence relevant to the debate, evidence that is timely and untainted by political interest. Ultimately, the important decisions are not made by sociologists. Too often, decision makers do not even take sociological evidence into account. But we will have done our job, as sociologists and citizens, if we have treated the debate and the evidence fairly and with respect.

REVIEW EXERCISES

For Discussion and Debate

1. Why do people believe that immigrants take more out of the economy than they put into it?

2. How is the immigration debate different from the multiculturalism debate?

3. "Through immigration, North America gains the talents of the most capable, educated, and dynamic people of the third world."

4. Are "middleman minorities" a benefit to American society or a problem?

Writing Exercises

1. "Only young, highly educated immigrants should be admitted to the country."

2. "A preference should be given to applicants for immigration who are wealthy."

3. "Immigrants should be told what part of the country they must live in for the first 5 years."

4. "Only countries that are large importers of American products should be permitted to send large numbers of immigrants."

Research Activities

1. Collect some basic information about immigrants living in your local community: how many there are, where they came from, when they came, what kinds of jobs they do.

2. Prepare a brief questionnaire on the experience of immigration that includes questions on why people left their home country, why they came to America and to this particular community, and how well they feel they have been accepted. Administer it to two immigrant members of your community and report your findings.

3. Sample issues of your local newspaper to see how it has discussed immigration and immigrants over the last 50 years. Do you detect a trend?

4. Focusing on one particular ethnic group in your community, collect information that would help you determine whether or not it is a "middleman minority."

SELECTED REFERENCES

ARCHDEACON, THOMAS J., Reflections of immigration to Europe in light of U.S. immigration history, *International Migration Review* (Summer 1992), 26, 2(98), 525–548.

BONACICH, EDNA, A theory of middleman minorities, *American Sociological Review* (October 1973), 38, 5, 583–594.

CARD, DAVID, The impact of the Mariel boatlift on the Miami labor market, *Industrial and Labor Relations Review* (January 1990), 43, 2, 245–257.

DONATO, KATHARINE M., THOMAS J. ESPENSHADE, and RICARDO ROMO, U.S. policy and Mexican migration to the United States, 1942–92, *Social Science Quarterly* (December 1994), 75, 4, 705–729.

FIX, MICHAEL, and JEFFREY S. PASSEL, Setting the record straight: What are the costs to the public? *Public Welfare* (Spring 1994), 52, 2, 6–15.

FREEMAN, GARY P., Migration policy and politics in the receiving states, *International Migration Review* (Winter 1992), 26, 4(100), 1144–1167.

HABERMAS, JURGEN, Citizenship and national identity: Some reflections on the future of Europe, *Praxis International* (April 1992), 12, 1, 1–19.

HEISLER, BARBARA SCHMITTER, The future of immigrant incorporation: Which models?

Which concepts? *International Migration Review* (Summer 1992), 26, 2(98), 623–645.

HUSBANDS, CHRISTOPHER T., The mainstream right and the politics of immigration in France: Major developments, *Ethnic and Racial Studies* (April 1991), 14, 2, 170–198.

KEELY, CHARLES B., The politics of immigration policy in the United States, *Migration World Magazine* (1993), 21, 1, 20–23.

KLENIEWSKI, NANCY, Immigration and urban transformations, *Urban Affairs Quarterly* (December 1994), 30, 2, 307–316.

KPOSOWA, AUGUSTINE J., The impact of immigration on native earnings in the United States, 1940 to 1980, *Applied Behavioral Science Review* (1993), 1, 1, 1–25.

LUTZ, WOLFGANG, and CHRISTOPHER PRINZ, What difference do alternative immigration and integration levels make to Western Europe? *European Journal of Population* (1992), 8, 4, 341–361.

MARTIN, PHILIP L., Immigration and integration: Challenges for the 1990s, *Asian Migrant* (April–June 1994), 7, 2, 46–51.

MASSEY, DOUGLAS S., The social and economic origins of immigration, *Annals of the American Academy of Political and Social Science* (July 1990), 510, 60–72.

MIN, PYONG GAP, Problems of Korean immigrant entrepreneurs, *International Migration Review* (Fall 1990), 24, 3(91), 436–455.

MOORE, STEPHEN, Who should America welcome? *Society* (July–August 1990), 27, 5(187), 55–62.

MURPHY, DWIGHT D., The world population explosion and the cost of uncontrolled immigration, *Journal of Social, Political and Economic Studies* (Winter 1994), 4, 481–510.

PEDRAZA-BAILEY, SILVIA, Immigration research: A conceptual map, *Social Science History* (Spring 1990), 14, 1, 43–67.

PUGLIESE, ENRICO, The new international migrations and the changes in the labour market, *Labour* (Spring 1992), 6, 1, 165–179.

RICHMOND, ANTHONY H., Race relations and immigration: A comparative perspective, *International Journal of Comparative Sociology* (September–December 1990), 31, 3–4, 156–176.

RYDER, NORMAN B., Reflections on replacement, *Family Planning Perspectives* (November–December 1993), 25, 6, 273–277.

RYSTAD, GORAN, Immigration history and the future of international migration, *International Migration Review* (Winter 1992), 26, 4(100), 1168–1199.

SATZEWICH, VIC, Migrant and immigrant families in Canada: State coercion and legal control in the formation of ethnic families, *Journal of Comparative Family Studies* (Autumn 1993), 24, 3, 315–338.

SCIORTINO, GIUSEPPE, Immigration into Europe and public policy: Do stops really work? *New Community* (October 1991), 18, 1, 89–99.

SIMMONS, ALAN B., and KIERAN KEOHANE, Canadian immigration policy: State strategies and the quest for legitimacy, *Canadian Review of Sociology and Anthropology* (November 1992), 29, 4, 421–452.

13. Religion

Some sociologists define **religion** as "a set of beliefs, symbols, and practices (rituals) based on the idea of the sacred, and which unites believers into a socio-religious community." This approach to religion follows in the steps of Emile Durkheim, who focused on the functions of belief and ritual in binding people together in social groups. Other sociologists, following in the steps of Max Weber, view religion as "any set of coherent answers to human existential dilemmas—birth, sickness, death—which make the world meaningful." Here, the concern is less with social cohesion and more with the role religion plays in interpreting the world for individuals.

In both definitions, religion includes all of the thoughts and practices that put people in touch with what are thought of as supernatural forces, powers, or experiences that transcend ordinary life. The followers of some religions believe the supernatural resides in natural objects like the ocean and natural forces like the wind. Others think of distinct supernatural creatures—gods, goddesses, nymphs, devils. Some religions have many gods, others have only one, whereas some religions—like Buddhism—have none. Some believe in an afterlife or in reincarnation, whereas others do not. Differences in ideas of good and evil and differences in ritual practices also distinguish the religions of the world.

In this chapter we consider three issues that illustrate the connection of religion to the rest of the social world. First, we examine secularization and ask whether religion is still important in people's lives. Second, we consider whether the church-state connection is still important—that is, whether religions should be involved in politics. Third, we look at the role and depiction of women in some of the world's religions and ask whether religions are typically hostile to women.

13.1

Is there still a place for religion?

<u>The issue:</u> In becoming a secular society, have we become an immoral society, with the result that there is even more need for religion today than ever? Some deny the premise that we are lacking in morality or even that religion and morality are necessarily tied together.

Introduction Emile Durkheim saw religion as expressing concepts and ideas that were central to any culture. Each culture and society developed its own religious expressions, and these would change as the culture changed. Other sociologists viewed religion differently, from the functionalist approach of discussing and enumerating the ways religion strengthened social ties and social cohesion to the Marxist concept of religion as the "opiate of the people," acting to maintain existing power structures. Today, sociologists view religious organizations and religious expressions as acting in complex ways, sometimes as mechanisms of social control and at other times as vehicles of resistance and empowerment. Many sociologists emphasize the need to consider how religion is implicit in people's construction of meaning in their lives, and so are moving away from examining religion merely in terms of its social functions, from either a functionalist or a conflict theory perspective.

THERE IS LITTLE PLACE FOR RELIGION IN A MODERN SOCIETY

The idea that religion is losing, or has lost, its importance is not a new one. Durkheim assumed that religion and religious expression would change as society changed. His work dealt with what holds society together, solidarity, and he defined two types of solidarity: mechanical and organic. *Mechanical solidarity* referred to societies where everyone did much the same thing so that households were self-sufficient, as among foraging peoples or small-scale agriculturalists. *Organic solidarity* referred to societies where people were interdependent; people's work differed greatly, but each person was reliant on many others for the necessities of life, as in present-day industrial societies. Mechanical solidarity was built on similarities of daily life, shared norms, beliefs, and ways of thinking. Organic solidarity consisted of obligations to other people within the society, however different they might be.

Durkheim studied the religions of aboriginal peoples of Australia and compared them with the religions in Europe. He concluded that religions form an expression of central values in society. When people engage in their religious practices, they are linking themselves to society. The deities they refer to and worship can be considered essentially personifications of their own society.

In one important respect, Durkheim illustrates a general feature of the sociological study of religion. Social scientists do not question whether "god" or "gods" or "goddesses" exist outside of people's social expressions. That is a topic for theology, a different discipline. Instead, like Durkheim, sociologists focus on the ways people create their understandings of divinity. Durkheim was not asking whether God exists, only how people relate to and worship their gods.

According to Durkheim, different concepts of deity are differently suited to mechanical and organic societies. Religious tensions, conflicts, and oppression are common in heterogeneous societies. For a complex organic society, the old ways of relating to divinity may be more destructive than productive. Durkheim hoped that regardless of people's personal beliefs and encounters with divinity, a form of humanism would become the "religion" of industrial societies—a religion in which people see their common humanity, not their specific religious beliefs, as what links them together.

Other theorists, often basing their work on that of Durkheim, have predicted that for complex industrial societies, religions will necessarily lose their importance. This process is spoken of as *secularization*. Many scholars have pointed to secularization within Western societies, noting a steadily diminishing influence of religion in public life. Sociologist Bryan Wilson, for example, points to three features of life in industrial societies that lead toward secularization: social differentiation, societalization, and rationalization.

Social differentiation forms part of the pattern of societies becoming increasingly complex, changing from little difference in what people do to great specialization and specificity. In the past, religion and its institution (which, following Durkheim, we can call a "church" regardless of the type of religious worship) was central to much of social life. Besides providing for worship and teaching about sacred things, the church taught basic skills, supported those in need, cared for the sick, served as a meeting place, and organized social events. In modern societies, these functions are taken care of by many separate institutions: schools, hospitals, government agencies, and social clubs, among others. This means that the church is no longer central to daily living but merely one institution among many. It is also one with which many individuals may have little contact, as it is no longer necessary to belong to a religious institution in North American or West European society, though it is seen as necessary for children to attend school and for sick people to visit a doctor's office.

The strength of religion is still its basis in community. But *societalization,* the second aspect of secularization, refers to how people increasingly relate, not to a community in which every person knows everyone else but to society in the abstract. In North America and Europe today, most people look to society—a large, amorphous unit with its organizations run on bureaucratic principles—to provide for their needs. People regularly find and work at jobs, read and watch the news, attend school, and vote in elections. All of these activities put them into contact with a society that sustains and regulates their activities. The interaction of people with society leaves little room for religion, which is increasingly viewed as personal, not societal, and indeed marginal to social life. Whether they are Buddhist or Roman Catholic, Protestant or Jewish, Muslim or Hindu or atheist, religion is not an important part of their dealings with society. They don't talk about it at work.

At its most important, religion helps people form meaning and identity through a community-wide understanding of relations to sacred things. But where people's chief attachment is to the wider society, religion is no longer a central, shared part of community life. Even though many people continue to engage in prayer and worship and attend synagogue or church, their religion has become something they engage in primarily as individuals, a lifestyle choice made out of interest or for personal development—a private matter when compared to the public pursuits of going to work or voting in elections.

The third feature of modern life that undercuts the importance of religion is *rationalization*—a focus on explaining the world and its events through ideas that rely on the logical interpretation of empirical evidence. The Judeo-Christian religions of the Western world themselves supported and encouraged the spread of rationalization, in part to reduce reliance on so-called superstition and folk-magic practices. Along with this emphasis on rationality, as Weber observed, modern religion has emphasized theology over myth. In most Christian denominations, the leadership emphasizes philosophical inquiry into the nature of people and their relationship with the divine, instead of the early Bible stories of the Creation. This is, indeed, the basic difference between mainstream and fundamentalist churches.

However, rationalization eventually acted against the churches. The major Western religions are ultimately based in faith, and tenets of faith are never susceptible to empirical testing. "Is there a God?" is not a question one can answer by applying the scientific method. The tendency in modern societies has been increasingly to view *all* religion as superstition, and faith as a possibly useful psychological crutch to help people deal with problems in their everyday lives. Marxists and feminists, for their part, view religion and faith as power structures erected to persuade people to follow codes of behavior that are not necessarily in their own best interests. Marx's comment about religion as the "opiate of the masses" particularly comes to mind.

Decreasing attendances and rationalization
Research has indicated that religiosity—expressed adherence to a religion and attendance at religious ceremonies—decreases as education increases. This is most noticeable in Western Europe. In the most secularized part of Europe—France, Belgium, and the Netherlands—in the early 1980s more than 26% of people reported having no religion. Only 37% of Catholics and 9% of Protestants attended church weekly. One-third of self-declared Protestants and one-fifth of self-declared Catholics never attended church at all. Young adults were less likely than their parents to attend or to say they had a religious affiliation. More recent figures indicate that both affiliation and attendance have continued to decline. In the Netherlands the proportion of the population that states they are Roman Catholic has fallen from 40% in 1960 to 35% in 1992, and today only 13% of Catholics attend weekly mass.

In an age of increasing education and falling church attendances, more people emphasize rational thought, and so the patterns of religious faith are being eroded. Yet for many people, religion remains a way of achieving personal growth and fulfillment. Some religious practices, doctrines, and beliefs are changing in an attempt to reclaim members. Recently, the Church of England officially reaffirmed its belief in the concept of Hell. However, this included changes from the medieval idea of a place of punishment; their theologians currently speak of it, instead, as a sense of absence of God.

Likewise, some Protestant churches have changed the way they present their religion, emphasizing the benefits of church membership in terms of social and psychological advantages, not faith in God or spiritual striving. Sermons in church reflect this change. For some people this is evidence that religion is in trouble. Others, though, see such changes as a natural adjustment to rapid changes within society and a sign that religion is still strong and healthy.

RELIGION IS NOT LOSING ITS IMPORTANCE

Church attendance may be lower in Western Europe and parts of North America than it was 30 years ago, but does that necessarily mean religion is less important? Could it be that we are seeing a change, not a loss, of religion—a separation of religion from the institutions that have dominated the construction of personal meaning for the last few centuries?

What is religion?   To answer that question, we need to expand on what we mean by religion. In *The Elementary Forms of the Religious Life*, Durkheim defined religion as "a unified system of beliefs and practices, relative to sacred things, which unite into a single moral community called a church, all those who adhere to them." However, many people have practiced their religion outside the bounds of official religious communities or organizations, though often in association with them. Think of the holy man or woman, the recluse, the hermit, the philosopher-mystics of the Middle Ages, such as Julian of Norwich. Sociologically, we must think of religious affiliation both as the formation of moral communities and as a quest for personal development and fulfilment. We can also examine it by inquiring to what extent the meanings and discourses developed within religious communities affect and influence the workings of society.

The obvious influence of religion on society is slight. Decisions in Congress or in Parliament are not made, for the most part, after ritual consultation of the Bible and consideration of the implications of its teaching for the decision (though some members of Congress or Parliament may do this). In many present-day societies we see an official separation of church and state. Where there are exceptions, as in England, we may discover on closer examination that the Church of England has little or no direct power over state decision making. The Church of England is "established" only in the sense that its clergy have an obligation to the people of England (but not to people in other parts of Britain) and cannot refuse to marry or bury them, and that it plays a part in English state ceremonies. However, we should consider the separation of church and state (discussed further in the next section) as part of a slow, long-term process of definition of religion within societies, not a recent phenomenon.

If we look at small, traditional societies such as hunter-gatherer bands, the concept of religion as we know it may be absent. That does not mean that people are not religious. Far from it! Instead, it means that their religion is closely interwoven with their daily lives. Rather than being concerned with an afterlife or even with a deity or deities, religion gives meaning to people's relations with the environment around them, the seasons of the year, the animals and plants that are their life support. There may not be religious specialists; however there are people who specialize in healing magic and ritual, in hunting magic and ritual, and in telling and enacting the myths of the society—the shared concepts of who people and animals are, how they came to be, and their relations with each other. The work of

these shamans and storytellers is an intrinsic part of the cultural life of society.

During the Middle Ages the vocation of theology—with the associated requirement that theologians be religious specialists who could debate points of religion apart from culture, history, and the workings of daily life—grew rapidly. However, it was not until the growth of science and rationality during the early modern period that religion became noticeably distinct from culture. With industrialization and modernization in Western societies, religion became conceptualized as a distinct social institution, a category of behaviors and beliefs that were important for people as individuals. A sociology of religion arose in which comparisons of different religions suggested an evolutionary progression from primitive animistic beliefs in spirits, through polytheism (belief in many different deities), to monotheism (belief in one deity, as in Islam, Judaism, and Christianity).

Roland Robertson, an eminent historian of religion, notes that "Against a long-drawn-out historical background . . . there crystallized at the end of the eighteenth century a view of religion centred on the place of individual religious commitment in the nationally constituted society" (1993, p. 13). As strong nation-states arose, along with the concept of the individual, there came a need in these nation-states for individuals to show loyalty directly to the nation-state and its society, not to their local community and the practices of their daily life. Societalization, instead of weakening the functions of religion, changed and strengthened it, making the concept of religion global (or all-encompassing). And with this globalization of religion came the concept of religious toleration, together with a separation of religion from the political workings of society. The church was no longer synonymous with the state. The church should not run the state, but churches should influence the people of that state and strengthen their attachment and loyalty to it.

Others point out that social scientists have, for a long time, been fond of predicting the death of religion, indeed have "particularly excelled in predicting the impending triumph of reason over 'superstition'" (Stark and Bainbridge, 1985, p. 1), but this has not come to pass. Religions lose some adherents but gain others, and new religions continually emerge. Church attendance may be down, but television audiences for religious programs continue to grow. More and more people consider themselves to be "detached believers" who pursue their religion in their own way, with little reliance on religious organizations.

Rather than say that religion is losing its importance, we can say that its importance has changed. This change is associated with long-term historical processes. Religion, even in parts of Europe where church attendance is lowest, shows no signs of losing its significance for the many individuals who either retain strong links to their churches, or create new religious organizations, or pursue their own studies in their chosen faith. As British sociologist James A. Beckford says, "Religious forms of sentiment, belief, and action have survived as autonomous resources. They retain the capacity to symbolize, for example, ultimate meaning, infinite power, supreme indignation, and sublime compassion" (1989, p. 171).

SUMMING UP

Is there still a place for religion in modern societies, or has religion lost its importance? There is evidence to support both sides of the argument. The debate depends on how we view religion. If we mean organized churches, well, in many Western countries these are no longer of obvious importance for the daily running of society, and this state of affairs has existed for quite some time. But in those states that have adopted Islamic governance, religion and state coincide, and Islamic law is based on the Qur'an. Importance of religion in this sense, therefore, depends on where you look. The growing role of Islamic societies in world affairs shows that religion is becoming more, not less, important.

Four out of five of the people of the world have a religion, but that religion is not necessarily the religion of their state. In many places, religion has come to be something that is personal and about which each person has a choice. The extent of that choice is associated with the extent to which religious tolerance is practiced within the chooser's own community. Instead of staying within a religion that has been learned since childhood—which is all the individual knows—many people today experiment with religion, moving from one to another or selecting humanism or atheism as a system that has meaning. It may be important for the sociology of religion to see this choice as a meaningful activity, not merely "dropping out." Many people who leave their religion may return at a later date or become permanent members of another religious organization.

Where religious tolerance permits choice, we see the development of many religious organizations. People who belong to them often stress the importance of understanding their religious group as a community. Within major denominations in North America, people often emphasize their liking for a particular church and a feeling of fellowship for others who attend there. For many, church attendance is as much a community-forming as a religious event. However, where people deliberately choose a religion or choose to return to a religion, they often do so on grounds of belief or shared philosophy. For many, then, religion has not lost its importance.

REVIEW EXERCISES

For Discussion and Debate

1. "Countries do best when there is one major religion that most people follow."

2. "How can existence have a meaning if people don't have religion?"

3. "When we can go to the moon, religion isn't relevant any more."

4. "Religion is important, but it isn't part of daily life."

Writing Exercises

1. "Religion is something that becomes important to people when they have kids."

2. "In large cities today, people create their communities based on religion."

3. "My own experience: The importance of religion in my life today compared to when I was a child."

4. "Why people search for religion."

Research Activities

1. Survey students in your class on religious membership. What is the spread of religion? (Note: Include atheism and humanism as religions.)

2. Interview three people whose religions affiliation is different from your own about their religious group membership. How did they become members of their religion—through birth or choice—and why is it important to them? What does this exercise tell you about your own choices?

3. Investigate statistics on religious membership or attendance in your geographic area over 10 years for three religions or denominations, at least one of which is not Christian. Is membership or attendance declining or increasing?

4. Collect newspaper articles on religion or religious institutions. What are most of the articles about?

SELECTED REFERENCES

BECKFORD, JAMES A., *Religion and advanced industrial society* (London: Unwin Hyman, 1989).

CHEAL, DAVID, Ritual: Communication in action, *Sociological Analysis* (Winter 1992), 53, 4, 363–374.

DEMERATH, N. J. III, and RHYS H. WILLIAMS, Secularization in a community context: Tensions of religion and politics in a New England city, *Journal for the Scientific Study of Religion* (June 1992), 31, 2, 189–206.

DOBBELAERE, KAREL, Church involvement and secularization: Making sense of the European case. In *Secularization, rationalism and sectarianism: Essays in honour of Bryan R. Wilson*, ed. Eileen Barker, James A. Beckford, and Karel Dobbelaere (Oxford: Clarendon Press, 1993), pp. 19–36.

EISEN, ARNOLD M., The rhetoric of chosenness, *Society* (November–December 1990), 28, 1(89), 26–33.

EISENSTADT, SHMUEL, The expansion of religions: Some comparative observations on different modes, *Comparative Social Research* (1991), 13, 45–73.

———, Culture, religions and development in North American and Latin American civilizations, *International Social Science Journal* (November 1992), 44, 4(134), 593–606.

ELLISON, CHRISTOPHER G., and MARC A. MUSICK, Conservative Protestantism and public opinion toward science, *Review of Religious Research* (March 1995), 36, 3, 245–262.

GOODY, JACK, Knots in May: Continuities, contradictions and change in European rituals, *Journal of Mediterranean Studies* (1993), 3, 1, 30–45.

HALLIDAY, FRED, Fundamentalism and the contemporary world, *Contention: Debates in Society, Culture and Science* (Winter 1995), 4, 2, 41–58.

HARLEY, BRIAN, and GLENN FIREBAUGH, Americans' belief in an afterlife: Trends over the past two decades, *Journal for the Scientific Study of Religion* (September 1993), 32, 3, 269–278.

HASTINGS, PHILIP K., and DEAN R. HOGE, Religious and moral attitude trends among college students, 1948–84, *Social Forces* (December 1986), 65, 2, 370–377.

HOOVER, DWIGHT W., Middletown: A case study of religious development, 1827–1982, *Social Compass* (September 1991), 38, 3, 273–284.

JELEN, TED G., Aging and boundary maintenance among American evangelicals, *Review of Religious Research* (March 1990), 31, 3, 268–279.

____, and CLYDE WILCOX, Religious dogmatism among white Christians: Causes and effects, *Review of Religious Research* (September 1991), 33, 1, 32–46.

LINDSEY, DONALD B., and JOHN HEEREN, Where the sacred meets the profane: Religion in the comic pages, *Review of Religious Research* (September 1992), 34, 1, 63–77.

MARTIN, DAVID, The secularization issue: Prospect and retrospect, *British Journal of Sociology* (September 1991), 42, 3, 465–474.

MISRA, JOYA, and ALEXANDER HICKS, Catholicism and unionization in affluent postwar democracies: Catholicism, culture, party and unionization, *American Sociological Review* (April 1994), 59, 2, 304–326.

OGUTCU, MEHMET, Islam and the West: Can Turkey bridge the gap? *Futures* (October 1994), 26, 8, 811–829.

ROBERTSON, ROLAND, Community, society, globality, and the category of religion. In *Secularization, rationalism and sectarianism: Essays in honour of Bryan R. Wilson*, ed. Eileen Barker, James A. Beckford, and Karel Dobbelaere (Oxford: Clarendon Press, 1993), pp. 1–18.

SCHMALZBAUER, JOHN, Evangelicals in the new class: Class versus subcultural predictors of ideology, *Journal for the Scientific Study of Religion* (December 1993), 32, 4, 330–342.

SKILL, THOMAS, JAMES D. ROBINSON, JOHN S. LYONS, and DAVID LARSON, The portrayal of religion and spirituality on fictional network television, *Review of Religious Research* (March 1994), 35, 3, 251–267.

STARK, RODNEY, and WILLIAM SIMS BAINBRIDGE, eds., *The future of religion: Secularization, revival, and cult formation* (Berkeley: University of California Press, 1985).

WALLIS, ROY, and STEVE BRUCE, Religion: The British contribution, *British Journal of Sociology* (September 1989), 40, 3, 493–520.

WILSON, BRYAN, The secularization debate, *Encounter* (1975), 45, 77–83.

WITTEN, MARSHA G., *All is forgiven: The secular message in American Protestantism* (Princeton, NJ: Princeton University Press, 1993).

13.2

Should churches mix in politics?

The issue: *The concern voiced by some that, in reviving religious enthusiasm, the so-called fundamentalists may have overstepped the line between church and state—a line that took centuries to draw and may have helped to prevent many religious wars.*

Introduction As stated in the preceding section, some countries of the world are Islamic states in which religion is intertwined with government. This section will not deal with these countries. The question of whether such states should run their governments in the ways they do is properly a subject for discussion within Islam. Instead, this section examines the general arguments for and against religion's involvement in politics in states where separation of church and state has occurred, as in many countries of Africa and Asia, in addition to Europe, North and South America, and Australasia.

For the most part, religious organizations in these countries do not form political parties or field candidates for election. They may, however, lend support to candidates of particular political parties. More often, local, national, or international religious leaders speak on political issues in nonpartisan terms, drawing the attention of political leaders and voters to social and political concerns. Should religions be involved in political matters in this way? Here we present the arguments both against and for such involvement.

RELIGIONS SHOULD STAY OUT OF POLITICAL MATTERS

There are two main arguments why religion should stay out of politics. One focuses on the effect involvement may have on politics; the other, on the likely effect of politics on religion.

If we look at what religion does in modern societies and how it operates, we can see many ways in which religions have adjusted to the modern world. One is the emphasis on individual fulfillment and the creation of community feeling—bonds linking members with others within their organization. Within a religious organization, therefore, people are held together by bonds of mutual support, belief, and commitment. The political arena is different. Within a democratic state, we look to individuals for ideas and debates. Every person is considered equal with every other and may contribute to the political process as she or he chooses.

Thus, the democratic ideology argues we should not allow religious institutions to become key actors in political affairs. Beyond that, there is evidence that when religions have become key actors in world history, the consequences have sometimes been disastrous. At the extremes, religions have promoted genocide (think of the Spanish Inquisition against Jews and Islamic Moors) and the suppression of particular groups

(whether women, religious minorities, or others with "unacceptable" attributes). In general, the Catholic Church played an antidemocratic role in European history, which is why the initially democratic Napoleon broke its hold wherever his armies were victorious. Some would say the Catholic and Islamic religions continue to support conservative and/or antidemocratic regimes in much of the world today.

The effect of religion on politics If a religious organization places support behind one or another political party, or one or another political cause, what are its members to do? Should they follow the dictates of their religious leaders, given that many churches have hierarchical, not democratic, power structures when it comes to making decisions about principles, morals, or right behavior? And if they do so, what happens to democracy?

This issue is particularly important for religions that claim jurisdiction over the actions of their members. If a priest suggests a possible course of action—say, actively supporting a candidate for election or canvassing for her or his campaign—should the priest then be permitted to check on the actions of parishioners? What if a parishioner feels obliged to confess that she did not support the candidate or even voted for someone else? A similar argument can be made for other forms of political behavior, such as lobbying or campaigning for or against policies. Religious organizations often hold strong sway over the minds, hearts, and loyalties of their members, and religious leaders can have great influence. If they wield this influence over political matters, people's political decisions are being made on grounds of belief, emotion, and loyalty, rather than on grounds of practicality and reason, as they are supposed to be.

We have all heard of situations in which people, swayed by emotion and religious fervor, even go to the length of committing criminal acts to support a cause. With this great power over the hearts and minds of people, religion should urge people to face their own faults and guide their own lives, not intervene in nonrational, nonpolitical ways in political decisions.

The effect of politics on religion   The separation of politics from religion in the West has been beneficial for religion. Previously there have been long periods in history when religious leaders have become power brokers or political leaders. Consequently, they and their followers have been subject to the same temptations and problems as lay people in the political world. Scandals of political corruption have affected religious leaders in the past. Where religious groups take a direct part in the political sphere, the leaders' ability to provide for the spiritual needs of their parishioners or followers may be severely compromised.

Religions in the present day chiefly serve the function of helping people develop and achieve fulfillment by exploring their potential for spirituality. This is not compatible with political involvement. In modern thought, politics deals with the material basis of life and with power and its operation; religion, with spiritual life and the relation of people to the divine. If religions advocate political courses of action, then they can no longer speak to all their followers but only to those who belong to particular political parties or espouse particular secular causes. If religions enter the political arena, they become merely pressure groups for political causes. If they compete for political favors, they lose the right, in the eyes of the general public, to speak to higher moral issues. That's why religions should stay out of politics—or at least, some people think so. But here's the other side.

RELIGIONS SHOULD PARTICIPATE IN POLITICAL MATTERS

We can see many examples of religious participation in politics. These include Catholic nuns who campaign for increased status for women and an end to spouse abuse, leading religious figures who campaign for peace, and outstanding examples where a single individual, as spokesperson for a religious movement, becomes associated with a civil cause. Anyone who has heard of South Africa's successful move to equality knows the name of Archbishop Desmond Tutu. And looking to the recent past, anyone who has heard of the American civil rights movement knows about the achievements of Dr. Martin Luther King, Jr. Both Tutu and King were, at least originally, religious and not political leaders; they used their religious insights and preaching skills to mobilize people for political causes.

From Durkheim on, social scientists have discussed religion's role in formulating and expressing the moral values of society. Religions do not only form a way for people to develop their spiritualities and their relations with the divine; they are also the custodians of society's moral standards. Some religions express these standards in the form of simple guidelines (such as the Ten Commandments); others, as more complex theologizing.

Politics involves making decisions about people and their environments. Accordingly, politicians look to what is possible and, often, to what will be popular with particular constituencies. But if religions are the custodians of morality and ethical behavior, religious leaders and their followers also have an obligation to involve themselves in the workings of society, in an attempt to ensure that society's decisions are made on a moral foundation. In theory, it would be desirable to bring ethics, not mere expediency, to bear on decisions about the way society is run, and religious leaders may be better equipped than politicians to do this.

In a society in which one religion or religious organization is dominant, such an association could lead to a merging of church and state. However, in North American society no single religious organization dominates. The majority of people follow a form of Christianity (though not all of them are churchgoers) but belong to many different churches or denominations. A sizable number belong to other religions, including Islam, Buddhism, and Judaism. Groups such as Unitarians even draw on the teachings of several religions and philosophies, including Christianity, Judaism, humanism, and others.

For many people, religious expression includes a strong component of social activism. Many churches and other religious organizations promote the concept of all people as equal, regardless of ethnicity or race, and encourage their members to campaign for social equality. Antipoverty issues also provide a focus for action that may include organizing charity events such as food-bank drives. In fact, it can mean anything from lobbying at a local government level to mobilizing and supporting antigovernment protest, as in the liberation theology of Latin American churches.

Problem areas: The example of same-sex marriages

A problem results, however, when some religious groups favor one political course of action and others another, particularly when these courses of action stem from different views of moral or right conduct. An example is the controversy over the legalization of marriage between same-sex couples. Within some religious doctrines, marriage is a sacrament that can occur only between a woman and a man. It is often viewed as an institution for the production of children, and groups holding these views may oppose legislation

to legalize same-sex marriage. Other religious groups view marriage as a social and religious recognition of love between two individuals, and they may campaign to have same-sex marriages legalized. Still other groups, probably constituting the majority, are divided; their members are unsure of what course they should take, or whether their faith's teaching on marriage should or could be a part of the public debate. All these groups are part of our society, and in a democratic society, all have a right to be heard.

Can religion and politics truly be separate?

There are other ways in which we can debate the rightful relationship between religion and politics. Religions exist within society, as part of it. Religious opinion and doctrine thereby become components of political ideology, concepts appearing and reappearing in political discourse. Political economy theorists have pointed to multiple links between dominant religion and other social structures. In Max Weber's discussion of the origins of capitalism, in his book *The Protestant Ethic and the Spirit of Capitalism*, religious theory, doctrine, and practice are closely associated with the rise of the capitalist elite, without requiring a conscious and deliberate involvement of religion in politics. The question becomes not *should* religion and politics be separate, but *can* they ever be separate?

So far we have dealt only with dominant religions and their links with politics. Here conflict theorists argue that the same concepts and discourses influence religious and political thought. Religion, they say, can be a form of social control. Through religion, people are encouraged to act in ways that benefit ruling sectors of society, to be meek, to not cause problems for employers. Instead of seeing this as religion's influence on politics, we could describe it as the influence of politics on religion. However, there are other ways in which religion and politics become linked, notably through the sense of religion as resistance.

The clearest examples come from situations where religion not only fosters identity as a group member but gives value to traditional ways of life and gives to both everyday and political events meaning that is different from the meaning these would be ascribed by the dominant society. In North America, for example, traditional religions of the Native peoples have recently been experiencing a revival. Native religions interpret the relation of people with the earth and with animals and plants in ways that show Native peoples as caretakers and conservationists, often in opposition to the European-American concept of "making use" of land, animals, and plants. Many people discover in these religions ways in which they not only can express themselves and identify with their communities but reinterpret political events and take political action to protect social and community rights. These religions are attractive both to many aboriginal people and to growing numbers of European Americans.

Many campaigners against poverty, racism, and violence in society trace the strength of their commitment to their religious (including humanist) affiliation. Their religion gives them a philosophy and a sense of purpose, as well as a feeling that by acting on their principles they can help create a better world. They use their religious commitment to actively oppose trends in society that they feel to be against their beliefs. People come together as religious groups to demonstrate their beliefs through marches, boycotts, political lobbying, or other active participation. Often they join with other groups, as occurred recently after several black Baptist churches in the United States were destroyed by arson. Then Unitarians and Mennonites (among others) joined forces to show their opposition to both racism and

intolerance by providing all the labor to rebuild the churches. Black Baptist churches themselves demonstrate how religious feeling can unite communities in political action. As already mentioned, Martin Luther King, Jr., a Baptist preacher, acted as his community's spokesperson against the injustices he saw.

SUMMING UP

Should churches or synagogues or mosques mix in politics? Napoleon didn't think so; that's why he took such pains to separate church and state wherever he took control in his nineteenth-century conquest of Europe. In this sentiment, he was supported by a great many revolution-minded Europeans. But for many in religious organizations today, prayer and contemplation is not sufficient. Their goals are not all related to speculation about an afterlife, and they feel a moral commitment to social action.

This is not true for every person who goes to a church, attends a synagogue, or thinks deeply about humanity and its relationship with its world. People make their own decisions in today's world on their religious and political commitment. Some believe that religion and politics can, and should, be separate. Others see them as inextricably intertwined, with religion indicating political routes that they are obligated to take. For such people, political action, which is not opposed to religion, becomes a necessary corollary to religious belief.

This section cannot resolve the question of whether religion and politics should be separate. This is a moral question each person must decide for herself or himself, and sociology cannot resolve problems of what should be. What sociology can do, however, is indicate that in many ways, and for many people, religion and politics go hand in hand.

From a sociological and historical perspective, the struggle to link, limit, and separate religion and politics is never-ending. And, like any major struggle, it brings out the best and the worst in human beings.

REVIEW EXERCISES

For Discussion and Debate

1. "Because some links between religion and politics are destructive, all political campaigning by religious groups should be banned."
2. "Can politics be kept out of religion?"
3. "Native religions are an important focus of resistance for Native communities. That's why they were suppressed by Europeans."
4. Pros and cons of religious leaders standing for public office.

Writing Exercises

1. "My own experience: How religion connects with political leanings in myself and those around me." (Remember to treat humanism and atheism as religions.)
2. "Politics needs the moral leadership of religion."
3. Alternative 'earth-based' religions and the environmental movement.
4. "How I react to political campaigns by religious organizations."

Research Activities

1. Observe a demonstration or protest march or look for newspaper articles of a march. From banners or other signs, what religions or denominations are present? What is the reason for the protest, and how does this connect with the philosophy of these religious groups, as far as you are aware of them?
2. Devise a questionnaire on how people's religion influences or connects with their political attitudes. Use this to survey 15 people and tabulate results for presentation to your class.
3. Search the World Wide Web for sites linking religion and politics. (Be aware that you may find links that you disapprove of, and remember that any site, on its own, may not speak for all members of the religion.) Discuss your findings with other students from your class.
4. Study popular materials produced by any religious organization (for instance, handouts given door-to-door), looking for information or advice on daily living and political activity. To what extent can these two aspects of life be separated?

SELECTED REFERENCES

Ashraf, Ahmad, Theocracy and charisma: New men of power in Iran, *International Journal of Politics, Culture and Society* (Fall 1990), 4, 1, 113–152.

Barker, Eileen, Behold the new Jerusalems! Catch 22s in the kingdom-building endeavors of new religious movements, *Sociology of Religion* (Winter 1993), 54, 4, 377–352.

Billings, Dwight B., and Shaunna L. Scott, Religion and political legitimation, *Annual Review of Sociology* (1994), 20, 173–202.

CHAVES, MARK, and LYNN M. HIGGINS, Comparing the community involvement of black and white congregations, *Journal for the Scientific Study of Religion* (December 1992), 31, 4, 425–440.

CHEHABI, H. E., Religion and politics in Iran: How theocratic is the Islamic Republic? *Daedalus* (Summer 1991), 120, 3, 69–91.

COLLINS, RANDALL, Liberals and conservatives, religious and political: A conjuncture of modern history, *Sociology of Religion* (Summer 1993), 54, 2, 127–146.

DAVIDSON, JAMES D., Religion among America's elite: Persistence and change in the Protestant establishment, *Sociology of Religion* (Winter 1994), 55, 4, 419–440.

DURHAM, MARTIN, Abortion and the politics of morality in the USA, *Parliamentary Affairs* (April 1994), 47, 2, 280–292.

HOROWITZ, IRVING LOUIS, The glass is half full and half empty: Religious conviction and political participation, *Society* (July–August 1991), 28, 5(193), 17–22.

MOALLEM, MINOO, The ethnicity of an Islamic fundamentalism: The case of Iran, *South Asia Bulletin* (Fall 1992), 12, 2, 25–34.

MOEN, MATTHEW C., From revolution to evolution: The changing nature of the Christian Right, *Sociology of Religion* (Fall 1994), 55, 3, 345–357.

MUELLER, CAROL, In search of a constituency for the "New Religious Right," *Public Opinion Quarterly* (Summer 1983), 47, 2, 213–229.

OLSON, DANIEL V. A., and JACKSON W. CARROLL, Religiously based politics: Religious elites and the public, *Social Forces* (March 1992), 70, 3, 765–786.

OOMMEN, T. K., Religious nationalism and democratic polity: The Indian case, *Sociology of Religion* (Winter 1994), 55, 4, 455–472.

RAYMOND, PAUL, and BARBARA NORRANDER, Religion and attitudes toward anti-abortion protest, *Review of Religious Research* (December 1990), 32, 2, 151–156.

REGAN, DANIEL, Islamic resurgence: Characteristics, causes, consequences and implications, *Journal of Political and Military Sociology* (Winter 1993), 21, 2, 259–266.

SANNEH, LAMIN, Religion and politics: Third world perspectives on a comparative religious theme, *Daedalus* (Summer 1991), 120, 3, 203–218.

SMITH, CHRISTIAN, The spirit and democracy, *Sociology of Religion* (Summer 1994), 55, 2, 119–143.

TIMMERMAN, DAVID M., and LARRY DAVID SMITH, The world according to Pat: The telepolitical celebrity as purveyor of political medicine, *Political Communication* (July–September 1994), 11, 3, 233–248.

VRCAN, SRDJAN, The war in ex-Yugoslavia and religion, *Social Compass* (September 1994), 41, 3, 413–422.

WARHOLA, JAMES W., The religious dimension of ethnic conflict in the Soviet Union, *International Journal of Politics, Culture and Society* (Winter 1991), 5, 2, 249–270.

WILSON, JOHN F., Religious movements in the United States, *Journal of Interdisciplinary History* (Autumn 1992), 23, 2, 301–307.

WUTHNOW, ROBERT, Understanding religion and politics, *Daedalus* (Summer 1991), 120, 3, 1–20.

13.3

Are traditional religions against women?

The issue: On one side, the strong need many have to believe in something beyond them-selves—a need traditionally fulfilled by religion. On the other side, the contention by many feminists that traditional religions teach the wrong kind of ideas about men and women.

Introduction   Are traditional religions misog-ynistic—that is, do they show hatred toward women? This question has been hotly contested within and outside traditional churches in North America and elsewhere. Proponents of the view that religions are against women say that not only have women been treated badly by conventional religions but that this treatment is intrinsically part of the religion, not something found in only a few problematic situations. Opponents of this view point out that more women than men are churchgoers. If women were badly treated, presumably they would not attend church as avidly as they do. This section questions whether traditional religions are against women and discusses the ways that people both inside and outside conventional churches may be attempting to deal with misogynistic elements.

TRADITIONAL RELIGIONS ARE NOT NECESSARILY MISOGYNISTIC

Many people within the churches spoken of as traditional in North America—that is, various denominations of Christianity and Judaism—have pointed to inequalities in the treatment of women and men. In this section we deal for the most part with Christianity. Some church members and also some sociologists deny that such inequalities exist. Many, however, think that they do, but give conflicting reasons. Some feminist theorists charge that inequalities stem from a basic misogyny within traditional religions. Others, including other feminists, think that religious organizations may merely reflect social inequalities of their times, so that the problems women face within traditional religions are transient and can be expected to disappear with church reforms as women achieve a higher status elsewhere in the public sphere and as women put pressure on church authorities.

Churches change with the times   One hundred years ago, women held no positions of authority within mainstream churches. They were not allowed to be preachers, ministers, priests, deacons, or bishops, and they could hold authority only over other women or children. Today, the picture is changing. Many churches have women in senior positions. The first woman moderator of the United Church of Canada was Lois Wilson, in 1980. Women have also been ordained by Anglican churches, even recently by the Church of England. Although many people threatened to leave the church if women were permitted to become priests, and a few did actually leave, the vote to have women as priests was carried by a majority.

If we look to the earliest writings of the Christian church, we find accounts of women as deacons—people who were recognized as knowledgeable and respected leaders in the emerging church. Later, these positions were filled only by men, and it is true that some of the writings and statements of these men do appear misogynistic. However, we have to take them in the context of their times. When society was misogynistic, so were its churches. Moreover, during many periods in European history, churches were organizations within which women had more choice than they did generally in society. Within the church, women who became nuns could have far more access to both scholarship and authority than other women. Senior members of female religious orders were widely respected, even venerated.

The worst times for women   During the period referred to as "the Burning Times"—roughly the fifteenth to the seventeenth centuries—large numbers of women were condemned by the church and accused of witchcraft, often for no other reason than that they were women. Some feminist scholars have said that this indicates misogyny. However, if we examine the evidence from that period, we find that, first, the numbers executed were small (approximately 100,000 rather than the millions that have been suggested), and that men as well as women were accused, although in almost all areas of Europe the numbers of women accused were higher.

It may be by chance that more women were accused. In many areas the witch became a convenient scapegoat, and all the ills affecting a district could be blamed on her or him. People who did not "fit in"—for example, who uttered curses or were seen as bad neighbors—were more likely to be targeted by an untutored peasantry as witches and as the source of local problems. Further, the witchcraze was conducted by civil authorities as well as by the churches, so it is unjust to blame the churches alone for this craze.

Important roles for women Since those unhappy times, many aspects of society have changed. The work people do, the distribution of that work, and its value for society all influence the ways women and men are thought of. Today in many churches women and their roles are once again highly valued. In some churches these roles are different from the roles of men. For instance, in the Catholic Church both women and men can be teachers and theologians, though only men can be called to the priesthood. Within Catholicism, priesthood represents a highly specialized position, and because all the first apostles were men, Catholic doctrine holds that their successors must be men also. Many Catholics point out that other positions are open to women, and that women within the church are highly respected, having their own spheres of influence and decision making.

Women have played an important role in religiously inspired movements in the past. Often movements for social change, linked to the churches, have been organized or headed by women or have taken up causes favored by women; the temperance movement is an outstanding example. Within church congregations, often the work of visiting, helping, and giving counsel and comfort is performed by women. These women are seen as the backbone of the church, central to its processes.

If we look at today's church congregations, we find that in almost all major denominations, the majority of church members and churchgoers are women. National surveys in the United States indicate that women are more likely than men to report attending a religious service in the past week (by 46% to 35%). They are also more likely to report their religious commitment as a positive experience and to see it as an important factor in their lives.

Major churches are strongly influenced by their memberships, and so women have a strong voice in decision making. If women require change, they have only to ask for it. Churches, therefore, are no more misogynistic than other social institutions, and indeed may be less so than the institutions of politics or business, for instance. There have indeed been examples of church-based misogyny, whether stemming from highly prejudiced individuals or occurring during times of exceptionally bad social treatment of women. However, churches are not necessarily misogynistic, and indeed, in these more enlightened times, they consciously minister to the needs of both female and male church members.

TRADITIONAL CHURCHES ARE MISOGYNISTIC

A number of feminist scholars and others charge that, since the times of the early church, social processes operating within the church have acted to exclude women from positions of power and decision making, and that both doctrine and practice have reflected this. Although women today have more chance to participate at a higher level, these processes remain in operation to a greater or lesser extent depending on the religious denomination. In the more conservative churches, exclusionary processes remain in force; in the more liberal churches, their operations are masked and contested, but they remain part of the church structure. Movements such as those for inclusive (i.e., nonsexist) language within churches are viewed as secondary or fringe interests, not essential to the basic operation of the church or even to the real challenges and issues facing churches today.

Participating in church and playing a large part in the organization of the everyday life of churches—from bake sales to visiting charity work and vast amounts of committee work—is not enough; women remain invisible. In part, because of this, increasing numbers of women are looking for and finding their religion outside traditional churches.

Women and church hierarchy   Mary Daly, well known as a critic of established churches, indicates that the structure, symbolism, and language of the churches are profoundly antiwoman. Churches promote the concept of hierarchy, with God at the apex, followed by men (in some churches, various levels of male priests, then laymen), women, and children. Even Protestant churches, which do not necessarily promote a hierarchy of clergy, have traditionally viewed men as closer to God. This hierarchy is strengthened and promoted by an overwhelming number of male images. Most often, God is still presented as male; images of Jesus abound in many churches; figures of the male apostles appear everywhere, from church windows to children's books.

Often, the only apparent female image is that of Mary, viewed as mother and described in ways that (as many feminist theologians and sociologists point out) make plain that she is set apart from "ordinary" women, and so cannot be truly emulated. Besides, she is spoken of as merely an "intercessor." Even as mother of Jesus, she has no power, and she does not form part of the male Trinity. When, in 1987, the world's first female Catholic theology professor, Uta Ranke-Heinemann, challenged the concept of the Virgin Mary as asexual, untainted, and pure—an impossible model for women—the church revoked her authority to teach theology.

Until recently, women were considered by mainstream churches to be incapable of acting as priests or ministers; and although in many Protestant churches women can now be ministers, this was not achieved without a struggle. The Catholic Church recently reiterated its position on the issue of women as priests. Bishop Angelo Scola stated that Christ was male and the apostles were male, and clearly he wanted to have only male priests. "The church does not have the power to modify the practice, uninterrupted for 2,000 years, of calling only men," Scola said, adding: "This was wanted directly by Jesus," and that the all-male priesthood is "objectively linked to the sex of Jesus." Feminists have been quick to point out that what was "wanted by Jesus" has been interpreted and reinterpreted by generations of male clergy.

The concept of women as spiritually different from men, in ways that matter for traditional religions, can be traced through the writings of theologians. According to the theologian Joanna Manning, "St Thomas Aquinas taught that in the natural or earthly order, only men possessed the fullness of humanity and women's defective humanity was derived through men's."

Another look at the witchcraze   The witchcraze, culminating in the sixteenth and seventeenth centuries, has already been referred to. During that period, civil as well as ecclesiastical courts condemned both women and men. The men were most often those associated with the women condemned as witches—their fathers, sons, or husbands, or men who tried to defend them. About 80% of those accused were women. It is no coincidence that this was also a period of the growing domestication and restriction of women. At the start of it, women acted in the public sphere as farmers, traders, craftspeople, midwives, and folk-healers. Some may have been involved in folk-religious practices akin to shamanic techniques of healing and prophesy found in many other parts of the world.

By the end of the period, a woman's place was as an adjunct to her husband, if she had one. Seen in a broader context, the process of accusation, trial, torture, and execution of thousands of witches proved to be one method by which men were able to restrict women's lives more in the early 1800s than ever before or since. And, in this context, one has to wonder whether the current enthusiasm for Jane Austen's nineteenth-century domestic novels represents a backlash against modern feminism and the actual liberation of women from second-class status.

The theology of the times made the witchcraze possible. Women were seen as the carriers of evil—susceptible to the advances of the devil from whom they derived their powers through a pact, sexually insatiable, the greatest danger to Christian society. The most famous witch-hunter's manual, *Malleus Maleficarum*, prepared by two Dominican priests, was published in 1486 and went through 6 editions before 1500, at least 13 by 1520, and another 16 by 1669. It was translated into German, French, Italian, and English, was intensively quoted in later manuals, and soon spread into civil law. Even enlightened judges, under the influence of church doctrine, sought supernatural explanations for phenomena such as the death of animals or sickness of people.

Today, most analyses of the witchcraze do not mention the intense misogyny inculcated by Christian doctrines or the determined hunting out of the remnants of folk-religious practices. Where it is mentioned, the witchcraze is seen as something "in the past," irrelevant to modern society. Many feminist scholars, however, point out that the effects of the witchcraze period are still with us, in popular images of women and especially in the ways we speak of older women, as well as troublesome women, women who protest, or are not obedient, as witches.

SUMMING UP

Are traditional religions against women? To the extent that they were misogynistic in the past and have yet to reform their practices, yes, they are. The witchcraze provides evidence that standard church doctrines and practices included a strong strand of misogyny. In some churches, women remain excluded from areas of religious life, and their qualifications to speak as theologians and teachers are under constant review. Harassment of women attending theological colleges is commonly reported, and the images of divinity presented today within Christianity are still overwhelmingly male.

Does this, however, constitute grounds for saying that traditional religions are misogynistic? Some feminist scholars and theologians argue that traditional religions are redeemable, and that constant pressure for reform will bring change, in time. Others, however, maintain that women can best express their spiritualities outside established churches.

Today, some writers are attempting to construct feminist theologies in which divinity is conceptualized as female, or as both female and male. Many other people in North

America are exploring their spiritualities through reconstructed practices based on the folk religions of Africa, America, and Europe. Native groups are working to reestablish indigenous North American religions. Others look to their background or ancestry, focusing on African traditions and beliefs, or on European Celtic and Nordic folklore and mythology. These practitioners reject the misogyny of the "Burning Times," conceptualizing divinity as female, male, neither, or both. Often they share a concept of Earth as the mother of all beings and become advocates for environmental awareness.

It is too early to tell what kind of challenge these reconstructed religions will pose to Christian hegemony in North America. It may be that in a postmodern world, with an atmosphere of more religious tolerance, each religion, however small, can hold its own and empower its adherents. Yet women who speak out are still viewed negatively, as "witches," and women and men who are followers of Wicca, Santeria, paganism, or heathenism may find that others in their community see them as a threat. The "Burning Times" may not be totally behind us.

REVIEW EXERCISES

For Discussion and Debate

1. "Using inclusive language in church is just being politically correct."
2. "Women need their own space to reclaim their spirituality."
3. Does organized religion control or oppress men?
4. The witchcraze—Was it an expression of women-hating?

Writing Exercises

1. The roles of women and men in a religious institution. (Choose your own institution.)
2. Why women seek the Goddess.
3. How people seek personal fulfillment in their religions.
4. "My own experience—Does religion empower me?"

Research Activities

1. Interview 10 women who are members of an established church. What do they see as problems facing women in their church? How can these problems be overcome? Present your findings to a group of students from your class.
2. Survey at least 20 students who are not members of your class on their attitudes toward followers of earth-centered spirituality, including pagans, Wiccans, heathens, and Goddess worshipers. (Many of these may be known as witches.) Discuss findings with other members of your class.
3. Draw up a short questionnaire on church attendance (including denomination and frequency of attendance) and views on changing roles of women. Using this, survey at least 15 people, and prepare your results for presentation to the class. (Remember that "church" can mean sociologically any religious organization.)
4. Conduct interviews with five women and five men who are active religious practitioners on the use of inclusive language within their religions.

SELECTED REFERENCES

ADLER, MARGOT, *Drawing down the moon*, 2nd ed. (Boston: Beacon Press, 1986).

ALDRIDGE, ALAN, Men, women, and clergymen: Opinion and authority in a sacred organization, *Sociological Review* (February 1989), 37, 1, 43–64.

BARSTOW, ANNE LLEWELLYN, *Witchcraze* (London: Pandora, 1995).

CHOKSY, JAMSHEED K., Women in the Zoroastrian Book of Primal Creation: Images and functions within a religious tradition, *Mankind Quarterly* (1988), 29, 1–2, 73–82.

CHRIST, CAROL P., *Laughter of Aphrodite: Reflections on a journey to the Goddess* (New York: HarperCollins, 1987).

———, Why women need the Goddess. In *Womanspirit rising: A feminist reader in religion*, ed. Carol P. Christ and Judith Plaskow (San Francisco: Harper, 1992).

DALY, MARY, *Beyond God the Father: Toward a philosophy of women's liberation* (Boston: Beacon Press, 1973).

ELLER, CYNTHIA, *Living in the lap of the Goddess: The feminist spirituality movement in America* (Boston: Beacon Press, 1993).

ERTURK, YAKIN, Convergence and divergence in the status of Moslem women: The cases of Turkey and Saudi Arabia, *International Sociology* (September 1991), 6, 3, 307–320.

FINLEY, NANCY J., Political activism and feminist spirituality, *Sociological Analysis* (1991), 52, 4, 349–362.

GHADBIAN, NAJIB, Islamists and women in the Arab world: From reaction to reform, *American Journal of Islamic Social Sciences* (Spring 1995), 12, 1, 19–35.

GOLDSCHEIDER, CALVIN, and WILLIAM D. MOSHER, Patterns of contraceptive use in the United States: The importance of religious factors, *Studies in Family Planning* (March–April 1991), 22, 2, 102–115.

GREEK, CECIL E., and WILLIAM THOMPSON, Antipornography campaigns: Saving the family in America and England, *International Journal of Politics, Culture and Society* (Summer 1992), 5, 4, 601–616.

GRIFFIN, WENDY, The embodied Goddess: Feminist witchcraft and female divinity, *Sociology of Religion* (1995), 56, 1, 35–48.

HOODFAR, HOMA, The veil in their minds and on our heads: The persistence of colonial images of Muslim women, *Resources for Feminist Research* (Fall–Winter 1993), 22, 3–4, 5–18.

HUNTER, JAMES DAVISON, and KIMON HOWLAND SARGEANT, Religion, women, and the transformation of public culture, *Social Research* (Fall 1993), 60, 3, 545–570.

INGERSOLL, JULIE J., Which tradition, which values? "Traditional family values" in American Protestant fundamentalism, *Contention: Debates in Society, Culture and Science* (Winter 1995), 4, 2, 91–103.

JELEN, TED G., Changes in the attitudinal correlates of opposition to abortion, 1977–1985, *Journal for the Scientific Study of Religion* (June 1988), 27, 2, 211–228.

KING, URSULA, Women and spirituality: Voices of protest and promise. In *Women in society*, ed. Jo Campling (London: Macmillan, 1989), pp. 91–105.

KINTZ, LINDA, Motherly advice from the Christian Right: The construction of sacred gender, *Discourse* (Fall 1994), 17, 1, 49–76.

LOTTES, ILSA L., and PETER J. KURLOFF, The effects of gender, race, religion, and political orientation on the sex role attitudes of college freshmen, *Adolescence* (Fall 1992), 27, 107, 675–688.

LOZANO, WENDY G., and TANICE G. FOLTZ, Into the darkness: An ethnographic study of witchcraft and death, *Qualitative Sociology* (1990), 13, 3, 211–234.

LUFF, TRACY L., Wicce: Adding a spiritual dimension to feminism, *Berkeley Journal of Sociology* (1990), 35, 91–105.

LUHRMANN, TANYA M., Resurgence of romanticism: Contemporary neo-paganism, feminist spirituality and the divinity of nature. In *Environmentalism: The view from anthropology*, ed. Kay Milton (London: Routledge, 1993), pp. 219–232.

MANNING, JOANNA, How the Vatican contorts itself in banning women as priests, *Globe and Mail*, January 28, 1997, p. A21.

MERNISSI, FATIMA, Muslim women and fundamentalism, *Middle East Report* (July–August 1988), 18, 4(153), 8–11.

OBERMEYER, CARLA MAKHLOUF, Reproductive choice in Islam: Gender and state in Iran and Tunisia, *Studies in Family Planning* (January–February 1994), 25, 1, 41–51.

PATTERSON, ORLANDO, The new Puritanism, *Salmagundi* (Winter–Spring 1994), 101–102, 55–67.

RALSTON, HELEN, Religious movements and the status of women in India, *Social Compass* (March 1991), 38, 1, 43–53.

Schüssler Fiorenza, Elisabeth, *In memory of her: A feminist theological reconstruction of Christian origins* (New York: Crossroad, 1983).

Sered, Susan Starr, Ideology, autonomy, and sisterhood: An analysis of the secular consequences of women's religions, *Gender and Society* (December 1994), 8, 4, 486–506.

Staats, Valerie, Ritual, strategy, or convention: Social meanings in the traditional women's baths in Morocco, *Frontiers* (1994), 14, 3, 1–18.

Starhawk, *Dreaming the dark: Magic, sex, & politics* (Boston: Beacon Press, 1982).

Touabi, Noureddine, Acculturation, value conflicts and the place of the sacred in family life in Algeria, *International Social Science Journal* (November 1990), 42, 4(126), 539–545.

14. Global Inequality

Global inequality—the economic and political inequality between different societies of the world—is signified by what social scientists call **imperialism**—the exercise of political and economic control by one state over the territory of another, often by military means. Imperialism's purpose is to exploit the indigenous population and extract economic and political advantages.

Early European imperialism occurred through **colonization**—the settlement and administration of foreign lands. However, domination of a foreign land does not always require colonization. In fact, economic domination is far safer, less costly, and more stable. By gaining control of a nation's economy—whether through ownership of lands or industries, the purchase of stocks and bonds, or monopolistic control of key resources (e.g., a long-term contract to buy all its oil, or cars, or wheat, or water at a certain price)—it is possible to control the political and social life of the country very effectively. As colonialism has declined, a more subtle form of imperialism, **neocolonialism**, has become common. Under neocolonialism, core states exercise economic control over countries that are formally politically independent.

In this chapter we consider three issues associated with global inequality and imperialism. First, we ask whether it is likely, desirable, or even possible that all societies can develop economically in the same way. Then we consider the role of foreign aid as an instrument that some believe helps societies develop and others believe serves as a veiled form of imperialism. Finally, we examine the effects of rapid, often externally funded, development on the global environment.

14.1

Is there only one road to modernity?

The issue: Historically, the West held itself up as the only or best model of modernization. All other paths were wrong. However, at the end of the twentieth century, the successes of Japan, Singapore, and China (among others) suggest that we may have to reevaluate our views of history and ourselves.

Introduction The arguments in this section deal with issues of modernity or development. We often talk about developed societies versus developing, or underdeveloped, or less developed ones. All these terms imply that development is of a particular nature, and that it is good. One aim of this section is to reconsider these terms and their implications.

A particular kind of development has led to Western society as we know it today. Is it the only possible kind of society, given the level of technology that we have? Has this development been universally "good"? Were other ways of developing equally possible? To ask these questions is to recognize that however good a lifestyle most of us think we have, there are always other possibilities. A further implication is that the current North American lifestyle may have disadvantages, and that these disadvantages may accrue to different people than the advantages, so we must ask ourselves whether, in order for me to live as I do, does someone else pay a penalty?

The three questions in this section are linked. Should all societies develop, or change, in the same way? Are there alternatives? What is development anyway?

ALL SOCIETIES DO (SHOULD) DEVELOP IN THE SAME WAY

Often we hear people talking about the "first world" or the "third world." Until the collapse of the Soviet Union and countries allied with it, the world was often described in terms of three economic blocs: the mostly Western "first world" (including Japan), said to be developed—technically advanced industrial producers—and comprising a trading bloc; the "third world" of non-Western countries; and the Soviet bloc, between the other two groups. China might variously be considered as belonging in the second or third groups. The collapse of state communism in the Soviet bloc has led to a disintegration of the second group, and it is unclear to what extent its members should now be counted as part of the first group. Nevertheless, the terms persist in popular usage, though the terms "North" and "South" are coming to replace them, as being generally descriptive of social and economic differences without being pejorative.

The nature of "modernization theory" The argument that all societies should develop in essentially the same way forms part of what is known as *modernization theory*. This theory looks at the technological development of Western societies such as the United States, Canada, and Germany and at the history of how this technological development came about. This path of development—modernization—is seen as the way societies should go, or eventually will go, although modernization theorists acknowledge that some aspects of the development will vary. For instance, development can occur faster in countries that are developing today. Some processes in Europe and North America took several centuries to evolve, but these same processes can be exported to third world countries in finished form. Health improvement through the use of Western medicine is an example here.

Modernization theory assumes that, until about two centuries ago, the entire world was poor. Some people were able to amass wealth, but overall, the standards of living and life expectancies were low. Then something happened in the Western world—the Industrial Revolution. In short order, people could produce far more goods and so live better. Knowledge increased at a vast rate—including knowledge of the human body and its needs and how to treat illnesses—and modern medicine was born. People began to live longer, birth rates dropped, and as families became smaller, people were more able to care for and educate their children. As a result, they could obtain better jobs, create more knowledge, invent more things that people needed, and take their places in a prosperous, industrialized world.

Industrial society There are similarities among industrial societies that may or may not be "capitalist" in the traditional sense. For this reason, many sociologists believe that our society is now best described as an industrial society. The term *industrial society* refers not only to a society in which industrial (mass) production prevails but to a whole package of associated features we consider basic to contemporary life. In the shift to an industrial society, subsistence farming disappears, the number of people in farming declines, and people produce for exchange with others, not for their own consumption. Alongside mechanization, workers begin to produce goods in large factories, large machines increasingly assist production, jobs and workers become highly specialized, and the number of wage laborers increases. Mechanization is also associated with *urbanization*: more people come to live in large cities, more people learn how to read and write, scientific research changes industrial production, and people become more concerned with efficiency.

In these respects, societies as different as the United States and China or Russia and Argentina are all industrial societies. Whatever the political system or economic ideology, industrialization leads a society to develop the features just listed. Sociologists have spent a lot of time identifying the features of industrial society. The factors that lead societies to industrialize are so many and complex that we can only discuss three main ones here.

One key feature of industrial society is a concern with improving human capital. Human capital theorists are concerned with improving people's general well-being through better health, education, welfare, and public security. After all, they argue, people are the key to creating wealth in an industrial order. Money invested in human well-being (i.e., human capital) is money invested in future economic growth.

Investment in human capital is expensive and slow in bringing expected payoffs. As well, such investment changes many parts of the economy and society in unexpected ways. One such change is the effect on class structure and the class struggle. Generally, an investment in human capital unsettles the population and mobilizes protest.

The rise of an industrial society also changes class relations. Cash relations replace customary feudal ties of mutual obligation. New social classes, especially, the bourgeoisie and proletariat, emerge as a result. But the class structure changes in other ways, too. For example, industrialization pushes and pulls the rural peasantry into cities and factories. More and more peasants are forced off the land and into wage labor as landholdings become larger and privatized, producing cash crops rather than subsistence crops. Many of these peasants work part time on the land and part time in factories.

The contrasts between Canada and India or Brazil and Nigeria point up differences between industrial societies (as a group) and nonindustrial or developing societies. Generally, industrial societies have: (1) a secular culture focused on efficiency, consumerism, and a high standard of living; (2) a highly developed state that provides health, education, and welfare benefits to its citizens; and (3) a class structure dominated (numerically) by the urban middle class. As a result, there are important similarities between industrial societies like the United States and Japan, which, a century ago, had almost nothing in common.

Convergence thesis The growing similarity of industrial societies around the world has produced what sociologists call the *convergence thesis*. Supporters of this thesis argue that as societies industrialize, their social patterns converge, or become more similar, despite previous differences. The convergence thesis is an important part of the theory of industrial society. It rests on the idea that industrialization gives rise to changes—like mass literacy, a nuclear family, and respect for the rule of law—that are linked to economic life. The linkages are easy to understand. For example, as people become literate, they become better informed, more politically active, and more eager to demand political liberties. The result is participatory democracy. Another common feature is the growth of a political rights-seeking middle class that manages large businesses. One emerged in Korea in the 1980s and another in Thailand in the 1990s. Similar changes seem to occur in *every* industrial society, though not always in the same sequence.

What is remarkable about convergence is the certainty of the process. The convergence thesis plays down capitalism as a crucial feature of economic life and puts industrial society in its place. It argues that what is important in world history is industrialism, not capitalism. With exceptions, non-Western experience has provided much support for the convergence thesis. Developing societies differ mainly in whether they merge selected modern ideas with their existing culture, as Japan has done, or rearrange their cultures around these ideas, as Singapore has done. However they do it, industrialization everywhere has certain key features. But it is not clear whether industrial societies converge because they must satisfy the same societal needs (e.g., for literacy) or because social practices spread from richer to poorer societies. There is evidence to support both views.

Development, in this paradigm, is a process of using science and technology to help achieve a higher quality of lifestyle, expressed as a higher standard of living. If people don't have enough to eat, or their harvests are at the mercy of extreme weather conditions such as droughts that occur every few years, modern scientific agriculture can feed them. If life expectancy is low, modern medicine can extend it. If people have large families and cannot support all of their children, scientific birth control can help prevent large families, ensuring greater prosperity for those who are born.

Along with the growth of science's role in social life goes the idea that only in societies where people share certain attitudes could industrialism have been invented. North Americans today, for the most part, are highly individualistic. They consider that each person's main goal in life is to work for his or her own advancement and support dependent children. They also believe they are autonomous in that they have, to a large extent, control over their own lives. How often have you heard people say, "She can do anything if she only sets her mind to it," or "Never mind what other people say, just do it!"

By contrast, in many developing countries, people are familistic. They want to do what other members of their group do and not stand out as being different. They carefully consider the effects of their actions on other family members, even on people that Americans would consider to be distant cousins. And they also appear fatalistic, in that they feel they will have little say in determining the course of their lives. Events happen to them, and they accept their fate.

So for third world countries to share in the prosperity of the advanced industrial nations, people must not only use the technologies of the first world but also adopt the attitudes that go with them, especially the beliefs that they can control their own destinies, have fewer children, and aim for personal success. The presumption implied by this theory is that by adopting modern science and modern attitudes, people will become better off.

But do such changes actually bring about modernization as predicted, and do they make people better off? The answer is, often, no; and this tells us that standard development practices may not work well for everyone.

ALL SOCIETIES DO NOT (SHOULD NOT) DEVELOP THE SAME WAY

Consider an example. In the 1960s, the Green Revolution promised food for the world's hungry. Large areas of Pakistan and India (notably the Punjab) and parts of Africa were planted with Western-developed, high-yield varieties of wheat and rice. These grains were "heavy feeders," requiring the application of chemical fertilizers to the soil, which in turn required machinery to apply them. They also required large-scale irrigation projects to provide steady moisture levels. Because one strain of wheat or rice would be planted over large tracts of land, there was an increased risk the crop might be wiped out by an attack of insect pests or diseases, so that chemical pesticides and fungicides were also required.

Some farmers did well from this, doubling or tripling yields. However many small farmers could not afford the chemicals and equipment. Also, over a period of 20 years, the fertility of the soil gradually declined. By the mid-1980s, a number of communities in Bangladesh were attempting to return to the indigenous varieties of grain their ancestors had farmed. While these might yield smaller harvests, they were more reliable, less prone to insect attack, and required fewer chemicals to grow.

At the same time, attempts were being made to encourage the use of western contraceptives and sterilization to lower birth rates. However, these had only a limited impact; few people made consistent use of them. Thus any advantages gained from the use of high-yield crops were cancelled out by population increases.

Modernization theory assumes that changes to the structure and culture of third world countries—making them more like so-called first world countries—will enrich the countries and their people, after a Western industrial pattern. But in the example we just considered, there was no net gain from modernization. In other cases, change has even resulted in impoverishment. This is most likely to happen when too little attention is paid to cultural or social conditions that limit or pervert the use of Western technology and productive practices. For example, Western models assume individual, or corporate, ownership of land. An assumption of colonists and policymakers has been that this ownership will be by males in a family. But in many peasant societies, extended families or lineage groups own land that is worked by women. These women have, therefore, rights to work the land and to control their own land parcels. Land reform programs make use of the male "head of family" concept, so that ownership becomes removed from the women—the people who are using the land to produce food for their own and their families' consumption.

An example comes from the Gambia. In 1984, village headmen had leased the women's land, along with unused swampland, to the Gambian government for a multi-million-dollar rice-growing project. The plan was to make the land productive. However, the headmen had also leased the land on which women grew rice crops to feed their families, and the women were prohibited from growing their rice, being promised food aid while the land was bulldozed and reapportioned. Fifteen hundred acres of ripened rice crop were bulldozed. In the end, crops were lost, but far more important than that, Western aid was used to deprive women of de facto control of farming land. In this way, it made relations between men and women far less modern than they had been before.

The demographic transition We are often told in America that the world has a population problem, but that the problem resides in other countries, not the countries of the North or the industrialized West. In Chapter 12 we discussed the idea that there is a population explosion that is taxing the resources of the earth and must be controlled. In line with this thinking, aid programs of countries of the North are often tied to requirements for underdeveloped countries to promote birth control programs, with, however, limited success.

Demographers who have studied the composition of the population in Europe and North America during the eighteenth and nineteenth centuries warn that popular thinking on this issue may be upside down. In Europe 200 years ago, families of 9, 11, 13, and even 20 children were not unknown. However, many of these children would die in childhood or infancy. Children who survived were the support of their parents in later life and contributed to the family income as economic producers from their childhood on. In the towns of England and France it was common for working-class women to be engaged in paid jobs while their children were too small to contribute economically, but to leave their jobs to become household managers when the children entered the paid work force.

Soon all that was to change. In the nineteenth century, child labor laws and compulsory education meant that children became expensive to raise: net consumers, not net producers. At the same time, better nutrition resulting from a greater availability of food meant that women, children, and men were healthier. Fewer children died in infancy. (This predated, and so should not be attributed to, modern medicine and standards of medical hygiene.) The birth rate dropped, even before modern contraceptives were available. And once contraceptives became available, they were widely used, as they made it possible for people to plan their childbearing. Delays in legalizing contraceptives, such as the diaphragm or the cervical cap, were due to the pro-natalist policies of legislators and governments that saw declining fertility as a problem, not a blessing. However, regardless of the methods of birth control used, the population went through a demographic transition.

History (and demographic transition theory) shows that in Europe lower rates of childbearing followed after, and was associated with, more security and a higher likelihood of children's survival. Materialists (i.e., Marxists and other conflict theorists) have concluded from this that, once people have enough to eat and are reasonably sure their children will not die, they are motivated to produce fewer children. It is the practicalities of life—food and security—that come first and influence people's ideas and opinions about how many children to have.

Some believe that this analysis contradicts modernization theory, which urges others to be like people in the West: "Have fewer children and you will prosper." In other words, modern behavior will follow from the adoption of modern values, and an improved standard of living will follow from modern behavior. However, other researchers consider that both demographic transition theory and modernization theory agree on one thing: the importance of technology and industrialization.

Is technology really the key?   Why did people in Europe start to have better levels of nutrition and lower levels of childbearing? Was it really all due to technology?

The eighteenth and nineteenth centuries were the years of European colonial expansion. People were going out from Europe to other parts of the world and claiming colonies for Germany or Britain or France, among others. We often think of this in terms of colonial administrators, people with education going to the colonies to make a name for themselves. However, many of the people who left Europe were poor, and many did not leave of their own volition. Social changes in Europe had created millions of landless people whose ancestors were peasants but whose land had been claimed by large-scale landowners.

An example is the Highland Clearances in Scotland. Landowners considered it more to their advantage to push out the peasants who had worked small farms for generations and turn the land over to sheep-grazing. Many of the displaced peasants headed for the cities, where they became workers in the factories emerging under the new system of capitalism. Others headed for the colonies. In the case of the Highland Clearances, they went to what would become Canada and the eastern United States. Other impoverished immigrants flooded into Australia, southern Africa, and other parts of the previously non-European world. Colonial practices were to turn these poverty-stricken immigrants into European-style farmers and miners, providers of resources and raw materials for the home countries. But the demographic transition theory does not mention the people they displaced from the lands they came to.

Not all of these colonized indigenous people were farmers. In what is today Bangladesh, colonial administrators found a thriving cotton textile industry, with its own patterns and styles of weaving and embroidery and its own markets, built up over centuries of trading. The textile industry in Britain was in crisis, and displaced tenant farmers and peasants were flooding into Britain's textile towns looking for work. The British government's solution was to collect textile patterns and send people to the colonies to learn weaving skills, then to close down the indigenous textile industries while supporting the weaving of these same patterns in factories in Britain. The famous Paisley pattern comes from the Indian subcontinent but gets its name from the Scottish town whose weavers learned to create its delicate designs and weave them into expensive shawls. These fabrics, made for the high-fashion market in Europe and its colonies, were even exported back to India for the wives and daughters of colonial administrators to wear. Part of the prosperity of nineteenth-century Europe, therefore, should be traced to its habit of exporting poverty along with its manufactured products. It was this export of poverty, as much as technological change, that led to the growth of wealth in industrial Europe.

And what of the receiving countries? Many have had a hard time industrializing. Is it because of faulty, "non-modern" values like familism?

Familism does not result in underdevelopment Part of the modernization hypothesis is that people in North American cultures are individualistic, and people in less developed countries are familistic. People with a familistic orientation do not try to get ahead and be successful, and they are slow to adopt new ideas and technologies. It is not hard to refute this argument. One of the leading, most successful industrial nations, Japan, is well known for the extent of its people's familism. In Japan, people are viewed as family members, aiding their family in its success. When a child is learning to walk, its first steps are taken, symbolically, with rice cakes bound to its back, to signify that this child, when it emerges from the security in which it is raised, will enter into the responsibilities of caring for its entire family.

In North America, some groups of people are more familistic than others. We occasionally see this familism given as a reason for their lack of success, in that they do not want to appear more knowledge-able, skilled, or successful than other family members. This is often cited as a reason for the assumed failures of Native American groups to become modern. Yet some Native groups have combined a familistic orienta-tion with successful group enterprise. In other groups, familism is credited with helping them to succeed, as family ties and loyalties strengthen the group as a whole and give support to its members. In a familistic culture, no one goes hungry while another family member has food.

Only under particular circumstances does familism become a problem to its members and to the group as a whole. It may be that, historically, these circum-stances were created by the colonial admin-istrators who attempted to destroy family ties and loyalties. In its place they put a structure that assumed that the values of white, middle-class colonial bureaucrats were the only values that counted.

SUMMING UP

Is there only one road to modernity? We don't think so. Many of the development advantages we associate with technology may be linked with advantages due to colo-nialism. Likewise, many of the disadvan-tages we associate with less developed societies may also be due to colonialism, not to familistic values which, under other circumstances, might work very well. The evidence suggests that there are many dif-ferent paths to economic development. People adopt new technologies when they can afford to, that is, when the technologies are available and pose little risk to their eco-nomic well-being. Improved material con-ditions are as attractive to familistic people as they are to individualistic people.

So, assuming that cultural change is needed before development is possible is a wrong reading of the evidence. Moreover, history shows us that a single development model is culturally destructive, as we have seen with the example of the Gambian women farmers. There is a profound danger in convincing people that they must re-adjust the relations of men to women, old to young, or individuals to families before economies can begin to grow. As we are seeing in Eastern Europe (and will discuss in a later section on individualism), the risks to social cohesion—even law and order—are very great.

Finally, what are we to learn from the European experience that can be useful in today's developing countries? If Europe developed by exporting its poverty, can India do this today? Where is left to colo-nize? Who, in this age of globally available nuclear weapons, can be safely overrun? The age of imperial solutions to local eco-nomic problems is nearly at an end. And even if it weren't, none of today's less developed countries would be in a position to exercise these options. Today's less developed countries cannot and will not develop in the very same way Western Europe and the United States did a century ago.

REVIEW EXERCISES

For Discussion and Debate

1. "Technology will always get us out of a fix."
2. "If people in the third world didn't grow so many cash crops, we wouldn't have our coffee."
3. "India could be just as rich as America. It's all a question of attitude."
4. "Getting ahead—on a global basis—is the name of the game."

Writing Exercises

1. Familism and its links with success.
2. How women farmers in the Gambia could win back their farmlands.
3. Your description of an ideal development project that would benefit everyone concerned.
4. "How I see links between population and prosperity."

Research Activities

1. Conduct some research on your own family history and background. Find a group of people, in any part of the world, that you are descended from. How did industrialization and/or colonialism affect this group? (Were they benefited, disbenefited, or was there a combination of effects?) From this, how has industrialization and/or colonialism affected who you are today?

2. Work with a group of your friends to list ways in which you are connected with countries of the South. (*Hint:* Look at your family histories, but also think of the foods you eat, the clothes you wear, and the music you listen to.)

3. Interview 10 people about what global development means to them. Analyze their ideas in terms of the competing paradigms presented in this section.

4. Collect media items on development and examine the ideas presented in these. Analyze the ideas in terms of the competing paradigms presented in this section. How do they compare with the opinions of the people you interviewed?

SELECTED REFERENCES

ARNOULD, ERIC J., Anthropology and West African development: A political economic critique and auto-critique, *Human Organization* (Summer 1989), 48, 2, 135–148.

BARRY, FRANK, Industrialization strategies for developing countries: Lessons from the Irish experience, *Development Policy Review* (March 1991), 9, 1, 85–98.

COLE, SAM, A conflict of visions: Reflections on African futures studies, *Futures* (April 1994), 26, 3, 259–274.

CROCKER, DAVID A., Toward development ethics, *World Development* (May 1991), 19, 5, 457–483.

DICKENS, DAVID R., The relevance of domestic traditions in the development process: Iran, 1963–1979, *International Journal of Contemporary Sociology* (January–April 1989), 26, 1–2, 55–70.

EVANS, PETER B., and PAULO BASTOS TIGRE, Going beyond clones in Brazil and Korea: A comparative analysis of NIC strategies in the computer industry, *World Development* (November 1989), 17, 11, 1751–1768.

EVERS, HANS DIETER, and SOLVAY GERKE, The culture of planning: Transmigration area development in East Kalimantan, Indonesia, *International Sociology* (June 1992), 7, 2, 141–151.

GORDON, APRIL, The myth of modernization and development, *Sociological Spectrum* (Spring 1989), 9, 2, 175–195.

Manzo, Kate, Modernist discourse and the crisis of development theory, *Studies in Comparative International Development* (Summer 1991), 26, 2, 3–36.

Mies, Maria, and Vandana Shiva, *Ecofeminism* (London: Zed Books, 1993).

Mukhopadhyay, Sudhin K., Adapting household behavior to agricultural technology in West Bengal, India: Wage labor, fertility, and child schooling determinants, *Economic Development and Cultural Change* (October 1994), 43, 1, 91–115.

Mytelka, Lynn Krieger, Rethinking development: A role for innovation networking in the "other two-thirds," *Futures* (July–August 1993), 25, 6, 694–712.

Parsonage, James, Southeast Asia's "growth triangle": A subregional response to global transformation, *International Journal of Urban and Regional Research* (June 1992), 16, 2, 307–317.

Pattnayak, Satya R., Integrating liberal-pluralist and dependency perspectives of development at specific levels of state capacity, *International Review of Modern Sociology* (Autumn 1992), 22, 2, 87–101.

Philip, George, The political economy of development, *Political Studies* (September 1990), 38, 3, 485–501.

Prigoff, Arline, Women, social development, and the state in Latin America: An empowerment model, *Social Development Issues* (Fall 1991), 14, 1, 56–70.

Quaye, Randolph, Planning the health care system in a decade of economic decline: The Ghanaian experience, *Crime, Law and Social Change* (November 1991), 16, 3, 303–311.

Schulman, Michael D., and Sheila R. Cotten, Adaptations to the farm crisis: Macro level implications of micro level behaviors, *Applied Behavioral Science Review* (1993), 1, 1, 93–111.

Shenhaw, Yehouda A., and David H. Kamens, The "costs" of institutional isomorphism: Science in non-Western countries, *Social Studies of Science* (August 1991), 21, 3, 527–545.

Sutton, Francis X., et al., Development ideology: Its emergence and decline, *Daedalus* (Winter 1989), 118, 1, 35–58.

Tenbruck, Friedrich H., The dream of a secular ecumene: The meaning and limits of policies of development, *Theory, Culture and Society* (June 1990), 7, 2–3, 193–206.

Tilley, Louise A., and Joan W. Scott, *Women, work and family* (New York: Holt, Rinehart & Winston, 1978).

Waring, Marilyn, *If women counted* (San Francisco: HarperCollins, 1990).

Weede, Erich, The impact of military participation on economic growth and income inequality: Some new evidence, *Journal of Political and Military Sociology* (Winter 1993), 21, 2, 241–258.

Woo, Myung Oc, Export promotion in the new global division of labor: The case of the South Korean automobile industry, *Sociological Perspectives* (Winter 1993), 36, 4, 335–357.

14.2

Does Western aid actually help?

<u>The issue:</u> Continued neediness in much of the southern hemisphere has combined with a growing withdrawal of aid by the Western industrial nations. For the West, is aid giving still a useful economic tool? Is it still a useful political tool? Is aid ever given with no strings attached?

Introduction   There are two main kinds of aid: public governmental aid and private charity aid. In practice, the two are not completely separate. Charities may work with governments and are subject to government regulation, in both donor and recipient countries, and governmental aid may be given to projects supervised or organized by charities.

It seems self-evident that aid, whether from a state or from a charity, must make things better. Aid, after all, is aid. If I have no food today and you feed me, I am better off.

I am no longer hungry, and perhaps tomorrow I will find work and so be able to feed myself, especially if you can tell me where the likely jobs are to be found.

Modernization theory looks to aid to assist with the modernizing of underdeveloped countries. It is through aid from wealthier states that new projects can be developed and old ones maintained; that work can be created for people; and that the effects of natural disasters, such as drought, can be alleviated. Finally, it is through aid that the recipient countries will become able to "catch up" to the donors in technology and standard of living.

It would seem on the face of it, then, that aid is an altogether good thing, at least from the standpoint of the recipient. Why, then, do we find criticisms of many aid programs and suspicion about the motives of many donors? Let's begin by considering how and why we think that aid is generally a good thing.

AID DOES MAKE THINGS BETTER

We have already considered why aid might be beneficial to countries that receive it. What about the donors? Aid is a cost to the donor nations and has to be justified to taxpayers by the governments that give it. But aid also has its benefits for donor nations. The giving of aid strengthens international links between nations, friendships, and bonds of mutual support. By helping to create a prosperous economy in a previously underdeveloped state, the donor country creates a trading partner, a market for its own goods and services, and a source of other goods and services that its people can purchase. Finally, by helping countries with their problems of poverty, disease, and unemployment, the donor country can prevent strife and conflict.

Now, let's turn this picture 180 degrees and look at it again. You know from your own experience that giving gifts establishes a bond between the donor and recipient. At the least, it establishes a need for reciprocity, and reciprocating a gift may be difficult if one of the parties to the transaction is significantly poorer than another. It may be even more difficult if there are strings attached to the gift— conditions defining when the return gift is expected and even what it should be.

Some gifts require very expensive upkeep. Imagine we give you a pet leopard and you have to feed it 50 pounds of fresh meat every day. Our gift of a pet pony will force you to find it a stable and room to run around. Other gifts are transparently self-serving. Imagine we give you tickets for one at a dozen movies to be shown at our theater. More likely than not, you will end up bringing someone and having to pay for the extra ticket, and that's money in our pockets.

Again, you can look at this in a positive or negative way. It's nice to get gifts: pet leopards, ponies, tickets to movies. On the other hand, it's a bother and a cost to have to pay them back, keep them up, or pay for peripherals. Believe it or not, these are the very same problems that arise when rich countries provide aid to poorer, less developed countries.

AID IS NOT NECESSARILY BENEFICIAL

Who benefits from aid?   The giving of aid can be seen as a self-interested act that increases the wealth and power of the donor nation. How can that be? First, the giving of foreign aid creates bonds of dependency. For example, a recipient nation may be obliged to support (i.e., defend) its donor nation in international conflicts for fear of losing the aid. Second, the donor country creates a trading partner that is bound to buy goods from the donor country and that will serve as a cheap source of raw materials. Third, by helping countries with their problems of poverty, disease, and unemployment, the donor can prevent people within the country from attempting to develop other systems of government that might threaten the existing world order and prevent the recipient nation from forming loyalties elsewhere.

These are the key tenets of *dependency theory*, a counter to modernization theory proposed by political economists, notably by Andre Gunder Frank. These theorists say that modernization theory, with its focus on development aid, ignores the problem of how nonindustrial countries of the South developed historically to become what they are today. Frank argues that these states are neither developed nor undeveloped, but have been deliberately underdeveloped to create dependency on the capitalist donor nations. The destruction of the textile industry of the Indian subcontinent, discussed in the previous section, is an example of deliberate underdevelopment. Under both mercantile and imperial colonialism, countries or regions were exploited for their raw materials. Their political and economic structures were dismantled. Infrastructures were designed for the convenience of the host country and the administrators. In many parts of Africa, roads lead to the nearest port, to facilitate export of raw materials, instead of to other parts of Africa along the old trade routes.

In the present day, colonial empires have been dismantled but economic dependence, referred to as *neo-imperialism*, remains. The South is still a source of raw materials for the North. Now, also, the South is becoming a source of cheap labor. Multinational corporations—with their headquarters in the United States or Germany or Britain or Canada or Japan—control large sectors of the economies of countries of the South. Through economic links and pressures, they also control many of the economic policies of the North, including aid-granting policies. Workers in the South are employed by multinationals to make goods for sale in the North (computer

components being a prime example), often at low rates of pay. Prime agricultural land is used to grow cash crops such as coffee and sugar cane, which deplete soils.

Against this economic backdrop, foreign aid can be given for several reasons. One is pure philanthropy, and there can be no doubt that many of the people who advocate giving aid are indeed motivated by philanthropy. But there are other reasons, as indicated above. Of these, commercial reasons take precedence. Much foreign aid is just a way of creating a market or hooking customers. Much of the aid money is spent within the country of origin on materials to be sent overseas and on the buying of expert services, creating many jobs. When this "aid" reaches its intended recipients, it requires further expertise to administer, operate, and maintain. Provision of tractors for an agricultural project, for example, means that later the recipients will have to buy tractor parts. Provision of seeds through the Green Revolution programs resulted in demands for chemical pesticides and fertilizers. In consequence, the net cost of foreign aid to the donor country may be zero or less.

Despite foreign aid programs, the net flow of funds is from South to North, not the other way. Dependencies created through imperial colonialism, mercantile colonialism, and neo-imperialism result in a reliance on Northern equipment and expertise. After all, large-scale projects are expensive to run. In theory, loans have to be repaid. But in practice, international North-South loans are not repaid but serviced; that is, the loan givers continue to collect interest on them. Further loans under the auspices of the World Bank and the International Monetary Fund (IMF) go either toward debt servicing or for projects designed to further exports to gain foreign currency to pay that loan interest. The goal of creating communities that are self-sufficient, grow their own food, and manufacture their own textiles from locally grown materials is not in line with the goals of the IMF, which are to further international trade.

Much of the so-called aid sent by countries of the North, therefore, goes to further dependency, including loan dependency. An example of the movement of funds from South to North is Brazil, which between 1979 and 1985 paid $69 billion in debt repayments, being deeper in debt at the end of the period than at the start. As a result, local conditions often worsen: "In the 1960s, a third of Brazilians suffered from malnutrition; in the 1980s, after 20 years of IMF-inspired development, two thirds did" (Engler, 1995, p. 135).

Is aid always wrong?   Almost everyone agrees that there are times—droughts, floods, disasters—when immediate, on-the-spot aid in the form of food, clothing, and other relief supplies may be crucial to saving lives. There have, however, been debates, even here, about how much of the aid reaches its intended recipients. If some is diverted, not only does it not benefit the people most in need; food aid may directly undercut the market sales of small-scale local producers, forcing them into bankruptcy and so out of production and thus result in later food shortages. However, this is not a reason to deny help in a grave crisis situation. It is a reason for countries that provide food aid to attempt to monitor how it is used, to listen to the voices of local people in need, and to work with local distribution networks.

We can consider other situations in the same way. Modernization theory holds that aid is a way countries of the North can assist those of the South in technological development. Dependency theory counters that aid works to maintain dependence and to get countries of the South deeper into debt. Each defines the terms of the argument in different ways. We can try to take another view of this question by asking: Are there types of aid that are useful? If so, what are they?

Useful aid   Here we have to define what we mean by "useful." Whose standards are we adopting? Some aid-administering organizations take the view that aid has to make things better on a small-scale, local level in ways that are not environmentally destructive and will last when the aid-granting agency is no longer present. In other words, aid should not encourage debt, though it may encourage local trade. The aid is to help communities become self-sufficient.

However, this may have unforeseen consequences. In the last section we mentioned the Green Revolution. Its dependence on expensive chemical fertilizers and imported seeds and machinery meant that agricultural aid was given to owners of medium-sized or large farms. Many small-scale peasant farmers in Bangladesh lost their land. Recently, workers paid by North American charitable agencies have been assisting peasants in founding cooperatives and gaining title to land. They have also assisted in finding seeds of indigenous varieties of grain and helping local communities establish their own seed banks. Workers have helped in developing composting facilities, so that the dependence on imported fertilizer is lessened. Most important, these workers have been working not as directors but as facilitators. One such project supervisor states that there is no point in trying to impose ideas from outside. The ideas must come from the local community members, or they will be jettisoned when the charity workers leave.

The aim of such aid is to provide expertise (including political and legal expertise) and cover start-up costs so that communities can develop their own technologies and self-sufficiency. Other examples include small-scale health initiatives that train local people in the provision of basic health services—midwifery, diagnosis of childhood ailments, rehydration techniques, contraceptive techniques. There is an emphasis on "appropriate technology," or working with what is available locally. Rather than nuclear power plants, these projects promote the local building of solar ovens.

A charge often heard against foreign aid is that it takes money from poor people in rich countries and gives it to rich people in poor ones. Many charitable organizations, such as Oxfam, Inter Pares, and the Unitarian Service Committee, attempt to show that this is not so by working directly with peasant farmers. They may find that this is not always easy to do. Governments control access to regions of the country, and peasant farmers generally have little political power. And even established plans can go awry when events such as currency devaluation, dictated by the IMF, intervene.

Here's another example of a plan that went awry: Villages in the Kigoma region of Tanzania were to receive oxen to assist them in ploughing their fields to grow their corn and beans. The oxen would make a tremendous difference to the amount they could grow. Oxfam had budgeted for eight oxen and their necessary veterinary supplies. But between the time the farmers received the grant and went to purchase their oxen, the price of the animals—like the price of just about everything else in Tanzania—had risen. Instead of eight animals, they could afford to buy only six. Worse, some supplies, such as pumps for spraying the oxen to kill deadly ticks and medicines for protection against the tsetse fly, were not available at all. These medicines are essential to the animals' survival, but like most veterinary supplies, they must be imported. To conserve funds needed to pay its foreign debt, the government imposed restrictions on these and other desperately needed imports. So in the end, the aided villagers received neither enough oxen, nor the medicines needed to keep them alive. Who's to blame?

SUMMING UP

Does Western aid actually help? It depends on the kind of help given and the strings that are attached. Foreign aid, which seems on the face of it such a good idea, does not always have the effect we would wish. Aid for large-scale projects—immense river dams or nuclear power plants, for example—often binds the recipient nation into long-running dependencies that result in more, not less, debt. These large-scale projects often leave thousands of people homeless or destined for resettlement on land of doubtful agricultural value. The effectiveness of aid is measured in dollar values or increases to the Gross National Product (GNP), which means that aid that results in transnational trade (through growing cash crops) counts as effective, whereas aid that acts to make families more able to feed themselves appears ineffective as these peasants no longer have to buy their food!

When there is a call for emergency aid—for example, for famine relief in the case of floods and droughts—North Americans do respond. Vast amounts of money are collected and sent off. This shows that large numbers of people in North America do believe they should try to help people in other parts of the world. They would like their aid dollars to be effective.

Sociologists can help by making the public aware of the problems associated with aid and its administration. We can draw the public's attention to successful aid programs. We can educate people about the role of the IMF and GATT. We can attempt to ensure that governmental aid programs become accountable not only to the IMF but to an aware, involved, and educated voting public, who evaluate aid on its effectiveness in human terms, not GNP. We can help to create foreign aid programs that really do make things better.

REVIEW EXERCISES

For Discussion and Debate

1. "Foreign aid workers shouldn't tell people what to do. They should just help them find the means to do it."

2. "The biggest problem faced by countries of the South isn't poverty. It's the countries of the North."

3. Food crops versus cash crops? Debate this by dramatizing a scene of villagers who grow traditional food crops, government representatives who wish them to grow cash crops for export, and aid workers who may take either side.

4. "Let the politicians look after the global development picture. We're too busy looking after ourselves."

Writing Exercises

1. A week in the life of an overseas aid worker.

2. "Why I (give)/(do not give) money to foreign aid charities."

3. A week in the life of a village where a new development program has just been announced.

4. A cooperative textiles project in a country of the South.

Research Activities

1. Examine statistics on foreign aid for the last 40 years. How much aid is sent, and what percentage is this of GNP? Attempt to find the countries that have chiefly benefited from this aid.

2. Conduct a detailed study of a charitable organization that is involved with overseas aid. Find out how money is gathered, what proportion of it is sent to projects, and how a typical project is administered.

3. Locate a movie that describes an aid project and watch it. Remember that the project will be differently described and analyzed depending on who is making and funding the movie.

4. With a group of four to six other students, plan and conduct a survey of people's attitudes toward foreign aid projects. Do people see them as beneficial to this country and to the recipient countries?

SELECTED REFERENCES

ANDERSON, MARY B., and PETER J. WOODROW, Reducing vulnerability to drought and famine: Developmental approaches to relief, *Disasters* (March 1991), 15, 1, 43–54.

ASLUND, ANDERS, Russia's road from communism, *Daedalus* (Spring 1992), 121, 2, 77–95.

BOHNING, W. R., Helping migrants to stay at home, *Annals of the American Academy of Political and Social Science* (July 1994), 534, 165–177.

BRADSHAW, YORK W., and JIE HUANG, Intensifying global dependency: Foreign debt, structural adjustment, and third world underdevelopment, *Sociological Quarterly* (Fall 1991), 32, 3, 321–342.

BRITAN, GERALD M., The future of foreign assistance, *Studies in Third World Societies* (April 1991), 44, 1–12.

BRYCESON, DEBORAH FAHY, Trade roots in Tanzania: Evolution of urban grain markets under structural adjustment, *Sociologia Ruralis* (1994), 34, 1, 13–25.

CARTY, R., Giving for gain: Foreign aid and CIDA. In *Ties that bind: Canada and the third world*, ed. R. Clarke and R. Swift (Toronto: Between the Lines, 1982).

ENGLER, ALLAN, *Apostles of greed* (London: Pluto Press, 1995).

FRANK, ANDRE GUNDER, "Sociology of development and the underdevelopment of sociology. In *Dependence and underdevelopment: Latin America's political economy*, ed. J. D. Cockcroft, A. G. Frank, and D. L. Johnson (New York: Doubleday, 1972).

FRIDERES, JAMES S., et al., From peasants to capitalists, *Community Development Journal* (April 1993), 28, 2, 129–140.

GAYDOS, JOEL C., and GEORGE A. LUZ, Military participation in emergency humanitarian assistance, *Disasters* (March 1994), 18, 1, 48–57.

GEORGE, SUSAN, *A fate worse than debt* (London: Penguin, 1989).

GREEN, MARSHALL, The evolution of U.S. international population policy, 1965–92: A chronological account, *Population and Development Review* (June 1993), 19, 2, 303–321.

HANLON, JOSEPH, *Mozambique: Who calls the shots?* (Bloomington: Indiana University Press, 1991).

HOOGVELT, A. M., *The sociology of developing societies* (London: Macmillan, 1976).

IHONVBERE, JULIUS O., The military and political engineering under structural adjustment: The Nigerian experience since 1985, *Journal of Political and Military Sociology* (Summer 1992), 20, 1, 107–131.

KELLY, MARION, and MARGARET BUCHANAN SMITH, Northern Sudan in 1991: Food crisis and the international relief response, *Disasters* (March 1994), 18, 1, 16–34.

MANNAN, MANZURUL, Women targeted and women negated: An aspect of the environmental movement in Bangladesh, *Development-in-Practice* (May 1996), 6, 2, 113–120.

MOSELEY, K. P., West African industry and the debt crisis, *Journal of International Development* (January–February 1992), 4, 1, 1–27.

RAO, J. MOHAN, Judging givers: Equity and scale in aid allocation, *World Development* (October 1994), 22, 10, 1579–1584.

SAXE-FERNANDEZ, JOHN, The Chiapas insurrection: Consequences for Mexico and the United States, *International Journal of Politics, Culture and Society* (Winter 1994), 8, 2, 325–342.

SHARPLESS, JOHN, World population growth, family planning, and American foreign policy, *Journal of Policy History* (1995), 7, 1, 72–102.

SHIVA, VANDANA, GATT, agriculture and third world women. In *Ecofeminism*, ed. Maria Mies and Vandana Shiva (London: Zed Books, 1993).

SMITH, BRIAN H., *More than altruism: The politics of private foreign aid* (Princeton, NJ: Princeton University Press, 1990).

STEWART, FRANCES, The many faces of adjustment, *World Development* (December 1991), 19, 12, 1847–1864.

VILAS, CARLOS M., Latin America in the "New World Order": Prospects for Democracy, *International Journal of Politics, Culture and Society* (Winter 1994), 8, 2, 257–282.

WALZER, MICHAEL, The politics of rescue, *Dissent* (Winter 1995), 42, 1(178), 35–41.

WEDEL, JANINE R., The unintended consequences of Western aid to post-communist Europe, *Telos* (Summer 1992), 92, 131–138.

14.3

Can everyone live like Americans?

The issue: **Is there some absolute goal to economic development—for example, the attainment of an "American way of life" by everyone? And can everyone hope to attain that goal?** Or would the attempt simply destroy the global ecology, even if the goal were attainable socially and economically?

Introduction "Catching up" has been the goal of economic development for the last 40 years or more. It has been promoted by governments in both the North and the South. Is it a workable goal? Opinions differ. Once again, in this section we consider modernization theory and dependency theory concepts. We also introduce ideas relating to the concepts of sustainable development and global ecology.

The presumption that helping less developed countries catch up is the goal of development rests on the notion of convergence: namely, that all industrial societies can and will be the same. It also makes the ethnocentric assumption that a Western—indeed, an American—way of life and standard of living are what every human being wants and needs. And related to this is the belief that human life is infinitely and universally perfectible, and the effort to achieve this perfection is unhampered by environmental or other constraints. We will have much more to say about these ideas shortly.

The supposed ability of all countries to achieve a North American standard of living has been promoted by both functionalist and conflict perspectives in sociology. How these arguments intersect and how they appear in the context of environmentalism form part of the debate.

OTHER COUNTRIES CAN CATCH UP

This has been the dominant view of both the North and South for about 40 years. In 1949, President Harry Truman, in his inaugural speech to Congress, for the first time defined as "underdeveloped areas" large sections of the world. This speech implied that all countries in the world were on the same track, but some had merely fallen behind in the race.

According to this perspective, technology and industrial advance have given the countries of the North a high and increasing standard of living, as measured by Gross Domestic Product (GDP)—that part of a nation's activities for which a monetary

value can be compiled. The goods and services of modern life, so measured, contribute to an enhanced quality of life for people in the society. Within a household, running water on tap, electricity and electrical appliances, and easily available food to cook in the appliances all make it easier to care for a family. The availability of television, books, newspapers, and computer e-mail networks means that family members will be informed about their world and entertained. Synthetic fabrics mean that people can be inexpensively clothed to keep them warm in winter; modern building standards, heating devices, and air conditioning help keep them secure and healthy, even in extreme climatic conditions. Surely everyone should have such basic amenities—or should they?

Rostow's stages of economic growth   Modernization theory sees "catch-up" development as the goal, and foreign investment, aid, and loans to technological projects as the means to achieve it. Walter Rostow's theory of stages of economic growth toward modernization spells out the stages of the way. Every country, Rostow claims, will necessarily go through the same five stages in the same sequence, these stages being:

Stage 1: *Traditional stage.* A stagnant economy, with agricultural subsistence and craft industries.

Stage 2: *Preconditions for takeoff.* Development of a market economy, with mining and cash crops for export and the development of roads and railways. Society run by a political and business elite who have an achievement orientation—that is, are motivated toward modernization. Investment is around 5% of GDP.

Stage 3: *Takeoff stage.* Investment rises to around 10% of GDP. Manufacturing industries start to grow, and social, institutional, and political structures arise that favor development.

Stage 4: *Drive to maturity.* Urbanization, mass public education, and high investment and growth in all sectors of the economy.

Stage 5: *High mass consumption stage.* The country now has an economy similar to those of advanced nations, with the availability of a wide range of consumer durables (such as kitchen appliances) and services. Its international importance is established.

Some societies have been able to move more quickly along this path than others. Those that were able to emphasize manufacturing have moved faster than those that emphasized the provision of services or exported raw materials. Critics of the theory have pointed, however, to imbalances in modernization as a drawback in many cases, saying that agricultural development must parallel that in manufacturing or the pace is slowed.

OTHER COUNTRIES CAN'T CATCH UP

A number of societies have indeed developed in the sequence Rostow would have predicted. However, critics point out that the idea of catch-up development rests on several major assumptions. These are, first, that people's quality of living is indicated by their standard of living, and that it makes sense for all peoples to emulate a North American model. Second, it assumes that economic and political conditions can be generated in any country similar to those under which economies of the North were able to take off. Finally, catch-up theory assumes that such development, including the worldwide growth of manufacturing, is possible, given the given biological, geolog-

ical, and atmospheric resources of the planet. We will look at each of these in turn.

The politics and economics of catching up   We have already talked about some of the factors that limit the possibility of catching up. Dependency theory notes that different societies begin their development at different starting lines in this "race." Largely, this is because the economic and political mechanisms of colonialism have already developed the countries of the South—that is, developed them as dependencies. Rostow's stages of economic growth model doesn't accommodate this fact. For example, where on Rostow's scale would we place a country that pays out in debt interest more than it takes in through both trade, and aid—regardless of the motivation of its economic elite? And where in his theory do international agencies such as the World Bank or the IMF enter the picture?

After 40 years of intensive global development, not only has the gap between frontrunners and stragglers not been bridged but, on the contrary, it has widened and one doubts it can ever be closed. As a result, the populous Southern countries make only a small contribution to the world's economic productivity. But is that contribution likely to increase?

Some countries—prime examples are in Southeast Asia and include Japan, China, South Korea, Hong Kong, and Taiwan—have been able to achieve success in the catching-up endeavor. Others—especially in Africa, Latin America, and the Middle East—have fallen farther behind. And if we look within countries to the people who live in them, we often find more extreme changes. Even if economic elites have indeed been "developed," the living conditions of the majority of the people have worsened. Prime examples are to be found in Russia and the formerly communist countries of

Eastern Europe. This may go along with an apparent increase in GDP and in the average standard, though not the quality, of living.

To understand these discrepancies and variations, we have to look at ways in which people earn their living. A small-scale farmer may be able to grow crops to feed her family for part of the year while she and other family members also engage in craft industry. However, her farming activities do not count as part of the country's GDP, nor do such craft activities as provide materials for household use. The GDP tallies only activities that result in items for sale. If the family is forced off the land—for instance, by a dam construction project—and moves to the city, it develops greater dependence on being able to buy food and other necessary items. Such transactions (if not conducted on the black market) *do* appear in GDP statistics, but the quality of life of the family may have suffered greatly in the meantime. Thus the GDP—the so-called "standard of living"—may be low even if families are secure and doing reasonably well; it may rise even when families are less secure and suffering a decline in their quality of life.

The question is: Does catching up mean increasing the standard of living or the quality of life? And who supports each outcome? Poor farmers and displaced peasants, who would tend to support the latter, have little voice on either a national or a global level; so the call remains from the South, as in the North, for more development, more catching up—a higher nominal standard of living. Development experts and national elites tend to believe that only the economy matters, whatever the impact of economic change on actual quality of life.

Ecological implications of catch-up development

When President Truman spoke in praise of development in 1948, he did not think of global resources running out or doubt the capacity of the earth to absorb the by-products of development. Almost no one was thinking of these issues. But in the years since, as development in the countries of the North has intensified, a growing number of biologists, geologists, and environmental scientists has been making us aware of the effect that human action has on the earth and its resources.

In short, the world is finite. There are limits to its resources and its regenerative capacities. With the kind of development we have in the North—and with a model that assumes there can always be more growth—we are pushing the limits of what is possible. We are affecting our environment in ways that in turn affect us. The model of unlimited growth in all areas (notably GDP, capital accumulation, and sheer numbers of goods) has led to a deterioration in our environment. The air in cities is not clean. Water is polluted. These have led to a deterioration in the quality of our lives here in the North and, indeed, everywhere on earth.

When we factor in these environmental concerns, the picture changes. It is the nations of the North, the developed nations, that chiefly contribute to global pollution and chiefly use nonrenewable global resources; 20% of the world's population who live in the North are using 80% of the world resources. In the long run, this pattern of consumption may destroy the natural foundations of life worldwide. However, many are reluctant to criticize and relinquish the North's consumption patterns and to warn the South against imitating the North. From a moral, if not ecological, standpoint, people in the South see this warning as an attempt by the North to keep them weak and powerless.

This would seem to lead to the conclusion that the only solution is to distribute more of our wealth through development aid to the poor in the South to enable them to catch up.

But as we have seen in the last section, development aid is an uncertain vehicle of assistance. Catching up is not possible, particularly if the North insists on maintaining economic growth and increasing its own development. Governments of the South, nevertheless, tend to feel that their nations are entitled to a Northern standard of living.

The nations of the North are also the chief consumers of renewable resources and of biomass. Research in the Netherlands has studied how much land every Dutch person uses on average within the Netherlands and outside it. It concludes that for every 1 hectare of land that a Dutch person uses within the Netherlands, he or she uses about 5 hectares outside it, in the third world.

Given the limited purchasing power of people in less developed countries, how can they compete with this? They cannot import much of what they need and must rely largely on their own resources, but many of these resources are being exported to the people of Europe and North America. At the same time, for a variety of reasons—increased soil salinity due to constant irrigation, erosion of forest cover, stress on the ecosystem—the biomass production of land in many less developed countries is decreasing. Is there another way out? Some think there is, and they have called for sustainable development.

The paradigm of sustainable development The phrase *sustainable development* was popularized by the Brundtland Report, published as *Our Common Future* in 1987. Sustainable development is continued economic growth of a kind that does not further compromise the environment and, in this way, "meets the needs of the present without compromising the ability of future generations to meet their own needs." The concept of sustainable development implies limits on the rate and type of growth. However, these limits are bound to change over time. They are imposed by the present state of technology and social organizations on environmental resources and by the ability of the biosphere to absorb the effects of human activities. Technology and social organization, the Brundtland Report argues, can be both managed and improved to make way for a new era of economic growth.

This gives hope to the business community of the North that wishes to combine ecologically sound capitalist production with economic growth. Critics argue that the two concepts are opposed, and for the time being that may be true. Perhaps sustainable development is a misguided goal. Perhaps countries and regions of the South will have to set their own goals, separate from the notion of catching up with the North, and the North will have to rethink its commitment to constant development.

Indeed, many grassroots movements in both the South and North are already working along these lines. Doing so requires new forms of social organization, and many of the new social movements display this concern with people-centered development, popular democracy, and social justice. Longer-term goals may include planned disengagement from international capitalism, regional self-sufficiency in food production, the satisfaction of basic needs for all, development from below through the termination of antirural bias, and concentration on relevant small and medium-sized enterprises.

Even environmentalists disagree over the meaning and usefulness of the concept of sustainable development. Some consider the concept imprecise and only a slogan, empty of meaning. Others believe it may be a useful concept if the two key components—sustainability and development—are examined separately; if growth is conceived of as other than GDP; and if the North, as well as the South, is seen as needing social transformation.

In the short term at least, the North and South have different goals. The North needs to work toward achieving sustainability while also dismantling or significantly reforming economic structures associated with Southern debt. Meanwhile, the South needs to focus on participatory development from the grass roots, or the poorest people, up. Such proposals are rooted in basic principles of democracy and justice. Though wide-ranging and wide-reaching, it is hard to see how sustainable development can be achieved with less.

SUMMING UP

Can everyone live like Americans? No, not if that means everyone in the world catching up to the current American (average) standard of living.

As we said in Section 10.1, today all countries of the world are inextricably linked, and many aspects of their cultures and economies are becoming integrated. This does not mean that one day we will all be members of the same culture or the same economy. It does mean that what happens in one country affects others, positively or negatively. We share an environment that is not only social and political but biological and geological. In short, we share the earth. Can we find ways of working with each other and with the earth that will let us value the diversity of human cultures? This is an area where sociologists must work with ecologists, development theorists, and politicians in an effort to solve the problems of global inequality and development.

The concept of catch-up development is still the dominant paradigm in development politics. However, even a little reflection indicates that it is unworkable, if what is to be caught up to is the throw-away, environmentally wasteful, though seemingly high standard of present-day North America. Yet if we can focus on quality of life, not standard of living, we may be able to achieve a different and better goal. Can sustainable development succeed? This is a challenge on which the future of all societies may depend.

REVIEW EXERCISES

For Discussion and Debate

1. "Sustainable development is the way everyone can benefit. It's a win-win situation." Agree or disagree?

2. "The concept of catch-up development ignores the extremes of poverty that exist in North America today." Agree or disagree?

3. "If the North persists in its development, it has no moral ground to tell the South it can't develop in the same way."

4. "For the South to get richer, the North will have to get poorer."

Writing Exercises

1. "How sociology can help people understand development issues."

2. "Problems I foresee in implementation of sustainable development."

3. Envisage a future in which development has proceeded unchecked within North America, but in which the rest of the world is becoming increasingly poorer. We have now reached the year 2150 . . . Describe the scenario and its outcomes.

4. Implications of the environmental movement for development theory.

Research Activities

1. For one week, monitor media stories on television and in newspapers and magazines covering development, the third world, and industrialization. What is the main focus of the stories? How often do you read or hear references to a possible decline in the standard of living of the first world?

2. Devise a questionnaire to measure people's attitudes toward reductions in the North American standard of living.

Survey at least 10 people, and discuss your findings with your friends. How do people react to the thought of having to make do with less, as a nation?

3. Conduct an Internet search for pages about sustainable development. What positions are adopted in these pages? What have you learned about the sustainable development debate?

4. Choose a country that is currently developing and conduct library and Internet research to familiarize yourself with the processes it is undergoing and the arguments connected with these. Remember to look at social class and gender issues.

SELECTED REFERENCES

AGARWAL, ANIL, and SUNITA NARAIN, Towards green villages. In *Global ecology*, ed. Wolfgang Sachs (London: Zed Books, 1993).

BARBIER, EDWARD B., Cash crops, food crops, and sustainability: The case of Indonesia, *World Development* (June 1989), 17, 6, 879–895.

BARBOSA, LUIZ C., The world-system and the destruction of the Brazilian Amazon rain forest, *Review* (Spring 1993), 16, 2, 215–240.

BLOWERS, ANDREW, Environmental policy: The quest for sustainable development, *Urban Studies* (May 1993), 30, 4–5, 775–796.

BRUNDTLAND REPORT, *Our Common Future* (Oxford: Oxford University Press, 1987).

BURNS, THOMAS J., EDWARD L. KICK, DAVID A. MURRAY, and DIXIE A. MURRAY, Demography, development and deforestation in a world-system perspective, *International Journal of Comparative Sociology* (September–December 1994), 35, 3–4, 221–239.

CHOGUILL, CHARLES L., Sustainable cities: Policies for the future, *Habitat International* (1993), 17, 3, 1–12.

CHOWDHRY, KAMLA, LINCOLN C. CHEN, and JUDITH TENDLER, Poverty, environment, development, *Daedalus* (Winter 1989), 118, 1, 141–154.

DEVLIN, JOHN F., and NONITA T. YAP, Sustainable development and the NICs: Cautionary tales

for the South in the new world (dis)order, *Third World Quarterly* (March 1994), 15, 1, 49–62.

EKINS, PAUL, Making development sustainable. In *Global ecology*, ed. Wolfgang Sachs (London: Zed Books, 1993).

FOSTER, JOHN BELLAMY, "Let them eat pollution": Capitalism and the world environment, *Monthly Review* (January 1993), 44, 8, 10–20.

GAN, LIN, Global warming and the World Bank: A system in transition? *Project Appraisal* (December 1993), 8, 4, 198–212.

GURUNG, BARUN, Towards sustainable development: A case in the Eastern Himalayas, *Futures* (November 1992), 24, 9, 907–916.

INMAN, KATHERINE, Fuelling expansion in the third world: Population, development, debt, and the global decline of forests, *Society and Natural Resources* (January–March 1993), 6, 1, 17–39.

KEMP, RENE, and LUC SOETE, The greening of technological progress: An evolutionary perspective, *Futures* (June 1992), 24, 5, 437–457.

KOUSIS, MARIA, Collective resistance and sustainable development in rural Greece: The case of geothermal energy on the island of Milos, *Sociologica Ruralis* (1993), 33, 1, 3–24.

LEE-SMITH, DIANA, and CATALINA HINCHEY TRUJILLO, The struggle to legitimize subsistence: Women and sustainable development,

Environment and Urbanization (April 1992), 4, 1, 77–84.

McCabe, J. Terrence, Scott Perkin, and Claire Schofield, Can conservation and development be couples among pastoral people? An examination of the Maasai of the Ngorongoro Conservation Area, Tanzania, *Human Organization* (Winter 1992), 51, 4, 353–366.

Mies, Maria, The myth of catching-up development. In *Ecofeminism*, ed. Maria Mies and Vandana Shiva (London: Zed Books, 1993).

———, The need for a new vision: The subsistence perspective. In *Ecofeminism*, ed. Maria Mies and Vandana Shiva (London: Zed Books, 1993).

Rau, William, and Dennis W. Roncek, Industrialization and world inequality: The transformation of the division of labor in the world, *American Sociological Review* (1987), 52, 359–367.

Rostow, Walter, *The world-economy: History and prospect* (Austin: University of Texas Press, 1978).

Sachs, Wolfgang, Global ecology and the shadow of "development." In *Global Ecology*, ed. Wolfgang Sachs (London: Zed Books, 1993).

Shiva, Vandana, Conflicts of global ecology: Environmental activism in a period of global research, *Alternatives* (Spring 1994), 19, 2, 195–207.

Stonich, Susan C., Struggling with Honduran poverty: The environmental consequences of natural resource-based development and rural transformations, *World Development* (March 1992), 20, 3, 385–399.

Taylor, Lance, The World Bank and the environment: The World Development Report 1992, *World Development* (May 1993), 21, 5, 869–881.

Vandermeer, John, The political ecology of sustainable development: The southern Atlantic coast of Nicaragua, *Centennial Review* (Spring 1991), 35, 2, 265–294.

Wood, Charles H., and Marianne Schmink, The military and the environment in the Brazilian Amazon, *Journal of Political and Military Sociology* (Summer 1993), 21, 1, 81–105.

Worster, Donald, The shaky ground of sustainability. In *Global ecology*, ed. Wolfgang Sachs (London: Zed Books, 1993).

15. Social Change

As we shall see, **social change** may begin at either a macro or micro level of society, but eventually its effects show up at both levels. Take the growth of high-tech industries. Automated manufacturing is gradually replacing human workers with machines and computers. In this way, it is changing the lives of thousands of workers and their families. Or consider people's decisions to delay childbearing, to have no children, or to have only one child. These are micro-level choices that people are making one person at a time, and their impact builds slowly. Yet, taken together, these choices are changing the whole world.

Contrary to popular belief, social change is rarely a result of great men and women having great ideas. Social change is happening all the time, a result of the actions of ordinary people. The difference between micro change and macro change is not in the number of people affected or the importance of the change. It lies in the point of origin. But whether a change begins at the macro or micro level, understanding it demands a macro level of explanation.

In this chapter we look at three types of social change that have both macro and micro aspects. First, we consider whether the natural environment (whose importance we examined in the last section) is getting better or worse, and with what social effects. Second, we look at the effects of technological change on society, specifically, the effects of the so-called information highway. Third, we ask whether the individualism that is stressed in Western (and especially North American) culture has become excessive and socially disruptive.

15.1

Is the environment improving?

The issue: A growing fear that humanity may be destroying Planet Earth and, with that, humanity's only chance at survival as a species. Some are optimistic that solutions will be found, but is the optimism justified?

Introduction We hear a great deal of talk these days about the environment. We debate issues of pollution, landfills, water supplies, and air quality. There is increased awareness that we live on a planet of finite resources. For a long time, people believed that we could always find more resources and always find a place to dump our unwanted products and by-products. Now,

most of us are aware that this is not the case. Environmental pollution and depletion have taken their toll on the health of plants, people, and animals.

There are new concerns about the future course of world history, and many of them have to do with the environment and ecology. We hear that the depletion of the ozone layer and the greenhouse effect are making it hazardous just to be out in the sun. The destruction of the Amazon rain forest and the emission of industrial pollutants threaten air quality. Oil spills and the dumping of industrial wastes threaten life in the rivers, lakes, and oceans. These new social problems face us *all*, regardless of class or political system. The former Soviet Union had its Chernobyl nuclear "mishap," just as the United States had its "accident" at Three Mile Island (although the former cost a great many lives while the latter did not). The third world suffers as much from such mishaps, and usually more, as the developed world. In Russia, despite dramatic changes in social organization, economic and health conditions have worsened significantly in the last few years.

In this section we review, first, the concerns about the environment, then pose the question: Is the environment improving? If not, have we caught the problem in time?

Why the concern for environment? People live in an environment and they modify this environment as they live in it. Think of your home, with paint, wallpaper, and pictures on the walls and rugs on the floor. What was the last modification you or your family made to your home? Adding a deck, perhaps, or painting the walls? Your environment, however, goes beyond the house you live in. The street you bicycle or drive through, the park you jog in, the college whose rooms you sit in, the restaurants and shops you frequent, the movie theater you were in last week— these, too, constitute "environment." Air circulates through this environment, water runs through it, people and other animals move in and out of it. You depend on your environment for what you need to live, as a biological organism: air, water, food, warmth, protection from the elements, shield from harmful rays. The provision of these needs, though, may result in problems in other areas.

"Is the environment improving?" may not be the most appropriate question to ask. It is neither accurate nor precise. "Improving" for what, and compared with what? Whose environment? However, it is a question often asked, or even more often, a statement that represents a belief that is often taken for granted. Yes, there were environmental problems, but now that we are on to them, we can fix whatever is wrong. This section will explore beliefs about the environment and whether it is improving, and attempt to summarize the situation as we perceive it.

THE ENVIRONMENT IS IMPROVING

In Rachel Carson's book *Silent Spring*, published in 1962, she pointed to the dangers of a buildup of toxins—derived from pesticides commonly used in agriculture—in the soil and in plants and animals, resulting in the destruction of many species and great reductions in others. The ghostly "silent spring" of her title would be one in which no birds sang; in some areas, this had already occurred. Moreover, in the future she feared people would not be immune to the effects of these toxins.

In the next decade, the Club of Rome produced the ground-breaking study *The Limits to Growth*. This was a frightening prediction of what would happen if humanity continued to use up natural resources and dump waste products at the current rate. The mathematical model underlying the book's predictions was instantly criticized as being too simple; and, indeed, the environmental problems we face today are not necessarily the ones predicted in that book. The model was also criticized for not taking account of new technological innovations and being too sweeping and frightening in its predictions. However, people have said since that it did not take sufficient account of such factors as atmospheric pollution. The study, an attempt to warn people that they live in a world of finite resources, and that the ability of the earth to cope with waste is also finite—has since proven to be more right than wrong.

These works and many others have influenced our awareness of the environment and what may be happening to it. But we must recognize that not all the effects on environment are caused by people.

Three kinds of environmental problems   In fact, there are three categories of environmental problems, which Kurt Cylke terms the ecosystem problem, the ecosystem crisis, and the biosphere crisis.

- *Ecosystem problems* can arise in many ways, and some are created by people. They include disruptions to the biosphere that threaten individual members of species, or, as in the case of human-created disasters, large numbers of people and other creatures. They do not, however, threaten the existence of an entire species. The Bhopal explosion was an example of a sudden ecosystem problem. Examples of chronic problems resulting from massive dumping of pollutants can be found in the toxic soils of Love Canal and Akwesasne.
- *An ecosystem crisis* stems from disruptions that threaten or eradicate entire species. These have occurred throughout the earth's history. However, the rate of species extinction has increased significantly due to ecosystem crises resulting from human activities, such as logging and dam building.
- *Biosphere crisis* includes events that render the biosphere unable to sustain life for most complex species, including humanity. Few human activities, other than a full-scale nuclear war resulting in nuclear winter, could cause damage on this scale. However, a biosphere crisis could be triggered by the occurrence of multiple ecosystem crises. Little attention is commonly given to biosphere crisis, possibly because it is unclear to environmental scientists what factors would lead to such an event. Hence, it is not clear what would prevent it. Both scientific and popular concern currently focuses on ecosystem problems and crises.

Environment in the news   One after another, environmental problems have hit the headlines. Oil spills and chemical spills grab our attention. The ozone layer is discussed each year. Cities continue to search for landfill space to solve their garbage problem. Global warming becomes a household term.

The extent to which these problems appear in the popular press indicates the extent of public awareness. Towns and cities implement recycling programs. Children's environmental clubs spring up in countless elementary and secondary schools, and many adults say that they have begun recycling as a response to pressure from the students living in their homes. The environmental movement has worked hard to bring problems to people's attention. Yet during the 1980s, attempts to convince governments to curb gaseous emissions and airborne particles in order to minimize acid rain were met with resistance from the Reagan administration. This controversy gave environmentalists a forum to bring their concerns to public attention.

The environment has suffered many problems, but some researchers believe it is not too late to deal with them. With warning and through education programs, we are able to curb pollution, restrict emissions, and recycle material (thus saving both energy and land-fill space). Pesticide use has been greatly reduced in the 35 years since Carson's warning of a coming "silent spring." With forethought and planning, we can ensure that the worst excesses are never repeated, and we can work together, citizens of many countries, toward creating sustainable environments. Or so at least some believe.

THE ENVIRONMENT IS NOT IMPROVING

The counter view is that, while recycling programs and other initiatives are beneficial, environmental improvement is illusory. It is true that an increasing number of people in North America and elsewhere are becoming aware of environmental problems. However, this awareness does not necessarily translate into action, and while action may target some problems, other problems go without remedy.

Action paradigms: Approaches to the environment

There are two main ways of approaching problems in the environment, and we may need to choose between them. The first, commonly termed the *dominant Western world view*, is based on the assumption that humans are fundamentally different from all other forms of life on earth: that we choose our actions, act within a world of vast resources, and have the ability to find solutions to the problems we face. Every problem will have its solution; the only difficulty is in finding it.

The second paradigm, termed the *new ecological paradigm (NEP)*, is based on different assumptions. In this way of thinking, humans are only one among many interdependent species. Human actions, as part of an intricate web of global cause and effect, may have unintended consequences. The world's resources available for human use are finite and impose restrictions on human possibilities, and humans do not have the infinite potential to provide solutions to all problems. In the end, ecological laws cannot be repealed.

Researchers have found evidence that increasing numbers of people in North America are moving toward, and even beyond, this NEP in their approach. Many now recognize that we humans have been rapidly depleting the earth's resources. We must change our practices if we want to avoid major environmental problems, and a necessary, but not sufficient, step toward coping with those environmental problems is the adoption of an *environmental ethic*. This ethic would stress the importance of humanity living in harmony with the earth's ecological systems. In short, we have to create societies that are permanently sustainable, a topic we touched on in the previous section.

There is evidence that over half of surveyed American respondents hold this point of view, with another quarter inclining toward it. Popular attitudes, therefore, are changing, and this change in beliefs has enormous importance. However, we can raise questions about this supposed transformation. Are people acting on their belief—that is, does changed belief actually result in changed practice? And if so, what are the visible results of these changes in practice? Are the people whose beliefs are changing the same people who are directly responsible for environmental pollution? Are attitudes also changing in other parts of the world? Can the environment recover, or are the changes in attitude and behavior too little and too late?

Species extinctions

We referred earlier to ecosystem crises that are responsible for extinctions of entire species. Many species are now threatened or disappearing. In 1992, Kurt Cylke found that three-fourths of the world's bird species are declining in numbers or threatened with extinction; one-third of North America's freshwater fish are rare, threatened, or endangered; one-third of U.S. coastal fish have declined in population since 1975; 100 species of invertebrates are lost to deforestation each day; and of the world's 270 turtle species, 42% are rare or threatened with extinction.

Going further afield, more than half of all the known species are to be found in the Central and South American forests. However, their habitats are threatened by land-clearing activities to create farmlands or grazing lands, mining activities, and felling of tropical hardwood trees for export. Rain forests in other parts of the world are similarly threatened.

Global warming that results from a buildup of greenhouse gases in the atmosphere has the potential to produce a biosphere crisis. Scientists disagree about the extent and results of this warming, some predicting a meltdown of polar ice with an associated rise in sea level, others, a thickening of the Antarctic ice cap. There is general agreement, however, that the past decade has been the warmest recorded by modern methods. In 1997, scientists noted that changes in temperature in Antartica had resulted in increased snowfall on coastal ice flows. In turn, this resulted in breeding-site problems for Adelie penguins and a subsequent reduction in their numbers.

Based on such data, we can see that the environment is not improving. Far from it. Diversity in both animal and plant species is being reduced, and when a species is gone, it is gone for good. True, the rate of species extinction can be slowed, but there is no evidence this is currently happening. Humanity is not making progress on this problem.

Differences in theory and practice   We can question to what extent changes in attitude are translated into practice. If more than half the population of North America favors an eco-

logical social paradigm, what changes in behavior are resulting from this? In fact, very few. Traffic congestion is increasing, CFCs (chlorofluorocarbons, which when released drift to the upper atmosphere, where they catalyze a reaction resulting in the breakdown of ozone molecules) continue to be used for refrigeration, and a variety of household chemicals, such as common bleaches, continue to cause problems of disposal. In supermarkets, products claiming to be environmentally friendly are generally priced above comparable products. This is odd, since truly "environmentally friendly" products should have received less processing and hence been less costly to produce.

A degree of schizophrenia with regard to paper products can be seen in the fact that, on the one hand, consumers are encouraged to recycle bond paper, yet products such as toilet paper and kitchen paper are generally not made from recycled materials. In some cases, people are being encouraged to use even more paper products than before. For example, women are being urged through advertisements to use paper "menstrual" products even on days when they are not menstruating. What this shows is an unrecognized conflict between environmentalism and capitalism, also between environmentalism and consumerism—an addiction to the "throwaway" culture.

If environmental concerns are being taken up by producers, it is for business reasons. No wonder environmental movements have recognized the need to convince businesspeople that environmentalism is in their interests because it is more efficient and hence more profitable. Environmentalism harnessed to the service of economic growth is likely to strike a responsive chord with Western producers and consumers; otherwise, it remains an empty word.

People who favor the ecological social paradigm are not, for the most part, the same people who shape social or business policy. At best, we are offered more environmentally friendly materials and services at a higher price, and with no guarantees that the materials are indeed more environmentally friendly. An example comes from the well-known episode of McDonald's polystyrene cups. After an outcry from schoolchildren, these were replaced by paper cups, which were neither more energy-efficient nor more easily recyclable, but in the public eye "better."

A basic problem with the currently popular concept of sustainable development is the idea of focusing attention on means of achieving development (or capital accumulation) so that such means do not cause irredeemable damage. Maintaining development in this way implies that societies such as those of North America can have their cake and eat it too, that by changing some practices, engaging in recycling, becoming more resource-efficient, North Americans can maintain and even expand their current standard of living.

But the truth is otherwise. An increase in resource efficiency alone leads to nothing unless it goes hand in hand with an intelligent restraint of growth. Instead of asking how many supermarkets or how many bathrooms are enough, one focuses on how all these—and more—can be obtained with a lower input of resources. Today's cars are far more energy-efficient than their predecessors. However, there are many more of them on the roads, so that the total amount of energy use and pollution, not only in transit but in car manufacture, is increasing.

And there are many instances where environmentalism has been co-opted in the service of capitalist production. However, capitalism is based on the concept of expansion, requiring an increasing demand for products, a growing market for which producers can compete. This tells us that the incompatibility between capitalism and environmentalism may be fundamental, not a matter of informing the public and making small gradual changes.

Several decades have passed since Garrett Hardin described the "tragedy of the commons." Imagine a situation in which all the villagers can graze their cattle on the common land. Each villager can profit by owning more cattle, so each, individually, sets more cattle to graze on the commons. The result is overgrazing and depletion of the common resource. Thus, the short-term interest of each is in conflict with the long-term interest of all.

This analogy has obvious parallels with the ecosystem problems and threatened ecosystem crises of the present—with overfishing of the Atlantic cod stocks, for instance. Hardin, however, has been criticized for the implication that this tragedy is inevitable. Some argue that it becomes inevitable only under certain types of highly competitive circumstances, such as those of present-day capitalism, under which producers compete to maximize their use of the resource pie, rather than to conserve the pie.

Others would argue that evidence from small, less economically developed bands suggests the problem is widespread. For example, nomadic tribes in Africa are blamed for ecological degradation in the Sahel, because (supposedly) overgrazing by their herds has largely led to the desertification of the region. Poor women in Africa and Asia are blamed for the destruction of forest areas because they must now search for fuel wood higher and higher in forest-covered hills. In this search for the guilty, the loggers, timber merchants, the furniture, sports, and paper industries, the cattle farmers, and the food export industry are seldom mentioned. The problems may indeed be of a similar nature, but differences in scale make an enormous difference to the ecosystem.

The lack of consideration of the social relations of power that surround environmental problems means that, for instance, public awareness is easily diverted onto the question of blame, at least where this blame attaches to someone else. Global warming is in the news. It has the potential to trigger a biosphere crisis. Production of greenhouse gases in the meantime continues—and in the popular mind the emission of carbon dioxide from North American car exhausts is equated with the emission of methane from Indian rice fields.

The environment is polluted, and despite an increasing public discourse of environmentalism, there is little indication that it is becoming less so. Instead of seeing a true improvement, we are seeing the emergence of new areas in which capitalist businesses compete: the creation of an environmental market going hand in hand with a concept of infinitely sustainable development. We are unlikely to see true improvement until we can ask where decisions are made, where power is located, and what level of material resources is enough.

SUMMING UP

Is the environment improving? That's a problematic question, for many reasons. The definition of environment is, to say the least, imprecise. Environment for what, or for whom? Living beings constantly modify their environment. We exist on this planet because early plants produced oxygen and so caused change. Today's people, however, change their environment rapidly and in ways that can threaten both their own well-being and that of other species.

Scientists have not reached a clear consensus about the nature of today's environmental changes or how to avoid biosphere crises. What will be the effects of global warming? What are the implications of the thinning of the ozone layer? In North America, people watch the news, express concern, engage to a greater or lesser extent in recycling programs, and put extra-strong sunscreen on their children. As individuals, there is little else we can do.

Sociologists have a different part to play. Sociology has no cure for environmental ills, not even a way of deciding who is really right among the wildly differing environmental forecasts. What sociology can do is help us understand how these forecasts are constructed and who are the interest groups involved in forecasting; how knowledge of environmental issues is communicated to the general public; and how social relations of production and power are implicated in the problems that ecologists debate. If we need to change the ways we are modifying our environment—and we do—we need to understand how these ways come about, and why some forms of social organization are more environmentally destructive than others. In short, we need to think sociologically about people and their environment in the context of their economic, political, and cultural organization.

REVIEW EXERCISES

For Discussion and Debate

1. "The major environmental problem is not that we're going to run out of resources but that we're going to cover the world with our garbage." Discuss.

2. "Business people are only interested in the environment if they think they can

make money out of people's interest." Discuss.

3. Which is more important, the environment or creating new jobs in industry?

4. What use are wetlands to the average person?

Writing Exercises

1. "How I could simplify my lifestyle to be more environmentally conscious—and what are the pressures on me to *not* do this."

2. "Think globally, act locally" (a common slogan of the environmental movement).

3. "Can we have environment and jobs too?"

4. "Reduce, reuse, recycle—does it make a difference?"

Research Activities

1. Investigate some of the pronouncements on how we can supply our energy needs during the next century. Examine statements by environmentalists, politicians, and power companies. Analyze these for how people's views connect with their jobs or social positions.

2. Conduct a search of the World Wide Web looking for statements by members of the Deep Ecology and Ecofeminist movements. What similarities and differences do you find in their statements?

3. Examine media coverage of an environmental issue in your area. How is the information presented? Whose views predominate in the media items you collect or hear? Discuss this with other students in your class.

4. Survey at least eight neighbors on their *attitudes* toward the environmental movement and recycling, and on their *practices*. Do they recycle? Do they commute by car? Do their practices match their views?

SELECTED REFERENCES

BLOWERS, ANDREW, Environmental policy: The quest for sustainable development, *Urban Studies* (1993), 30, 4–5, 775–796.

BRULLE, ROBERT J., Environmental discourse and social movement organizations: A historical and rhetorical perspective on the development of U.S. environmental organizations, *Sociological Inquiry* (1996), 66, 1, 58–83.

CARSON, RACHEL, *Silent spring* (Boston: Houghton Mifflin, 1962).

CYLKE, F. KURT, JR., *The environment* (New York: HarperCollins, 1993).

FREUDENBERG, NICHOLAS, and CAROL STEINSAPIR, Not in our backyards: The grassroots environmental movement, *Society and Natural Resources* (1991), 4, 3, 235–245.

GIBSON, DONALD E., The environmental movement: Grass-roots or establishment? *Sociological Viewpoints* (1992), 8, 92–124.

GORDON, CYNTHIA, and JAMES M. JASPER, Overcoming the "NIMBY" label: Rhetorical and organizational links for local protestors, *Research in Social Movements, Conflicts and Change* (1996), 19, 159–181.

HARDIN, GARRETT, The tragedy of the commons, *Science* (1978), 162, 1241–1252.

HARDIN, JESSE WOLF, Deep ecology: A quarter century of earth minstrelsy, *Humboldt Journal of Social Relations* (1995), 21, 1, 95–109.

KRUTILLA, KERRY, and CLARE BREIDENICH, The GATT and environmental policy: An analysis of potential conflicts and policy reforms, *Policy Studies Review* (1993), 12, 3–4, 211–225.

MANNING, ROBERT E., and ROBERT GOTTLIEB, Forcing the spring: The transformation of the American environmental movement, *Forum for Applied Research and Public Policy* (1996), 11, 1, 145–146.

MEADOWS, DONELLA H., and DENNIS MEADOWS, *The limits to growth: A report of the club of Rome's project on the predicament of mankind* (New York: Universe Books, 1972).

MERCHANT, CAROLYN, *Radical ecology: The search for a livable world* (New York: Routledge, 1992).

MIES, MARIA, and VANDANA SHIVA, *Ecofeminism* (London: Zed Books, 1993).

PETERSON, ABBY, and CAROLYN MERCHANT, "Peace with the earth": Women and the environmental movement in Sweden, *Women's Studies International Forum* (1986), 9, 5–6, 465–479.

PULIDO, LAURA, *Environmentalism and economic justice: Two chicano struggles in the Southwest* (Tucson: University of Arizona Press, 1996).

ROGERS, RAYMOND A., Doing the dirty work of globalization, *Capitalism, Nature, Socialism* (1995), 6, 3, 23, 117–134.

RYCROFT, ROBERT W., Environmentalism and science: Politics and the pursuit of knowledge, *Knowledge* (1991), 13, 2, 150–169.

SCHREPFER, SUSAN R., and KIRKPATRICK SALE, The green revolution: The American environmental movement, 1962–1992, *Journal of American History* (1995), 81, 4, 1832–1833.

SHIVA, VANDANA, *Staying alive: Women, ecology and development* (London: Zed Books, 1988).

SIMMONS, JAMES, and NANCY STARK, Backyard protest: Emergence, expansion, and persistence of a local hazardous waste controversy, *Policy Studies Journal* (1993), 21, 3, 470–491.

STREETER, CALVIN L., and JACQUELINE GONSALVEZ, Social justice issues and the environmental movement in America: A new challenge for social workers, *Journal of Applied Social Sciences* (1994), 18, 2, 209–216.

VAN DER HEIJDEN, HEIN ANTON, RUUD KOOPMANS, and MARCO G. GIUGNI, The West European environmental movement, *Research in Social Movements, Conflicts and Change* (1992), supplement 2, 1–40.

YEARLEY, STEVEN, Environmentalism: Science and a social movement, *Social Studies of Science* (1989), 19, 2, 343–355.

ZIMMERMAN, MICHAEL E., The threat of ecofascism, *Social Theory and Practice* (1995), 21, 2, 207–238.

15.2

Will the information highway change social life?

The issue: The optimistic enthusiasm people have about the potential for human betterment provided by new information technology (also known as the information highway, cyberspace, the Web, and Internet). Is this just end-of-millennium lunacy, or are we truly at the start of a new social revolution?

Introduction In North American society, many people make daily use of the so-called "information highway." This means they have rapid access to information through the Internet and other means of swift electronic communication. But many other people do not; they have no computers or Internet access. What are the implications of this technology, and access to it, for society and social change? Is the Internet merely another way of exchanging information, or has it the potential to alter how we perceive ourselves and our world? Will it change how society is structured?

In this section these views are explored. Other issues touched on include the ques-tions of Internet censorship, privacy and security of information, and who can or should control access.

THE INFORMATION HIGHWAY WILL NOT GREATLY CHANGE SOCIAL LIFE

It is easy to get overly excited about new gadgets and gizmos. (Your garage may be littered with things that seemed like miracles for $29.95 when you saw them advertised on television, but quickly lost their value when you got to know them better.) So it is necessary to approach new technologies like the Internet with a certain degree of skepticism. It's true we've never had the Internet before, but we have had other new technologies—including new information technologies—before, so we know something about what they can and can't do. We also know about how they usually prove less revolutionary than we expected.

Take the telephone, a very important device that has speeded up the rate at which we can communicate with people all over the world. But if you ask questions like these—Has the telephone transformed the ways in which people relate to one another as human beings? Has it solved any of the world's pressing social problems? Has it improved the quality of life for society's most vulnerable citizens?—in all honesty you would probably have to answer "no."

Today, much social change results from new technology. Genetic engineering and *informatics*—the combination of computing and communication technologies—are two of the newest major influences on our society. However, in discussing new technology, we must be careful to avoid the dangers of technological determinism. *Technological determinism* holds that social and cultural change are usually the result of changes in technology. Like other single-minded theories, this theory assumes that one particular factor—in this case, technology—always has the same effects.

Technological determinists propose that technology has the same social effects, whatever the culture, society, or sociohistorical setting in which it is being used. A prime example of this view is Marshall McLuhan's famous slogan, "The medium is the message." By this, McLuhan meant that television influences us all by the way it conveys information, not because of the information it conveys. He believed that changes in communication technology would change the world's culture.

And, in fact, it has. Still, it is easy to overstate this view, to believe that technology does, or can do, more than is really possible. Without denying technology's importance, we cannot agree that social and cultural life are *determined* by technology. Like ideas, new technologies are neither sufficient nor necessary for social change to occur. Societies are too complex for that.

The evidence shows people use the same technology differently in different organizations, societies, or cultures. The precise effect of a new technology depends on the context into which it is introduced. The motives and attitudes of people who control the technology and the prevailing culture—the beliefs, cultural practices, and existing technology—all make a difference. We can see this in the ways different people and different societies make use of already available technologies, ranging from the telephone and automobile to the computer and the Internet. The Internet, for example, can be used for good or ill depending on the kind of information it carries and the way that information is organized and used. In turn, the organization and use of Internet information is a social product; like all social products, it is shaped by culture, political power, class interest, and the value placed on efficiency.

Even today, we see a vast number of different uses made of computing technology. Computer use varies from one society to another and from one organization to another within the same society. People determine computer use, not vice versa. But some of the most influential of these people are the ones who design computers and computer software, like Microsoft's Bill Gates. Computers and other new technologies have the most impact where they are dealing with problems that are readily "technifiable." These are problems that have a few very characteristic features. The problems are specific and practical—for example, how to get money out of your bank account on a weekend or at 3 A.M. (ordinary people are hoping for new technology in that area) or how to build cheaper, more reliable cars that do not pollute the air. The technology is powerful, meaning that it requires little instruction and can do a great deal for the user. A microwave oven, a computerized chess game, and a reference library on CD-ROM are examples of this.

Often, making a technological change is too complicated and costly to be worthwhile. Things remain the same, even though better solutions are possible. Nevertheless, we are in the midst of a microelectronics revolution that is transforming many aspects of our society. With proper use, computers can become instruments of human betterment; with wrong use, they can become instruments of domination. We have seen that this is true of *all* technology.

People today can communicate faster than ever before, using a variety of different means. In the past, newspapers received written reports that correspondents sent through the mail; they took days or weeks to reach their destination, so that "news" was never new and always out of date at its source, though to readers of the newspapers, the information was fresh and indeed "news." Then came telegraph and telephone communications, speeding up the process. Correspondents could now send their reports that would be in the next day's papers. Business and scientific information could also be exchanged more rapidly, and whole segments of the economy came to depend on the availability of access to rapid information.

Today information can readily be sent from one part of the world to another by means of electronic signals. Fax machines and computers enable us to exchange news, stock-market prices, or scientific findings almost instantaneously. Only the fingers of the typist slow down the rate of transfer. So for industries that depend on rapid exchange of information, the information highway is invaluable. It does nothing more than the earlier telephone and telegraph communications did—it just sends the information faster. But sometimes faster is better.

For people requiring fast information, therefore, the information highway is a highly useful tool. However, even those who regularly use the Internet find the quality of information on it variable. It is a good place to find documents of government agencies or nonprofit organizations. But much of the other material available is of poor quality, often outdated or produced by students as part of their reports. Unless dealing with government material or official statistics, we cannot rely on Internet information.

But many people have little connection with the Internet. They do not own fax machines or computers. For the majority of people in the world, the information highway is irrelevant to their everyday life. Many people encounter the Internet in school or college. Even then, some will ignore it. Others experiment, use e-mail, even make friends through news groups. The main use they make of the Internet, though, is in finding information for class assignments, connecting to sites for games, and participating in MUDs (Multi-User Domains, based on the Dungeons and Dragons game, and played interactively by many people at their own terminals or computers) or IRC (Internet Relay Chat). After graduation they lose their computer accounts and Internet access unless they work for a company that makes a lot of use of computers. Even then, their main Internet use is likely to be product-related or focused on maintaining e-mail links with colleagues and friends.

Some businesses have attempted to use the Internet for sales purposes. However, this practice has not taken off. Many people are reluctant to buy products from a Web page or even use e-mail, when they have to give out their credit card number. There is a perceived security problem. Everyone has heard of hackers who can obtain information and use it illegally; and indeed, some Internet browser programs give out warnings that information submitted is insecure. Attempts to overcome this problem with encryption of sensitive data have so far not caught on among potential buyers.

The extent to which the information highway will change social life, therefore, is small. It will enable some people to keep in touch, speed the flow of information, and provide for increased distractions at work or home. It will not likely result in major social change. At least, that is what some skeptical observers claim; but there is another point of view on this.

THE INFORMATION HIGHWAY MAY PROFOUNDLY CHANGE SOCIAL LIFE

The counter argument is that changes resulting from the information highway will indeed be far-reaching. The information highway is not only about how information is transferred from place to place and person to person; it also has the potential to transform the type of information and the use to which it is put, and in the process, to restructure the social relations underlying the construction and use of information or knowledge. Though we know this potential exists, it is not yet clear what forms new social relations of knowledge will take.

Knowledge as a commodity in the modern world

We are now living in what has been called the Information Age. As a species we have more information about more concepts than at any time in history. We make use of this, exchange it. Information is a commodity, to be bought and sold.

Five centuries ago, scholars could decide on what constituted the appropriate body of knowledge within any one literate society—be that society Chinese, European, or otherwise. It was still possible for someone to imagine becoming an expert—a knowledgeable person—in *everything*. (The Renaissance scholar Erasmus has been thought of in these terms, and some would speak of Leonardo da Vinci the same way.) Even 50 years ago, scholars could still demarcate the boundaries of knowledge—what was known and knowable. However at that time the demarcated body of knowledge was far beyond the reach of a single person, so that we required specialization even within specific fields (e.g., within chemistry, anthropology, or literature).

This concept of the demarcated body of knowledge—of what educated people should know—was produced by the technology of the day, along with the question of whose was the knowledge. Until the invention of the printing press, people did not have a concept of "authorship" in the modern sense. In Europe, monks spent time copying manuscripts (deemed to be the word of God). However, most knowledge or information—information about growing crops or doing blacksmith work, or weaving, or about the other activities that were part of everyday life—was transmitted orally from person to person. The printing press changed this by making possible the rapid copying of what had previously taken months or years. Knowledge was now a *thing* that could be disseminated among strangers, and printers became seekers after material to print. Still, the concept of authorship took several centuries before it gained its modern form.

With the concept of authorship, or of ownership of knowledge, came ideas about standards for knowledge. Eventually the standard, in the popular mind, became what was printed. Mirroring this, we currently distinguish between knowledge producers and knowledge consumers. *Producers* are people who, for whatever reason, are viewed as experts and who can get their works into print, whether as academics through peer-reviewed journals and monographs, or as hands-on experts through the medium of popular books, or as reporters in far-off places who tell us through newspapers and magazines what is happening in the world.

Consumers, by contrast, are people who use the knowledge so produced, who buy the thousands of "how-to" books. They go to school and college to gain knowledge and skills from their teachers and then into the world of work, in theory at least, to use this knowledge and these skills, only to find that they require *more*. Producers are themselves consumers, and as such must make clear distinction in academic publications between what is "their" knowledge and what has come from other people. The ownership of knowledge is important, both for its own sake and for its market value. Knowledge is a commodity, to be owned and sold.

How does the Internet affect this relationship among consumers, producers, and knowledge? The Internet may change the whole way we view information and also change the relations of its production. But before exploring these ideas, let us first examine who uses the Internet and how and where they do so.

Who uses the Internet? The American Internet Survey was conducted in November and December of 1995 as an attempt to characterize American users of the Internet. The numbers of actual users found then were small—only 9.5 million American users, comprising 8.4 million adults and 1.1 million children under 18. Of all U.S. households, only 6.4% had one or more Internet users. (These figures did not include people who used only e-mail.) However small, what the survey results showed was a dramatic growth. Over half of surveyed users had begun using the Internet during 1995. Further, of all users, 7.3 million—two-thirds—used the Internet from home, and 37% used it exclusively from home. Of the new users, almost half used the Internet exclusively from home.

Nearly 6 million adults reported using the Internet for business activities, and 6 million for personal activities; 60% used it for both. The most popular single use was e-mail. That is, people used the Internet primarily for purposes of communication; finding information was a secondary use. When users were asked how they saw the future of the Internet, a majority listed future use for information access, communications, and/or education. Smaller fractions reported the Internet's likely usefulness in advertising and marketing, entertainment, buying and selling, and/or community service.

More recent surveys show increases in the population of users, to 23% of those aged 16 and over in the United States; 23% of the combined populations of the United States and Canada had Internet access in August 1996. Most likely, these figures have increased once more since these surveys, though the rate of increase by mid-1996 had slowed.

It should be remembered that the Internet implies not only users' communication and information sessions but the technology hardware and software and networks of suppliers and technicians that make the communications possible. Some estimate that by the year 2000, the global Internet market will soar to $23 billion.

It is time to look more closely at how the Internet is used and the implications of this use. Business use permits shifting the location of work to home, and allows companies to further spread their functions among a number of locations, be they towns, regions, or countries. The Internet also facilitates a change in the ways goods are ordered and inventoried, resulting from the speed of computerized communications. Businesses are moving to what is known as "just in time" production and delivery. No longer are retail businesses required to maintain substantial inventories; instead, they can function as information distributors, contacting suppliers instantly to arrange delivery "on time."

Such changes are important in terms of business organization. They may also result in altered patterns of employment in some business sectors. Fewer people will be needed to manage inventory and more will be needed to track orders—important changes for the people concerned. However, these changes are part of a long-term change stemming initially, as previously mentioned, from telegraph and telephone communications. Are they sufficiently far-reaching to warrant the claim of profound social change?

Other researchers have pointed to deeper implications. The point of the Internet revolution, they say, is neither that it leads to adjustments in employment, nor that consumers use the World Wide Web directly to purchase products. Instead, the revolutionary potential of the Internet is that it re-creates information as something that is commonly shared and exchanged, not a commodity that is owned. The Internet is described in phrases such as the "commons of information" and the "agora" (the marketplace of ancient Greek cities where people walked and talked). And let's not lose sight of the scale of this marketplace area. Some see it as being totally out of control, impossible to map accurately, and being used far beyond its original intentions. These unknowns and uncontrolled elements are, from a certain standpoint, highly beneficial, since they give ordinary people the chance to return to being producers, rather than only consumers, of knowledge.

Another fascinating aspect of the electronic agora is that it is made up of people who have probably never physically met each other but who share beliefs and ideologies, give mutual support, and exchange ideas on a regular basis. The result is a creation of worldwide *virtual communities*—communities of interest and shared viewpoint that are unhampered by distance and many of the social factors (age, race, gender, class) that often keep otherwise similar people from meeting or interacting with one another.

The Internet, unlike other media of information, is not centralized and not restricted; anyone who can gain access to a computer and modem can participate. Community nets (or Freenets) are developing in many towns and cities, often with terminals installed in public libraries, to give access to those who do not have computers at home or work. This opportunity is not guaranteed to continue, however. In *The Virtual Community*, Howard Rheingold speaks of it as temporary, threatened by commercial interests that seek to control and to impose centralization. If we citizens do not develop a clear vision for ourselves of how we want the Internet to grow, it seems likely the future will be shaped by large commercial and political powerholders.

Numerous writers have pointed to problems in who gets to use this technology. Internet users today are overwhelmingly white and male (though surveys show that women are rapidly becoming users). By some estimates, only 3% to 5% of U.S. users are African American. Again, however, though the percentages are small, they are growing rapidly, as Afrocentric Web pages increase in number. Native peoples of North America are also extending Internet contacts, not only within the United States and Canada but to groups of indigenous peoples elsewhere. Women's pages, like Afrocentric pages, are rapidly increasing in number. However, centralization, censorship, and monitoring of the Internet may have the effect of hindering both access and the spread of ideas among alternative groups and communities.

The control issue Currently the Internet is anarchic. There is no centralized control, and from some points of view, this is a good and healthy thing. However, periodically there are attempts to censor the information available through it. The question of the type of information available is a difficult one to deal with. If access to the Internet is free and open, anyone can post what he or she wants. This leaves scope for new ideas to surface— and for hate literature and obscenities as well. How can the Internet community control the latter without removing the ability of people to speak freely on issues that matter deeply to them?

Many Internet providers are attempting voluntary controls, requesting that people not post "offensive" material on their sites. To an extent this does work. However, there are campaigns to censor whole categories of material, and some countries have gone beyond this. The United States, at least in theory, can impose penalties on Internet providers who transmit obscene material, even unknowingly. Germany bans some news groups, to prevent racist hate literature from being broadcast into the country. China has stringent regulations preventing access, in an attempt to prevent dissemination of ideas that might be subversive. While there is a long step between the Chinese government's current position and that of the

United States or Germany, it is clear that any censorship of the Internet can prevent important ideas from being openly debated.

As an example, numerous commercial "Internet nanny" programs are available that are designed to prevent children or adolescents from finding material that parents do not wish them to read. These work by screening out sites or news messages containing certain words. Screening all messages for the word *rape* will prevent reception of violent pornographic messages that contain this word, but it will also remove feminist discussion of problems of date rape among adolescents. However, these programs give purchasers a choice, to use or not to use them. State censorship gives no choice. Currently, a blue ribbon campaign is attempting to prevent Internet censorship, and many Web pages carry its logo.

SUMMING UP

Without vigilance on the part of users, the Internet could go from being an anarchic network of information providers and communicators to a means of surveillance. Already there is potential to track the messages and Web site accesses of individual users. The threat here is of the Internet becoming the *panopticon*—the all-seeing eye that allows those in authority to monitor people's thoughts and communications. Some Internet users are campaigning on issues of privacy and security of information, including the information they transmit when they connect to any site.

We do not know what the future of the Internet is. We do know that it has the potential to change society. In whose interests the change may be is not yet clear. But what the Internet issue does is throw into clear relief the somewhat abstract issues of rights to information property, liberty versus authority, geographic community versus constructed community, and technology-in-theory versus technology-in-social-use. Much of the twenty-first century will be taken up with democratically resolving issues that before this century and the rise of the Internet were of only theoretical interest.

REVIEW EXERCISES

For Discussion and Debate

1. "The Internet is just a big waste of time for most people. More work hours are lost on the Internet than through sick days or people sleeping on the job."

2. "Free, rapid exchange of information—Will it change your life?"

3. "The Internet has revolutionary potential as great as that of the printing press."

4. Censorship of the Internet—pros and cons.

Writing Exercises

1. "Women and the Internet: Why women are a numerical minority online."

2. "My own experience. How I use the Internet, and why."

3. "Why members of minorities should (or should not) invest time in the Internet."

4. "The Internet as an agora."

Research Activities

1. Find current statistics on the growth of the Internet and examine them. How has the Internet grown since you left high school? Since this book was written? *Hint*: Find these statistics on the Internet. Some possible sites are http://etrg.findsvp.com/internet/highlights.html; http://etrg.findsvp.com/graphics/internet/usrftr.gif; http://www.cyberatlas.com/market.html; and http://www.webcom.com/pcj/it/it-fr1.html.

2. Search for the use of the Internet by members of any small-scale group who share a common goal or orientation to the world, such as an environmental group or a non-mainstream religion (or even fans of a TV show or a music band). How do group members use the Internet to create community?

3. Survey 10 students on their Internet use. What are the most common uses (e.g., e-mail, MUD, news, WWW surfing), and how much time do they spend in Internet use? How many are information producers via the Internet in addition to being information consumers?

4. Conduct a study of a Usenet Newsgroup. Sort the messages according to whether they fall into the categories of NOISE (extraneous comments, hellos or "me too" messages, insults or "flames," or "spams" attempting to sell products across a wide range of newsgroups), or SIGNAL (messages that actually attempt to convey information or add material to a discussion). Share your findings with friends who have studied different newsgroups. What would you recommend to a sociologist seeking information about people's opinions or behavior about using newsgroups as a source of material?

SELECTED REFERENCES

BLAIS, PAMELA, How the information revolution is shaping our communities, *Planning Commissioners Journal* (Fall 1996) (http://www.plannersweb.com/articles/bla118.html).

ESCOBAR, ARTURO, DAVID HESS, ISABEL LICHA, and WILL SIBLEY, Welcome to Cyberia: Notes on the anthropology of cyberculture, *Current Anthropology* (June 1994), 35, 3, 211–223.

FARRELL, DAVID, Will Internet set African Americans free? *Detroit News,* February 4, 1996 (http://detnews.com/cyberia/daily/34539.html).

FORESTER, TOM, Megatrends or megamistakes: What ever happened to the information society? *Information Society* (July–September 1992), 8, 3, 133–146.

GUMPERT, GARY, and SUSAN J. DRUCKER, From the agora to the electronic shopping mall, *Critical Studies in Mass Communication* (June 1992), 9, 2, 186–200.

HADDON, LESLIE, and ALAN LEWIS, The experience of teleworking: An annotated review, *International Journal of Human Resource Management* (February 1994), 5, 1, 193–223.

HINES, ANDY, Jobs and infotech: Work in the information society, *Futurist* (February 1994), 28, 1, 9–13.

KROKER, ARTHUR, and MICHAEL A. WEINSTEIN, The political economy of virtual reality, *Canadian Journal of Political and Social Theory* (1994), 17, 1–2, 1–31.

KURLAND, DANIEL J., and DAPHNE JOHN, *Internet guide for sociology* (Belmont, CA: Wadsworth, 1997).

LYON, DAVID, An electronic panopticon? A sociological critique of surveillance theory, *Sociological Review* (November 1993), 41, 4, 653–678.

MANTOVANI, GIUESEPPE, Is computer-mediated communication intrinsically apt to enhance democracy in organizations? *Human Relations* (January 1994), 47, 1, 45–62.

MARKUS, M. LYNNE, TORA K. BIKSON, and MAHA EL-SHINNAWY, Fragments of your communication: Email, Vmail and fax, *Information Society* (October–December 1992), 8, 4, 207–226.

MARX, GARY T., The new surveillance, *National Forum* (Summer 1991), 71, 3, 32–36.

MENZIES, HEATHER, *Whose brave new world? The information highway and the new economy* (Toronto: Between the Lines, 1996).

MITCHELL, WILLIAM J., *City of bits: Space, place, and the infobahn* (Boston: MIT Press, 1995).

MYERS, DANIEL J., Communication technology and social movements: Contributions of computer networks to activism, *Social Science Computer Review* (Summer 1994), 12, 2, 250–260.

RAKOW, LANA F., and VIJA NAVARRO, Remote mothering and the parallel shift: Women meet the cellular telephone, *Critical Studies in Mass Communication* (June 1993), 10, 2, 144–157.

RHEINGOLD, HOWARD, *Virtual reality* (London: Secker and Warburg, 1993).

———, *The virtual community*, 1996. Available on the World Wide Web at http://www.well.com/user/hlr/vcbook/vc bookintro.html. (Not available, at the time of writing, in bookstores.)

SACHS, HIRAM, Computer networks and the formation of public opinion: An ethnographic study, *Media, Culture and Society* (January 1995), 17, 1, 81–99.

SCHROEDER, RALPH, Virtual reality in the real world: History, applications and projections, *Futures* (November 1993), 25, 9, 963–973.

SEWELL, GRAHAM, and BARRY WILKINSON, "Someone to watch over me": Surveillance, discipline and the just-in-time process, *Sociology* (May 1992), 26, 2, 271–289.

SNIDER, JAMES H., Democracy on-line: Tomorrow's electronic electorate, *Futurist* (September–October 1994), 28, 5, 15–19.

SPENDER, DALE, *Nattering on the Net: Women, power and cyberspace* (Toronto: Garamond, 1995).

TRIBE, LAWRENCE, The constitution in cyberspace: Law and liberty beyond the electronic frontier, *Humanist* (September–October 1991), 51, 5, 15–21.

TURKLE, SHERRY, Constructions and reconstructions of self in virtual reality, *Mind, Culture, and Activity: An International Journal* (Summer 1994), 1, 3, 158–167.

WALTHER, JOSEPH B., JEFFREY F. ANDERSON, and DAVID W. PARK, Interpersonal effects in computer-mediated interaction: A meta-analysis of social and antisocial communication, *Communication Research* (August 1994), 21, 4, 460–487.

WEBSTER, FRANK, What information society? *Information Society* (January–March 1994), 10, 1, 1–23.

WILSON, ROBERT H., Rural telecommunications: A strategy for community development, *Policy Studies Journal* (1992), 20, 2, 289–300.

15.3
Has individualism become excessive?

The issue: Life, liberty, and the pursuit of happiness. People have flocked to America from around the world to follow their own individual dreams. But is it actually possible to build a society on energetic individualism? The loneliness and anxiety of many Americans suggest something else is needed.

Introduction The question of individualism ties in with both that of the Internet, currently a vehicle for individual expression, and that of environmental change (discussed in an earlier section). Individualism has different meanings to different people. To some it means an emphasis on self-actualization, which in turn can be viewed as either a search for personal fulfillment or the selfishness attributed to the "me-generation" of the 1980s. That is not where we will be going in this section.

Instead, we outline the development of "the individual" in Western society and point to differences between Western and non-Western interpretations of relations between individuals and society. We examine the view, first, that there is too much emphasis on the individual, that it indeed has become excessive. Then we turn to an examination of how this concept has benefited people in society and how it is used today. Finally we tally up both problem and benefits, and ask if there is any route society can take that emphasizes both individual and community.

The concept of the individual has grown up over time and varies from one culture to another. This notion seems strange to many Westerners, for whom the idea of being an individual is natural and self-evident. Society is made up of people, and each person feels herself or himself to be an individual, right? Well, not exactly.

If we look around the world, we can see societies in which this concept of the individual does not exist. People are first and foremost members of clans, lineages, kin groups, or families. Instead of acting in the world as individuals, they act as representatives of these groups, indeed as extensions of them, and they think about themselves in these terms. This view has sometimes been described as familism and disparaged by advocates of Western-style modernity, as we saw in an earlier chapter.

Consider a few differences between the Western individualistic perspective and the community-based orientation described by ethnopsychologists. For instance, among the Ifaluk, a people who live on a Pacific atoll, it is the community, not the individual, that has rights, and the community, not the individual, that owns property. Even cigarettes are viewed as community property, and a failure to share them will arouse anger in the community.

In Western society today, individualism is both an orientation of people toward their everyday world and an orientation of social scientists who study that world and these people. In the discussions that follow, we first take up the popular conception of individualism, then look at individualist versus sociohistoric paradigms of understanding society.

What is an individual? Interest in and concern with the individual has a long history in Western thought, but it has rarely been as prevalent as it is today. In the literature of the Middle Ages we can find narratives of people whose behavior, though related to society and based on social concepts of proper conduct, is portrayed as individualistic, with unique properties and feelings. Examples come from the poetry and prose of northern Europe, in the old English epic of *Beowulf*, or sagas such as that of Grettir the Strong. At this time the dominant ideology was that of every person with a place in society, but there was room for individualism of a type we might recognize today. It was later that the concept of the individual became central to Western society. The American and French revolutions had their philosophical bases in liberalism—a reaction against the old order of the feudal system. Liberal individualism suggested people acted in rational self-interest, to pursue and achieve goals that seemed good to them. Society came to be seen as composed of interacting, goal-directed people.

In the nineteenth century, the philosopher John Stuart Mill wrote that we could understand society by understanding the motivations, actions, and goals of its individual people.

> Men . . . in a state of society are still men: their actions and passions are obedient to the laws of individual human nature. . . . Human beings in society have no properties but those which are derived from, and may be resolved into, the laws of the nature of individual man.

Today, following Mill, the philosophical concepts of "freedom," "the individual," and "individual rights"—the basis of philosophical liberalism—are everywhere mentioned in political, constitutional, and everyday discourse. However, some fear we have lost too much through this emphasis on the individual.

INDIVIDUALISM HAS BECOME EXCESSIVE

In North America, there is a strong emphasis on the individual and his or her thought, freedom, and rights. Each person is urged to be an individual. The focus, in popular thought, is on seeing each person apart from all others. In this view, a community is a collection of individuals who have chosen to live together for their mutual benefit. Each one of us has the right to further our own interest as best we can, to succeed to the best of our ability.

This easily leads to a view that each person is in competition with all others for resources. In the sections on the environment, we saw the results of this. The "tragedy of the commons" occurs when individual people are motivated—even obligated—to maximize their interests at the eventual expense of the community through the destruction of resources previously available to all. Further, the search for individual success or individual expression can be detrimental to relationships within communities and families. Communities succeed because people cooperate within them, to their mutual advantage. But if each person stands for her or his own interests, the community does not automatically thrive; often, it disintegrates.

Think of this in the context of the smallest human community—the family. In the 1950s, Betty Friedan wrote of "the problem that has no name" in her book *The Feminine Mystique*. A generation of women were feeling themselves to be trapped as homemakers in a world that did not value their domestically based work. For many of these women and their present-day descendants, the solution was to seek fulfillment as individuals in the public world of work and politics. The result has been a generation of children growing up in households in which their care has been relegated to paid assistants, because both parents (in the case of a two-parent family) are heavily involved with outside interests, and where pressure on these parents—to appear successful and self-reliant, economically, emotionally, and spiritually—is still increasing.

The intense focus on the individual results in the high level of stress displayed by many people today. Workplace health programs advertise stress-reduction courses in which people are told to engage in recreation activities and to delegate responsibilities. The programs do not identify the source of stress in the extreme levels of performance required of people as individuals. Within the workplace, all people have to perform to the same standards and show themselves willing to put in the same long hours, regardless of the other responsibilities that lie on their shoulders. Here, individualism has gone too far.

Politically, an extreme individualist position suggests that individuals, and by extension the society that is composed of many individuals, does best when individuals are free to act as they wish. In the words of a classic movie, "we don't need no damn organizations" to run our lives or make decisions for us. This position takes the stance of rugged individualism or self-sufficiency. Yet a little sociological reflection indicates that for people today, self-sufficiency can never be total but must go hand in hand with the ability to exchange the product of one household with that of another.

The organizations of society may be in need of reform, but they represent the sum of people coming together to create a community in which all can benefit. In the United States and Canada, the government is accountable to the electorate. Abolition of governmental organizations does not result in greater freedom for all. In fact, governmental regulations have reduced the freedom of some—to oppress, to use racial slurs, to pay wages so low that people cannot live on them—in the interests of increasing the freedom of the many people who make up our society. To reduce the role of government may be to revert to what Thomas Hobbes described as "the war of all against all." Philosophical liberalism did not take such a Hobbesian position but argued that the rights of some must be weighed against the rights of all—for example, the rights of some people to breathe smoke against the rights of all to breathe clean air.

Political parties, including those in government, often take positions that many people disagree with. This is the nature of politics within a democracy. Different groups propose their solutions, and then the electorate can decide. In a pluralist state, groups cannot merely count the weight of numbers of their own supporters but must show how their policies are beneficial for all within the state. In this area, the extreme individualist position may too easily lead to the horrors of ethnic nationalism (discussed in Section 5.3). When all are out for themselves, each is likely to distrust and fear people whose goals are most opposed to their own. Not all people are natural leaders, and they will seek leaders to follow. They are easy prey for demagogues, who seek to further their own interests through attracting a following that does not question their motives but accepts a simple-minded rhetoric.

The extreme popular individualism of the present-day is attracting increasing numbers of supporters. It forms part of the ideology of North America—each person for herself or himself, self-reliant, self-sufficient, and with the rights of the individual in opposition to the rights of the entire community. This is a philosophy profoundly attractive to many people holding high positions in large corporations. In recent years we have seen the development of a technique used to prevent people from banding together and making use of state agencies on, in particular, environmental issues: the SLAPP, or Strategic Lawsuit Against Public Participation.

This works as follows. A developer, for instance, has purchased land and plans to start building on it. Local residents are concerned about the effect on wetlands. They debate the issue and petition the Department of Environmental Protection, asking for a review of the environmental impact. They receive notification that they, each as an individual, are being sued for character defamation and for interfering with the developer's right to use his or her property. The result of such SLAPP actions has been to silence some activists and make others cautious about what they do.

In this situation people's collective rights to assembly and to approach government by peaceful means are being seriously eroded. The government agencies that should assist them are also being targeted. The call for less government (and lower taxes) in people's lives results in decreased funding for many government agencies and programs, with environmental agencies, education, and social programs high on the list for cutbacks. The doctrine of individualism holds that people must achieve on their own merits, and so welfare programs and Head Start programs lose funding.

Individualism has also been attacked from the right or conservative tradition by social theorists who promote what is called "communitarianism." Their idea is that individual lives are lived—can only be lived—within the context of communities; it is only within communities that individual rights and opportunities become available. Thus defense of the community is properly seen as a form of enlightened self-interest for everyone. Seen in this way, traditional virtues such as commitment, loyalty, faithfulness, sociability, and even conformity to social standards are strategies for self-preservation and personal development. They also make people better spouses, parents, workers, and friends. Conversely, without these personal traits and healthy relationships, human life is isolated, rapacious, and unfulfilling.

Communitarians (among others) put an increasing emphasis on the role of civil society as the source of social organization and personal development. This is that portion of social life that exists in neither the economy nor the state, but includes families, clubs, churches—indeed, all voluntary associations. The claim is that just as we cannot expect to get everything we need through our isolated individual pursuits, neither can we expect to get it in the marketplace or through a government program. Not only does civil society make available what other social structures do not; the very process of creating and maintaining a civil society is essential to a meaningful human existence.

If we see modern society as Durkheim did—not as a collection of individuals but as a complex web of interdependence—we must regret and reject this individualism that makes us unable to see society for looking at the people within it. Today, we are unable to see the forest for the trees.

INDIVIDUALISM IS NOT EXCESSIVE AND CAN BE HELPFUL

But now, let us try to imagine the same situation without a concept of individualism—for example, if we had modern technology but no private property. What would be the pressures on the community to develop, regardless of environmental concerns? Who would control the decision making? Who would have the final say?

It is not clear what the outcome would be. Many traditional communities around the world do not share our Western concept of the individual. Many communities attempt to control and resist the influx of developers who seek to "improve" and modernize land use, such as the determined protests of the tribal people of Gandmardhan against Bauxite mining. These people seek to defend their lifestyle and their land, where their identity as a tribal people is inextricably linked to the land and its use.

Whether successful or not, a communal orientation makes possible such protest. However, we can look also to the old Soviet Union, where an official ideology privileging community and state over the individual was linked with excesses of overproduction and pollution, rivaling anything achieved by the excesses of Western individualistic capitalism. State communism did show itself capable of controlling the rise of ethnic nationalism within the former Soviet Union and its satellite countries, but it did so only by means of suppressing traditional practices and beliefs, even languages. With the lifting of restrictions in the countries of Eastern Europe has come a massive wave of nationalistic sentiment, resulting in the revivals of old hatreds and bitterness.

And what about the SLAPP lawsuits? We view them as the manifestation of extreme individualism, preventing the communal responses of community-minded and environmentally minded citizen groups. However, there are other ways they can be viewed. The dominant ideology in North America has tended to distance people from their environment conceptually. We can indeed say that the idealization of the individual has formed part of this distancing. Yet in North America we now see people from many different backgrounds uniting, because of the beliefs and values they have chosen as individuals to adopt, in order to resist threats to their common well-being.

The concept of the individual, arising along with Western capitalism, was initially that of the rational person (envisaged as male) acting to maximize self-interest or profit within the opportunities offered by the economic, social, and physical environment. From this followed the concept of individual rights and freedoms. One result has been the acknowledgment that

people as individuals must be free to choose lifestyles and beliefs, and that these choices are shaped by culture and education. The environmental protests are brought by people who have a right as individuals to protest and a right to join with others to make the protest communal. Looked at this way, SLAPP lawsuits are as much an attack on individual rights as they are on community rights.

Threats to welfare and education programs are evident in both the United States and Canada. They may stem, in part, from a position of extreme individualism, and they gather support from people who adhere to such a view. But the defenses of these programs are also individualistic. Social programs benefit communities by giving individuals within them the opportunities to make something of their lives.

In North America and across the world, people are contacting others, listening to their stories, and making common cause with them. The individualism of North America leads to innovation, not only of technology but of ideas. With today's methods of communication, people are able to exchange news and views through the Internet. Rather than eroding community values, today's individualism permits people to create their communities and feel that they have a say in how these communities develop.

There are excesses of individualism and abuses of power. However, on balance, Western individualism has the potential for great good within the societies in which it presently flourishes, so long as it is tempered with a recognition that responsibilities go along with rights, and that other people, as individuals and societies, have rights also.

What is missing in the argument?   Our view of individualism lies between the pessimism of the first argument and the optimism of the second. Both are views that are commonly expressed. Something, however, is missing from both of them. Let us examine what it may be.

With the "tragedy of the commons," the problem is not that individualism drives each farmer to compete until resources are extinguished. Rather, the structure of the economy is such that continuous expansion is the only way for enterprises to remain in business. Individual competition is not the problem; instead, it is a symptom of particular kinds of economic pressures. Competition between villages, or regions, or nations can be just as devastating. The state communism—or state capitalism—of the former Soviet Union provides an example.

The two perspectives both result from an idealist philosophical approach to the world: the notion that people's actions are driven by their ideas and concepts. Although this is a popular viewpoint, many sociologists reject it. People plan their actions and base their behavior on what they know, surely, but they act within the real constraints of the resources available to them. Within a materialist perspective of history and society, it is the concepts of what people are that track the practicalities of what people do, not the other way about. Thus, instead of seeing individualism as causing social changes of one type or another, we can see its spread as a result of Western capitalism. An individualist outlook is beneficial to certain kinds of capitalist development. The concept of individual property ownership facilitates capitalist development. It is in the interests of developers, therefore, to encourage ideas that are individualist rather than communalist. (This gives another slant on the concept of "everyone as an individual," taught in schools.)

Yet individualism, in maintaining that each person has potentially the same rights, holds that each person has the right to self-expression, to have his or her case heard. In practice, some people find that these rights are easier to exercise if they band together with others, and so new communities of ideas and association are born.

Individualism has developed over time in the Western world along with capitalism. Today it is part of dominant North American culture, and as such it is implicated in both the excesses of development and resistance to it, as we saw in earlier sections. Individualism can be exceptionally problematic for many in North America, particularly people who do not form part of the dominant culture and who do not necessarily place the same emphasis on it. However, as mentioned, that same individualism has alerted many people within the dominant culture to the fact that they must, to be true to their principles, support the rights of other people to find their own identities within their cultures.

SUMMING UP

This section concludes with questions instead of answers, and with one further example. At times, it does seem that individualism may hinder the search to solve social problems. An example can be found in prison populations in the United States and Japan, countries that have diametrically opposed views of how to deal with criminals. American prison populations are large and expanding, and offenders are generally repeat offenders. Prison populations in Japan are small and declining, with the proportion of repeat offenders being small. The dominant ideologies of who has responsibility for crime are very different in the two countries. In Japan, crime is seen as an offense against society. Criminals are expected to admit that they have offended, accept responsibility for the offense, apologize, and try to make good the offense by serving society through a form of community service. The attitude is that separating the offender from society only prevents him or her from taking appropriate action. In return, the community of neighbors and kin accepts the responsibility of helping to keep the offender from offending again; if he or she does, this brings great shame on that community.

In North America, an offender is separated from the community, which takes no official responsibility for his or her actions. Instead, the offender is sent to live with other offenders. This the Japanese see as merely giving him or her the opportunity to learn how to be a better offender. Meanwhile, vast sums in Western economies go to the building, maintenance, and staffing of prisons, which remain full to overflowing, as we saw in the earlier chapter on prisons.

Japan has perhaps struck a better balance—a culture that places importance on both the individual and community and sees both as having responsibilities and rights. Each society, ours included, has to find its own balance; but now the pendulum has swung very sharply away from community interests.

REVIEW EXERCISES

For Discussion and Debate

1. "It takes a whole village to raise a child," some people say. Who should have responsibility for child care, individuals or the community?

2. "There is no true individualism today, because we're all expected to behave just like everybody else."

3. Every individual has a responsibility to make the most of his or her life chances.

4. The cult of individualism actively promotes conformity in North America today.

Writing Exercises

1. "How can I be myself, and not a part of my community?"

2. The philosophy of Western liberalism is based on a concept of the individual as a white, male European who acts out of rational self-interest. What relevance does this have for the present day?

3. How can we achieve true community, which at the same time acknowledges people as individuals?

4. "My family and how they form part of who I am today."

Research Activities

1. Work with a group of four to six others. List which of your attributes seem to be most individualistic and most communalistic. Discuss.

2. Media research: Watch 3 hours of TV, noting commercials you see in this time. Analyze how people are portrayed: as individuals or as members of an ethnic, religious, or gender group?

3. What is individualism? Devise a questionnaire on the characteristics and prevalence of individualism and use it to interview 15 to 20 people. Tabulate results for presentation to the class.

4. Interview three people who are as different as possible from each other—for example, members of different ethnic groups or age groups. Ask them to explain who they are and to tell you something of their background and life history. Analyze the interviews to show how history and community form part of their identities.

SELECTED REFERENCES

ALEXANDER, JEFFREY C., and PHILIP SMITH, The discourse of American civil society: A new proposal for cultural studies, *Theory and Society* (April 1993), 22, 2, 151–207.

ARATO, ANDREW, Revolution, civil society and democracy, *Praxis International* (April–July 1990), 10, 1–2, 24–38.

BELL, DANIEL, "American exceptionalism" revisited: The role of civil society, *Public Interest* (Spring 1989), 95, 38–56.

BENDIX, REINHARD, State, legitimation and "civil society," *Telos* (Winter 1990–1991), 86, 143–152.

CALHOUN, CRAIG, Civil society and the public sphere, *Public Culture* (Winter 1993), 5, 2, 267–280.

COHEN, JEAN L., and ANDREW ARATO, *Civil society and political theory* (Cambridge, MA: MIT Press, 1992).

DOLD, CATHERINE, SLAPP Back! In *Social problems: The search for solutions*, ed. Frank R. Scarpitti and F. Kurt Cylke, Jr. (Los Angeles: Roxbury, 1995).

ETZIONI, AMITAI, Too many rights, too few responsibilities, *National Forum* (Winter 1992), 72, 1, 4–6.

———, TIMOTHY WILLARD, and DANIEL M. FIELDS, The community in an age of individualism, *Futurist* (May–June 1991), 25, 3, 35–39.

FRIEDAN, BETTY, *The feminine mystique* (New York: Norton, 1963).

GELLNER, ERNEST, Civil society in historical context, *International Social Science Journal* (August 1991), 43, 3(129), 495–510.

GITLIN, TODD, After the failed faiths: Beyond individualism, Marxism, and multiculturalism, *World Policy Journal* (Spring 1995), 12, 1, 61–68.

HALL, JOHN A., After the fall: An analysis of postcommunism, *British Journal of Sociology* (December 1994), 45, 4, 525–542.

HAYES, JEFFREY W., and SEYMOUR MARTIN LIPSET, Individualism: A double-edged sword, *Responsive Community* (Winter 1993–1994), 4, 1, 69–80.

JENSEN, LENE ARNETT, Habits of the heart revisited: Autonomy, community, and divinity in adults' moral language, *Qualitative Sociology* (Spring 1995), 1, 71–86.

KATEB, GEORGE, Individualism, communitarianism, and docility, *Social Research* (Winter 1989), 56, 4, 921–942.

KUMAR, KRISHNAN, and CHRISTOPHER G. A. BRYANT, Civil society: An inquiry into the usefulness of an historical term, *British Journal of Sociology* (September 1993), 44, 3, 375–395.

LODGE, GEORGE C., Ideology and national competitiveness, *Journal of Managerial Issues* (Fall 1992), 4, 3, 321–338.

LEYS, COLIN, Rational choice or Hobson's choice? *Studies in Political Economy* (1996), 49, 37–79.

MULHALL, STEPHEN, and ADAM SWIFT, *Liberals and communitarians* (Cambridge: Blackwell, 1992).

MUNDY, LIZA, The success story of the war on poverty. In *Social Problems: The Search for Solutions*, ed. Frank R. Scarpitti and F. Kurt Cylke, Jr. (Los Angeles: Roxbury, 1995).

PHILLIPS, DEREK L., *Looking backward: A critical appraisal of communitarian thought* (Princeton, NJ: Princeton University Press, 1993).

SAMPSON, EDWARD E., *Social worlds, personal lives* (San Diego: Harcourt Brace Jovanovich, 1991).

SELZNICK, PHILIP, *The moral commonwealth: Social theory and the promise of community* (Berkeley: University of California Press, 1992).

SHILS, EDWARD, The virtue of civil society, *Government and Opposition* (Winter 1991), 26, 1, 3–20.

SHIVA, VANDANA, Homeless in the "global village." In *Ecofeminism*, ed. Maria Mies and Vandana Shiva (London: Zed Books, 1993).

TAYLOR, CHARLES, and PARTHA CHATTERJEE, Modes of civil society, *Public Culture* (Fall 1990), 3, 1, 95–118.

TRIANDIS, HARRY C., Collectivism and individualism as cultural syndromes, *Cross Cultural Research* (August–March 1993), 27, 3–4, 155–180.

WALZER, MICHAEL, Multiculturalism and individualism, *Dissent* (Spring 1994), 41, 2(175), 185–191.

WILDAVSKY, AARON, Why self-interest means less outside of a social context: Cultural contributions to a theory of rational choices, *Journal of Theoretical Politics* (April 1994), 6, 2, 131–159.

WILEY, NORBERT, History of the self: From primates to present, *Sociological Perspectives* (Winter 1994), 37, 4, 527–545.